decision making and the WILL OF GOD

Garry Friesen with J. Robin Maxson

Multnomah Books

DECISION MAKING AND THE WILL OF GOD
published by Multnomah Books

Revised and updated edition

International Standard Book Number: 978-1-59052-205-9

Cover image by Stephen Johnson/Getty Images

Published in the United States by WaterBrook Multnomah, an imprint
of the Crown Publishing Group, a division of Random House Inc., New York.

Printed in the United States of America

For information:
MULTNOMAH BOOKS
12265 ORACLE BOULEVARD, SUITE 200
COLORADO SPRINGS, CO 80921

Library of Congress Cataloging in Publication Data
Friesen, Garry, 1947–
Decision making and the will of God.
Includes indexes.
1. God—Will. 2. Decision-making (Ethics)
3. Christian life—1960–
1. Maxson, J. Robin, 1947– joint author. II. Title.
BV4501.2.F767 248.4 80-24592
ISBN 0-88070-024-6 (pbk.)
ISBN 1-59052-205-2

09 10 — 34

To the wonderful women who have graced my life:
Lucille "Muz" Friesen (1924–1991),
Lonie (Friesen) Tucker (1953–1997),
Alice (Timm) Friesen, Cindy (Friesen) Dombrowski,
Barbara (Rosslip) Friesen, Brittany and Erica Friesen,
and to Robin's wife, Louise Maxson,
without whose intervention this would have been a much longer book!

To the students of Multnomah Bible College and the men
of Aslan's How who make community in Christ a reality.

To the believers at United Evangelical Free Church
of Klamath Falls, OR, who helped to nurture this book.

CONTENTS

Part 4
Deciding the Big Ones:
The Wisdom View Applied

FOREWORD TO THE FIRST EDITION

Sacred cows make the best hamburger, but the meat can be hard to swallow.

Christians cherish a mythology that, along with their theology, shapes and directs their lives. Perhaps no myth more strongly influences us than our understanding of how to know the will of God. We want to make right decisions, for we realize that the decisions we make turn around and make us. As we choose one end of the road, we choose the other. When we select a life's work, a life's partner, or a college, we desire God's direction in those choices.

Yet when we ask, "How can I know the will of God?" we may be raising a pagan question. In the ancient world kings and generals consulted the oracles to gain guidance from the gods for their plans. The oracles provided such direction by vague and illusive counsel, and worshipers could read into the enigmatic responses what their hunches told them to do. Convinced that their plans had the stamp of the gods, generals could lead their troops into battle with unfounded courage. By 300 B.C., however, the oracles had gone out of business. Too often they had led their devotees to staggering defeat.

If we ask, "How can I know the will of God?" we may be asking the wrong question. The Scriptures do not command us to find God's will for most of life's choices, nor do we have any passage instructing us on how it can be determined. Equally significant, the Christian community has never agreed on how God provides us with such special revelation. Yet we persist in searching for God's will because decisions require thought and sap energy. We seek relief from the responsibility of decision making and we feel less threatened by being passive rather than active when making important choices.

In this book, Dr. Garry Friesen insists that we must change the question. Instead of wondering, "How do I find the will of God?" a better question to pursue is, "How do I make good decisions?" Answering that question stands as the central purpose of this book. While the author challenges the traditional Christian approach to decision making as both unbiblical and unworkable, he does not stop there. He moves on to give us specific practical principles that we can apply when making everyday decisions that range from minor choices to vital problems. Through a study of these pages we are delivered from two crippling extremes: unwarranted delay and vacillation on the one hand, and impulsive, emotionally loaded judgments on the other. As a result, we achieve freedom to live spiritually productive lives.

The Bible does not provide a map for life, only a compass. But through this book you will discover how the compass can guide you over the bewildering terrain.

Haddon W. Robinson
Harold J. Ockenga Distinguished Professor of Preaching
Gordon-Conwell Theological Seminary

FOREWORD TO THE REVISED EDITION

My brother and I grew up with the principles of *Decision Making and the Will of God* as theological background music for our lives. We heard our father give the talk about decision making enough times that we could reprise the basic outline at will. And we enjoyed showing our friends where we were mentioned by name in "Daddy's book" (as examples of the blessings of marriage).

Neither of us actually read *Decision Making* until we got to college and found ourselves surrounded by thoughtful young Christians, on our own for the first time, and faced with myriad important decisions that would shape the rest of our lives. What major should I choose? What career should I pursue? Should I get married, and if so, to whom and when? Although Mike and I were not necessarily any more certain than our peers about the answers to such weighty questions, we noticed that we were often significantly less anxious about them, because the theological paradigm we had picked up liberated us from the fear of missing God's individual will for our lives. And so we found ourselves, time and again, in the cafeteria, the coffee shop, the dorm lounge, explaining the basic critique of the idea that God has a secret, individual will for the life of each believer that it's our job to figure out, and describing the freedom and responsibility that we each have to make wise choices about our lives. As we learned how to answer our friends' thoughtful challenges and questions, we gained a clearer understanding and renewed appreciation for the approach to decision making that was virtually second nature to us.

As I came to follow in the footsteps of my "Uncle Garry" and entered graduate school in Bible and theology, *Decision Making and the Will of God* undergirded my confidence in both the process and the particular conclusion of my vocational decision. With prayer for wisdom and the guidance of wise counselors, I had found a line of work that was a good match for my gifts, temperament, and passions, and was grateful that God sovereignly provided opportunities to pursue it. Moreover, I believed that this work need not be an impractical, ivory tower pursuit, but could make a positive difference in people's lives. This was not simply a theoretical conviction for me, but something I had firsthand evidence of. Over the years, as I on occasion had outlined the major theses of *Decision Making* for my friends, one of the most common responses I encountered was delighted recognition. While my friends did not necessarily recognize the names of the authors (especially the one in small print), more often than not at least one of them remembered reading the book and attested that it had given them freedom and confidence to more faithfully live out their Christian lives. *Decision Making and the Will of God* has thus been for me the foremost example of theology not as an abstract exercise, but as a tool for equipping God's people to apply their faith to every aspect of their lives.

At the beginning of my career as a theologian, I am grateful for this model of theological writing that glorifies God and serves the church. It is a theology that is thoroughly rooted in the Word of God—ambitious in its scope, endeavoring to do justice to the whole counsel of Scripture, and responsible in its approach, eschewing simple proof-texts for careful exegesis. It is also a theology driven by the practices and problems of Christian living. It is not detached from the real-life concerns of the faithful, but is motivated by the intensely practical question of how we are to be faithful to God in decision making. These are the central reasons, I believe, that this book in the first edition has been so helpful to so many. It is my hope that this edition will provide encouragement, insight, and liberation for another generation of believers.

Rachel E. Maxson, Duke University

ACKNOWLEDGMENTS

We were thrilled when Rod Morris accepted the assignment to be editor of the second edition, as he was for the first. His expertise and irenic spirit have improved this book. Send any negative reviews to him.

Thank you to Wayne Strickland, Rex Koivisto, and Multnomah Bible College's Academic Dean's Council for granting me sabbatical time to finish this second edition.

Thank you to supportive family: Bill Friesen, my father, Joe Dombrowski, Tom and Vickie Tucker, Kevin Friesen, Doug and Deidre Timm, Kirk and Gayle Johnston.

Thank you to the believers at Community Bible Fellowship and Trinity Fellowship, including the Ichthus team, who have nurtured my faith and taught me to worship. Appreciation goes to Dick and Martha Sleeper and the members of the Eagle and Child reading group for instilling in me the love of good books (may this be one of them).

For their models of great commission living: Norm and Muriel Cook, Ray and Jill Davis, Swede and Sandi Ekholm, Tom and Bonnie Kopp, Jack and Cheryl Shiflet, Norm and Linda Vissering, Mark and Karen Wagner, Gary and Pauline Williams, my heroes in missions. May the chapter on missions encourage more servants like these.

For longtime friends in Christ: Mike and Chris Bauslaugh, Ron Frost, Ed and Kay Klotz, Emi Koe, Glen and Linda Letellier, Gregg and Renee Naslund, Daniel and Kim Scalberg. May these relationships and this book speak the truth in love.

introduction

IS IT WORTH ANOTHER LOOK?

Is it worth another look? The answer to that question will depend, in part, on who is asking it. For as I submit a revised edition of a book first published over twenty years ago, I realize that I now address readers in two audiences. One audience consists of those who have never encountered the content or perspective of this book. Perhaps the book was recommended by a friend. Or maybe you're intrigued by a presentation that claims to be a biblical alternative to other books on God's will. Possibly you're like the quarter-million readers of the first edition who had reason to explore an approach that differed from the standard teaching on the subject. For you, the question, "Is it worth another look?" means, "Should I consider another viewpoint on decision making and the will of God?" You want to know, what's this all about?

Those in the second audience are already familiar with the original version. You're curious about any alteration in my views. Perhaps you wonder if the questions you had after reading the first edition have been addressed. Or maybe you want to know how (and whether) the viewpoint of this book has matured over two decades. For you, the question, "Is it worth another look?" means, "Should I revisit the 'way of wisdom' to see if deeper insight may be gained?" You want to know, what's new?

Begging the patience of my friends in audience number two, I will respond to new readers by narrating how this book came to be written in the first place, and by giving you a sneak preview of its main points. Then I'll unveil what's new in this edition.

The personal research that culminated in the writing of this book was initially motivated by frustration. Like most Christians in evangelical churches, I had received instruction on discerning God's guidance. Yet when I followed the steps normally taught, I didn't always obtain the clear picture that was supposed to materialize. Are believers like laboratory rats consigned to an intricate maze of decisions while God just watches? Surely not. But my efforts to apply the traditional teaching only yielded confusion.

My serious quest for answers began when I was about to graduate from high school. Entering young adulthood I had to decide, on my own, where I would spend the four formative years of college life. A full year before the deadline, I narrowed my choice to two colleges. One was in Detroit and the other in Arkansas—John Brown University. Which was God's will? Frankly, they seemed equal. I carefully and prayerfully followed the steps I had been taught. Yet evaluation of circumstances, scriptural principles, inner impressions, and advice from counselors did not decisively narrow my decision to a single, perfect choice.

I had never been encouraged to put out a circumstantial "fleece" unless other methods had failed. However, twelve months dwindled to two weeks and I had to do something. I resorted to a fleece. "I'll ask my father which of two job offers he thinks I should take just before entering college," I thought to myself. "If he says 'radiator shop,' I'll go to John Brown; but if he says 'camp worker,' I'll go to the college in Detroit." Dad was not aware that he was deciding the next four years of my life by answering a simple question. I asked him. He thought for a moment and then said, "I think you should take the job with your Uncle Reiny in the radiator shop."

"Okay," I said to myself, "God is sending me to John Brown University."

I was content with the choice I had made, but the complexity and uncertainty of the process was disconcerting. I arrived in Arkansas with a theological issue. Why had it been so hard to find God's will when I had so sincerely sought it? Secondarily, was this "fleece" method really plumbing the mind of God? Was I the only one who did not have 100 percent certainty for every decision? A new possibility struck me. Perhaps my understanding of the nature of God's will was biblically deficient. Maybe there was a better way to understand *how* God guides.

For the next ten years I searched the Scriptures for clues about God's guidance. Second Timothy 3:16–17 spurred me on: "All Scripture is inspired by God and profitable for teaching...so that the man of God may be adequate, equipped for every good work." Further research provided enough data for my doctoral dissertation. That material was presented in seminars and conferences and underwent further refinement. Finally, five years of writing resulted in the publication of the first edition of *Decision Making and the Will of God* in 1980.

Since that time, the book has been read, critiqued, and questioned. Over a thousand readers have written letters. Good questions have been asked—both by those who agreed with the book and by those who emphatically did not. Insightful observations exposed places where the original book was unclear or where further analysis was required. And so this second edition has been prepared as a much-needed update, presenting the same thesis about God's guidance, but I hope with more clarity, additional biblical support, and answers to the most frequently asked questions.

Decision Making, like many books before and after it, seeks to clarify God's teaching on personal guidance. Where it differs from others is in some of its conclusions. Thus, it is called an "alternative to the traditional view." Many of the books that have been published on this subject over the past two decades continue to follow a common approach to finding God's will. Hence, the traditional view of my youth continues, with some refinement, to be propagated.

Ironically, my research into the history of this teaching indicates that its origin is relatively recent. It appears that what has become the traditional view was developed by British and American Bible teachers connected with the Keswick Movement. Arising from spiritual life conferences that began in 1875 in Keswick, England, and spreading to America, this movement became a powerful force for the cause of world missions. Through its influence, many believers around the world have been taught this traditional view, believing it to be the only view.

To my surprise (but not shock), I learned that the material I present in this book was not a discovery of anything new. It turns out that many spiritual traditions prior to Keswick taught the "wisdom view" presented here. So from a historical perspective, which position is indeed "traditional" could be debated. The significant question, however, is not which view came first. Rather our concern must focus on which understanding best expresses the teaching of Scripture. This book will seek to fairly critique what has become the traditional view, and then offer a biblical alternative.

A Sneak Preview

In part 1 the traditional view is presented. The fictional seminar I employed in the first edition has been replaced by a more concise, expanded outline.[1] Part 2 is a critique of the areas where the traditional view needs correction. The key material is expounded in chapter 4 where relevant Scriptures used by the traditional view are carefully reexamined in context. Part 3 presents the biblical alternative called "the way of wisdom." It gives my answer to the question, "How does God guide?" Finally in part 4 the biblical principles of guidance are applied to specific important decisions: singleness and marriage, choosing a vocation, and how to disagree with other believers without starting the newest church split.

"So," you ask, "what is the 'way of wisdom'?" In the first edition of *Decision Making,* I didn't tip my hand for 150 pages. That was too long for some readers to wait—including my mother. Many couldn't stand the suspense and cheated by reading the conclusion first. To forestall such temptation, this time I'm going to reveal right up front how the story ends. I hope this summary will whet your appetite and motivate you to keep chewing until you digest the full meal.

If you've been raised under the traditional view of guidance and are comfortable with the application of it in your life, a brief summary of the "way of wisdom" may not seem right at first reading. Furthermore, I won't even try to prove that it is correct until part 3. On the other hand, if your experience has been like mine, and you have felt frustrated in the application of traditional steps to guidance, you have reason for hope. In the next few pages you will learn that there is a refreshing biblical alternative to what most Christians have been taught about "finding God's will."

God's guidance according to the way of wisdom can be summarized in four simple statements:

1. Where God commands, we must obey.
2. Where there is no command, God gives us freedom (and responsibility) to choose.
3. Where there is no command, God gives us wisdom to choose.
4. When we have chosen what is moral and wise, we must trust the sovereign God to work all the details together for good.

Part 3, "The Way of Wisdom," will give proof for each of these principles from Scripture, supported by reason and experience. Right now I will expand these four principles to assure that you can see the forest of guidance before we inspect the specific trees.

In the Bible, the term "God's will" most often refers to all the commands, principles, and promises that God has revealed in the Scriptures. This first biblical meaning of "God's will" is best described as God's moral will. It is fully conveyed in the Bible and so does not have to be "found"—just read, learned, and obeyed.

Though this book has been called controversial, there is nothing controversial about the concept of God's moral will. Virtually all Bible teachers agree (including those who promote the traditional view): *Where God commands, we must obey.* Yet this simple truth cuts deeper into real life than we usually realize. Every action, thought, motive, attitude, and plan is affected by God's moral will because its commands go beyond outward actions to search the motives and intents of our most secret desires (1 Samuel 16:7).

The second principle is the point where I part company with the traditional view. (It has been called "heretical" by opponents, "revolutionary" and "liberating" by those who have been transformed by it.) This principle must be denied by proponents of the traditional view or their position cannot stand. It starts to answer the question, "What do you do when there is no specific command in the Bible to determine your decision?"

Where there is no command, God gives us freedom (and responsibility) to choose. The principle actually is not as radical as it may sound. It does not say that God does not care what we decide. It does not mean that there is no further guidance from God (there are two more principles). It does not say that our decision does not matter or that we can do our own selfish thing. It *does* say that we are morally free to decide. This freedom is God-given. But alongside that freedom is a God-given *responsibility* to decide.

Grasping the reality of freedom and responsibility has resulted in a very common response to the first edition of the book: "This book is both liberating and sobering. With freedom comes relief that I am not missing God's will. At the same time, being responsible for my decisions means that I cannot blame bad decisions on God."

Principle three says, *Where there is no command, God gives wisdom to choose.* We are never free to be foolish, stupid, or naive. The freedom in the second principle is limited by the guidance God gives through wisdom. Put differently, wisdom is commanded of believers by the moral will of God and must be applied to all noncommanded decisions.

I will support this principle by citing numerous biblical commands that exhort believers to act and choose wisely. I will also illustrate it with scriptural terminology and examples. The wisdom books of the Old Testament make a great contribution and can be taken at face value as models of God's primary method of guidance. In the area of freedom, it is God who promises to give wisdom when we ask.

Principle four states, *When we have chosen what is moral and wise, we must trust the sovereign God to work all the details together for good.* God's sovereign superintendence of all the particulars assures that after we have followed His guidance in the first three principles, God secretly works all the unknowns and details together for good. He is involved in the smallest particulars even when He does not tell us exactly what to do. This work of God gives the peace of mind that God is guiding in everything.

These four principles form the core of the way of wisdom. It takes the rest of the book to explain them, prove them from Scripture, and apply them to life.

New and Improved

Now, how is this revised edition different from its predecessor?

First, this update contains a *clearer presentation* of the view. Years of interaction with students and readers have resulted in the discovery of statements that were confusing to people or inadvertently led to faulty inferences. There is more than one way to get across an idea, and some ways of saying things are clearer than others. The most obvious example of this is the vocabulary used to express the four fundamental principles of the way of wisdom. These simpler, shorter statements are less subject to misunderstanding.

Second, this edition discusses *additional key passages*. One of the distinctive features of *Decision Making* is a thorough examination of relevant biblical texts carefully analyzed in context. During the past two decades, I've encountered additional key passages that were overlooked in writing the first edition. Some of these passages were identified by readers who asked "What about...?" A few surfaced in other books on the will of God. My own Bible reading brought me into contact with some very helpful verses. So this edition includes exegetical treatment of previously omitted passages inserted in the appropriate sections of the book.

Third, while some sections of the original book have been pared down, *new material* has been added. For instance, my explanation of the traditional view in Part 1 has been reduced from fifty-seven pages to eight, from three chapters to one. Instead of a narrative, I've provided an outline. That was done in part to make room for new content, most of which was added to the chapters on the "way of wisdom" in part 3. This new material reflects the impact of twenty years of living with the way of wisdom and learning additional insights about God's marvelous guidance.

Fourth, this edition includes my replies to *frequently asked questions.* I owe a lot to hundreds of students and readers who have raised significant questions about the concepts in the first edition. Some of these questions have called for clarification of central points. Others have explored inferential or applicational ramifications of the way of wisdom. With the advent of the computer age (the first edition was written on typewriters!), most current readers are familiar with "frequently asked questions" (FAQs) from Internet websites. So the best of these questions (and my answers) have been packaged in that format. A list of the questions is included in the index.

Fifth, this edition adds an appendix containing brief *reviews of fifteen books on God's will* that have been published in the intervening years. One good way to increase our understanding of a position is to see how it contrasts with others, so each review focuses mainly on those areas where my views differ from those of the author.

Sixth, a *group study guide* originally published separately is included with this edition.

And finally, both Robin and I are older and our youthful *pictures* on the first edition now qualify as false advertising. I hope we not only look more mature, but have written a more mature exposition of the wisdom view.

So, is it worth another look? Well, I think so. That's why I wrote, then rewrote this book. But I can't answer that question for you. That's one decision you'll have to make for yourself.

1. Readers familiar with the first edition of *Decision Making and the Will of God* may want to go directly to chapter 3. The longer presentation of the traditional view from the first edition is available at www.gfriesen.net.

part one

you have HEARD IT SAID

The Traditional View Presented

chapter one

ON MARRIAGE AND MISSIONS

Bill Thompson's concentration on the computer screen was so focused that he literally jumped at the sound of his secretary's voice on the intercom.

"I'm sorry to disturb you, Pastor," she said, "but Ted Bradford just came in and asked if he could talk with you. I thought you might want to see him."

Bill's initial irritation at her contravention of his "do not disturb" order melted instantly and a smile erased the frown from his face. He hit the "save" button on the computer as he replied, "You're right, Charlene. Send him in."

He got up from his chair and noticed that it felt good to stretch. He wondered how long he had been hunched over his keyboard as he moved toward the door to admit Ted to his office. Genuinely glad to see a young man he considered one of his protégés, he extended his hand in welcome. "Hi, Ted. Good to see you!"

"It's good to be home, Pastor," Ted replied, shaking Bill's hand. "I've been looking forward to semester break for a long time, or so it seems."

Bill motioned to the chair facing his desk. "Have a seat. You don't look too much the worse for wear. I like your mustache."

Ted grinned and self-consciously brushed his lip with his fingers. "I've gotten used to it. I almost forget it's there. My folks haven't decided what they think about it yet."

Bill laughed. "Don't worry about them. They'll adjust. They always do."

"Yeah, I guess so."

Bill sat down in his swivel chair and leaned back. "So, how does it feel to be one semester away from graduation?"

"I'm pretty excited about it for the most part."

"For the most part?"

"Well, that's what I wanted to talk to you about, Pastor. I'm going to have to make some pretty big decisions in the next few months, and I'd like to get your advice on some of the things I've been thinking about."

Bill leaned forward in his chair. "Before we go any further, I want you to know that my advice is free—and worth every penny."

Ted grimaced appropriately and continued. "I'll bear that in mind." He hesitated. "I'm not sure where to start. It's all gotten kind of complicated."

"Complicated, huh?" Bill leaned back and arched his eyebrow. "What's her name?"

Ted was momentarily startled. "How did you know?" Then he laughed. "Her name is Annette—Annette Miller. And she's a remarkable girl."

"She'd have to be to get your attention," Bill chided. "Does she like mustaches?"

"She doesn't let them get in her way. Not this one, at least."

"I bet with a little arm twisting you could be persuaded to produce a picture of this young lady."

"Thought you'd never ask." Ted extracted a photograph from his wallet and passed it across the desk to the pastor. "It's a little worn around the edges, but I think it bears a close resemblance to the real thing."

Bill studied the picture for a moment. "Annette Miller is one very attractive young lady, Ted. I can see why you would notice her."

"She really is a remarkable girl, Pastor."

"You said that already," Bill replied as he handed the picture back. "Tell me something objective about her, if that's possible."

"Well, she enrolled in the one-year Bible program at the beginning of this school year. Before that she graduated with a B.A. from the state university with a major in African history and a minor in anthropology. I met her during the first week in a Bible class. She was so easy to talk to, Pastor, I didn't even have to work up courage to ask her out for the first time. I took her to a reception for new students and we really had a great time. The relationship just kind of took off from there."

"She sounds very impressive," Bill said. "Where does she live?"

Ted hesitated. "I'm never really sure how to answer that one. You see, her folks are missionaries in Kenya. That's where Annette grew up. When they come back to the States, their home base is Chicago. Of course, Annette is pretty much on her own now, so I guess her home is wherever she happens to be going to school."

"Well, that accounts for the major in African history," Bill said. "It sounds like she's preparing to return to Kenya as a missionary herself."

"She's not positive that she should go to Kenya specifically, but she does feel that the Lord has called her to a ministry in Africa. Of course she's most familiar with Kenya, but the tribe her parents have been working in extends across national boundaries. For that matter, she's not even sure yet that she should return to that same tribe. She's just preparing as much as she can so that when she does receive a more specific call, she'll be ready to go anywhere."

"It sounds like she's very committed to the Lord."

"Yes, she is, Pastor. That's what I appreciate most about her." Ted paused and looked down at the floor. It was quiet in the study for a few moments.

"Do you love her, Ted?"

Ted raised his head and looked Bill in the eye. "Yes, I do—very much."

"Do you want to marry her?"

"Yes."

"Does she know that?"

"We've talked about it quite a bit."

"How does she feel about the idea?"

"She'd like to marry me, too."

"So what's the problem?"

Ted's gaze returned to the floor and he sighed. "There seem to be several problems, Pastor, and they're not going away. The more I think about them, the harder they seem to get, and the more confused I become."

"Why don't you just list them one at a time," Bill said. "Sometimes a forest seems more manageable when you tackle one tree at a time."

"All right." Ted paused to think a moment. "One thing that concerns me is that I don't know whether it's the Lord's will for us to get married. When we first started dating, I never stopped to think about whether Annette might be the girl God had chosen for me to marry. I know that the Lord has a plan for my life, and I know that plan includes the person I should marry. I also know that the same thing is true for Annette and her future husband. We're just not sure we were meant for each other, you know, as far as God's plan is concerned."

"Are you willing *not* to marry Annette if it's not the Lord's will?"

"I've agonized over that question a lot, Pastor. And I think I can honestly say that I'm willing to give her up if that's His will. Both of us realize that if the Lord doesn't mean for us to marry it would be a big mistake for us to go ahead on our own. We want the Lord's best for our lives—for both of our lives..." Ted hesitated for a moment. "In fact, we've kind of broken things off until we get a clear answer on this from the Lord."

"I imagine it's been kind of rough on you."

Ted nodded.

"I really have a lot of admiration for you two," Bill said. "It takes considerable inner strength to do what you've done. I think you are demonstrating real maturity and sincerity in this matter. The Lord will reward that, I'm sure."

Ted took a deep breath and cleared his throat. "Annette and I have had a wonderful relationship. I'm glad that I don't have to be ashamed of any part of it. And there are several things that indicate that we'd make good marriage partners. We seem to complement each other in personality and abilities and things like that. The only major indicator that might point in a different direction is this Africa business."

"You don't want to go to Africa?" Bill asked.

"Oh, I'd be willing to go. It's just that Annette has had such a strong feeling that that's where she should serve the Lord, and I haven't received any kind of a call. Until I met Annette, I never thought about Africa at all."

"What do you plan to do after graduation?"

Ted shrugged his shoulders. "I haven't had any strong leading in any specific direction. I've been thinking about going to seminary. In fact, I've applied to a couple of different schools. But even that was frustrating."

"Why? I think you'd do real well in seminary. I'm glad to hear you're thinking about it."

"I'm excited about the idea. It's just that on the application forms they wanted me to describe my 'call to the ministry of the gospel.' I had to tell them that I don't yet know exactly what the Lord wants me to do. But I feel that I need more training in the Word for whatever it is."

"I see," Bill said.

"The thing is, I don't see how Annette and I can be married unless we both feel called to the same ministry. Or at least our calls should be compatible. Another thing that bothers me is that since we began discussing marriage, Annette has been wondering about her commitment to Africa. What if she didn't go there because she married me instead? That's the question that's been haunting me."

"Perhaps the Lord wants Annette to spend a term in Africa while you go to seminary," Bill said.

"That's a possibility, Pastor. And I think we're both willing to do that, as hard as it would be. I guess the thing I really want to know is, how can we know for sure what the Lord wants us to do? We have to make some decisions pretty soon, and we need to know clearly what God's will is for us."

"That's very interesting," Bill mused as he stared off into space.

Ted laughed. "I thought you'd think so. Are you going to give me any of that free advice you promised?"

"As a matter of fact, yes. But not right now."

"Not now?"

Bill waved at the materials on and around his desk. "You see all that chaos? It just so happens that I was asked to lead a seminar on 'Knowing God's Will for Your Life' at our district's annual youth conference. I've been working on it for several weeks. In fact, that's what I was doing when you came in."

Ted's eyes registered his amazement as he surveyed the materials on the desk and the volumes in the cardboard box next to the pastor's chair. "Are all those books on the will of God? You must have twenty-five paperbacks alone!"

"Well, I've been collecting them for a couple of years, but new titles seem to come off the press faster than I can read them. The subject is very popular—always has been."

"I guess that means I'm not the Lone Ranger when it comes to questions about God's will for my life."

"Exactly. I've probably been asked more questions on that subject than any other—especially by young people. That's why I've been working so hard on this seminar presentation."

"So when is this conference?" Ted asked.

"This weekend. I think they have me down for Saturday morning."

Ted's face fell. "That's not going to work for me. Our family will be out of town at my cousin's wedding. And then I'm off to Camp Maranatha where I'm working this summer. I'm literally just passing through."

"There's more than one way to skin the proverbial cat." Bill pointed back at the pile on his desk. "I'm pretty much done with these books. I'd be happy to lend them to you."

Ted sighed. "No offense, but I'm kind of 'booked out' right now. Is there just one book that summarizes what I need to know?"

Bill smiled. "You could read part 1 of the first edition of *Decision Making and the Will of God.* It gives an excellent account of my presentation."

Ted looked puzzled. "I guess that could work..."

"Or I could give you a copy of my outline. It won't have all the narrative and illustrations, but you've heard this material before. All you need is a good overview. Besides, those first chapters in *Decision Making* go on forever!"

"That sounds good, Pastor Bill." Ted rose from his chair, and the two men shook hands. "I'll come back and pick up that outline tomorrow morning." He started toward the door, then stopped and turned back to Bill. "Lord willing, of course."

chapter two

THE TRADITIONAL VIEW: AN OUTLINE

In the original version of *Decision Making and the Will of God,* I presented the traditional view of guidance through a fictitious seminar. Following the meeting between Pastor Bill Thompson and Ted Bradford, I devoted the next three chapters to Pastor Thompson's presentation. In this edition, I present the same material in outline form. (I will flesh out some of the points of this outline in my critique in part 2.) My assumption is that the traditional view is widely understood and that a summary outline is adequate for the purposes of this book.

The longer version is available at www.gfriesen.net and in the quarter-million copies now in print of the first edition of *Decision Making*—some of which may be found in church or school libraries or (alas!) used bookstores. The scholarly documentation in the doctoral dissertation is still available also.[1]

I. Premise: For each of our decisions, God has an ideal plan that He will make known to the attentive believer.

A. Rather than asking "What is best for me?" or "What will bring me the greatest amount of happiness?" the Christian should always ask "What is God's will for me in this decision?"

B. Given God's desire and ability to communicate, the believer can have confidence that God's will can be known with certainty in any situation.

C. Failure to discern and/or obey God's leading results in anxiety, frustration, and discouragement that come from living outside the center of God's will.

II. Definition: The phrase "will of God" is used in three ways in the Bible.

A. God's *sovereign* will = God's secret plan that determines everything that happens in the universe (Daniel 4:35; Proverbs 16:33; 21:1; Revelation 4:11; Ephesians 1:11; Romans 9:19; 11:33–36; Acts 2:23; 4:27–28). Because God's sovereign will is secret, it does not directly affect our decision making.

B. God's *moral* will = God's revealed commands in the Bible that teach how men ought to believe and live (Romans 2:18; 1 Thessalonians 4:3; 5:18; 2 Corinthians 6:14; plus all other direct commands in Scripture). Where God has spoken in the Bible, the believer must obey. But God's moral will does not directly address many specific decisions faced by an individual.

C. God's *individual* will = God's ideal, detailed life-plan uniquely designed for each person (Colossians 1:9; 4:12; Romans 12:2; Ephesians 5:17; 6:6; Proverbs 3:5–6; 16:9; Psalm 32:8; Genesis 24). God's guidance for decision making is given through the indwelling Holy Spirit who progressively reveals God's life-plan to the heart of the believer through a variety of means. *This is the aspect of God's will that is usually of greatest concern to those facing life's decisions.*

1. Some writers use the visual image of a target to describe the "very center of God's will." Within the larger circle of God's moral will, finding the dot in the center is essential to making correct decisions in daily life.

The Center of God's Will

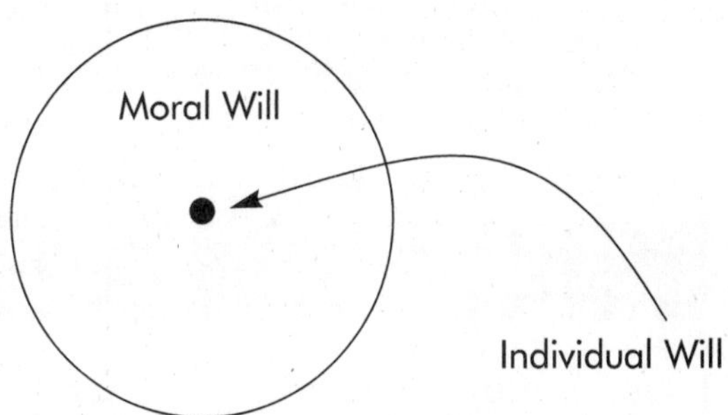

2. Choosing apart from God's perfect will ("missing the dot") will likely result in experiencing God's "second best," or living within God's "permissive will."

Summary: We gain clarity in understanding biblical usages of the phrase "God's will" by comparing and contrasting the individual will with the sovereign will and moral will of God.

COMPARING AND CONTRASTING GOD'S INDIVIDUAL AND SOVEREIGN WILLS

God's Individual Will	God's Sovereign Will
1. A detailed plan for all decisions in a believer's life.	1. A detailed plan for all events in the universe.
2. The believer is able to find and know it.	2. It is hidden—the believer cannot find and know it.
3. Believers are expected to find it as part of the Christian life.	3. Believers are not expected to find it as part of the Christian life.
4. Believers can miss it by failure to discover or obey it.	4. Believers cannot miss it because it always comes to pass.

God's Individual Will	God's Sovereign Will
5. Includes only that which is good and ideal.	5. Includes both good and evil.
6. Must be discovered before a decision can be made.	6. Can only be discovered after it happens.
7. Directly Ideal Plan: It is in harmony with the Bible and is always the most ideal decision and so brings glory to God.	7. Indirectly Ideal Plan: Though it includes evil acts and foolish decisions, it will ultimately lead to God's glory.

COMPARING AND CONTRASTING GOD'S INDIVIDUAL AND MORAL WILLS

God's Individual Will	God's Moral Will
1. A detailed plan for all decisions in a believer's life.	1. A body of general commands and principles for life.
2. Believers are expected to find and do it.	2. Believers are expected to find and do it.
3. Believers can miss it by failure to discover or obey it.	3. Believers can miss it by failure to discover or obey it.
4. It is being revealed to the hearts of believers and cannot be found at all in the Bible.	4. It was revealed to apostles and prophets and can be found completely in the Bible.
5. It is revealed by the Holy Spirit through inward impressions using many means.	5. It was revealed by the Holy Spirit through supernatural revelation.
6. Its directives are specific for one specific believer ("Marry Jane next month in Portland").	6. Its directives are general for all believers ("Marry only a believer").

III. Proof: How I can know that God has a plan for my life

A. *Reason:* We know that God knows all things; that He is a God of order (1 Corinthians 14:40) who makes plans; that He loves His children individually and cares for our welfare. Therefore, it just makes sense that He would have an individual will for each life. This idea is supported by biblical images of God as our King, our Shepherd, and our Father (Matthew 6:26; Psalm 23).

B. *Experience:* Historical examples (Martin Luther, John Wesley, William Carey, David Livingstone, Hudson Taylor, Adoniram Judson) show the effectiveness of following God's individual will.

C. *Biblical example:* Many persons in the Bible show obedience to God's individual will, such as:

1. Jesus (Hebrews 10:7–9; John 4:34; 5:36; 6:38; 7:17; 8:26, 42; Luke 22:42)
2. Paul (1 Corinthians 1:1; Galatians 1:1; Acts 13:1–2; 16:10; 16:6–7)
3. Philip (Acts 8:26–29)
4. Ananias (Acts 9:10–11)
5. Peter (Acts 10:20)
6. Jerusalem Council (Acts 15:28)
7. Joseph (Genesis 50:20)

D. *Biblical teaching:* Several verses directly teach that God has a perfect individual will for each believer.

1. Colossians 1:9–10: a prayer for "knowledge of His will"
2. Romans 12:1–2: an exhortation to "prove" what God's will is
3. Proverbs 3:5–6: a promise that God will "direct the paths" (NKJV) of those who trust in Him
4. Isaiah 30:21: a promise of direction to the right "way"
5. Psalm 32:8: a promise of instruction and counsel in "the way which you should go"
6. Ephesians 2:10: direction into specific "good works"
7. Genesis 24: an example of guidance in finding the right spouse

IV. Process: How I can discover God's individual will

A. Erroneous expectations that bring confusion in finding God's will.

1. "God will unveil His plan all at once—like a course syllabus." No, God usually unfolds His will progressively, step by step—more like a scroll.
2. "If I tell God I don't want to go to Japan as a missionary, that's where He'll send me." This picture of God as a "celestial killjoy" is a caricature. The place of greatest joy is in the center of His perfect will.

3. "God only reveals His will to people with special 'callings'—like ministers and missionaries." No, God's vocational call is for every believer.
4. "Only mature Christians can discern God's will." No, a young believer who has an open heart and is well taught can know God's will too.
5. "If God wants me to do something specific, I can expect a heavenly flash of lightning—like Saul on the Damascus Road." No, God normally speaks through the "still small voice" (1 Kings 19:12, NKJV) of His Spirit as He did with Elijah.
6. "God is only truly concerned about my major, life-shaping decisions." No, His will includes the details of life that lead up to (and away from) the "big decisions."

B. Reliable road signs that bring assurance in finding God's individual will

1. *The Word of God:* Since the individual will of God is always found within the moral will of God, the Bible is the place to start. It provides perfect guidance, and God's will is always in harmony with it. The Bible should always be interpreted according to the author's intent; beware of "reading into" a passage a message that is not there.
2. *Circumstances:* Since they are controlled by God, circumstances can point to His will. He uses "open and closed doors" (though sometimes a door that is closed only means that we should wait). And God uses "fleeces"—a providential sign, determined beforehand, that indicates a "yes" or "no" from Him. (Example: "Lord, if you want us to sell our home, please have someone inquire about it next week without our advertising its availability.") Putting out a circumstantial fleece (Judges 6:36–40) should be done only rarely, with great care and much prayer.
3. *Inner witness of the Spirit:* Guidance is an important ministry of the Holy Spirit (John 16:13; Romans 8:14; Galatians 5:18). He leads through inner impressions in our heart and gives confirmation through a settled, supernatural sense of peace (Philippians 4:7; Colossians 3:15; see Nehemiah 2:12).
4. *Mature counsel:* Proverbs 24:6 underscores the value of wise counselors who can help us discern God's will.
5. *Personal desires:* If we avoid the two extremes of automatically distrusting our own desires (because they are tainted with sin—Jeremiah 17:9) or of automatically equating them with God's

will (insisting that "He will give me the desires of my heart"—Psalm 37:4), our own inclinations can be useful (since God is working in us to desire what He desires—Philippians 2:13).

6. *Common sense:* Church leaders are expected to be wise, prudent, and sensible (Acts 6:3; 1 Timothy 3:2; Titus 1:7–8), so common sense is a valuable asset in knowing God's will. We must remember, though, that divine guidance—like that received by Noah, Abraham, Joshua, and Philip—may appear foolish to others.
7. *Supernatural guidance:* God has led through audible voice, angel, vision, prophecy, or miracle (Acts 8:26; 9:3–6; 10:1–20; 13:2; 16:9–10). He does not promise such guidance, but there is nothing in the Bible that rules it out.

V. Certainty: How I can know for sure God's individual will

A. Certainty comes by *agreement of the road signs.* One sign is not enough to confirm God's will, but when the three main signs agree (Bible, circumstances, and inner witness of the Spirit), you may be confident that you have found God's will.

B. Certainty comes through *prayer* (James 1:5; 4:2). Prayer makes your heart willing and helps you to hear God's still small voice.

C. Certainty comes through *communion* (Psalm 32:8–9; James 4:8; John 10:1–16). The closer you are to God, the more you will instinctively recognize His voice and understand the guidance He is giving us.

D. Certainty comes from the *results* of the decision. God will bring peace and blessing from His individual will and thus confirm the correctness of your decision. If you erred, God may use a closed door to redirect you to the right path.

VI. Common (if not Frequently Asked) Questions about finding God's will (according to the traditional view)

A. "Why do some books talk about only two definitions for God's will instead of three?"

Answer: Some books combine the moral will of God and the individual will of God. There are similarities since both are desired by God and must be discovered. However, the distinction between them is important because of the differences. God's moral will is fully revealed in the Bible for all believers, but God's individual will is revealed to the believer's heart and is specific for each believer.

B. "How do I know what college courses I should take when God has not revealed what my vocation should be?"
Answer: God's guidance is revealed one step at a time. As you choose your courses, you should follow the road signs to finding God's will. God will insure that they harmonize with His future guidance for you.

C. "How can I distinguish my personal desires from those coming from the Spirit?"
Answer: God-given desires will not contradict the Bible and will have His distinct stamp upon them. They will often be wise and holy beyond what you could have generated on your own. Sooner or later as you wait on Him, the difference will become clear. Hunches that surface unexpectedly will either fade or grow stronger with time, and God's hand in them will become obvious.

D. "Does God have an individual will for individual churches?"
Answer: The experience of the church in Antioch (Acts 13:1–4) indicates that God has an individual will for local churches. Knowing this should help a church to be unified when all members are listening to Christ, the Head, and following His direction.

E. "Could I use spiritual counsel as a 'fleece'?"
Answer: Counsel is helpful in finding God's direction, but don't make the mistake of automatically equating such advice with God's will. This would be misuse of the legitimate value of counsel rather than a correct use of a fleece.

F. "What if God calls you to do something that you do not know how to do?"
Answer: Usually God prepares people before He sends them. But sometimes He uses believers because of their *availability* rather than their

ability. In such cases, God will give the ability to accomplish the task He has guided you into—like He did for Gideon, Amos, and Paul (2 Corinthians 12:9).

G. "What do you do when you are not certain of God's individual will, but have a deadline?"
Answer: When the deadline comes, you must admit your failure to discern God's will, pray for the outworking of His sovereign will, and then make the decision that you think would most please God. If you have made a mistake, then you should go back and start over again with the decision.

H. "What do you do when two options appear to be equal?"
Answer: Understand that they only *seem* equal. God knows that one choice is superior in its future implications. That is why He chooses one as His will for you. Be sure to look at both options very carefully. In such cases the inward witness of the Spirit is very important. Submit the whole issue to the umpire of God's peace (Colossians 3:15). Picture each option in your mind as you pray and then listen carefully to God's still small voice in the form of His peace concerning the correct choice.

VI: Summary: Principles of Decision Making (The Traditional View)

A. *Premise:* For each of our decisions God has a perfect plan or will.

B. *Purpose:* Our goal is to discover God's individual will and make decisions in accordance with it.

C. *Process:* We interpret the inner impressions and outward signs through which the Holy Spirit communicates His leading.

D. *Proof:* The confirmation that we have correctly discerned the individual will of God comes from an inner sense of peace and outward (successful) results of the decision.

---

1. Garry Lee Friesen, "God's Will as It Relates to Decision Making" (PhD diss., Dallas Theological Seminary, 1978), 7–148.

part two

the case of the MISSING DOT

The Traditional View Critiqued

chapter three

DOES GOD HAVE THREE WILLS?

In this chapter we begin a critique of the traditional view. And I start with this alert: reading such a critique can be unsettling for someone used to applying the traditional view to decision making. For this presentation brings to the surface inconsistencies of biblical interpretation and experiential tensions that believers inevitably encounter when they try to operate within this framework.

The traditional view promises clarity. It must do this because the God who makes His will known "does not stutter" when He speaks. And yet I suspect the reading of Bill Thompson's seminar outline did not make things easier for Ted Bradford. For when one carefully follows the steps laid out by the traditional view, the result is not always an unambiguous message from heaven. I'm not the only high school graduate who had a hard time figuring out where God wanted him to go to college.

So how does one make sense of this difficulty? If the traditional view is correct, there can be only one explanation: The person seeking God's guidance must be spiritually defective. But that explanation is hard to take, especially when the seeker is being as sincere as she can be. There is no obvious solution to that problem. Trying harder often makes matters worse. So most people just decide not to think about the dissonance between their understanding (of how things are supposed to work) and experience (which does not always conform to their expectations). They assume that the problem must be with them, but they don't know what to do about it—other than reading another book on guidance.

I don't think Ted Bradford's frustrations are due to his lack of sincerity or an unwillingness to follow wherever God might lead. I think there are problems with Bill Thompson's outline! *Ted Bradford is not spiritually defective; the traditional view is biblically deficient.* If that conclusion proves correct, then the frustrations that follow from trying to apply the traditional view (which I explore in detail in chapters 5–6) are actually predictable.

All I ask from the dubious reader is a mind open enough to look at Christian decision making, and the factors that enter into it, from another angle. The intent of my critique is not to perturb people, but to open the way to a better understanding of the biblical truth that sets us free. Sometimes in order to understand what is right, we have to first recognize what is wrong.

Sometimes in order to understand what is right, we have to first recognize what is wrong.

We begin with the question: What does the expression "God's will" mean?

Two Out of Three

The traditional view says that God's will may be understood in three ways: God's *sovereign* will, His *moral* will, and His *individual* will. We need to determine whether each of these categories is biblical.

Does God have a sovereign will? The traditional view says "Yes," and I agree. The Bible clearly teaches that God has a sovereign will, "a secret plan for everything that happens in the universe," as defined in part 1. Most traditional view proponents accept this doctrine, and even for those who reject it, their view makes little difference to their overall position on God's individual will. God's sovereign will has an important bearing on the believer's decision-making process, so this aspect of God's will is further explored in chapters 12 and 13.

Does God have a moral will? The Scriptures clearly reveal all of the moral will of God. While evangelicals agree about the reality of God's moral will, they disagree on the extent to which that moral will provides guidance in making specific decisions. The traditional view holds that the Bible (God's moral will) gives *most* of the guidance needed to make a decision, but also that knowing God's individual will is essential for complete leading to the correct choice. The view put forth in this book is that the Bible is *fully sufficient* to provide all guidance needed for a believer to know and do God's will. This concept will be developed in chapter 8, "Your Word Is Truth."

Does God have an individual will? Here we have come to the crux of the matter. In the traditional view, the concept of an ideal plan uniquely designed for each believer lies at the very heart of the whole system. The traditional view says, "It is important to make one's decisions within the larger circle of God's moral will. But finding the dot in the center—God's specific individual will—is essential in making correct decisions in daily life."

I am using *individual will* in a precise way here. It is the term used by the traditional view to designate "God's ideal, detailed life-plan uniquely designed for each person." No writer on biblical guidance equates this individual will with God's sovereign will. Obviously, God's sovereign will is specific for each person and in that sense, individual. But God's sovereign will can neither be found in advance nor missed. So that is not what the traditional view means by God's individual will.

My contention is that an *individual will* of God for every detail of a person's life is *not found in Scripture*. If I am right, the most startling ramification is that many believers are wasting a great deal of time and energy searching for something that does not exist. The search for the proverbial needle in a haystack holds a greater promise of success than the quest for the elusive dot.

Rather than assuming the reality of this individual will (which is where many presentations on guidance begin), I invite a reconsideration of this centerpiece of the traditional view. Pastor Thompson's outline cited reason, experience, biblical example, and biblical teaching as the bases for the individual will. We will examine each line of evidence in this order[1], addressing the first three in this chapter (reason, experience, and biblical example) and biblical teaching in the next (chapter 4, "Does Scripture Teach the Dot?").

THE ARGUMENTS FROM REASON

The traditional view says reason suggests several arguments for the individual will of God. The first line of evidence is based upon the combination of two of God's attributes: orderliness and omniscience. God's insistence upon order (1 Corinthians 14:40) and His advance knowledge of the outcome of every possible decision (Matthew 11:21–22) suggest that He would construct an individual will for each person. For all of creation, from the configuration of the galaxies to the intricacies of molecular structure, testifies to the orderliness of the Master Designer.

Given God's orderliness and omniscience, He certainly *could* develop an individual will for each person. But must we conclude that God's orderliness *demands* the existence of an individual will for people? I think not. The possibility of such an individual plan is not contrary to reason, but the necessity of such a plan is not required by reason.

Consider this illustration. A man might drive down Main Street on his way to work because that is the shortest route. But he does not *have* to go that way. He may take a longer route that, because of lighter traffic and fewer signal lights, allows him to get there more quickly. Reason permits either alternative.

Twinkle, Twinkle, Little Star

Everyone agrees that the Creator is orderly. But the design of the galaxies is the product of God's sovereign will, not His individual will.[2] The universe contains inanimate objects that function in an orderly fashion because of their conformity to God's laws of nature. The galaxies do not discover God's plan for them or choose to obey it. There is a major difference between particles and people: Only people make moral decisions.

And so, while the concept of an individual will of God is acceptable to reason, it is hardly required by it. Furthermore, reason can account for the orderly guidance of God in other ways, one of which will be presented later in this book.

Father Knows Best

The traditional view argues from reason that the imagery of God as our Father, Shepherd, and King indicates the reasonableness of an individual will. It says that a good father, king, or shepherd would have a detailed plan for his charges.

But is that true? Does a wise father guide his child through a plan that covers every detail of the child's life? Does he reveal that plan step-by-step as each decision must be made? Of course not. The truly wise father teaches his child the basic principles of life. He teaches right and wrong, wisdom and foolishness. He trains the child to make his own decisions within those moral guidelines. He is overjoyed when he sees his child grow into a mature adult capable of making wise decisions. This very picture is developed by the apostle Paul in Galatians 4:1–11. Throughout history, God has dealt with His people as a wise father would rear his children. As children grow, they are given increased responsibility. With increased responsibility comes greater freedom and fewer restrictions.

The other images indicate a similar pattern. A good shepherd sets boundaries for his sheep, but allows freedom of movement within those boundaries. He establishes limits for the safety of the sheep, but does not point out which specific tufts of grass ought to be eaten by each animal.

Likewise, an effective king does not seek to legislate every activity of his people. He establishes basic laws to promote order and uses penalties to promote compliance. He does not desire a nation of slaves, but a kingdom of people who respect his wisdom and appreciate his protection. When such a relationship exists, the people will act responsibly within the limits of the law.

God does guide His people like a father, shepherd, and king. But these figures do not prove the existence of an individual will of God. If these figures argue anything, they demonstrate that God guides through the basic principles of life given in the Bible (His moral will), thereby teaching His children to wisely use their freedom in the application of those principles to the decisions of life.

THE ARGUMENT FROM EXPERIENCE

The second line of proof advanced by the traditional view for the individual will of God is based on *experience*. Bible teachers agree that experience alone cannot determine truth. It can, however, give support for truth. If it can be shown that experience conforms to the teaching that God has an ideal plan for each believer, such evidence would provide valid support for that viewpoint.

Accounting for Hudson Taylor

Hudson Taylor was highly successful in his missionary endeavors in China. How can we account for his success? The traditional view is that Hudson Taylor's success can be attributed to his obedience to God's call to take the gospel to China. Because he followed God's individual will for his life, God blessed him.

If God does have an individual plan for each believer, this explanation is indeed possible. But is it the correct explanation? Are there any other factors that might account for such success? I believe there are. It seems equally possible that Hudson Taylor's accomplishments in evangelism stem from his obedience to God's *moral* will. Spiritual success is *promised* to the one who will obey God's Word (Psalm 1:2–3; 1 Kings 2:3; 1 Chronicles 22:13). God's moral will is given "so that you may be careful to do according to all that is written in it; for *then you will make your way prosperous, and then you will have success*" (Joshua 1:8).

Blessing is the result of knowing and obeying the revealed moral will of God (John 13:17; 2 Timothy 3:16–17). How successful would Hudson Taylor have been if he had gone to Africa rather than China? We have no way of knowing, but if his spiritual success was attributable to his obedience to the great commission (Matthew 28:19–20), there is good reason to believe he would have been an effective witness for Christ wherever he took the gospel, whether to China or Chinatown.

Of course we cannot prove that Hudson Taylor would have had success in endeavors he did not undertake. But in raising that possibility, I am insisting that experience proves only that Hudson Taylor did have success in China. It does not prove the reasons for that success. Scripture indicates that spiritual success comes because the sovereign God is working through believers who are obedient to His moral will wherever they are. This appears to be an acceptable explanation for Hudson Taylor's success.

A Still, Small Nudge?

What is one to make of those strong inward impressions that seem to point to a specific course of action? Personal examples of such promptings are common and appear to offer valid support for an individual will. Some who have followed such impulses have seen genuine spiritual results. These experiences are usually considered convincing demonstrations of the reality of God's precise, individual will.

This is an important question, and it will be discussed at length in chapter 6, "Impressions Are Impressions." For now, two observations will suffice. First, many such inward impressions lead nowhere. Promptings lead to dead ends as often as to avenues of service. For inward promptings to have value as proofs for the existence of an individual will, they would have to uniformly produce spiritual effects, with some degree of consistency. Second, spiritual accomplishments that result from following inner leading can be accounted for in the same way as Hudson Taylor's success. That is, the believer in question seized upon the opportunity presented to minister in accordance with God's moral will (Ephesians 5:16–17). Obedience brings blessing whether accompanied by an impression or not.

To sum up, experience neither proves nor disproves the existence of an individual will of God. There are other adequate explanations for spiritual success.[3]

THE ARGUMENT FROM BIBLICAL EXAMPLE

Having considered the arguments for the individual will from reason and experience, we may now turn to *biblical examples* that some construe to indicate an ideal plan for individual believers.

Examples in Scripture must be handled with care. Many of the events in the Bible are included primarily because they were unique or highly unusual occurrences. It must be determined whether each example referred to was intended to illustrate *normative* Christian behavior or experience. Should believers today practice the holy kiss (1 Corinthians 16:20)? Should one expect a light and a voice from heaven to accompany a call to the ministry (Acts 9:3–4)? God spoke to Balaam through a donkey (Numbers 22:28–30). Should each believer keep one in his backyard just in case? These suggestions may be extreme, but they remind us that while scriptural examples have real value, they must be carefully interpreted.

The scriptural examples shown in support of an individual will invariably cite instances where God gave supernaturally revealed guidance that was much more specific than God's moral will. The Old Testament includes accounts of people who received direct guidance to take certain vocations (such as leader, prophet, king) or to do certain things (e.g., Jonah 1:2). The book of Acts records numerous divine directions that Paul and others received. Paul was called, literally, to be an apostle by vocation (Acts 9; 1 Corinthians 1:1; Galatians 1:1). He was sent out as a missionary (Acts 13:1–2). During Paul's missionary work he was directed to specific places of ministry and away from others (Acts 16:6–10; 18:9–10; 22:17–21; 23:11). Peter was told to go to Cornelius's house (Acts 10:17–20) after Cornelius was directed to find Peter (Acts 10:5). Later Peter was led out of Herod's prison (Acts 12:7–8). Philip was directed to a desert road (Acts 8:26) to join a particular chariot (Acts 8:29), from which he was dispatched to the town of Azotus (Acts 8:39–40). Ananias was ordered to find Saul of Tarsus after the Damascus Road experience (Acts 9:10–16).

There is no doubt that these occurrences involved guidance that was more specific than the general moral commands of Scripture. The question is whether such examples prove that God has an individual will for every believer.

Consistently Sporadic

The traditional view has weaknesses at this point. The first weakness is that the *number of recorded cases is not sufficient* to constitute normative experience. In the first thirty years of the church's history recorded in Acts, there were only fifteen to twenty instances of direct, personal guidance. Many of these directions were given to Paul. Yet throughout his ministry, relatively few of his decisions were determined by such leading. Most of the time he had to weigh the apparent merits of various options before settling on a course of action.[4] In other words, he had to decide (Acts 15:36; Acts 20:16; Romans 1:10–13; 1 Corinthians 16:4–9; 2 Corinthians 1:15–2:4). The cases of direct guidance are clearly the exception to the rule, even in Paul's case.

Second, *these examples are not sufficiently comprehensive.* God's individual will for the believer's life should cover every decision made. But the examples do not touch upon life's ordinary decisions. Most of the instances in Acts had some direct bearing on the spread of the gospel; specific leading was given by God to insure evangelistic outreach during the formative years of the church. Such a purpose is clearly seen in the guidance given to Peter, Cornelius, Philip, Ananias, Barnabas, the church at Antioch, and Paul. In the book of Acts, there is no indication of any specific word from God on the more ordinary decisions of life.[5]

The third weakness of arguing for an individual will from such examples is that *most of the recipients of specific guidance occupied a special place in the outworking of God's program.* They were people selected by God to play a major role in His plan.

Most of the examples in Acts occur in the ministries of Peter and Paul—*apostles* who received special revelation because of their unique office in the church. The nonapostolic recipients of direct guidance—Philip, Ananias, Cornelius, and the church at Antioch—found themselves at strategic historical crossroads in the spread of the gospel beyond the house of Israel. By virtue of their reception of divine revelation and their obedience to it, they became key figures in the worldwide propagation of the gospel.

Old Testament examples are usually prophets, judges, kings, or other leaders, not the general populace. This is partially explained by the fact that most of biblical history focuses on "special" believers. Still, to argue from these cases that God has an individual will for all believers is unwarranted in the absence of further substantiation from the Epistles.

We have seen that the examples of detailed divine guidance in Scripture are infrequent, limited in scope, and directed to persons who play a special role in God's program for earth. Such selectivity on the part of God weakens rather than strengthens the support for the concept of an individual will for all Christians.

One more factor worthy of consideration is the *means of communication.* The traditional view holds that supernatural revelation is not normative experience for all believers. Yet all of the examples given in support of individual guidance are clearly instances of *supernatural revelation.* In Acts, such guidance came through visions (9:10–16; 10:3–8; 10:17; 16:9–10; 18:9; 22:17–21), angelic messenger (8:26; 12:7–8; 27:23), physical miracle (8:39), an audible voice from God (8:29; 9:3–6; 10:19–20; 23:11), or a prophet who had received direct revelation (13:1–2; 21:10–11). There are no recorded examples where detailed guidance was given through a means other than supernatural revelation.

One could argue that God *may* give a believer guidance that is more specific than that found in the Bible. But if He does, it will be through supernatural means.

SUPERNATURAL GUIDANCE—WHAT NEW TESTAMENT EXAMPLES SHOW

- Supernatural guidance for specific decisions was the exception to the rule.
- Supernatural guidance was given to people who played a strategic role in the drama of world evangelization.
- Supernatural guidance was provided only at critical points during the formative years of the church.
- Supernatural guidance was always communicated by means of supernatural revelation.

The absence of indisputable examples of the traditional view's approach to decision making is striking. In the Bible, no believer asks, "What is God's individual will for me in this matter?" Much of the vocabulary and many of the concepts in the traditional presentation are absent from the Bible. One does not read of the "specific will," "center of God's will," "right decision," "putting out a fleece," or even "finding God's will."

Even more startling is that no decision is ever explained on the basis that it was "God's individual will." Today we often hear people say, "I did this because I knew it was God's will for me," or "I felt in my heart God wanted me to do it." The apostles often gave reasons for their decisions, but never in such terms.[6] If their decisions were based upon God's individual will, it is remarkable that they never mentioned it. What is so common and essential to the traditional view is passed over in silence in the New Testament.

There are no examples in Scripture of ordinary believers making decisions in the manner outlined by the traditional view. Proponents of that view have had to water down examples of supernatural guidance to support what they contend is normative guidance. This approach to biblical interpretation is dubious, to say the least.

For example, we read in Acts 8 that God supernaturally guided Philip to explain the gospel to the Ethiopian eunuch. Is it valid to deduce from this that God will put impressions in the heart of the believer to point out people they should witness to? Unless there is a specific teaching of Scripture that promises such guidance (and I contend there is none), this deduction is not warranted. The difference between "an angel of the Lord" who spoke to Philip (Acts 8:26) and an inward impression in the heart of a contemporary believer is just too great.

What Would Jesus Do?

One final matter needs to be addressed: the example of Christ. Proponents of the traditional view are very cautious with this "biblical example" of an individual will of God. Jesus is the supreme model of one who knew God's will perfectly and fulfilled it completely (Luke 22:42; John 4:34; 6:38; Hebrews 10:7–9). While He is set forth as the believer's example, there is an awareness that He was unique in His person and in His relationship to His Father. My own conclusion is that Christ was given specific guidance by the Father beyond the moral will of God. Like earlier examples, this guidance came through supernatural direct revelation. In His case this revelation was abundant since He was the God-man, Prophet, Priest, and King.

Virtually everyone agrees that Christ's life was not normative for Christian experience at every point. His relationship with the Father is different from that of everyone else. God is "His own Father" which means that He is "equal with God" (John 5:18). It is not normative experience for the believer to follow the example of Christ by being equal with God, or regularly performing miracles, or speaking authoritatively on every interpretation of Scripture, or receiving worship, or calling for absolute allegiance, or reading the thoughts of opponents, or giving others the authority to do miracles, or exercising any other prerogative of deity.

The nonnormative character of Christ's life is further underscored by His office as a prophet (Deuteronomy 18:15, 18; Matthew 11:21; John 6:14; Acts 3:20–23). As a prophet, He would regularly receive direct revelation from God—a privilege not experienced by all believers.

Christ perfectly obeyed God's will for His life. He said, "My food is to do the will of Him who sent Me and to accomplish His work" (John

4:34). He also said "BEHOLD, I HAVE COME...TO DO YOUR WILL, O GOD'" (Hebrews 10:7). Jesus repeatedly said that the work He did was the work which the Father had for Him to do (John 5:19, 30, 36; 6:38; 8:28–29, 42; 10:37–38; 12:49–50; 14:31; 15:10; 17:4). The question is, what was the "will of God" for Jesus Christ?

It must have included the moral will of God revealed in the Bible for all men since He was a true man (John 9:4; 1 Timothy 2:5). It must have included, in particular, all those passages written for the Messiah to fulfill (Luke 4:18–21). It must have included all communication between Father and Son, from eternity past until the Incarnation, about the words and works of the Son when He became the Messiah. Finally, the will of God for Jesus must have included the direct revelation that passed between Father and Son during Christ's incarnation on earth. The content of this last category of communication is known only to the Godhead, but it did include whatever Christ said He was seeing and hearing the Father do (John 5:19, 30).

For all these reasons it is valid to believe that Christ received specific guidance by direct revelation for many of His actions. It is even possible that direct communion between Father and Son touched every detail of Christ's life. These details would harmonize perfectly with the moral and sovereign wills of God.

But the uniqueness of Christ is so pervasive, one must be cautious in suggesting where Christ's life provides a normative example for the believer today. In the Epistles, Christ is declared to be our example, but the extent to which He is our model is not open-ended. He is our example in specific ways. Whenever the Bible calls God, or Christ, our example, it delineates the area of likeness. Those areas cited include: humble service (John 13:1–15), holiness (1 Peter 1:15–16), righteousness (1 John 3:7), purity (1 John 3:3), love (Ephesians 5:1–2), forgiveness (Colossians 3:13), compassion (Ephesians 4:32), endurance (Hebrews 12:2–4), submission (1 Peter 2:21–24), humility and obedience (Philippians 2:5–8), kindness (Luke 6:35), and generosity in giving (2 Corinthians 8:1–9).

Significantly, the areas in which believers are told to imitate Jesus Christ *concern the manner in which He fulfilled the moral will of God.* Just as Jesus obeyed His Father's moral will, so the sons and daughters of God should obey their Father's will. The difference is this: For the only begotten Son of God, His Father's will was revealed through a variety of means; for the born-anew sons of God, their Father's will is fully revealed in His Word, the Bible.

To sum up, a survey of the biblical examples of specific guidance shows that they do not prove an individual will of God for every believer. They show only that God has broken into history at infrequent times to give specific guidance through supernatural revelation to selected people, usually for the purpose of evangelism. The exceptional proves only the exceptional. Such guidance is not normative according to any viewpoint. Nor is it necessary for normal decision making in the Christian life.

Although the examples do not prove an individual will of God, they do not disprove it either. The direct teaching of the Word of God must act as the final arbiter.

frequently asked question

> *Question:* In the first edition of *Decision Making*, you did not discuss Acts 22:14–15 in which Ananias told Paul that he would know God's will for him. Doesn't that indicate that God had an individual will for Paul? And if God intended for Paul to know His will, shouldn't we expect the same for all believers?

Okay, this was an *infrequently* asked question. But this passage has been brought up by enough readers to warrant a reply, and it does refer directly to "knowing God's will." Here is what the passage says:

> "And [Ananias] said [to me, Paul], 'The God of our fathers has appointed you to know His will and to see the Righteous One and to hear an utterance from His mouth. For you will be a witness for Him to all men of what you have seen and heard.'"

This passage is one of three that describes Paul's conversion (Acts 9:1–19; 22:1–21; 26:9–23). What is the content of "His will" in these verses? A believing response to the gospel is the first step of obedience to the moral will of God for unbelievers like Paul. The immediate result of this Damascus Road revelation was Paul's salvation and baptism (Acts 22:16).

It is probable that "His will" also encompasses God's revelation of Paul's apostleship and ministry to the Gentiles declared at the same time.

In later writings, Paul refers back to his apostolic appointment as being "according to the commandment of God" (1 Timothy 1:1) and "by the will of God" (2 Timothy 1:1). The statements in Acts 9:15 and 22:15 that Paul is "a chosen instrument of Mine [Christ's]" and "a witness for Him" likely refers to Paul's apostolic commissioning, since the apostles were the chosen and inspired eyewitnesses of the resurrection (Acts 1:22).

"God's will" for Paul, then, was that he believe in the message of the gospel and accept his appointment as an apostle to the Gentiles. While the former is part of God's moral will for all men (1 Timothy 2:3–4; 2 Peter 3:9), the latter is unique to Paul. These two facets are sufficient to explain "His will" in this text without reading the theology of an individual will into the passage.

So my answer to the question is no. The fact that God's moral will for Paul included details that were revealed to the apostle by divine revelation does not imply that God has an individual will for all believers revealed to their hearts by impressions of the Holy Spirit.

---

1. Most Bible teachers agree that direct biblical teaching is what ultimately matters—arguments from reason, experience, and biblical examples properly serve a corroborative role. And yet I suspect that many Christians actually acquire their picture of "God's plan for my life" from these auxiliary lines of evidence, which they then read into the passages that explicitly teach on God's will. (I expand on this theme in the next chapter.) So it is necessary to carefully analyze these supplementary arguments as well.
2. Again, our established definitions for the terms *individual will* and *sovereign will* of God must be carefully observed here. Each star in the universe is one "individual" part of God's sovereign plan; but there is no *individual will* of God for each star, as defined by the traditional view. This distinction applies in the same way to people. Every person has an "individual" part in God's sovereign plan. But that is not what the traditional view means when it speaks of God's individual will for a person.
3. I have assumed (for the sake of discussion) a definition of spiritual success that equates it with some positive and identifiable response to ministry. That is, when people respond to the proclamation of God's Word in repentance and faith, we tend to label such ministry "successful."

   But in Scripture, spiritual success is described as faithfulness to the commands of God (1 Corinthians 4:2; 2 Corinthians 2:14–17; Hebrews 11:32–39). For faithful service always glorifies God and matures God's servant whether the outcome is a great revival or a slammed door.

   On the other hand, there have been situations where God has sovereignly chosen to reap a spiritual harvest through the efforts of men who were motivated by wrong attitudes (Philippians 1:12–18; Jonah 3–4). Spiritual results? Certainly. Obedience to God's will? Hardly. For God's will encompasses both action and attitude (Philippians 2:3; Romans 2:8).

Since faithfulness in ministry does not always yield "positive" results, and since sinners are sometimes brought to repentance through the agency of carnal heralds, *any* argument from experience is of dubious value. For it is impossible to judge the success of an action or a ministry strictly on its observable outcome.

4. The actual processes by which the apostles determined most of their decisions are analyzed at length in chapters 10, 11, 14, and 15. Additional illustrations from the New Testament are interspersed throughout the applicational chapters of part 4, "Deciding the Big Ones."
5. For completeness it should be noted that examples outside the book of Acts could be cited that seem to show detailed guidance in common, everyday decisions. Such examples might include the Shunammite woman who received specific directions to move in order to avoid a famine (2 Kings 8:1–2); Saul, who received guidance in finding his donkeys (1 Samuel 9:20); the wandering Israelites, who experienced guidance in daily travel from a pillar of cloud (Numbers 9:15–23); and the twelve disciples, who received direction from Christ on where to seat and how to serve the five thousand (John 6:10–12).

   But even these additional cases do not alter the point. To show that God's usual means of guidance involves specific direction for each decision, the traditional view must offer much more than a few sporadic examples.

   Furthermore, though they concern everyday matters, the examples do not purport to indicate the nature of normative guidance. The Shunammite's guidance, for instance, demonstrated the prophetic authority of Elisha, who was miraculously enabled to predict the famine. It also showed God's care for the woman who had earlier aided His prophet (2 Kings 4:8–17). Even in this example, the guidance did not specify the location she should move to. It was left to her to go "wherever you can sojourn" (2 Kings 8:1). Evidently, Philistia was her selection (2 Kings 8:2).

   The direction that enabled Saul to find his donkeys was not provided as normative guidance, but as evidence of Samuel's authority as a prophet. For Samuel was preparing to anoint Saul as king. The finding of the donkeys was one in a series of signs that were given to prove that God had chosen Saul to be Israel's first king (1 Samuel 10:1–13).

   The pillar of cloud was provided as evidence of God's special care for Israel so that the people would learn at the inception of the nation to trust Him. When Israel entered the land of Canaan, the cloud was removed. It was a temporary provision that was no longer needed.

   The guidance received by the twelve disciples of Jesus from time to time can hardly be considered normative. Christ was God-in-the-flesh, and the disciples were appointed to a unique office. Yet even in their daily life with the Son of God, the Twelve were not specifically told what they should do in every decision.
6. Again, the actual processes by which the apostles determined most of their decisions are analyzed at length in chapters 10, 11, 14, and 15.

chapter four

DOES SCRIPTURE TEACH THE DOT?

Virtually all evangelical Bible teachers agree that while reason and experience can support a doctrinal position, they cannot prove it. Likewise, scriptural examples can add strong support if they are shown to be normative. But in the final analysis, the straightforward teaching of Scripture itself must determine and establish our viewpoint on any issue. And so the question is, what does God's Word teach about an individual will of God? Can an ideal plan for each individual be proved from the sacred text?

In this chapter we will consider the Scripture passages most often quoted by the traditional view as teaching an individual will. For the person who assumes that God has an individual will for each life, each of these passages will, upon first reading, appear to confirm that presupposition. However, closer scrutiny of these verses in context shows that, in most cases, it is more likely that the writer is referring to the *moral* will of God. What this chapter establishes, then, is that these key passages do not prove an individual will of God for each person; rather a stronger case can be made for understanding them in terms of the moral will of God.

As we launch into the crux chapter of this critique of the traditional view, Acts 17:11 comes to mind: "Now the Bereans were of more noble character…for they received the message with great eagerness and *examined the Scriptures every day to see if what Paul said was true*" (NIV). I am by no means equating these pages with apostolic authority. I invite the reader to emulate the noble Bereans in the sincerity of their examinations of the Scriptures. For I have no desire to persuade anyone of anything that is contrary to the biblical text. This chapter is best read at a slower, deliberate pace with a Bible close at hand. Since I will be making repeated references to the contexts of the key verses (and no passage should ever be studied apart from its context), an open Bible will help you to evaluate the accuracy of my explanations. And I welcome that.

PSALM 32:8

I will instruct you and teach you
in the way which you should go;
I will counsel you with My eye upon you.

In the King James Version, the second clause is translated: "I will guide thee with mine eye." The verb translated "guide" has the sense of "counsel," as it is rendered by the New American Standard Bible above. Such counsel is given in the form of instruction and teaching, which represents a kind of guidance. The traditional view understands the speaker to be the Lord, who is promising specific guidance for a particular "way"—i.e., the individual will of God.

The speaker could be God, but some respected commentators believe that David himself is speaking. This idea stems from the relation that Psalm 32 bears to Psalm 51. Psalm 51 is David's prayer for forgiveness and restoration after his sin with Bathsheba was exposed by God's prophet. In that prayer, David promised that if God forgave him, he would teach transgressors God's way (Psalm 51:10–13). Psalm 32 records David's response when he received word that God's forgiveness had been granted. What David had promised in Psalm 51:13, he fulfilled in Psalm 32:8.[1]

The phrase "the way which you should go" refers to the course or manner of life we should follow. This is the way of righteous living, which the law revealed and David taught.[2] If God, however, is the speaker, He is seen teaching His way of righteousness intended for all believers, not an individual way for each believer. This customary usage fits the context, so an individual will is not in view.

Virtually all commentators struggle with the last phrase "with My eye upon you." The best explanation is that David is giving counsel to sinners as his eye of concern is upon them.

In all likelihood, if the word "guide" had not been used in the rendering of the King James Version, this verse would never have been used in presentations on guidance. For it is simply reiterating the message of so many other Old Testament passages that describe instruction in the life of righteousness provided by the law, the moral will of God.

PROVERBS 3:5–6

Trust in the LORD with all your heart
And do not lean on your own understanding.
In all your ways acknowledge Him,
And He will make your paths straight.

This passage may be the most frequently quoted verses in discussion of God's will. Usually, it is the King James Version that is quoted, for the translation "and he shall direct thy paths" seems to give credence to personal leading according to an individual plan.

Still the interpreter must ask what the original writer meant by that expression. In order to answer that question, it is important first of all to determine the most accurate translation of the original Hebrew statement, and then to note other usages of that same expression by the same writer to get additional light on its meaning.

Hebrew lexicons and commentaries on the Psalms and Proverbs agree that the correct translation of Proverbs 3:6b is: "and He shall make your paths straight, (or) smooth, (or) successful."[3] Both the NASB and NIV translations render it "make your paths straight."

The noun "path" is frequently employed in the Psalms and Proverbs. But it does not have the idea of an individual will of God. Hebrew writers use it to describe the general course or fortunes of life (see Proverbs 4:18–19; 15:19). When the verb "make straight, make smooth" is connected with "paths," the meaning of the statement is, "He shall make the course of your life successful." This meaning is clearly indicated in Proverbs 11:5:

> The righteousness of the blameless will *smooth his way*,
> But the wicked will fall by his own wickedness.

This verse contrasts the righteous man who experiences true success in life with the wicked man who brings trouble upon himself by his devious behavior. This is a common theme in Proverbs (4:18–19; 11:5; 15:19; 22:17–21).

The point of Proverbs 3:5–6, then, is that those who trust God, and trust in His wisdom rather than their own worldly understanding, and acknowledge God in each part of their life, will reap a life that is successful by God's standards. This understanding fits the larger context precisely. Proverbs 3:1–10 is a series of two-verse couplets. Each couplet describes the blessings that come to the person who acknowledges God. Here is a summary of the couplets:

Keep my commandments and have long days and peace (1–2).

Keep kindness and truth and find favor and good repute (3–4).

Trust in the Lord and He will make the course of your life successful (5–6).

Fear the Lord and it will bring healing to your body (7–8).

Honor the Lord with your wealth and your barns will be filled with plenty (9–10).

The means by which we acknowledge God in all our ways is by believing and obeying the law of God rather than trusting and following man's finite, worldly philosophy for success and happiness. Proverbs 3:5–6 is not dealing with specific guidance into an individual "path" marked out by God. Old Testament scholar Bruce Waltke confirms this:

> All of us have had the shock of discovering that a favorite verse in the King James Version was inaccurate.... I recall the astonishment of one of the committee members assigned to translate the Book of Proverbs for the New International Version when he discovered that Proverbs 3:5–6 had nothing to say about guidance.... [W]hen confronted with the linguistic data he had to admit reluctantly that the verse more properly read "and He will make your path smooth."[4]

The true intent of Proverbs 3:5–6 is to set forth a pattern the believer should follow to experience true success in life—a pattern in which he demonstrates his trust and obedience of God by following the directions of God's moral will.

PROVERBS 16:9

The mind of man plans his way,
But the LORD directs his steps.

Those who cite this verse in support of the traditional view infer a meaning that could be paraphrased: "The mind of man improperly tries to make his own plans, but it is the LORD who should do the directing into His will." This sounds like the warning in Proverbs 3:5: "do not lean on your own understanding." Instead, seek God's direction into His individual will—or so it is assumed.

This verse, however, is a sample of several passages that describe *not* the moral will of God, nor a so-called individual will, but God's sovereign will. A better paraphrase is, "Man makes plans, but the ultimate outcome is directed by God." The proverb is not about guidance for believers only; it is true of all men. No matter how independent an individual may think he is, his steps are ultimately controlled by God's sovereign direction. This Hebrew proverb appears in other languages as well. In English it is: "Man proposes, but God disposes." In German, "Der Mensch denkt, Gott lenkt." Despite man's freedom to plan and scheme, God ultimately determines the direction of those plans and whether they succeed or fail.

Proverbs 16:1 (in the near context) communicates a similar idea:

The plans of the heart belong to man,
But the answer of the tongue is from the LORD.

Old Testament commentator Derek Kidner sees Proverbs 16:1 teaching the same truth as 16:9. "The meaning is…that for all his freedom to plan, man only…advances God's designs."[5]

Another proverb expresses the same idea differently:

Many plans are in a man's heart,
But the counsel of the LORD will stand. (Proverbs 19:21)

Delitzsch adds an apt application. The one who knows that God is sovereignly guiding the final outcome should "do his duty and leave the rest, with humility and confidence, to God."[6]

Proverbs 16:9 promises sovereign guidance for the believer and unbeliever alike. It is detailed. When dice are thrown, the outcome is determined by God (Proverbs 16:33). These and other verses in the Proverbs tell of God's sovereign work on the earth (see also Proverbs 20:24; 21:30–31; Psalm 33:10–11). They are not referring to the individual will of God as taught by the traditional view.

ISAIAH 30:20–21

Although the Lord has given you bread of privation and water of oppression, He, your Teacher will no longer hide Himself, but your eyes will behold your Teacher. Your ears will hear a word behind you, "This is the way, walk in it," whenever you turn to the right or to the left.

This passage is often quoted by proponents of the traditional view as describing the inward work of the Holy Spirit giving specific guidance into God's individual will. It is suggested that whenever a believer strays from the pathway of God's will for his life, the Spirit will communicate that fact and give directions for returning to the proper road.

Three interpretive questions need to be answered about this passage. First, who is the "teacher" who will be seen and heard? Second, what is "the way" in which the people are to walk? Third, in what sense does the message of the teacher come from "behind" them?

Now concerning the identity of the teacher, the translators of the New American Standard Bible made an interpretive decision that I consider doubtful (and the editors of the New International Version and the New King James Version concur). In capitalizing "Teacher" and adding the italicized "He" (a pronoun not in the original text), they indicated their conclusion that the teacher who gives the directions is the Lord. But there is a better explanation. It is more likely that the teacher was a prophet sent to teach the people.[7] For since the time of wicked King Ahaz, the prophets had to be in hiding for their safety, a fact mentioned even in the near context (Isaiah 30:8–11). This is reflected in the NIV translation, "your teachers will be hidden no more; with your own eyes you will see them." (NKJV: "Yet your teachers will not be moved into a corner anymore, but your eyes shall see your teachers.")

This being the case, the "eyes" and "ears" in this passage should be taken literally. The promised blessing was that when Israel repented (Isaiah 30:19), God would bring the prophets out of hiding. When He did that, they would see their teacher with their eyes and hear him with their ears.[8] (If the teacher was the Holy Spirit, it is difficult to grasp in what way He could be seen with the eyes. Literal interpretation, which fits the context well, removes that difficulty.)

This understanding suits the larger context as well. In Isaiah 30:1–17, God declares His judgment against wayward Israel. Then in verses 18–26, He lists the blessings that would come upon the repentant nation. One of those blessings would be the needed return of the teaching prophets.

The message of the prophets is significant: "This is the way, walk in it." It is true that the prophets predicted future events, but the primary prophetic function was to appeal to the nation to return to the Lord and live in obedience to His moral law. The prophets were to teach and preach the precepts of the law so that the people could repent and avoid God's certain judgment.

Whether the speaker in this passage is the Lord or a prophet, "the way" is the way of God's law. This is the consistent meaning of the term throughout the Old Testament (recall the discussion of Psalm 32:8 and Proverbs 3:5–6, above). And frequently, warnings to obey the law fully are given in negative terms as "[do] not turn aside to the right or to the left" (Deuteronomy 5:31–33; see Deuteronomy 17:18–20; 28:13–14; Joshua 1:7; 23:6). For example, in Deuteronomy 5:31–33, "the way" is defined as "all the commandments and the statutes and the judgments." From this teaching Israel was commanded "you shall not turn aside to the right or to the left." Clearly, "the way" was the righteous way of the law, God's moral will for them.

Now this voice that the people of Israel would hear is not described as an inward voice of the Spirit,[9] but as a voice *behind them*. The word "behind" probably indicates that if Israel did depart from the way of the Law, the people would be turning their backs on God's commands, and the prophets would call to them from behind to return to the pathway of righteousness. In any case the description of the voice better fits the teaching of the prophets than the inward impressions of the Holy Spirit.

Isaiah 30:20–21 reveals that teachers are a great blessing from God. Good teachers clearly instruct us in the way of God's moral will and call us to return to the path of righteousness when we stray as Israel did. There is danger to the right and to the left, but God's way of righteousness is the way of success (Joshua 1:7–8).

JOHN 5:19

Therefore Jesus answered and was saying to them, "Truly, truly, I say to you, the Son can do nothing of Himself, unless it is something He sees the Father doing; for whatever the Father does, these things the Son also does in like manner."

In recent years a new passage has been used to support the traditional view of guidance. Jesus' words in John 5:19 are set forth as the normative model for discovering God's individual will.

This version of the traditional view claims that the key to finding God's will is to see what God is doing in the world and then join Him. In Jesus' case, He kept watching the Father's activity around Him so He could unite His life with the Father's activity. The suggested application is that the believer should look for the ways God is working and then join Him, knowing that this is His individual will for that person. God's work involves things that only He can do: drawing people to Himself; revealing spiritual truth; and convicting the world of sin, righteousness, and judgment.

The book *Experiencing God* gives an example of this approach. An evangelistic team was considering whether God wanted them to plant a church in a town where they had conducted meetings. They believed that to make the decision based upon a population survey would be an exercise in self-planning and the application of "human logic." Instead they wanted to "find out if God [was] at work." One team conducted a Vacation Bible School. When several parents attended the closing program on Friday night, the leaders asked a question. "We believe God may want us to establish a Baptist church in this town. If any of you would like to begin a regular Bible study group and maybe become a part of a new church, would you just come forward?" Several people who had been praying for a church responded favorably.

The prospective church planters concluded, "We didn't have to take a survey. God had just shown us where He was at work!"[10] I may be missing the nuance of this example, but it looks like they did conduct a survey. They surveyed a specific population, found a fertile area, and did what was wise.

Is this illustration a valid application of John 5:19? It is true that John 5 clearly emphasizes how Christ did God's will rather than His own (John 5:30, 36). The main point of this passage, however, is to prove that Jesus was equal to God. His opponents accused Him of "making Himself equal to God" (John 5:18) and Jesus asserted that He was guilty as charged. Jesus saw the Father at work and did the same works (John 5:19). The initial work appears to be the miraculous healing that started the debate (John 5:1–16).

More pertinent are the two further works that Jesus claims to do in John 5:17–29. The first work is giving life to the dead. The Father raises the dead and so does the Son (John 5:21). The second work is judgment. The Father judges and has given this judgment to the Son (John 5:22) as well as equal honor (John 5:23). These two works will be even more dramatic in the future when the Son will speak and those in the tombs will be raised and judged by the Son (John 5:28–29). The works that the Father does He gives to the Son to do. The Son does them and the works are a witness that the Father has sent the Son (John 5:36–37). As Wescott points out, this is not mere "imitation by the Son, but by virtue of the sameness of nature with the Father."[11]

The traditional view seems to be building on the coincidence of the wording of John 5:19 rather than Jesus' meaning. We commonly speak of "seeing God at work." We mean that we see His influence in a particular circumstance—blessing, conviction, revival, and so on. By "joining God in the work" we mean that we pray and get involved with people and ministries. Our common expressions are similar to that of

Jesus in John 5:19, but the meaning is quite different.

Jesus means that He *actually* does the *same* works that He sees His Father doing—resurrection and judgment. He is equal to the Father. We don't see the Father directly within the Godhead as Jesus does. We do not do the same works that the Father does—resurrection and judgment. These things are quite different from seeing God's influence in circumstances and joining in to minister.

And so I conclude that the suggested interpretation of John 5:19 is flawed. At the same time, I commend the approach taken in the illustration. There is nothing wrong with finding people who are praying for a church and sending a church planter to them. Paul would call this an "open door" for ministry (1 Corinthians 16:8–9; 2 Corinthians 2:12; Colossians 4:3).[12] So there is a perfectly good, biblical rationale for the church planting strategy. It just doesn't come from the words of Jesus recorded in John 5, nor do those words support a theology of an individual will.

To sum up, John 5 presents Jesus as a model for obeying the Father and doing His will. Verse 19, however, does not set out a way of discerning the individual will of God by watching circumstances in the world.[13] Jesus is presenting evidence of His equality with God. That equality is based upon direct access to the Father and upon His supernatural works like those of the Father.

JOHN 10:3–4, 16, 27

"To [the shepherd] the doorkeeper opens, and the sheep hear his voice, and he calls his own sheep by name and leads them out. When he puts forth all his own, he goes ahead of them, and the sheep follow him because they know his voice."

"I have other sheep, which are not of this fold; I must bring them also, and they will hear My voice; and they will become one flock with one shepherd."

"My sheep hear My voice, and I know them, and they follow Me."

Using the imagery of a shepherd and his sheep, Jesus spoke repeatedly of the sheep "hearing" and "knowing" the shepherd's voice. According to proponents of the traditional view, this parable teaches that Jesus conveys His individual will to those "sheep" who "hear His voice." The closer I walk to the Shepherd, the clearer I will be able to hear the Shepherd's specific directions revealing His individual will.

The parable is not difficult to follow. It is a response to the conflict between Jesus and certain Pharisees over the healing of a blind man (John 9). The parable is addressed to Jesus' opponents (9:40–10:1). He is the Good Shepherd who lays down His life for the sheep (10:11); He is also the "door" to salvation (10:9). They are thieves, robbers (10:1, 8), strangers (10:5), and hired hands (10:12–13). The sheep are those who believe in Him.

So what does Jesus mean when He says, "My sheep hear My voice"? Is He speaking solely of auditory recognition? No. In the context, Jesus is explaining a grim reality. There are others who would permit or do harm to the sheep. These others call out to the sheep, and the sheep hear them, in a literal sense. But the sheep do not "hear" the imposters (10:8) the way they hear the shepherd in confident trust. The subject of the parable is not guidance, but salvation. And the point is that only Jesus is the true Shepherd, and all who are true sheep believe Him, follow Him, and receive eternal life (10:26–28).

This teaching explains the experience of the blind man just healed by Jesus (John 9). In a literal sense, he heard both the voice of Jesus (9:7, 37) and the voices of the Pharisees (9:13–17, 24–34). But in the end he rejected the "call" of the Pharisees and "heard" (that is, he believed and accepted) the words of Jesus who claimed to be the Savior (9:37). "Lord, I believe," he said, and he worshipped Him (9:38).

The interpretation of the traditional view founders at three points. First, as we have just seen, the parable is not about guidance. It is about the identity of the true Savior and faith in Him for salvation.

Second, the traditional view makes a distinction between some believers who hear God's voice and others who are not walking intimately with God and so do not hear Him—or hear Him indistinctly. Those who do not recognize God's leading, it is said, are too far away from the Shepherd. In contrast, John 10 teaches that *all* God's sheep, all believers, hear clearly and accept the words of His voice (10:4–5, 16). Because the sheep hear and believe, they are given eternal life (10:26–28).

Third, the traditional view assumes that God's voice is an impression in the heart. In contrast, Jesus is referring to His actual spoken words and His message of salvation. The question at issue is, of the many voices calling to the sheep, which one will they follow?

The interpretation that equates "hearing the Shepherd's voice" with guidance into God's individual will by means of inner impressions is an instance of reading one's theology into the passage. It is invalid to infer from this text that a believer who is sufficiently close to the Shepherd will be able to discern which impression among many is the guiding voice of God. The reality is that if God gives further revelation, you could not miss it if you wanted to. But that would be no inner impression; it would be a real voice—or the equivalent.

It is valid to say (on the basis of passages other than John 10) that walking close to God will help you to *judge* impressions. The closer you are following the Spirit the better you will be able to separate sinful impressions from holy ones, to distinguish foolish impressions from wise ones.[14] But impressions do not equal God's revelation, so no amount of discernment will identify some of them as the pure voice of God.

John 10 addresses the moral will of God (that sinners trust in Jesus for eternal life [10:26–28]) and the sovereign will of God (that those who so believe will never perish [10:28–29]). But any claim that this parable teaches how Christians may discern God's guidance into His individual will is mistaken and foreign to the passage.

Romans 12:1–2

Therefore I urge you, brethren, by the mercies of God, to present your bodies a living and holy sacrifice, acceptable to God, which is your spiritual service of worship. And do not be conformed to this world, but be transformed by the renewing of your mind, so that you may prove what the will of God is, that which is good and acceptable and perfect.

This is the first passage in which we encounter the specific terminology "will of God." So our first step is to determine the sense in which it is being used.[15] Was Paul challenging the Romans to prove God's sovereign will, His moral will, or His individual will? Proponents of the traditional view frequently cite this passage to show that we must prove or find God's individual will, and that personal surrender is a prerequisite to finding it. God's sovereign will does not fit the context, but the moral will and the individual will both do. The verb "prove" can also mean "approve after proving," but in either case the idea of "prove" or "discern" is involved.[16] And the verb will fit either the moral or individual senses of God's will. There are, however, some positive indications that the moral will is in view in this passage.

First, the twelfth chapter of Romans marks the beginning of the second major section of the epistle. The first eleven chapters contain a closely argued exposition of doctrine. Chapters 12 through 16 follow through with exhortations regarding appropriate behavior that corresponds to the doctrine taught. Paul's thrust in Romans 12:1 is: on the basis of God's mercies, which have just been explained in detail, surrender your body to God for obedient living. Then beginning with verse three and extending into the next four chapters, he spells out the commands that ought to be obeyed. In other words, as soon as he completes his exhortation to "prove what the will of God is," he begins giving specific examples of that will. Significantly, those examples are moral commands addressed to all believers. The immediate context says nothing about such things as finding our vocation, choosing our mate, or anything else that is so specific as to be part of God's individual will. Rather, there are commands concerning the use of our gifts (12:6–8), love (12:9), devotion to other believers (12:10), diligence in serving the Lord (12:11), rejoicing (12:12), hospitality (12:13), blessing persecutors (12:14), and so on. These obviously reflect the moral rather than the individual will of God.

Second, the three words that qualify "the will of God"—"good and acceptable and perfect"—closely resemble a similar threefold description employed earlier in the letter of the law of God, which is His moral will: "So then, the Law is holy, and the commandment is *holy and righteous and good*" (Romans 7:12).[17]

Third, the moral will best fits the general contrast between conformity to the world and transformation of the mind. For in other passages of Scripture, it is specifically the Word of God (His moral will) that effects that spiritual metamorphosis. For instance, in 2 Corinthians 3:18, Paul uses "transformed" in a context where exposure to the mirror of God's Word is the key element in the transforming process (2 Corinthians 3:14–18; see also James 1:25).[18]

Fourth, in Ephesians 5:10 a similar use of the word "prove" occurs in the expression "trying to learn [lit., *proving*] what is pleasing to the Lord." In that context, finding out what is pleasing to the Lord is to be accomplished by walking in light, goodness, righteousness, and truth (Ephesians 5:8–9)—namely, the moral will of God. The vocabulary of Romans 12:2 occurs again in Ephesians 5, most notably in verse 17 where "the will of the Lord" appears to be directly related to a list of moral commands (Ephesians 5:18–21, see pp. 69–70). This is consistent with Paul's use of the term "His will" earlier in Romans (2:18) where the sense of moral will is clearly indicated.

Romans 12:1–2 is important for believers to understand. Christians are urged to surrender themselves wholly to God as a living sacrifice. They are to work this self-dedication out through resistance to worldly conformity and conscious involvement in a divine process of transformation. The process of transformation is carried out as the mind is renewed by the Word of God, thereby enabling the believer to prove what God's moral will is. Thus the believer knows that God's moral will is good, acceptable, and perfect for his life. Romans 12:1–2 does not summarize a process for discovering detailed guidance for specific decisions, but rather urges a basic approach to the entirety of our Christian life—an approach in which the moral will of God plays a central and transforming role.[19]

Ephesians 2:10

For we are His workmanship, created in Christ Jesus for good works, which God prepared beforehand so that we would walk in them.

This verse is not often emphasized by traditional view writers. This is surprising, for it offers stronger possibilities for their position than many of the verses that are used. Those who do employ it point out that this verse establishes that God has prepared in advance certain good works for a believer to do. It is appropriate, then, that the Christian should seek the leading of the Lord to learn which good works God has chosen for him to do. Such an interpretation makes good sense.

There are, however, two other possible interpretations of the verse that also make good sense. And neither of them requires an individual will that must be discovered. The first alternative interpretation is that the works referred to in this passage are described only in general terms. There is no article or adjective qualifying "good works." Since good works are one of the purposes for which Christians are created, the idea could be that God prepared those works "beforehand" by providing what was needed for their accomplishment. That is, He created new creatures with new hearts capable of producing good works. Then He gave those creatures the Holy Spirit for enablement, and gave clear instructions in the Word of God to direct them in the use of His power to accomplish good works.[20] All of these provisions precede the good works, and so by His equipping of saints with divine power and instruction, He "prepared beforehand" the good works.

A second alternative interpretation views the good works "prepared beforehand" from the perspective of God's sovereignty.[21] In Romans 9:23, the only other verse in the New Testament where "prepared beforehand" is used, Paul is obviously referring to God's sovereign plan. The concept is very close in meaning to Paul's description of that plan in Ephesians 1:4–5, a similarity that is even more apparent in Greek than in English.[22]

This second alternative also fits well with the verses that immediately precede Ephesians 2:10, for they speak of God's sovereign work in our salvation. The point of the well-known passage Ephesians 2:8–9 is that salvation is by God's grace and is not of ourselves; nor is it the product of our good works. The idea is reinforced in verse 10 when believers are called "His workmanship" and described as "created in Christ Jesus." It is that same sovereign grace that has prepared in advance good works in which the believer will walk. Just as salvation is of God, so also are the good works that flow from it. Believers are involved in both, but the ultimate cause or source is God. He sovereignly "prepared beforehand," in eternity past, that we should walk in good works (even possibly in specific good works) through which we will help to carry out His sovereign plan. Within this interpretation the elements of enablement and instruction are also incorporated as part of God's means in His sovereign work.

While I prefer the second alternative interpretation, I concede that these three possible interpretations come closer to being equal than any of the others discussed thus far. The most that can be said, then, is that either side could use this verse in support of their position, but neither side could use Ephesians 2:10 to *prove* their position.

> EPHESIANS 5:15–17
>
> Therefore be careful how you walk, not as unwise men but as wise, making the most of your time, because the days are evil. So then do not be foolish, but understand what the will of the Lord is.

Here is a command to understand the will of God, so the sovereign will is immediately ruled out. The alternatives once again are the moral will and the individual will. If we are to make the most of our time in these evil days and avoid living foolishly, what aspect of God's will are we to understand? Is it necessary for the believer to understand God's individual plan for his life if he is to buy up every opportunity? Or will his grasp of God's moral will give him the direction he needs for wise living?

Even a casual reading of the fifth chapter of Ephesians should answer our question. The context, both preceding and following this passage, points without ambiguity to the moral will of God. Verses 1–14 of this chapter provide a general contrast between the believer's walk in light and the unbeliever's walk in darkness. The intent of the contrast is to highlight the lifestyle of goodness, righteousness, and truth, which "is pleasing to the Lord" (5:6, 9–10). As was established earlier in the discussion of Romans 12:1–2, this whole exhortation can only be seen as an appeal to follow the moral will of God.

Further confirmation of this viewpoint comes from a side-by-side comparison of the relevant portions of verses 8–10 and 15–17:

"walk as children of Light	"walk… as wise [men]
trying to learn	do not be foolish, but understand
what is pleasing to the Lord" (8, 10)	what the will of the Lord is" (15, 17)

There can be little doubt that Paul was giving the same message, in different terms, in the two segments.[23] This equation of "what is pleasing to the Lord" with "the will of the Lord" (both referring to the moral will of God) corresponds to what is indicated elsewhere in the New Testament (see 1 Thessalonians 4:1–2; 2 Corinthians 5:9–10; Romans 14:18; 1 John 3:22; Hebrews 13:21).

The context that follows verse 17 gives added confirmation of this. Immediately after the command to understand the will of the Lord, there follows a series of examples that include being filled with the Spirit (5:18), spiritual singing (5:19), giving of thanks (5:20), and appropriate submission (5:21). The theme of submission is applied to the various relationships within the believer's household (5:22–6:9). Of specific interest is the exhortation to slaves (6:5–8), where these believers are told to do "the will of God from the heart" (6:6). Such compliance includes obedience, respect, sincerity, and diligent labor, "as to the Lord" (6:7). These statements show that God's will throughout this context means God's moral will.

The instruction of Ephesians 5:15–17 follows these lines: Christians are to avoid foolish living. Wise living understands the folly of immorality and the value of doing whatever is pleasing to the Lord. The days are so evil, and the need for properly functioning, serving Christians is so great, wise Christians will make good use of their time, taking opportunities for ministry as they come. Knowledge of the moral will of God will give discernment not only between good and evil, but between what is wise and what is foolish.

COLOSSIANS 1:9

For this reason also, since the day we heard of it, we have not ceased to pray for you and to ask that you may be filled with the knowledge of His will in all spiritual wisdom and understanding.

Did Paul pray that the Colossians might know God's sovereign will, His moral will, or His individual will? Again, sovereign will can be immediately ruled out because it is hidden and cannot be known in advance.

Whatever sense of His will is presented in this verse, it can be known. Furthermore, such knowledge is desired for Christian living, and that knowledge could be missed. So far, these characteristics apply to both the moral and individual wills. On what basis can a judgment be made for correct interpretation?

In this case, the context of the verse proves decisive.[24] The next three verses say:

> so that you will walk in a manner worthy of the Lord, to please Him in all respects, bearing fruit in every good work and increasing in the knowledge of God; strengthened with all power, according to His glorious might, for the attaining of all steadfastness and patience; joyously giving thanks to the Father, who has qualified us to share in the inheritance of the saints in Light. (Colossians 1:10–12)

The first indication that Paul was praying for knowledge of God's *moral* will follows from the stated purpose for the knowledge of that will. The purpose was that believers might *walk worthy* of the Lord and be pleasing to Him. When Paul used that same terminology in other passages, he was referring to the *moral* will of God. In Ephesians 4:1, the worthy walk is described as obedience to the general moral commands that immediately follow. In fact, Ephesians 4:1 introduces the section of that epistle devoted to moral commands concerning Christian behavior. A "worthy walk" would conform to all of the exhortations in chapters 4, 5, and 6 of Ephesians.

Paul uses the same terminology in writing to the Thessalonians (1 Thessalonians 2:12; 4:1–3). His directions on how they should "walk and please God" are termed "commandments" (4:2) and "the will of God" (4:3). The will of God in this context is clearly God's *moral* will.[25] So Paul's concept of a Christian "walk" that is "worthy of the Lord" and "pleasing to the Lord" is consistently connected with God's moral will. (See also 2 Corinthians 5:9–10; Romans 14:18; Ephesians 5:10, 17; 6:6; and 1 John 3:22.)

The immediate context of Colossians 1 gives a second evidence that "His will" means His moral will. For in the clauses that follow verse 9, God's will and the worthy walk are further defined by a series of actions. Do these things that follow from the knowledge of God's will fit the concept of an individual will of God, or do they fit the more general goals of God's moral will? The list includes: bearing fruit in every good work, growth in the knowledge of God, strengthening by God's power, steadfastness, patience, joy, and thanksgiving. God's moral will encompasses every item on that list. God desires those things to be true of every believer. And in 1 Thessalonians 5:18, thanksgiving is specifically declared to be God's moral will for believers.

The point of Colossians 1:9 is very important for Christian living. It is vital that the believer be filled with the knowledge of God's moral will, for such knowledge is foundational to a worthy walk that pleases God! We might legitimately develop the following applicational paraphrase of Paul's request: "I pray that you might study the Word so that your mind will be filled with knowledge of His revealed will as the foundation for all spiritual wisdom and understanding. May God give us pastors who faithfully and accurately teach the Scriptures. May you develop a hunger for His truth that compels you to seek out spiritual insights and principles by which to govern your daily walk."

On the basis of the consistent teaching of Paul throughout his epistles, and the immediate context of this exhortation, it seems clear that in Colossians 1:9 the moral will of God is in view as that which must be known for godly living.

Colossians 4:12

> Epaphras, who is one of your number, a bondslave of Jesus Christ, sends you his greetings, always laboring earnestly for you in his prayers, that you may stand perfect and fully assured in all the will of God.

Again, the identification of "the will of God" is the issue of importance. The request that the Colossians "may stand perfect and fully assured" does not appear to fit the sovereign sense of God's will. But either of the other two categories would make sense within the immediate context.

Here the evidence points again to the moral will of God. First, such an understanding is consistent with Paul's usage of the phrase in Colossians 1:9. In both passages, the reference to God's will occurs in the context of intercessory prayer. It would be strange if Epaphras, in his prayer for these people, meant something entirely different from what Paul intended by the same expression.

Second, the request that the Colossian believers "may stand perfect and fully assured" is almost an echo of Paul's statement in Colossians 1:28 about the goal of his ministry: "so that we may present every man complete [or perfect] in Christ." In other words, what Paul was striving for, and what Epaphras was praying for, were the same—the perfection, the maturity of the saints. The means by which Paul hoped to accomplish his goal is significant here: "We proclaim Him [Christ], admonishing every man and teaching every man with all wisdom" (Colossians 1:28). Paul was bringing the moral will of God to bear upon the lives of those to whom he ministered to bring them to maturity. That being the case, Epaphras's prayer that the believers might stand perfect and fully assured in all the will of God is a request that the moral will of God would accomplish its purpose in those believers' lives.

Finally, there are indications from the wider context of Paul's teaching throughout the epistle that God's moral will is in view in the prayer of Epaphras. Paul's concern in the letter was to refute heretical teaching that was a composite of Jewish and Gnostic elements. His antidote for such poison was a correct belief in the doctrine of the person and work of Christ (2:16–23). This wider context dovetails perfectly with our understanding of Epaphras's prayer. The Colossians were being influenced by false beliefs and practices, but Epaphras was striving in prayer that they would be mature and fully assured in the true doctrine of the Word of God—that is, His revealed moral will.

Therefore, even though the immediate context of the verse does not allow us to say with absolute certainty which sense of God's will is intended, the wider context of the epistle indicates that the moral will better corresponds to the flow of Paul's thought.[26]

The passages of Scripture discussed in this chapter are very helpful for the guidance of the believer. They are not, however, proof for guidance by means of an individual will of God. In each case the context does not require the interpretation of the traditional view. Rather, there is better evidence that "God's will" indicates His moral will. Most of these passages underline the vital place the *moral will* of God—*not* an *individual will*—has in directing the believer. It is, in fact, essential for us to know the moral will of God so that we might "walk in a manner worthy of the Lord, to please Him in all respects" (Colossians 1:10).

Scripture Does Not Teach the Dot

Our study of the biblical support for the traditional view raises a logical question: If proper interpretation of the key passages fails to substantiate the concept of an individual will for each decision, why has that idea been taught and *accepted as biblical* by so many for so long?

Without being dogmatic, I suggest that the basic reason is imprecise hermeneutics. It appears that the idea of an "individual will of God" stems from *a synthesis of biblical teaching and biblical examples.* Using two representative verses by way of example, we could diagram that synthesis in the following manner:

"BIBLICAL SUPPORT" FOR THE TRADITIONAL VIEW

Biblical Examples	Traditional View of Guidance	Biblical Teaching
GOD GUIDED BELIEVERS *Example:* "A vision appeared to Paul in the night: a man of Macedonia was standing and appealing to him, and saying, 'Come over to Macedonia and help us.'" (Acts 16:9)	God has an ideal, detailed life-plan uniquely designed for each person, which He reveals to the heart of the believer through inward impressions and outward signs.	GOD PROMISES GUIDANCE *Example:* "And the LORD will continually guide you. . . ." (Isaiah 58:11) "For such is God, our God forever and ever; He will guide us until death." (Psalm 48:14)

A superficial reading of the passages seems to provide a scriptural foundation for the traditional view. But closer scrutiny reveals that foundation to be inadequate. For in order to arrive at the conclusion of the traditional approach, it is necessary to *water down* the biblical examples and *spice up* the biblical teaching. Examples are watered down to be less miraculous than they really are. Biblical teaching must be spiced up to be more specific than it really is.

This chapter has demonstrated that careful exegesis of the relevant passages fails to support the basic premise of the traditional view.

"BIBLICAL SUPPORT" FOR THE TRADITIONAL VIEW SHOWN TO BE INADEQUATE

Biblical Examples	Traditional View of Guidance	Biblical Teaching
GOD GUIDED BELIEVERS *Example:* "A vision appeared to Paul in the night: a man of Macedonia was standing and appealing to him, and saying, 'Come over to Macedonia and help us.'" (Acts 16:9)	~~God has an ideal, detailed life-plan uniquely designed for each person, which He reveals to the heart of the believer through inward impressions and outward signs.~~	GOD PROMISES GUIDANCE *Example:* "And the LORD will continually guide you...." (Isaiah 58:11) "For such is God, our God forever and ever; He will guide us until death." (Psalm 48:14)
However 1. In every example, the means of communication is supernatural revelation. 2. Such direct guidance for specific decisions was the exception to the rule.		**However** 1. Each passage concerns God's moral or sovereign will. 2. No passage indicates communication of God's will via inner impressions.

My response to the question, "Does God have a plan for my life?" is this: If God's plan is thought of as a blueprint or a dot in the "center of God's will" that I must discover, the answer is no. On the other hand, God does have a plan for our lives—a plan described in the Bible in terms that we can fully understand and apply. But more on that in part 3.

---

1. C. F. Keil and F. Delitzsch, *Commentary on the Old Testament*, vol. 2: *Biblical Commentary on the Psalms*, by F. Delitzsch, trans. Francis Bolton (Grand Rapids, MI: Wm. B. Eerdmans Publishing Co., 1950), 398; Joseph Addison Alexander, *The Psalms: Translated and Explained* (Grand Rapids, MI: Baker Book House, 1975), 139.
2. Charles Augustus Briggs and Emile Grace Briggs, *A Critical Exegetical Commentary on the Book of Psalms, The International Critical Commentary*, 2 vols. (Edinburgh: T&T Clark, 1906), 1:281.
3. Frances Brown, S. R. Driver, and Charles A. Briggs, *A Hebrew and English Lexicon of the Old Testament*, s.v. ישר. See also: Keil and Delitzsch, *Commentary on the Old Testament*, vol. 6: *Proverbs, Ecclesiastes, Song of Solomon*, by F. Delitzsch, trans. M. G. Easton, 232. Delitzsch gives this translation and cites Proverbs 3:6 as a parallel example of this usage. See also: Crawford H. Toy, *A Critical and Exegetical Commentary on the Book of Proverbs, The International Critical Commentary* (Edinburgh: T&T Clark, 1899), 222; John Peter Lange, ed., *A Commentary on the Holy Scriptures*, vol. 10, *Proverbs, Ecclesiastes, Song of Solomon*, by John Peter Lange, trans. Philip Schaff (Grand Rapids, MI: Zondervan, n.d.), 58.
4. Bruce K. Waltke, "Dogmatic Theology and Relative Knowledge," *Crux* 15, no. 1 (March 1979).
5. Derek Kidner, *The Proverbs: An Introduction and Commentary* (London: InterVarsity Press, 1964), 118.
6. Delitzsch, *Proverbs, Ecclesiastes, Song of Solomon*, 340.
7. Joseph Addison Alexander, *Commentary on the Prophecies of Isaiah* (Grand Rapids, MI: Zondervan, n.d.) 2:481; the plural form is attributed to the context by Delitzsch in Keil and Delitzsch, *Commentary on the Old Testament*, vol, 7: *Biblical Commentary on the Book of the Prophet Isaiah*, 2:35.
8. Edward J. Young, *The Book of Isaiah: The English Text, with Introduction, Exposition, and Notes* (Grand Rapids, MI: Wm. B. Eerdmans Publishing Co., 1969), 2:356–57; Delitzsch, *Isaiah*, 2:35.
9. This understanding excludes guidance by subjective impressions, but does not exclude the biblical teaching that inward convincing of the Spirit will accompany the outward proclamation of the Word. John Calvin, *Commentary of the Book of the Prophet Isaiah*, trans. William Pringle (Grand Rapids, MI: Wm. B. Eerdmans Publishing Co., 1948), 2:371–72; E.H. Plumptre, "Isaiah," *Ellicott's Commentary on the Whole Bible: A Verse by Verse Explanation*, ed. Charles John Ellicott, vol. 4, *Job-Isaiah* (Grand Rapids, MI: Zondervan, 1959), 499.

10. Henry Blackaby and Claude V. King, *Experiencing God* (Nashville: Broadman & Holman Publishers, 1994), 77. For a more complete evaluation of *Experiencing God*, see appendix 1.
11. Morris quotes Wescott, "not in imitation, but in virtue of His sameness of nature." Leon Morris, *The Gospel According to John, The New International Commentary on the New Testament* (Grand Rapids, MI: Wm. B. Eerdmans Publishing Co., 1971), 313.
12. See our discussion of "open doors" in chapter 13, "God's Sovereign Will and Decision Making."
13. Indeed, "reading providence" (interpreting circumstances as a means of divining God's direction) is not a biblically sanctioned approach to decision making. See our discussion of this idea in chapter 13, "God's Sovereign Will and Decision Making."
14. See the extended discussion on "Benefiting from Impressions" in chapter 17, "A New Way of Seeing."
15. There are several Greek words that are translated as "will" in the New Testament phrase "will of God." Unlike other Greek synonyms, the distinctions in meaning are not determined by the specific vocabulary words so much as they are by the context. Both the *boulomai* word group and the *thelō* word group can refer to the desired (moral) or determined (sovereign) will of God. As a result, for nearly every word in these two groups, examples of God's moral will and His sovereign will can be found. In each case, the context must determine in which sense the Greek word is being used. (However, a case can be made that when *boulē* is used of God in the New Testament, it invariably denotes His sovereign will. See Luke 7:30; Acts 2:23; 4:28; 13:36; 20:27; Hebrews 6:17; Ephesians 1:11.) Cf. John Murray, *The Epistle to the Romans, The New International Commentary on the New Testament* (Wm. B. Eerdmans Publishing Co., 1965), 2:115. Murray gives a list of references that demonstrate two uses of the term "God's will." His titles are "will of determinate purpose" and "will of commandment." The older theologians often use the similar titles of decretive will and preceptive will.
16. William F. Arndt and F. Wilbur Gingrich, trans., *A Greek-English Lexicon of the New Testament and Other Early Christian Literature,* 2nd ed. (Chicago: University of Chicago Press, 1979), s.v. δοκιμάζω.
17. Murray, *Romans*, 2:115 notes the parallel between the two passages.
18. Ibid., 2:114. Murray calls 2 Corinthians 3:18 a fuller explanation of the same process of transformation.
19. That the moral sense of God's will is intended here is also supported by Murray, *Romans*, 2:115–16; C. K. Barrett, *A Commentary on the Epistle to the Romans, Harper's New Testament Commentaries*, gen. ed. Henry Chadwick (New York: Harper and Bros., Publishers, 1957), 233; John Calvin, *The Epistle of Paul the Apostle to the Romans and to the Thessalonians, Calvin's Commentaries*, trans. Ross MacKenzie, ed. David W. Torrance and Thomas F. Torrance (Grand Rapids, MI: Wm. B. Eerdmans Publishing Co., 1960), 265; William G. T. Shedd, *A Critical and Doctrinal Commentary upon the Epistle of St. Paul to the Romans* (New York: Charles Scribner's and Sons, 1879), 359; R. C. H. Lenski, *The Interpretation of St. Paul's Epistle to the Romans* (Columbus, OH: Lutheran Book Concern 1936), 758.
20. William Hendricksen, *Exposition of Ephesians, New Testament Commentary* (Grand Rapids, MI: Baker Book House, 1967), 124.
21. S. D. F. Salmond, "The Epistle to the Ephesians" in *The Expositor's Greek Testament* (Reprint ed., Grand Rapids, MI: Wm. B. Eerdmans Publishing Co., 1974), 3:290.
22. The reference is simply to the similar *pro* as a prefix to *proorisas* (Ephesians 1:5) and *proetoimasen* (Ephesians 2:10).

23. Francis Foulkes, *The Epistle of Paul to the Ephesians: An Introduction and Commentary, The Tyndale New Testament Commentaries*, R. V. G. Tasker, gen. ed. (Grand Rapids, MI: Wm. B. Eerdmans Publishing Co., n.d.), 150.
24. T. K. Abbott, *A Critical and Exegetical Commentary on the Epistles to the Ephesians and to the Colossians, The International Critical Commentary* (Edinburgh: T&T Clark, 1897), 202.
25. John Calvin says, "The knowledge of *the divine will*, by which expression he rejects all inventions of men and all speculations foreign to the Word of God. For His will is not to be sought anywhere else than in His Word." John Calvin, *The Epistles of Paul the Apostle to the Galatians, Ephesians, Philippians and Colossians, Calvin's Commentaries*, trans. T. H. L. Parker, ed. David W. Torrance and Thomas F. Torrance (Grand Rapids, MI: Wm. B. Eerdmans Publishing Co., 1965), 304.
26. Charles John Ellicott, *A Critical and Grammatical Commentary on St. Paul's Epistles to the Philippians, Colossians and to Philemon, with a Revised Translation* (Philadelphia: Smith, English, and Co., 1976), 60; R. C. H. Lenski, *The Interpretation of Colossians and Philemon* (Columbus, OH: Wartburg Press, 1937), 203; Clark paraphrases, "That ye may stand firm, perfectly instructed, and fully persuaded of the truth of those doctrines which have been taught you as the revealed will of God." Adam Clark, *Clark's Commentaries: Romans–Revelation* (Nashville: Abingdon, n.d.), 300.

chapter five

MORE DOUBTS ABOUT THE DOT

To this point in part 2, I have responded to the first three points in the outline of the traditional view. To the question "What does God's will mean?" I have expressed my essential agreement with the traditional view that the sovereign and moral aspects of God's will are scripturally valid. I do not agree, however, that the Bible reveals an individual will for each person. This individual will is often pictured as the center of a target or a dot—the very center of God's will. But I have substantial doubts about the dot. I presented my reasons in chapters 3 and 4 through a critique of the arguments cited by the traditional view in support of an ideal plan for each life—arguments based on reason, experience, biblical example, and biblical teaching.

Consequently, to the question, "Does God have an individual plan for my life that I must discover?" I gave a qualified negative. *Scripture does not teach the dot* or an individual will for each believer. God's plan for our lives must be understood in a manner that is fundamentally different from the traditional view.

Now we can consider the next point in the outline: "How can I discover God's will?" Of course, for the traditional view, "God's will" means the *individual* will. If I am correct in my conviction that there is no such thing as an individual will, then it follows that I cannot discover it. There is simply no point in looking for something that does not exist.

Having determined that, I am also confident that such an ideal individual will is *not necessary* for making good decisions in the Christian life. Looking at the matter from one angle, if God has revealed only the actuality of His sovereign will and the content of His moral will, we may expect them to be fully adequate for our decision-making needs. That this is indeed the case will be established and explained in part 3, "The Way of Wisdom."

If the individual will does not exist, believers who are looking for it will encounter frustration.

From another viewpoint, we would expect that if the individual will does not exist, believers who are looking for it will encounter frustration. As noted in chapter 3, such frustration has indeed been experienced in different ways and in varying degrees as Christians have attempted to pinpoint that elusive dot in the center of God's will. The popularity of seminars on God's will is evidence that many have difficulty finding this dot, and in sessions I have conducted, participants have admitted this difficulty. Some even say they are *never* 100 percent sure they have found God's individual will.

Mum's the Word

There was a time, though, when such confessions were few and far between. Before I began my study of God's will, it seemed that everyone else was successful in finding this dot that so often eluded me. I heard others give testimony of their certainty in finding God's individual will. I never stood up to testify that I had a hard time finding God's will. No one else did either. Mum was the word.

That silence is not hard to explain. The traditional view was taught by godly speakers whom we respected, and there was no alternative framework for interpreting our experience. So we could only conclude that our frustrations must have been the result of sin or insincerity in our hearts. For we continually heard, "God will always clearly reveal His will to the sincere seeker."

When Sincerity Begets Anxiety

For a small segment of believers, the situation is more than just frustrating—it is critical. One woman told me that she began enjoying her Christian life for the first time when she jettisoned the traditional view. That wasn't just overstatement. Though sincere in her search for God's individual will, she still was never certain that she had found it. So she made no decisions until she was absolutely forced to decide. The results were feelings of anxiety before and feelings of guilt after every decision. Her consistent commitment to the traditional view only made matters worse.

Previous chapters showed that Scripture fails to support the concept of the traditional view's individual will. In the next two chapters I will address the experiential difficulties that come from consistently trying to apply the traditional approach.

THE PROBLEM OF "ORDINARY" DECISIONS

The first practical problem encountered by those who try to consistently live out the traditional view in everyday life may be put quite simply: It cannot be done. At some point, everyone abandons the traditional view's approach to making decisions. That may sound like a bold statement, but you can check it yourself with this little test: During the past week, in what percentage of the decisions that you made did you have certainty of knowing God's individual will in advance? Don't overlook such choices as which route you took to work, which seat you occupied at church, which shoe you put on first each morning, and which particular fruit you selected at the grocery store.

Such decisions, and hundreds of others like them, are made each week. Speakers or writers on God's will often say, "God's will for your life is detailed, so you can expect guidance from Him in every decision." That statement is perfectly consistent with the traditional view.

But in the small, seemingly unimportant decisions, specific guidance does not seem to materialize. Those sincere Christians who conscientiously attempt to seek God's direction for every decision either give up after a few hours or end up in some mystical fringe group. As a result, in the small decisions where no command is involved, virtually all

Christians habitually make those decisions on the basis of what seems best to them at the time. This does not square with the teaching of the traditional view, but it is the only livable approach.

Drawing the Line

What is required, then, is that people believe one way and live another. Each person must draw a vertical line through the decisions of life.

LIFE'S DECISIONS	
Important Decisions: I Must Know God's Will!	**Ordinary Decisions:** I Must Use Good Judgment Without Wasting Time.
Shall I marry?	What shall I wear today?
Whom shall I marry?	What should I have for lunch?
Should I go to school?	How shall I get to work?
Which school?	Where shall I sit in class?
Where should I live?	Where should I buy gas?
What vocation?	When should I have devotions?
Which car should I buy?	Which cologne shall I wear?

All decisions to the left of the line are "important," and thus require knowledge of God's individual will before a choice is made. All decisions to the right of that line are "ordinary" or "common" and must be made to the best of our ability without lengthy deliberation. Such a line may prove practical, but it is inconsistent with the traditional view and not taught by Scripture. An alternative theology is needed that consistently deals with all decisions, large and small.

THE PROBLEM OF EQUAL OPTIONS

A second practical problem for the traditional view is the matter of equal alternatives. In many of the choices we face, two or more of the options seem to be equal in value, making a decision all the more complicated.

To be consistent, the traditional view teaches that in such cases the equality is only apparent. One option, and one only, is God's will.

Again, the small decisions most reveal the weakness of the traditional view. The reason is simply that with smaller decisions, the options are more nearly and more often equal. Consider the matter of getting dressed in the morning. "Which pair of shoes should I wear today? Which of three pairs of brown socks should I wear? Which shoe should I put on first?" and so it goes. Are the options equal? They sure seem to be. Does the final choice really matter? Probably not. But to be consistent, the traditional view has to say that, in principle, it does matter.

While this inability to explain and deal with equal alternatives is most obvious in small decisions, it also affects those that are more important. For there are situations, like my own choice between two schools described in the introduction, where the options in a major decision appear equivalent. In such cases, the person who is convinced of the traditional view is stymied, and the frustration level soars. Instead of rejoicing that he has two good opportunities, he is anxious that he will miss God's will. The anxiety is increased because both options look good, but only one is believed to be correct.

APPLICATIONAL DIFFICULTIES OF THE TRADITIONAL VIEW

1. *Ordinary Decisions:* The traditional view must be abandoned in making the minor decisions of life.
2. ***Equal Options:* The traditional view must deny equal options, generating anxiety over missing the dot.**

THE PROBLEM OF IMMATURITY

A third practical difficulty with the traditional view is its inability to reckon with immaturity on the part of the decision maker. What do we say, for instance, to the two young believers who meet on a weekend college retreat and announce at its conclusion that God has revealed in their hearts that He wants them to get married? What counsel can be given to the young man who is about to drop out of Bible school in the middle of his second semester because he feels that the Lord has called him into a full-time ministry of evangelism? Neither of those decisions is antibiblical, but more mature Christians might have good reason to be apprehensive about their long-range consequences. Concerned friends would probably feel compelled to approach such young people and counsel them to wait awhile before following through on their respective courses of action. Good reasons could be given in support of wiser plans. But if the final, determining factor in making the decision is the conviction that "God told me to do it," little more can be said.

The reason for such a dilemma is not hard to see. The traditional view teaches that there is one ideal choice to be made in every decision. And it holds that any sincere believer can discover this ideal individual will. Furthermore, God gives final guidance in each decision only to the specific person involved. So as long as the decision that is made is within the moral will of God, it is not open to refutation by others who may be more mature. If God has indicated His verdict, there can be no higher court of appeal—unless, of course, we are prepared to challenge *His* wisdom!

But sincere Christians *do* make foolish decisions. Immature believers tend to make immature decisions—at least with a higher degree of frequency than more mature saints. And the problem is not lack of sincerity. Often, it is the enthusiastic babe in Christ who is most anxious to do whatever God wants him to do. If he becomes convinced that the Lord has directed him to dive into a thimble, he will run for his swimming trunks and snorkel! The observer might wonder, "Did God really intend for him to do such a foolish thing?" But if the act is not forbidden in Scripture, and the believer is convinced of the Lord's guidance, there is little room for discussion.

Clearly something is wrong. If it is true that God has made the decision in question and has revealed it to the young believer, then the decision should be ideal, not immature.

Can't Argue with God

The problem becomes compounded when Christians justify foolish behavior to others by announcing that it was God's decision, not theirs. And so, inadvertently, the traditional view tends to actually *encourage* immaturity. For it provides a means of defending unwise behavior that can be neither verified nor critiqued by the scrutiny of others.

There are, in addition, several other ways the traditional view promotes immaturity. It is often taught that we should not make a decision until there is certainty concerning the Lord's direction. We must be careful not to "run ahead of the Lord" in such matters. Now I concur that we should not be hasty, especially in making important decisions. But often a long delay occurs because the decision maker is not 100 percent certain of God's individual will. While the traditional view calls this "waiting on the Lord," it soon begins to look like common indecisiveness.

Unnecessary delay may have at least two undesirable consequences. The first is loss of valuable time. In some cases, time is an important factor in the execution of a decision that has been made. Time wasted in making the decision subtracts from the time available to carry it out.

The second, related consequence is that circumstances come to dominate the decision to a greater and greater degree. With the passing of time, some alternatives may be eliminated. Or the circumstances surrounding the decision may become altered, forcing the decision maker to make adjustments that would not have been required had he acted earlier. Waiting too long to buy an airplane ticket will often limit our choice to a more expensive seat on a less convenient flight.

Redeem the Time

The mature believer learns that some decisions should be made earlier than is absolutely necessary, provided there is a sufficient basis for making a choice. The immature believer, on the other hand, may actually find comfort in having the decision made for him circumstantially. But in taking such an approach to decision making, he loses the ability to engage in long-range planning. Indecision due to lack of certainty may crowd the decision-making process to the point where there is no longer any decision to be made, or it may significantly reduce the full potential of an opportunity due to lost time or changed circumstances. The Christian who is stymied by lack of a clear go-ahead on a particular decision may experience any or all of these undesirable consequences.

The traditional view of God's will lies behind other questionable approaches. When I followed the traditional view, I would often respond to apparently equal options by choosing the one I least desired. An observer might conclude that I had a perverted view of God's goodness, but I employed this methodology as a hedge against self-centered motivations. On the assumption that it was my fault for failing to discern God's perfect will, I chose the least preferable option to assure that I did not add the sin of a self-centered decision. My reasoning was based on a sincere effort to maintain pure motives; but it promoted immaturity and resulted in Christian experience robbed of potential joy.

If She Answers on the First Ring...

Then there is the "phone fleece" method of dating. I used to be quite good at it. When I did not know which girl the Lord might want me to take out on a particular date, I would set up "providential signs" in advance: If no one answered the phone, that meant God wanted me to call back later; a busy signal was a closed door—I shouldn't call back (maybe some other fellow was asking her out); if she answered but turned me down, then God did not want me to take her out (nor did the girl); if she answered the phone and accepted my invitation, she was the one!

I was encouraged to use a fleece by an imagined concern. If I dated the wrong girl and became interested in her as a potential life partner, I might end up marrying the wrong person. That would be bad enough. But the problems only escalated. If *I* was married to the wrong person, then *my wife* would also be living outside of God's will. Furthermore, the woman I was *supposed* to marry would also wed the wrong spouse since I was not available. And my (wrongly chosen) wife would create the same problem for the man designated by God for her. It was not hard to see how one wrong date could eventually mess up the whole universe!

I once thought that my "phone fleece" method of dating was a private arrangement between me and the Lord until I began encountering a number of fellows who followed the same procedure. One day I confessed my approach when teaching a seminary theology class, much to the delight of the students. Then I added, "You're laughing, but I bet some of you used to do that same thing in your sincerity to find God's perfect will." Some were sheepishly nodding when a voice said, "What do you mean *used* to?" God appreciates such sincerity, no doubt, but I imagine that a few of the angels must get a good chuckle when they see some of the things we have done to find the elusive dot.

One of my greatest concerns about the theology of the traditional view is that it may give undue confidence to young, immature believers. They are taught that they can make perfect decisions since all that is required is sincerity and God will make His choice perfectly clear to them. At the time when they most need the wisdom of mature believers, they may be confidently reading the impressions in their heart. The reality is that immature believers tend to have immature impressions.

Most advocates of the traditional view are careful to teach against opening the Bible at random to seek guidance for a specific decision. That such warnings are so common indicates that many follow this method when they are at the end of their decision-making rope. Their logic: "God's perfect will is not clear yet and the decision is imminent. If there's any place where I can find a word from God, it ought to be in the Word of God." They then pray and open their Bible, looking for words to fit their specific decision. They choose a college in Texas because they read the word "south" in the Scripture. They believe they have made a decision that comes from God's authority, but in reality, they have turned their Bible into a kind of divining rod, which more resembles magic than faith. The teachers of the traditional view do not encourage this approach, but the logic of the traditional view too often moves sincere believers to use this method.

THE TRADITIONAL VIEW PROMOTES IMMATURE DECISIONS:

1. By permitting justification of unwise decisions on grounds that "God told me"
2. By fostering costly delays because of uncertainty of God's individual will
3. By influencing the rejection of personal preferences when facing equal options
4. By encouraging putting out a fleece and letting circumstances dictate
5. By giving young believers confidence that they can make perfect decisions (apart from mature counsel) if they are sincere
6. By inadvertently moving believers to misuse their Bibles to get needed guidance

In this chapter we have seen various practical problems that the traditional view creates in its search for an individual will of God. First, in the ordinary decisions that we make all day, every day, the traditional view approach must be abandoned. Second, the traditional view has no room for equal options. And third, the traditional view promotes immature approaches to decision making by insisting on the certainty of one right decision.

APPLICATIONAL DIFFICULTIES OF THE TRADITIONAL VIEW

1. *Ordinary Decisions:* The traditional view must be abandoned in making the minor decisions of life.
2. *Equal Options:* The traditional view must deny equal options, generating anxiety over missing the dot.
3. ***Immaturity:* The logic of the traditional view promotes immature approaches to decision making.**

A fourth practical difficulty is the problem of subjectivity. Because I view this as the most significant applicational problem of the traditional view, I have devoted the following chapter to its discussion.

chapter six

IMPRESSIONS ARE IMPRESSIONS

While engaged in a ministry to high school students in eastern Oklahoma, I once began a youth meeting with the following declaration: "This afternoon, I have a message from the Water Tower Monster." I gained immediate attention as their curiosity was piqued. "The Water Tower Monster is an awesome specter who lives beneath the water tower just outside of town beside Highway 59. His message is this: He wants everyone in town to believe in him. He says that if there are any unbelieving residents remaining at the end of one year, he will destroy the whole town. When you believe in him, you will experience an unmistakable shiver in your liver. The stronger your faith becomes, the more he will communicate with your inner being. Are there any questions?"

After a few moments of restless silence, one student decided to humor me. "I live pretty close to that tower. Why haven't I ever seen this monster?"

"The Water Tower Monster is only visible to believers," I replied.

Another spoke up. "Then you have personally *seen* the monster with your own eyes?"

"Oh yes. Not, however, with my physical eyes. I see him with the eyes of my heart."

"The eyes of your heart?"

"Right. As I grow closer to the Water Tower Monster, the liver shivers become stronger and his presence is more clearly confirmed within."

One boy looked especially perplexed. "Wait a minute. Are you talking about the eyes of your heart, or the eyes of your liver?"

"That's right," I said.

A girl probed further. "Has anyone else ever felt these liver shivers?"

"Of course. All true believers have them."

"But how do you know the difference between a genuine 'liver shiver' and liver disease?" she continued.

"When you experience the real thing, there is no doubt about it. The inner message is as distinct as if the Water Tower Monster were speaking audibly."

"This is ridiculous!" one of the kids said, to the obvious approval of all present.

"Tell me," I replied, "is your belief in God substantially different from my 'faith' in the Water Tower Monster?"

What followed was a lively discussion of the foundation of Christian belief. And many of those young people came to appreciate more than ever that their faith was built not upon a wholly subjective foundation, but upon the solid rock of God's entrance into human history and His objective revelation to man.

THE PROBLEM OF SUBJECTIVITY

Subjectivity touches many aspects of religious experience. People with widely divergent, even contradictory convictions testify to personal experiences that seem to be alike. And yet the reputed cause of the experiences differs according to the religious perspective of the individual reporter. What is needed is an objective standard by which these claims may be evaluated. In the area of decision making and the will of God, the *lack of such an objective source of knowledge* constitutes the greatest applicational weakness of the traditional view.

The word *subjective* can have several positive or neutral meanings. It can refer to the mind and feelings in contrast to outward objects. Or it can mean personal in contrast to nonpersonal. In this chapter, however, I will be using *subjective* in the technical sense of an opinion that cannot be substantiated by an objective source of truth. The connotation of our usage is negative and points to a flaw in the traditional view.

By way of illustration, let's say that two men see an automobile strike a pedestrian. Both are called to testify at the trial of the driver. At issue is whether the car was exceeding the speed limit of 25 miles per hour when it hit the person.

The first man, who saw the accident from the street corner, testifies for the prosecution. When asked to judge the speed of the car prior to impact, he replies, "I believe the car was going at least 35 miles per hour."

In the cross-examination, the defense attorney says, "My client insists that he was traveling no more than 25 miles per hour. What makes you so sure that he was doing 35?"

"I can tell the speed of a car," the witness says, "and I'm sure that vehicle was doing at least 35—maybe faster."

The other witness, who saw the accident from his own car, testifies for the defense. "I was following the car in question for several blocks. Just prior to the accident, I remarked to my traveling companion how hard it is to keep your speed at or below the speed limit in residential areas. I was saying that if it wasn't for the car in front of me, I'd probably be going too fast. We both glanced at my speedometer and noted that we were traveling just under 25 miles per hour. Then the accident occurred."

The jury would undoubtedly disregard the testimony of the former witness on the grounds of subjectivity. By contrast, the testimony of the second man has credence because his judgment was based on an objective standard (the speedometer) by which the truth could be reliably determined.

God has provided two objective sources for certain knowledge of His will: His Word and direct revelation from Himself. But the traditional view does not claim that God's individual will may be learned from either of these sources. The Bible reveals only God's moral will, but His individual will is more specific. And direct revelation (God's verbal communication to the individual) is not to be sought or expected. So when someone holding the traditional view says, "I have discovered God's will about which school I should attend," he is not claiming to have received supernatural revelation, nor did he find such leading from a direct statement of Scripture.[1]

What we shall see is that the traditional view relies almost entirely on subjective elements to determine God's individual will for a specific decision. And that creates a tremendous dilemma: How can the traditional view obtain certain knowledge of God's individual will without an objective source of knowledge?

That question corresponds precisely with the fifth point in Bill Thompson's outline: "How can I know God's individual will for sure in a specific situation?" My answer, which I develop in this chapter, is that you cannot. For if the source of our knowledge is subjective, then the knowledge will also be subjective and therefore uncertain.

If the source of our knowledge is subjective, then the knowledge will also be subjective and therefore uncertain.

Consider the Source

Let's look again at the means put forth by the traditional view for discerning God's will. How is God's individual will communicated? The key ingredient is the indwelling Spirit of truth (John 16:13). One of His ministries in the life of the believer is that of "leading" (Romans 8:14; Galatians 5:18). The means by which He does this is variously described within the traditional view: the still small voice, inner voice, inward pressure, inward urging, guiding impulse, inner impression, and so on.

The traditional view does not equate such inner impressions with supernatural revelation. The divine revelation Ezekiel or Paul received was much more definitive and authoritative than guidance individual believers receive today. In fact, the traditional view instructs Christians to test inner impressions by the other "sign posts" because much of the time, the inner impressions are downright vague.

Everyone who has approached decision making in this manner has experienced this lack of clarity. And the sense of ambiguity is in no way dispelled by labeling such impulses "impressions of the Holy Spirit." For the first question usually uttered by the sincere seeker of God's will is: "How can I tell whether these impressions are from God or from some other source?"

This is a critical question. For impressions could be produced by any number of sources: God, Satan, an angel, a demon, human emotions (such as fear or ecstasy), hormonal imbalance, insomnia, medication, or an upset stomach. Sinful impressions (temptations) may be exposed for what they are by the Spirit-sensitized conscience and the Word of God. But beyond that, we encounter a subjective quagmire of uncertainty. For in biblically noncommanded areas,[2] Scripture gives no guidelines for distinguishing the voice of the Spirit from the voice of the self—or any other potential "voice." And experience offers no reliable means of identification either (which is why the question comes up in the first place). And yet the traditional view requires that the source of those impressions must be identified if the believer is to discern God's guidance. Tremendous frustration has been experienced by sincere Christians who have earnestly but fruitlessly sought to decipher the code of the inward witness.

Inner impressions are not a form of revelation. So the Bible does not invest inner impressions with authority to function as indicators of divine guidance. Impressions are real; believers experience them. But impressions are *not authoritative*. They do not constitute the authoritative voice of the Spirit. They may be useful in pointing the way to wisdom, but on the issue of their authority, impressions are just impressions. They may be "spiritual" or reflect the influence of the Spirit, but they fall short of direct revelation and thus fall short of authoritative guidance. Impressions by any other name confuse the issue and confound the believer in decision making. Impressions are still just impressions.

An Impressive Commentary

One area where an appeal to inner impressions is deemed invalid in decision making is in *biblical interpretation*—the science of hermeneutics. There are many accepted principles for the study of God's Word, but tuning in to inward impulses is not one of them.

Some Bible passages are difficult to understand, and while the author intended a single meaning, the text is often interpreted by modern readers in more than one way. Bible commentators usually explain the plausible views on the passage in question before stating their own interpretation and giving appropriate reasons for the choice.

If a commentator were to adopt the traditional view of decision making and apply it to matters of biblical interpretation, he might write something like this: "In response to my prayer for guidance, the Spirit has indicated to my heart through His still small voice that the correct interpretation is the last one listed above."

Such a rationale should raise red flags in the mind of the reader. How is a layman to decide which commentator is correct? Should he follow the opinion of the man he considers to be the most spiritual? Or should he add up the number of scholars supporting each view and go with the majority?

Of course the entire hypothetical situation is absurd. A commentator might write such an opinion as the one suggested above, and he would be consistent with the traditional view.[3] But his book would be rejected for publication by any reputable publisher (and rightly so) on grounds of improper methodology and irresponsible scholarship. If such an approach was permitted in the field of hermeneutics, there would be nothing to prevent scholars who espouse opposing views from making the same claims to divine guidance. That, in turn, would make a mockery of genuine biblical scholarship and impugn the Spirit of truth as the author of confusion. Instead, claims to speak *ex cathedra* on matters of biblical interpretation are rejected as nonauthoritative at best and contrary to Scripture itself at worst.

Impressions may be good commentaries of our present feelings, but they are not trustworthy guides for determining proper interpretation of Scripture or finding specific guidance from God.

Pick a Sign, Any Sign

A proponent of the traditional view might reply: "I know that I cannot prove clear guidance on the basis of inner impressions alone, but there are other signs that point the way to God's will."

That is a remarkable statement. For it is a tacit admission of the very point I have been making. If the inner impressions, which reportedly provide the most personal and direct indication of God's will, are really from the Holy Spirit, why is there any need of confirmation from other signs? If God were to choose to reveal His will in that manner, His communication would be crystal clear. His voice might be "still" and "small," but it would certainly be understandable.

On the other hand, if we grant the validity of multiple signs for the sake of discussion, the problems are hardly resolved. For the other signs are subject to the same difficulties encountered with inward impressions.

Consider, for example, the sign of circumstances. Do circumstances give clear direction of God's will? God is sovereign over circumstances, but is He trying to tell us something specific through them?

I will develop this subject at greater length in chapter 13, "God's Sovereign Will and Decision Making." But for now it will suffice to observe some of the difficulties the traditional view encounters with circumstances. In order for circumstances to give direction, they must be interpreted. And, again, Scripture gives no guidelines for reading providence. And so the subjective element creeps back in.

When, for instance, does a circumstance constitute a "yes" sign? How do we distinguish between an "open door" and one that is only ajar? And who opened that door—God, or Satan, or neither of them? Conversely, when we encounter an obstacle in pursuit of some goal, is that obstruction a roadblock, a closed door, or a test of faith? Circumstances are complex, seldom pointing conclusively in a single direction. And the traditional view has not provided an objective means for interpreting them. The result, once again, is uncertainty.

Subjectivity and consequent ambiguity characterize every one of the so-called signs. The traditional view gives a significant role to *counselors*, but it undermines the value of such advice with the warning that human beings are fallible, and the reminder that God's will is revealed ultimately only to the individual seeking it. *Common sense* must also be exercised, it is said. However, we must also be open to guidance that may not, at first glance, seem so logical. After all, what would have been accomplished by Noah, Joshua, Gideon, or Naaman the Syrian if they had followed common sense? So, does the traditional view promote the exercise of common sense? Well, yes and no.

Time and time again, the traditional view points to the road signs. But the instructions and warnings about reading these signs underscore the difficulty in determining an accurate interpretation. Certainly such factors as circumstances, counselors, and common sense ought to have an important bearing on our decisions. But when they must be read as a "yes" or "no" indicator of God's individual will, they cannot yield the desired certainty.

Compounding the Uncertainty

At this point someone might respond: "All right. I can see that an individual sign by itself is subjective; but *agreement* of the signs will produce guidance that is objective."

But will it? What happens if a believer, whose perspective becomes distorted either by zeal or sin, incorrectly reads several of the signs as indicating "yes"? Does such "agreement of the signs" yield a positive indication of what God wants him to do? Of course not.

And how often do we find incontestable unanimity among the signs? If I am "pretty sure" that the circumstances are positive and "quite sure" that the inner impressions give the go-ahead, the combination of the two can never rise above "pretty" or "quite" sure. If anything, the addition of the two reduces the level of certainty.

How many of the signs must agree? Most presentations of the traditional view stress the importance of agreement among the Big Three: the Word, circumstances, and the inner voice. But whether we must reconcile three signs or twenty-three, the problem remains the same: If the elements that make up the whole are uncertain, the whole will also be uncertain. Uncertainty plus uncertainty yields uncertainty. As we add more signposts to the equation, the subjective factor is multiplied and the degree of uncertainty is magnified.

Of all the signs, the only one that provides the desired objectivity is the Bible. It can clearly disqualify an option that violates moral standards. But it gives no positive indicators in noncommanded areas. To specific questions of vocation, marriage, or education, for instance, the Bible cannot say "yes." It can only indicate what is, and is not, permissible. The traditional view must appeal to the other signs for more specific direction, thereby denying the decision maker the confidence that only an objective source of knowledge can give.

Too Many Cooks Spoil the Broth

The uncertainty is compounded not only by adding more signs to the equation, but by adding more people. Many decisions, such as those made by a church board or the congregation of a local church, are group decisions. When two, ten, or two hundred people must all have the same inward leading, the process grows increasingly complicated. Should a church require unanimity of thought before proceeding with a decision? The work would grind to a standstill. And so most congregational churches make decisions based on a majority or two-thirds vote. But that does not square with the theology of the traditional view. By definition, a nonunanimous vote signifies that a segment of the decision-making group somehow missed God's leading. This fact creates a real tension in the minds of some people.

I once sat in on a congregational meeting of a church I was attending, though I was not a member. That church had to make a difficult decision, and the members had given the matter much thought, discussion, and prayer. However, they could not reach a consensus. Godly men and women lined up on opposite sides of the issue.

One lady stood up and said, "I have talked with several others here who are earnestly seeking God's perfect will in this matter. Apparently, the Holy Spirit has told some of us to vote 'yes' and some of us to vote 'no.' How can we resolve the question when the Holy Spirit is telling us two different things?"

The traditional view cannot solve this problem.

SUBJECTIVITY PRODUCES UNCERTAINTY

1. Impressions are not direct revelation and thus cannot give certainty.
2. All of the traditional guidance signs except Scripture are subjective and cannot give certainty.
3. A compounding of subjective signs cannot give certainty.
4. A multiplying of decision makers adds to the subjectivity and uncertainty.

What we have seen, then, is that the subjectivity that is an inescapable factor in the traditional approach rules out any possibility of attaining certain knowledge of God's individual will. When we add that deficiency to the problems discussed in the previous chapter, we are reminded of at least four areas of frustration encountered by those who follow the traditional view.

APPLICATIONAL DIFFICULTIES OF THE TRADITIONAL VIEW

1. *Ordinary Decisions:* The traditional view must be abandoned in making the minor decisions of life.
2. *Equal Options:* The traditional view must deny equal options, generating anxiety over missing the dot.
3. *Immaturity:* The logic of the traditional view promotes immature approaches to decision making.
4. ***Subjectivity:* Certainty of God's individual will is impossible without an objective source of knowledge.**

But doesn't the Bible teach that one of the ministries of the Holy Spirit is to lead believers?

The answer, of course, is yes. The issue, however, is not *whether* God leads, but *how*. It is to that question that we turn in the next chapter.

---

1. This is generally true of most evangelicals. Some charismatic believers claim they are getting direct revelation, not impressions. If they can show miraculous confirmation of such revelation, their claim must be taken seriously. Usually, however, when questioned closely, their "revelation" appears to be the same as what other believers call "an impression from the Spirit."
2. In the first edition of *Decision Making*, I spoke of decisions not directly governed by biblical command as "nonmoral decisions." In this edition I have changed my terminology to "biblically noncommanded" decisions (or, more simply, "noncommanded" decisions). The reasons for this are set out in the Frequently Asked Questions section at the end of chapter 9, "God-Given Freedom (and Responsibility) to Choose." In that context, I begin to describe such decisions as being "within the area of freedom."
3. By "consistent with the traditional view" I do not mean that proponents of the traditional view actually do it or espouse it. I mean that it is consistent with the method of decision making presented by the traditional view. I would assume in the illustration that the interpretation did not contradict other Scripture and that it was not illogical, showing agreement of the "signs." I am convinced that in actual practice quite a few immature believers do in fact follow such a procedure.

chapter seven

THE LEADING OF THE HOLY SPIRIT

If the Holy Spirit is not leading believers into His individual will by means of inner impressions, what is the nature of His leading ministry? We have already examined the primary passages cited by the traditional view in support of an individual will of God (chapter 4). It remains for us now to investigate the key texts on the leading of the Holy Spirit and the peace of God.

> ROMANS 8:14
>
> For all who are being led by the Spirit of God, these are sons of God.

This verse is often quoted as proof that the Holy Spirit leads believers through inner impressions into the ideal will of God. The word "led" certainly looks like guidance, and the agent of leading is the Holy Spirit. The context, however, deals a deathblow to such an understanding of this passage.

First, the context is not dealing with daily decision making in noncommanded areas. Second, neither the verse itself nor the near context gives any indication that the *means* of the leading is by inward impressions. Furthermore, there is no hint that the goal of the leading is the individual will of God. Not one of the distinctive features of the traditional view is present in Romans 8:14 or its context. The word "led" is a common, nontechnical word that does not in itself indicate either the goal or the means of the leading.[1]

What the apostle Paul is discussing in this passage is righteous living.[2] The answers to the problems of slavery to sin (raised in Romans 7:7–25) are given in Romans 8:1–17. The issue is set forth in a series of vivid, mutually exclusive contrasts: good versus evil (7:19); the law of sin and death versus the law of the Spirit of life (8:2); life according to the flesh versus life according to the Spirit (8:5); being hostile to God versus pleasing God (8:7–8); being in the flesh versus being in the Spirit (8:8–9); being indwelt by the Spirit versus not having the Spirit of Christ (8:9); and, finally, living according to the flesh versus putting to death the deeds of the body (8:13, which is the immediate context). This passage has nothing to do with choosing between two possible home sites or the decision to buy a new suit. What Paul is talking about is experiential conformity to the *moral* will of God.[3]

"Being led by the Spirit of God" is another way of describing life "according to the Spirit" in which the Christian is "putting to death the deeds of the body" (8:13).[4] The leading is guidance into the moral will of God to do what is pleasing to Him. Obedience to that will would be impossible apart from the life-changing presence and empowering of the Holy Spirit (8:6, 13). While the means of the Spirit's leading is not emphasized, the goal of His direction is the clearly revealed, moral will of God (7:12, 14, 22; 8:3–4).

Romans 8:14 must not be interpreted apart from its context (see extended discussion below). Even considered alone, the verse would not prove guidance through inner impressions indicating an individual will of God. But in context, the meaning is transparent: Sons of God are those who are led by the Holy Spirit to put to death the deeds of the flesh and accomplish the moral will of God.

Romans 8:15–16

> For you have not received a spirit of slavery leading to fear again, but you have received a spirit of adoption as sons by which we cry out, "Abba! Father!" The Spirit Himself testifies with our spirit that we are children of God.

These two verses describe the Spirit bearing witness with our spirit and may be evidence of God using impressions to speak to our inner person. The traditional view sometimes uses this passage to say that God is leading us (8:14) by speaking or impressing our human spirit directly.

C. E. B. Cranfield outlines two possible interpretations for Romans 8:16, and neither of them give support to the traditional view.[5] The differences between the two views stem mainly from the fact that "spirit" (of adoption) can refer to the human spirit or the Holy Spirit. Second, the word "bear witness" (or "testify") can be a general term meaning "assure," or it can signify "to witness along with [another]."[6]

The bottom line is that neither interpretation gives support for the traditional view. One interpretation says that the Spirit takes the gospel and assures believers that they are children of God. The second one says that *both* the believer's human spirit *and* the Holy Spirit witness *together* to assure the believer that he is a child of God.

Although either option can be reasonably argued, I hold the view that there are two witnesses to our salvation—our human spirit and God's Spirit. In the phrase "spirit of slavery," the term "spirit" is certainly not God's Spirit (8:15). It follows that the regenerated believer has the "spirit of adoption" (small *s*) and so is able to cry out "Abba! Father!" Our own confession of salvation is significant, but it is joined by that of the "Spirit Himself" who confirms the Word of God and testifies with us that we are "children of God" (8:16). Thus, the Spirit bears witness *"with"* our spirit. The sense of "with" is made clearer in Moffatt's translation: "It is this Spirit testifying along with our own spirit that we are children of God." (8:16). Moule describes this wonderful truth. "'Doubtless thou art His own child,' says the Spirit. 'Doubtless He is my Father,' says our wondering, believing, seeing spirit in response."[7]

Clearly, these verses do not say God "leads" us to make correct daily decisions by impressions to our human spirit from the Holy Spirit. I have argued against impressions having authority as the direct voice of God. However, I believe it is biblically correct to say that the Spirit takes the objective Word of God and convinces our inner spirit that it is true. This gives a conviction and an assurance that the gospel is 100 percent true and we are God's children. His convincing is not subjective in the negative sense because it can be confirmed as identical with the objective revelation of God. This work of the Spirit happens every time someone believes the gospel and is given assurance that he is a child of God.

GALATIANS 5:18

But if you are led by the Spirit, you are not under the Law.

This verse, which is very similar to Romans 8:14, is often cited with it in support of the traditional view of guidance. But the context of Galatians 5 makes an even stronger case for ruling out such an interpretation.

In this passage, Paul describes the conflict between the believer's fleshly pulls and the pulls of the Holy Spirit. The key to overcoming the lust of the flesh and fulfilling the desire of the Spirit consists in walking by the Spirit (5:16) and being led by the Spirit (5:18). Failure to do so will result in immorality (5:19–21). However, being led by the Spirit will result in love, joy, peace, patience, kindness, goodness, faithfulness, gentleness, and self-control (5:22–23).[8]

In addition, the Spirit leads the way in fulfilling the law to love one's neighbor as oneself (5:13–14). This is great guidance! But this passage cannot be construed as a proof-text for the traditional view. For this leading is unquestionably related to the moral will of God as revealed in Scripture (Matthew 22:36–40).

The traditional view seems to take the verb "led" in this passage and read into it examples of specific guidance as found in the book of Acts. Their amalgamation fits neither the moral content of Galatians 5:16 nor the supernatural context of the events in Acts. It is a fallacy to superimpose Paul's Macedonian call (Acts 16:9) onto his comments about "being led by the Spirit." Yet it is apparent that many have done this.

John 16:12–14

"I have many more things to say to you, but you cannot bear them now. But when He, the Spirit of truth, comes, He will guide you into all the truth; for He will not speak on His own initiative, but whatever He hears, He will speak; and He will disclose to you what is to come. He will glorify Me, for He will take of Mine and will disclose it to you."

Some have cited Christ's promise in these verses of the guiding ministry of the Holy Spirit in support of the traditional view. "All the truth" could appear to encompass knowledge needed to make decisions not specified by Scripture but part of God's individual will. It is usually suggested that this guiding ministry is effected through the inward impulses of the Spirit.

The text, however, will not permit such an interpretation. In context, "all the truth" must refer to spiritual truth such as the teaching Jesus' hearers had received from Him in John 14–16.[9] This is required by verses 12 and 14. In addition, any broader interpretation must make the inner expression exhaustive in scope (all the truth whatsoever). But no one interprets it that way. In this passage, Jesus is promising guidance into spiritual understanding.

Also, there is no hint in the passage that the Holy Spirit's guidance will be provided through inner impressions.

Finally, the promise was made to the apostles—the men Jesus was speaking to. It is difficult to determine with certainty the nature of the promise. One view is that Christ was making provision for revelation yet to come—truth that would be written down and passed on in the pages of the New Testament.[10] Another good possibility is that Jesus was promising these men future illumination to grasp the necessity and significance of His imminent death and resurrection.[11]

If this passage has a direct application to believers today, it is a promise of the Spirit's ministry of illumination that enables believers to understand spiritual truth (1 John 2:20, 27).

These explanations harmonize with the immediate context and with the doctrine of the Holy Spirit in all the New Testament. The Spirit did reveal truth to the Church through the apostles and He does indwell believers to illumine that truth to them. This clearly demonstrates the Spirit's guidance into God's moral will, whether by revelation or illumination, rather than inward leading in everyday decisions.

> NEHEMIAH 2:12
>
> And I arose in the night, I and a few men with me. I did not tell anyone what my God was putting into my mind to do for Jerusalem and there was no animal with me except the animal on which I was riding.

This passage does not mention the Holy Spirit, but it uses vocabulary that matches what the traditional view describes as God putting his individual will in the mind of a believer. Did God lead Nehemiah by giving him an inward impression? It looks like this verse (and Nehemiah 7:5—where the terminology "put into my heart" appears) could be taken that way. Ironically, this passage is seldom if ever cited by the traditional view, and we did not address it in the first edition of *Decision Making.*

When Nehemiah said that God put an idea in his mind, it is possible that he considered that direct revelation. But later, when he sought to persuade the city's leaders to join him in rebuilding the wall, he made no reference to an authoritative command from God (such as, "God told me to do this!"). If he thought he had received divine revelation, it seems likely that he would have passed this along to the leaders as the most persuasive reason for their participation.

A better view is that Nehemiah clearly saw God's hand in this plan, but not by means of direct revelation. How then was God involved?

First, note what Nehemiah was *not* saying. He did not claim that when he first had the idea, he knew it was from God. From his prayer in chapter 1, it is apparent that he was uncertain as to the outcome of his plan; so he asked God for favor with the king. After the fact, when he was writing the book, he had the advantage of looking back on the event and seeing the hand of God. It was not the thought itself that convinced him it was from God. It was only by looking backward with hindsight that he knew for sure.

Second, Nehemiah's thought was from God in the sense that it had the moral will of God as its goal. Yahweh's determination to make Jerusalem His dwelling place was part of His covenant with Israel (Nehemiah 1:5, 9). It was God's promise to bless and regather those who turned to Him and return them to Jerusalem (Nehemiah 1:9). Thus, Jerusalem had to be rebuilt as a viable city. Nehemiah knew that his plans corresponded to God's covenant.

Third, God's providence brought about the success of Nehemiah's idea. When Nehemiah turned his prayer into a request of the king, the king gave him leave to return, guaranteed safe passage through enemy territory, and even supplied the building materials (Nehemiah 2:5–8). Nehemiah said this happened "because the good hand of my God was on me" (2:8). The result of the work showed that the idea was from God.

Fourth, when Nehemiah challenged the dispirited leaders of the community to join him in the wall-building project, he did not appeal to the divine origin of the plan. Rather, he gave two other reasons that motivated them to move forward. His first appeal was that rebuilding the wall would remove the reproach on Jerusalem (2:17). Second, he observed that since God's hand had been upon him in a remarkable way, they could expect success in their pursuit of God's covenant purposes (2:18, 20). Since this plan corresponded to the moral will of God as expressed in the covenant promises of God (1:8–9), and since God had to that point answered Nehemiah's prayer for success by the exercise of His sovereign will, the leaders said, "Let us arise and build" (2:18).

Nehemiah did not have subjective certainty when the idea entered his mind. But, when an idea is in harmony with God's expressed purposes (moral will) and God orchestrates circumstances to bring about its completion (sovereign will), it is scripturally valid to deduce in retrospect that the idea came from God.

THE PEACE OF CHRIST

For many who follow the traditional view, one final factor indicates either God's stamp of approval or His red flag of warning—the peace of

God. Since peace is a fruit of the Spirit (Galatians 5:22), many view it as one of the means at His disposal to communicate His will to the believer. As Pastor Bill Thompson explained, the Holy Spirit "leads through inner impressions in our heart and gives confirmation through a settled, supernatural sense of peace (Philippians 4:7; Colossians 3:15)." Accordingly, when trying to choose between two apparently equal options, he advised, "Submit the whole issue to the umpire of God's peace. Picture each option in your mind as you pray and then listen carefully to God's still small voice in the form of His peace concerning the correct choice."

COLOSSIANS 3:15

Let the peace of Christ rule in your hearts, to which indeed you were called in one body; and be thankful.

PHILIPPIANS 4:7

And the peace of God, which surpasses all comprehension, will guard your hearts and your minds in Christ Jesus.

Appealing to the Umpire

The biblical basis for this concept is created by connecting phrases from Colossians 3:15 ("Let the peace of Christ rule in your hearts") and Philippians 4:7, which refers to God's peace "which surpasses all comprehension." Drawing on the imagery from the Greek word for "rule" in Colossians, writers explain that this peace functions as an umpire that "calls" each decision in question.[12] So long as the believer is living within the center of God's will, he experiences an inner quietness of heart that cannot be explained on merely human grounds ("surpassing comprehension"). The umpire of peace is calling "Safe!" But if the Christian begins to move in the wrong direction, he experiences increasing restlessness and inner anxiety—an indication that he is in danger of being called "Out."

It is not difficult to see the logic of this explanation, and it corresponds beautifully with the other aspects of the traditional view of guidance. Unfortunately, it does not correspond to the meanings of the passages it is based on. For the "peace" Paul wrote about to the Colossians is very different from the "peace" he promised to the Philippians. And neither one fits within the framework of the traditional view.

Broadly speaking, *peace* is presented in two ways in the New Testament. One kind of peace is internal—*within* an individual. Defined negatively, it is the absence of anxiety (Philippians 4:6–7) or fear (John 14:27). It is an inner assurance gained from faith in God's sufficiency and sovereignty. It is not lack of trouble, but is expected in the midst of tribulation (John 16:33) and in every circumstance (2 Thessalonians 3:16). Absence of this kind of peace may indicate a lack of faith in God's sufficiency, not perplexity in the area of guidance. While there is a superficial resemblance between the peace described by the traditional view (where one has a sense of confidence concerning God's direction) and the inward peace described in passages about trust in God's sovereign care, they are not the same. Where there is faith, there is peace; it is a fruit of the Spirit (Galatians 5:22).[13]

The other kind of peace is external—*among* individuals. It replaces hostility and division between persons with oneness and harmony (Ephesians 2:14–15). And this is clearly the sense in which it is being used in Colossians 3, where Paul wrote, "let the peace of Christ rule in your hearts." In context, that statement is part of a paragraph that runs from verses 12 through 17. That paragraph begins with an exhortation for believers to "put on" certain virtues: compassion, kindness, humility, gentleness, patience, forbearance, forgiveness, and above all, love, "which is the perfect bond of unity" (3:14). These virtues are to replace discarded vices such as immorality, greed, anger, abusive speech, lying, and the like (3:5–11). Such evil manifestations of "the old self" are the cause of the tremendous divisions we see in the world. But the tensions that exist between "Greek and Jew, circumcised and uncircumcised, barbarian, Scythian, slave and freeman" are not to exist in the church. Rather, believers are to be characterized by unity—a unity that will grow spontaneously as Christians put on the garments of love (3:12–14), *submit to the peace of Christ* (3:15), share the word of Christ (3:16), and do all things with thanksgiving in the name of the Lord Jesus (3:17).

Bible commentator T. K. Abbott correctly concludes: "The immediate reference here [in Colossians 3] is not to inward peace of the soul; but to peace with one another, as the context shows."[14] Therefore, the whole appeal of Colossians 3:12–17 is for believers to demonstrate

Christlike attitudes and virtues that will result in an experiential unity among believers. Such harmony reflects a supernatural change that replaces hatred and animosity with love and peace. Any interpretation of Colossians 3:15 that explains it as inner guidance in decision making is foreign to the context.

Disturbing the Peace

In addition to the exegetical problems described above, the traditional view has a secondary, experiential problem with its appeal to the peace of God. It is the same problem that has emerged like a monotonous refrain throughout this chapter: the inherent subjectivity in accounting for the experience of peace—or more precisely, the lack of it.

For the sake of argument, let's return to the traditional view's definition of peace as inner quietness of heart or the absence of anxiety. Now when a believer experiences "lack of peace" in the process of decision making, the question that must be asked is, what is the source of the anxiety? Is it always an indication of the Spirit's guidance, or could it be explained by other factors?

Sometimes a lack of peace is the result of facing great difficulties that have nothing to do with guidance or disobedience.

A moment's reflection will yield several potential disturbers of the peace. One likely suspect in certain cases is the conscience. If the Christian begins to pursue a course of action in violation of God's revealed moral will, the Spirit-sensitized conscience will produce the first symptoms of guilt. This disruption of peace is designed to be an alarm system warning the believer to change his direction and get back on the path of righteousness (see Ephesians 4:25–32). Of course, in such instances, obedience to the moral will of God is in question.

However, even when faced with choices within God's moral will, Christians often experience a lack of peace. Again, the potential causes are numerous: insomnia, illness, concern for a loved one, occupational stress, an approaching deadline, nagging uncertainties, timidity, a new experience, and so on. Sometimes a lack of peace is the result of facing great difficulties that have nothing to do with guidance or disobedience. Christ was greatly troubled, but it was not the result of sin (John 12:27).

There Goes the Groom

I was once the best man for my friend, Mike, who was getting married in North Dakota. In order to go to our position backstage without being seen, we had to crawl through the church baptistery. Doubling as the unofficial photographer, I took a picture of the groom as he crawled through the baptistery. Then I focused the camera on Mike as he sat by the entrance door biting his fingernails with the wide-eyed look of a condemned convict.

The pose was made in jest. But suppose he had looked up at me at that moment and said, "Garry, I've prayed a lot about marrying Chris. But right now I feel so unsettled inside, I think the Lord must be telling me not to go through with it." What should I have done? Should I have stopped the wedding? Isn't that what best men are for?

Of course, he didn't say that. And I didn't stop the wedding. Nor would I have—not without a more legitimate reason. If all marriages were called off because of nervous grooms, there would be few weddings. Such "lack of peace" is normal when we face a major new step in life.

A disturbance of our quietness of heart can be accounted for in all sorts of ways. Furthermore, Scripture gives no criteria by which we may distinguish the negative leading of the Spirit from other disquieting influences.

As important as God's peace is in the life of the believer, its presence or absence is not to be construed as a sign of God's leading in biblically permitted decisions. Peace cannot function as such, nor was it so designed.

To summarize the last two chapters, the problem with the traditional view is not that it recognizes the reality of inner impressions, but that it requires too much of them. Since it is impossible to define with certainty either their source or their meaning, it is also impossible to derive from them objective guidance pointing to one "right" decision. God's Word does not grant authority to subjective sources of knowledge. We must not either.[15]

Behold the Forest!

Lest we lose our way among the individual trees of our presentation, let's pause momentarily to review where we've been. Then we should be able to see where we need to go. Based on the outline presentation in part 1, the distinctive features of the traditional view are as follows:

THE TRADITIONAL VIEW OF DECISION MAKING

Premise: For each of our decisions, God has a perfect plan or will.

Purpose: The goal of the believer is to discover God's individual will (find the dot) and make decisions in accordance with it.

Process: The believer interprets inner impressions and outward signs, which the Holy Spirit uses to communicate God's individual will.

Proof: The confirmation that one has correctly discerned the individual will of God comes from an inner sense of peace and outward (successful) results of the decision.

As I promised, part 2 has been mainly critical. In these chapters, I have worked to establish a single major point, and several corollaries. The *major point* is this: God does not have an ideal, detailed life-plan uniquely designed for each believer that must be discovered in order to make correct decisions. The concept of an "individual will of God" cannot be established by reason, experience, biblical example, or biblical teaching (chapters 3 and 4).

The *corollaries* are: First, attempts to find a dot that does not exist have generated needless frustration. I have shown, for instance, that practitioners of the traditional view are forced to abandon the process in the minor decisions of everyday life. Second, the traditional view provides no adequate means for dealing with genuinely equal options. Third, the traditional view tends to promote immature approaches to decision making. And finally, since the traditional view can appeal only to subjective sources of knowledge, the seeker of guidance is denied the possibility of objective certainty that he has found God's will (chapters 5 and 6). Not only is the individual will of God not found in Scripture, but the suggested process for finding it is absent as well.

Thankfully, the Christian is not left to his own devices when he must make decisions. God's provisions are abundant and practical. It is into that portion of our theological forest—the doctrine of the nature of guidance—that we may now proceed.

1. William F. Arndt and F. Wilbur Gingrich, trans., *A Greek-English Lexicon of the New Testament and Other Early Christian Literature*, 2nd ed. (Chicago; University of Chicago Press, 1979), s.v. ἄγω.
2. John R. W. Stott, *Men Made New* (Downers Grove, Ill.: InterVarsity Press, 1966), 93.
3. W. H. Griffith Thomas, *St. Paul's Epistle to the Romans: A Devotional Commentary* (Grand Rapids, MI: Wm. B. Eerdmans Publishing Co., 1946), 215; John Murray, *The Epistle to the Romans, The New International Commentary on the New Testament* (Grand Rapids, MI: Wm. B. Eerdmans Publishing Co., 1959), 1:293–95.
4. Stott, *Men Made New*, 92–93.
5. C. E. B. Cranfield, *Romans: A Shorter Commentary* (Grand Rapids, MI: Wm. B. Eerdmans Publishing Co., 1985), 189–90.
6. Arndt and Gingrich, trans., *A Greek-English Lexicon of the New Testament*, s.v. συμμαρτυρέω, 786.
7. Handley C. G. Moule, *The Epistle of St. Paul to the Romans* (New York: A. C. Armstrong and Son, 1894), 224.
8. John R. W. Stott, *The Message of Galatians* (Downers Grove, Ill.: InterVarsity Press, 1968), 152.
9. Leon Morris, *The Gospel According to John, The New International Commentary on the New Testament* (Grand Rapids, MI: Wm. B. Eerdmans Publishing Co., 1971), 700, n. 30.
10. Merrill C. Tenney, *John: The Gospel of Belief* (Grand Rapids, MI: Wm. B. Eerdmans Publishing Co., 1948), 238–39.
11. Charles Caldwell Ryrie, *The Ryrie Study Bible* (Chicago: Moody Press, 1979), 1632.
12. The idea of umpire comes from the fact that *brabeuo* was used for the umpire who "ruled" over an athletic game. The traditional view understands the word to mean more than overall supervision, but to mean making specific decisions in specific cases. However, the context of Colossians 3:15 favors the general sense of "rule" or "control."
13. Scott L. Kaseburg, "The Place of Inward Peace in the Believer's Determination and Confirmation of God's Will in Decision-Making," (unpublished thesis, Western Conservative Baptist Seminary, 1980).
14. T. K. Abbott, *A Critical and Exegetical Commentary on the Epistles to the Ephesians and to the Colossians, The International Critical Commentary* (Edinburgh: T&T Clark, 1897), 289. See also F. F. Bruce, "Commentary on the Epistle to the Colossians," in *Commentary on the Epistles to the Ephesians and the Colossians, The New International Commentary on the New Testament* (Grand Rapids, MI: Wm. B. Eerdmans Publishing Co., 1957), 282.
15. To say that impressions lack authority does not mean they lack value. In the way of wisdom, impressions play a legitimate role in decision making. I further discuss the origins of impressions and how Christians should respond to them in chapter 16, "Making a Good Thing Better."

part three

the way of WISDOM

The Wisdom View Explained

chapter eight

YOUR WORD IS TRUTH

The expression *will of God* is used in the Bible in two ways. God's *sovereign will* is His secret plan that determines everything that happens in the universe. God's *moral will* consists of the revealed commands in the Bible that teach how people ought to believe and live.

To these biblical usages (moral and sovereign wills), the traditional view has added a third. It is commonly taught that for each person, God has an *individual will*—an ideal, detailed life-plan for each person. In this traditional view, the key to decision making is to discover God's individual will, and then do it. Accordingly, the burden of most books on guidance is to explain how to discern God's specific leading in each situation.

By contrast, the emphasis of Scripture is on God's moral will. In fact, the Bible reveals nothing of an "individual will" governing each decision. Rather, the teaching of Scripture may be summarized by these basic principles:

PRINCIPLES OF DECISION MAKING
THE WAY OF WISDOM

1. Where God commands, we must obey (chapter 8).
2. Where there is no command, God gives us freedom (and responsibility) to choose (chapter 9).
3. Where there is no command, God gives us wisdom to choose (chapters 10 and 11).
4. When we have chosen what is moral and wise, we must trust the sovereign God to work all the details together for good (chapters 12 and 13).

These four principles form the thesis of this section and summarize the "way of wisdom" that will be developed, explained, and illustrated throughout the chapters of part 3.

In part 1, Pastor Thompson provided an accurate explanation of the sovereign will and moral will of God. Since these concepts are foundational to the Christian's decision-making process, it is appropriate at this point to establish in greater detail both the genuineness and character of each of these biblical senses of God's will. Then we will be prepared to recognize the important bearing that each has on our decisions.

THE REALITY OF GOD'S MORAL WILL

I had studied long and hard, and I thought I had a good grasp of the material. The exam was taxing, but it was a fair test of how much we had learned. I knew I had done well; the only question was whether I would get an *A* or a *B*.

I lived with the suspense for a week or so. At last, the graded exams were returned—the moment of truth had arrived. Or had it? What was the letter in the upper right-hand corner? It was neither an *A* (as in "astute"), nor a *B* (as in "brilliant"). It was a *D* (as in "dumbbell")! How could that be?

I quickly paged through the exam, finding that I had done even better than I expected on pages one, two, and three. But page four was a disaster. I had missed nineteen out of nineteen true or false questions. I could have done better flipping a coin! Then I saw the problem: I had put a *T* or *F* in each answer blank whereas the instructions had specifically directed me to spell out *True* or *False*. The penalty never did seem completely fair to me, but I did learn a valuable lesson: Before you begin an exam, read all of the instructions carefully.

In C. S. Lewis's classic book *The Silver Chair*, much more was at stake than a grade on a test. The great Lion, Aslan, assigned to Jill and Eustace the task of finding the lost prince. In this danger-filled adventure, they would have the assistance of Puddleglum, the Marshwiggle. Aslan promises success if they will carefully follow four signs. These four directives are to be learned, memorized, believed, and obeyed. They are to be rehearsed each morning and evening, and as they walk in the way. Nothing else matters, they are told. The world around them will be deceptive, but believing the signs will bring them through. In the dramatic moment of the book, the lost prince asks them for something "in Aslan's name"—the final sign! They are afraid to obey, but Puddleglum knows what he must do, whether he lives or dies. Trusting Aslan's promise, he acts on the prince's plea. The evil enchantment is broken, and the prince is rescued!

Whether we are taking an exam or rescuing a captive prince, following the instructions is the key to success. The same principle applies to our spiritual lives. God's instructions are always fair, and they bear careful reading. Those instructions, which are clearly set forth in the Bible, constitute the moral will of God.

Bookworm's Delight

God's moral will is the perfect and complete guide for the Christian's faith and practice. Most Christian books are concerned with God's moral will. Bible commentaries interpret God's moral will as it is presented in the text of Scripture. Books on theology and doctrine organize God's moral will into various subjects and categories. Ethics books wrestle with proper application of God's moral will to complex, real-life situations. Devotional books inspire us to follow God's moral will in daily living.

As we noted in chapter 4, "Does Scripture Teach the Dot?," this moral aspect of God's will was a common subject of biblical writers. One clear example is found in Romans 2:18. Addressing the unbelieving Jew, the apostle Paul said, "[you] know His will…being instructed out of the Law." In this statement, Paul could not have been speaking of God's sovereign will (which cannot be known), nor His individual will (which is neither revealed in the law nor ever discovered by unbelievers). Rather, Paul was speaking of God's moral will.[1] For in the law, God's moral laws and requirements are revealed to all Jews, believing and unbelieving alike.

Again, in 1 Thessalonians, Paul directly equated God's will with specific moral commands. For instance, sanctification of life, including sexual purity, is called "the will of God" (4:3), and, "in everything give thanks; for this is God's will for you in Christ Jesus" (5:18). ("God's will" may actually encompass the whole list of terse commands that immediately precede the directive to give thanks [5:12–17].)

Moral Is Good, but Love Is Better

I have selected the term *moral* to describe God's revealed will. I could have employed another word to describe this aspect of God's will—a word used by Jesus when He was hard pressed by His opponents.

> And He said to him, "'YOU SHALL LOVE THE LORD YOUR GOD WITH ALL YOUR HEART, AND WITH ALL YOUR SOUL, AND WITH ALL YOUR MIND.' This is the great and foremost commandment. The second is like it, 'YOU SHALL LOVE YOUR NEIGHBOR AS YOURSELF.' On these two commandments depend the whole Law and the Prophets." (Matthew 22:37–40)

That key word, of course, is *love*. Every command of the moral will of God is a specific expression of the greatest command to love.

The law is what love would do.

Love is the foundation and motivation for all the other commands. Our love for God and people is the basis for "the whole Law and the Prophets" (Matthew 22:40). The greatest command is not just first in importance, but all other commands "depend" upon it. As the apostle Paul put it: "He who loves his neighbor has fulfilled the law" (Romans 13:8); and "The entire law is summed up in a single command: 'Love your neighbor as yourself'" (Galatians 5:14, NIV). One of my seminary professors concluded: "The law is what love would do."

How is this command to love to be understood in practical terms? Jesus stated it this way in His famous Golden Rule: "In everything, therefore, treat people the same way you want them to treat you, for this is the Law and the Prophets" (Matthew 7:12).

THE NATURE OF GOD'S MORAL WILL

The guidance God provides through His moral will is more pervasive than many realize. The abundance of this provision is more keenly appreciated when we explore four distinct facets of the moral will of God.

Like Father, Like Son

First, the moral will of God is *the expression*, in behavioral terms, *of the character of God*. Perhaps the most succinct statement of divine expectation is Peter's quotation of the Old Testament imperative: "You shall be holy, for I am holy" (1 Peter 1:16; Leviticus 11:44–45). Now, how am I to guide my life so as to "be holy...in all...behavior" (1 Peter 1:15)? By obeying the moral will of God, which, like God Himself, is "holy and righteous and good" (Romans 7:12). Put differently, God's children are to manifest the family likeness by obeying the Father's will (Ephesians 5:1; 1 John 5:3).

Ironically, what Satan sought to usurp ("I will make myself *like the Most High*" [Isaiah 14:14]) and tempted Eve to pursue ("you will be *like God*" [Genesis 3:5]) has been part of God's design for mankind from the very beginning. Created in the image of God, Adam and Eve were already "like God." His purpose for them was that they would reflect the Creator's likeness on the finite level (Genesis 1:26–31).

No lesser purpose defines God's "new creature" (2 Corinthians 5:17), which, through the redemptive and recreative activity of the Godhead, is being progressively renewed and will ultimately conform precisely to the Creator's image (Colossians 3:10; Romans 8:29). The capacity and the resources people need to manifest the character of God have been granted by His grace (2 Peter 1:3–4). Consequently, one of the most frequent and fundamental motivations for godly living in the New Testament is the reminder of what God is like. Specifically, the following traits are among those that are to characterize the believer *because they characterize the Godhead*: holiness (1 Peter 1:15–16), righteousness (1 John 3:7), purity (1 John 3:3), love (Ephesians 5:1–2), forgiveness (Colossians 3:13), compassion (Luke 6:36), endurance (Hebrews 12:2–4), submission (1 Peter 2:21–24), humility and obedience (Philippians 2:5–8), kindness (Luke 6:35), and generosity in giving (2 Corinthians 8:1–9).

Second, God in His grace has made His moral will known to us, for it is *fully revealed in the Bible*, our final and complete authority for faith and practice (2 Timothy 3:16–17; Hebrews 1:1–2). It was authoritative for Jesus Christ (Matthew 4:4–10; 5:18; 22:29) and His apostles (2 Peter 1:19–21). (See the "Frequently Asked Question" at the end of this chapter for further discussion of this point.)

God is not concerned simply with what we do; He's equally concerned with why we do what we do, as well as how we do it.

Third, if the moral will of God is the expression of His character, then we would expect it to govern much more than merely external behavior. The imperatives of God's moral will *touch every aspect and moment of life* because they prescribe the believer's goals, motives, and attitudes, as well as his actions. To put it differently, God is not concerned simply with what we do; He's equally concerned with why we do what we do, as well as how we do it. The purpose, the process, and the product are all directed by His moral will. Furthermore, it shapes the believer's perspective of reality, which serves as the context in which his decisions are made.

The End Just As the Means

These generalities are more clearly seen via specifics. So we will look more closely at the guidance God has given us in Scripture concerning our goals, our attitudes, our means for achieving our objectives, and our frame of reference for decision making.

Goals, by their nature, are more general than behavioral commands. In Scripture, the believer's primary goals reflect God's purposes for His children during their earthly lives. A good example of God's will for our goals is found in 1 Peter 4:10–11:

> As each one has received a special gift, employ it in serving one another as good stewards of the manifold grace of God. Whoever speaks, is to do so as one who is speaking the utterances of God; whoever serves is to do so as one who is serving by the strength which God supplies; so that in all things God may be glorified through Jesus Christ, to whom belongs the glory and dominion forever and ever. Amen.

Here, the believer's ultimate goal is to glorify God in all things (1 Corinthians 10:31; 2 Corinthians 5:9; Colossians 1:10). Toward that ultimate end, intermediate objectives are established. They include ministering to others ("serving one another"; 1 Corinthians 10:23; Romans 14:19), and fulfilling God-given responsibilities ("as good stewards"; Ephesians 5:22–6:9; Galatians 6:9–10).

Other important assignments given elsewhere include evangelization of lost people (1 Corinthians 10:31–33; 2 Peter 3:9), and production of spiritual fruit and good works (John 15:8; 1 Corinthians 6:12; Ephesians 2:10; Colossians 1:10).

Such directives plainly state God's moral will for our lives. When the Christian adopts those imperatives as his personal goals, he has *concrete guidance* that is applicable even to situations that may not be directly addressed by Scripture. When considering an opportunity, for instance, the believer can often clarify his options with this question: If I take this opportunity, will it help or hinder me in accomplishing my God-given goals? Similarly, a choice between two or more options should raise the question: Which choice will maximize the fulfillment of my spiritual objectives?

A second category of life in which we receive guidance from God's revealed moral will is that of *attitudes*. Scriptural exhortations appealing for God-honoring attitudes are legion. The chart below represents only a portion of these directives, and is offered as a "pump primer" for the reader's personal study.

GOD'S WILL FOR OUR ATTITUDES		
Is...	**Not...**	**Key Passages**
Love	Lust	Mark 12:28–31; Romans 14:13–19; 1 Corinthians 13:1–3; Romans 13:14
Reliance	Independence	Proverbs 3:5–6; Galatians 5:16
Humility	Pride	James 4:6; Philippians 2:5–8
Gratitude	Presumption	Colossians 3:17
Clear conscience	Guilt	Romans 14:22–23
Integrity	Irresponsibility	Colossians 3:17, 22
Diligence	Laziness	Colossians 3:23
Eagerness	Compulsion	1 Peter 5:2
Generosity	Selfishness	1 Timothy 6:17–19
Submission	Self-advancement	1 Peter 5:5–6
Courage	Cowardice	John 16:33; Matthew 10:26–28
Contentment	Greed	Hebrews 13:5; Philippians 4:11

A third area governed by God's moral will is the *means* Christians use to accomplish their goals. Most decisions permitted by Scripture, and most questions about decision making and the will of God, actually concern means to ends. For very few of our activities are done for their own sake. They are part of an overall process by which we strive to fulfill our plans. In that sense, such disparate choices as which shoes to put on and which person to marry are means-related decisions. Both have to do with the fulfillment of personal objectives.

The moral will of God for appropriate means for our goals may be summed up in two broad principles: First, our means must be biblically *lawful*—that is, they may not be outside of the revealed moral will of God (Ephesians 5:1–14); second, our means must be *wise*—that is, the believer may not make a decision he knows to be foolish (Ephesians 5:15–17; cf. Luke 14:28–32). These principles will be developed further in subsequent chapters.

Since no decision is made in a vacuum, the degree to which we pursue godly goals with righteous attitudes and wise actions will be largely determined by our *perspective on life*. In particular, the Christian whose worldview is shaped by Scripture will have a sense of self-identity different from the world's. Knowing that she is loved by God with a love she did nothing to earn (and which, therefore, she can do nothing to forfeit, Romans 8:31–39), she will face life with a deep sense of security. Being aware that God has equipped her to participate meaningfully in the outworking of the eternal purposes of God (Ephesians 2:10; 1 Peter 4:10–11), she has a clear grasp of her personal worth. A strong sense of security and significance in Christ frees the Christian from self-promoting motivations in decision making, releasing her to focus more on the needs of others (Philippians 2:1–5).

Other passages remind the Christian that she is on assignment for God in enemy territory (Ephesians 6:12), that physical life on this earth is preparatory for "real life" in heaven and that what she invests for God now will be repaid with interest later (Matthew 6:19–21; Romans 8:18; 2 Corinthians 4:17). And she will recognize that the unseen forces and resources of heaven are involved in her behalf as she seeks to carry out God's will on earth (Hebrews 1:14; 11:1; 2 Kings 6:16–17).

God's moral will insists that we resist having our viewpoint molded by the world (Romans 12:2). Instead, we are to "walk by faith" (2 Corinthians 5:7), seeing our lives, and therefore our decisions, through the "glasses" of God's Word.

To sum up: Because God's moral will prescribes our goals, attitudes, actions, and perspective, it touches every aspect and moment of life.

Finally, since the Bible expresses God's own character, contains God's complete revelation pertaining to faith and life, and touches every aspect and moment of life, it is *able to equip believers for every good work.* This is explicitly stated by the apostle Paul:

> All Scripture is inspired by God and profitable for teaching, for reproof, for correction, for training in righteousness; so that the man of God may be adequate, equipped for every good work. (2 Timothy 3:16–17)

By contrast, human traditions do not have this authority and often divert people from God's moral will by encouraging a violation of it (Matthew 15:1–6; Colossians 2:8, 16–23).

> **THE NATURE OF GOD'S MORAL WILL**
>
> - *Origin*: It is the expression, in behavioral terms, of God's character.
> - *Communication*: It is fully revealed in the Bible.
> - *Scope*: It touches every aspect and moment of life: goals, attitudes, means, and perspectives (why, how, and what).
> - *Impact*: It is able to equip believers for every good work.

The Most Important Decision

It is the moral will of God that each person believes on Christ and has eternal life. It is possible that your genuine interest in spiritual things has caused you to read this book, but you are not certain of eternal life. Believing in God's existence is not enough; heart trust in Christ is what is needed. The difference is like that of believing in doctors over against *trusting* your doctor in major surgery. The first is commendable, the second is lifesaving.

God does not have a low self-image that needs a boost from a lot of people affirming that He exists. God's existence will not be altered by the percentage of people who believe or disbelieve in Him. The issue is man's sin. God's holiness has been violated, and the just penalty is God's wrath. God's love has not ignored His holiness, but satisfied it by paying the price for sin. The price was death, and the perfect Christ paid it in full. As a result of Christ's sacrifice, God can offer forgiveness and eternal life as a gift—a gift purchased with a precious price. It is God's moral desire that everyone accept this gift.

> This is good and acceptable in the sight of God our Savior, who desires all men to be saved and to come to the knowledge of the truth. For there is one God, and one mediator also between

> God and men, the man Christ Jesus, who gave Himself as a ransom for all. (1 Timothy 2:3–6)

In fact, God's judgment against sin has been "postponed" so that all will have time to respond.

> The Lord is not slow about His promise, as some count slowness, but is patient toward you, not wishing for any to perish but for all to come to repentance. But the day of the Lord will come. (2 Peter 3:9–10)

No excuse for rejecting Christ is excusable. A pastor friend of mine likes to put it this way: "If you refuse Christ, be sure that you have a real good excuse thought up because it's the excuse you will give when you stand before God on judgment day." It is the moral will of God that everyone trust Christ. It is the sovereign will of God that those who do will certainly have eternal life.

> For this is the will of My Father, that everyone who beholds the Son and believes in Him will have eternal life, and I Myself will raise him up on the last day. (John 6:40)

Do you intend to live your life according to God's will? The very first step of obedience is to turn to God in repentance and receive His salvation through faith in Christ. If you have never done that, you would be wise to stop reading this book long enough to express your faith to God in prayer. Whatever words you can find to express the trust in your heart will suffice.

THE BELIEVER'S RESPONSE TO GOD'S MORAL WILL

The moral will of God has been well illustrated as the area enclosed by a circle. The interior of the circle contains all the commands and principles that are morally binding upon the believer. Any thought, attitude, or action that conforms to the scriptural imperatives is acceptable and pleasing to God. But any thought, attitude, or action that falls outside of that circle is sin (1 John 3:4). Thus, it is of supreme importance that the believer learn where the perimeter of that circle runs. Jesus told His disciples, "If you know these things, you are blessed if you do them" (John 13:17). The blessing of obedience is impossible apart from fulfillment of the first "if"—"if you *know* these things."

Accordingly, the Christian's first responsibility is to *gain a good understanding* of what is included within God's moral will. The source of such knowledge, as we have emphasized, is God's Word. The process for gaining such an understanding includes reading (1 Timothy 4:13), careful consideration (2 Timothy 2:7), search and inquiry (1 Peter 1:10–11), diligence in study (2 Timothy 2:15), meditation (Psalm 1:2; Joshua 1:8), memorization (Psalm 119:11), and learning from gifted Bible teachers (Philippians 4:9; 1 Corinthians 12:28–29; Galatians 6:6). This requires time and effort! The Bible student should strive to progress in his understanding, moving on from the "milk" of God's truth (as is appropriate for infants) to the "meat" of the Word (which is enjoyed only by the more mature; 1 Corinthians 3:1–4; Hebrews 5:12–14).

The believer can expect that God will be at work within him to give understanding as he studies. Paul exhorted Timothy, "Consider what I say, for the Lord will give you understanding in everything" (2 Timothy 2:7). The Holy Spirit of truth does not work to illuminate the Bible's meaning apart from our diligent study, but rather works through it.

Your Wish Is My Command

As the Christian grows in his understanding of God's moral will, he must also *grow in his obedience* to it. Obedience is one of the most important responsibilities believers have during this life. In the early years of the church, there was a great debate over whether a Gentile believer should become circumcised or remain uncircumcised. In the minds of many, it was an earthshaking issue. But the apostle Paul wrote: "Circumcision is nothing, and uncircumcision is nothing, but *what matters is the keeping of the commandments of God*" (1 Corinthians 7:19).

Such obedience has always been of paramount importance to God's people. Moses summarized the whole point of revelation with this statement:

> "Now, Israel, what does the LORD your God require from you, but to fear the LORD your God, to walk in all His ways and love

> Him, and to serve the LORD your God with all your heart and with all your soul, and to keep the LORD's commandments and His statutes which I am commanding you today for your good?" (Deuteronomy 10:12–13)

In this declaration, Moses stated a theme reiterated throughout Scripture: Whatever outward response we make to God's declared will must be a genuine expression of the heart to be acceptable to God (1 Samuel 16:7; Mark 12:28–31). Just as God's moral will addresses the inner man at the level of his goals and attitudes, so the believer's obedience is to be an activity of the soul as well as the body. The spirit of the law, not the letter, is of supreme importance to God. And so it should be for the believer.

This commitment of believers to the moral will of God is possible because of the nature of faith. Genuine faith takes the statements of the Bible as absolute fact. Faith in the promise of God fully expects the promise to be fulfilled. Faith in the command of God obeys—convinced that it is the most important thing to do. Faith's stance toward the moral will of God consists of trust, expectation, and obedience. Faith and the moral will of God will always be in harmony.

You Can't Know the Players Without...

The keeping of the moral will of God is so significant that believers are distinguished from unbelievers on the basis of their response to God's commands. Jesus said that those who do the moral will of God will enter the kingdom of heaven, while those who do not will not (Matthew 7:21; 21:31). Using different terms, Christ said that those who obey God's will are part of His spiritual family (Matthew 12:50).

In his first epistle, the apostle John made a vivid contrast:

> Do not love the world nor the things in the world. If anyone loves the world, the love of the Father is not in him. For all that is in the world, the lust of the flesh and the lust of the eyes and the boastful pride of life, is not from the Father, but is from the world. The world is passing away, and also its lusts; but the *one who does the will of God lives forever.* (1 John 2:15–17)

John expected that the one born of God will give evidence that he is a new creature by his obedience to the moral will of God as a pattern of life. Throughout the epistle, he describes what such a lifestyle looks like: keeping the commands of God (2:3–6), living a life of love (4:7–8), and believing in true doctrine (2:21–23; 4:1–3; 5:1). These characteristics are not the basis for our salvation, but are rather the evidence of it. We are saved by grace through faith (Ephesians 2:8–9), but genuine saving faith can never be separated from good works, which follow from it (Acts 26:20; Ephesians 2:10; James 2:14–26). Obedience to the moral will of God is of supreme value. It is not optional.

Significantly, that very obedience is the key ingredient in successful living. When God commissioned Joshua to lead the nation of Israel into the Promised Land after the death of Moses, He gave him this prescription for success:

> "This book of the law shall not depart from your mouth, but you shall meditate on it day and night, so that you may be careful to do according to all that is written in it; for then you will make your way prosperous, and then you will have success." (Joshua 1:8)

This promise to Joshua was declared to be a universal principle, applicable to all of God's people, by the psalmist:

> How blessed is the man who does not walk in the counsel
> of the wicked,
> Nor stand in the path of sinners,
> Nor sit in the seat of scoffers!
> But his delight is in the law of the LORD,
> And in His law he meditates day and night.
> He will be like a tree firmly planted by streams of water,
> Which yields its fruit in its season
> And its leaf does not wither;
> And in whatever he does; he prospers.
> (Psalm 1:1–3; see also Ecclesiastes 12:13)

Moses reflected this same understanding when he told Israel that God's commandments were "for your good" (Deuteronomy 10:13). And the apostle John affirmed from experience the beneficial nature of God's moral will when he wrote: "For this is the love of God, that we keep His commandments; and His commandments are not burdensome" (1 John 5:3).

Eat, Drink, and Be Mature

Our Lord gave equal emphasis to the importance and value of obeying God's will. Early in His ministry, Jesus used two elements basic to physical life—food and water—to instruct a thirsty woman and hungry disciples about spiritual necessities. To the woman at the well, He offered the ultimate thirst quencher: His salvation, which would cover her sins and supply the dynamic gift of eternal life (John 4:10, 13–14). The disciples, on the other hand, had already been satisfied at Christ's salvation fountain. To them He explained that the purpose of believers is to do the moral will of God. Such service has the same nourishing effect on the soul that eating does for the body. Jesus said, "My food is to do the will of Him who sent Me and to accomplish His work" (John 4:34).

Do you desire the spiritual success described in Joshua 1:8 and Psalm 1:2–3? Is your greatest goal in life to please the heart of God? If you are His child through faith in Jesus Christ, the process is clear: Learn, love, and obey the moral will of God. If you read only this far in this book, you will know how to become a person like King David, of whom God said, "I HAVE FOUND DAVID the son of Jesse, A MAN AFTER MY HEART, who will do all My will" (Acts 13:22).

How did this "man after God's heart" regard God's moral will? Reflect on these words of David. For when you perceive and respond to God's Word as David did, your life, too, will be pleasing to God.

> The law of the LORD is perfect, restoring the soul;
> The testimony of the LORD is sure, making wise the simple.
> The precepts of the LORD are right, rejoicing the heart;
> The commandment of the LORD is pure, enlightening the eyes,
> The fear of the LORD is clean, enduring forever;
> The judgments of the LORD are true; they are righteous altogether.
> They are more desirable than gold, yes, than much fine gold;
> Sweeter also than honey and the drippings of the honeycomb.
> Moreover, by them Your servant is warned;
> In keeping them there is great reward. (Psalm 19:7–11)

LEARNING GOD'S MORAL WILL: PRACTICAL SUGGESTIONS

While many Christians express a keen interest in knowing God's will for their lives, they often fail to give appropriate attention to the abundant guidance already supplied. This striking irony is perhaps understandable if we expect a mystical sort of direction for our decisions. But the biblical pattern calls for the believer to become a student of the Scriptures, exerting personal effort to learn the instructions already given by the God who has spoken (Hebrews 1:1; 2 Timothy 2:15; Ezra 7:10).

Dr. John G. Mitchell was one of the founders of Multnomah Bible College in Portland, Oregon. At the entrance to the college library that bears his name, a large plaque is inscribed with his oft-repeated challenge: "Don't you folks ever read your Bibles?" Dr. Mitchell put his finger on what is perhaps the greatest deficiency in the practice of guidance-seeking believers. The only will of God that must be "discovered" was never lost—it's just ignored. One consequence is expressed in J. I. Packer's observation that Christianity in North America is three thousand miles wide and a half inch deep.[2] Too many of us are like Dale Hinshaw, Philip Gulley's character in the Harmony series. Hinshaw "knew just enough Scripture to be annoying, but not enough to be transformed."[3]

I'm not talking about seminary training here. It is true that some folks are intimidated by the fear that they might err in their interpretation of a biblical passage. And such concern is commendable, for we must be careful to discern the meaning the biblical authors intended rather than imposing our own ideas onto the text. But I contend that the greater problem is *biblical illiteracy* of the sort Dr. Mitchell referred to. Before we worry about what the Bible means, we have to know what the Bible says.

Having spent most of my adult life challenging college students to study the Bible, I have three suggestions for those who want to upgrade their knowledge of God's moral will. The first, introduced to me by my friend and colleague, Ron Frost, is a simple "read through" program in which a person covers a large portion of Scripture in a short amount of time in partnership with a friend or a group.[4]

By way of example, I once had to decline an invitation to speak at a weekend retreat because I didn't have time to prepare the four messages required by the schedule. But I made a counteroffer: I would be willing to facilitate a "read through" of the book of 2 Samuel. We would call it, "Finding Out What Made David a Man After God's Own Heart." There would be no recreational activities that weekend. Saturday would be spent in individual reading of 2 Samuel in ninety-minute increments. Each reading period would be followed by group discussion of what we had learned. The worship time on Sunday would employ worship songs that reflected truth from 2 Samuel, prayers that used words or concepts from 2 Samuel, and readings from favorite passages in that book. My offer was accepted and the retreat was scheduled.

Many of the twenty participants began reading 2 Samuel weeks before the retreat and were already in serious reading mode by the start of the weekend. Almost everyone had read through the whole book once and many made it through as many as five times. During sharing sessions we were not allowed to raise questions about the text; we only interacted on passages we understood and insights that had helped us. (We reserved discussion of problem passages and questions for mealtimes. At dinner we enjoyed a stimulating discussion about David, polygamy, and war.)

The weekend in 2 Samuel was so well received that a year later I was asked to lead another "read through" retreat. We took our second foray through the book of Acts. Our theme was "God's Spirit in the Life of the Church."

A similar format can be followed as part of a discipleship program. Two people might decide to cover a specific Bible book or segment over a period of weeks or months. They would each read on their own, but meet once a week to discuss what they had learned. Some small groups using this approach have read through the entire Bible in three months. One advantage of this format is that it helps the reader to get the big picture of a section of Scripture. She also has the encouragement of partners to whom she is accountable and the benefit of their shared insights as they participate in the adventure of Bible reading together.

Recently, Josh, a student living in my house, suggested devoting a day to reading the whole New Testament aloud. We invited others to join us for this "Bible Marathon." Fifteen of us started early Saturday morning, and we finished Revelation Sunday morning (which happened to be Easter) at 2:15 a.m.! (It takes nineteen hours to read the entire New Testament aloud taking five minute breaks every two hours.) Before we finished the day, several asked, "When are we going to do the Old Testament?"

The Bible Marathon was difficult, but the encouragement of the body in community aided our alertness. It was difficult, but the commitment of a day to Scripture helped us drink deeply from God's Word in the midst of a busy culture. It was difficult, but we saw key themes all the way through the New Testament. It was difficult, but the very bigness of the challenge attracted many, and the event itself was easy to plan and flexible enough for any number of people.[5] Since that first marathon, we have conducted a dozen similar "read throughs" that ranged from four to eighteen hours.

You Will Forget Everything You Read

A second useful approach to learning God's moral will is more traditional—memorization of Bible verses. My appreciation for the value of Scripture memory began in high school through my participation in a Youth for Christ quiz. Infused with all the fervor and exertion of varsity athletic contests, these quizzing competitions elevated Bible knowledge to the level of serious business. Each year the teams were challenged to master one or more specific books of the Bible. Members of championship-caliber teams not only read and studied those books; they actually memorized them! During my wonder years, I memorized 1 Corinthians and Jude one year, Matthew and Psalm 119 the next. It was an excellent way to fill up vast, empty tracts of an adolescent mind.

In the years that followed, however, I had to confront a disappointing reality. By the time I was in college, I could barely quote more than fifty verses from the myriad I had learned. My claim that I had memorized hundreds of verses sounded more like the man who boasts that he has quit smoking hundreds of times.

Roger, a friend in seminary, introduced me to a Scripture memory system that transformed my practice. His approach takes into account both the strengths and limitations of the human mind. It is based on the premise that while people forget most of what they read, they remember most of what they *review.* It was based on one simple principle: *Review* as much *and* as little *as you must to hold on to verses perfectly.* This principle created a change of focus for me. Rather than simply adding new verses to my memory bank, I learned the importance of devoting time to the retention of passages previously learned.

How can we effectively hide God's Word in our heart (Psalm

119:11)? I found that it requires a workable system of review, and in appendix 2, I have included a description of a system that has worked for me. The plan involves an organized schedule of review with diminishing frequency. New verses are reviewed daily until they are learned; they are moved to the weekly review list until they are locked in; monthly review makes them second nature; and bimonthly review establishes permanent retention. The minimum requirements for success are a plan and disciplined time commitment. I invest about two hours a week in Scripture memory and review, but a half hour a week will bring great benefit. Five minutes a day is a good place to start. Some folks have found that Scripture memorization has transformed their daily commute from a necessary evil to a spiritually productive exercise.

What verses should you memorize? Printed verse cards are available through your Christian bookstore, but I suggest that you develop your own list from a "read through" or some other form of Bible study. Memorizing passages chosen from your own experience with the text is the culminating step in effective Bible study. What began with reading and reflecting is sealed with memorization and review. Thus, not only will you learn God's moral will for your life, you will also remember it (Psalm 119:16)!

The Olympic Decathlon

There is a third approach to Bible study that I impose on my students in the Pentateuch course at Multnomah Bible College. In the middle of the school term, they tend to grumble about the effort it takes. But at semester's end, their course evaluations consistently rate this assignment as among the most helpful aspects of their instruction. If the "read through" is like a marathon, this exercise resembles a decathlon.

The assignment in my class is to memorize short titles for every chapter in Genesis, Exodus, Leviticus, and selected chapters from Numbers and Deuteronomy. When the students learn over 125 chapter titles, they have a mental "table of contents" for the books of Moses. It organizes the Bible in their mind so they are able to recall in an instant where to find the Ten Commandments (both places) or the sacrifice of Isaac. They also know the main subject of Genesis 48 or Exodus 28 or Leviticus 17 or Numbers 31 or Deuteronomy 13.[6]

Any Bible student would benefit from creating his own chapter titles from his study of the text. Start by writing a one-sentence summary of each paragraph in a chapter. Then try to capture the dominant idea of the chapter in a single phrase or two. Your goal is not to cover every topic in a chapter, but the main one—which will, in turn, remind you of other points included.

You can write these chapter titles on cards and add them to your review system for memorizing Scripture. Whenever possible, I try to use the key words used in the text as part of a chapter title. My title for 2 Corinthians 7 is "Sorrowful Letter," since that phrase appears several times in my translation.

To sum up, I have suggested three techniques to improve our understanding and retention of the moral will of God. "Read throughs" with friends provide meaning-filled overviews of significant portions of God's Word. An effective plan of Scripture memorization increases our recall of key passages. And chapter titles provide a framework for staying oriented within the Bible.

The cumulative effect of these three methods of study can be dramatic. The Bible student who has practiced these disciplines over a few years is able to find subjects, verses, and doctrines in the Bible without hauling around a trailer full of reference books. It is both satisfying and useful to hear a verse recited and be able to pinpoint it by book and chapter. I have students who like to test me with a quote. When I know the reference, they are amazed. When I am wrong, they are amused. I prayed for the gift of a photographic memory, and God gave me chapter titles. (You have to work with what you've got. If you have a photographic memory, disregard these suggestions.)

We must not lose sight of our objective. We are not in training for an appearance on *Jeopardy!* or a game of Trivial Pursuit. We are in training for godliness (1 Timothy 4:7–8). Specifically, we are concerned with making decisions that are pleasing to God. If our decisions are going to conform to God's moral will, we must have access to God's moral will. The revelation that God has graciously and abundantly given is of no use to us if it remains confined to the pages of a Book. It needs to be ingrained in our hearts (Psalm 119:11). To the degree that a disciple has mastered and absorbed the content of God's written instruction, to that degree he has moment-by-moment access to the wisdom of God and will be able to draw upon that wisdom *at the point of decision making.*

So, if you have a system for learning God's moral will, keep at it.

And if you don't, I invite you to join me in the marathon and the decathlon.

PRINCIPLES OF DECISION MAKING
THE WAY OF WISDOM

1. Where God commands, we must obey (chapter 8).

frequently asked question

> *Question:* In this chapter you state that the moral will of God is fully revealed in the Bible. But wouldn't special revelation expand the content of God's moral will beyond what is contained in the Bible?

Yes, it would. And that did happen during the biblical era. For example, when the Spirit directed the church at Antioch to send out Barnabas and Saul as missionaries (Acts 13:1–2), that instruction represented an addition to the great commission. And it became God's moral will for them—they were obliged to obey. Later, the "Macedonian vision" (Acts 16:9–10) did the same thing for Paul. His travel options were reduced by special guidance that expanded God's moral will for him. So any divine guidance to an individual by means of supernatural revelation is God's moral will for that person.

Is special revelation being given today? Some Bible scholars rule out that possibility. They maintain that with the closing of the canon of Scripture, God's revelation has ceased until the second coming of Christ. While I understand the arguments for that position, I don't see a conclusive case in the Bible itself. It seems preferable to leave open the possibility of divine revelation and subject specific claims to biblical tests—including supernatural means of communication and harmony with existing Scripture. Accordingly, in the first edition of this book, I included another category of God's will—special guidance: "In unique cases God may supernaturally guide believers by divine voice, angel, dream, or miracle according to special revelation."

On the other hand, while special guidance is possible, it is not promised nor do most believers have reason to expect it. When the Bible instructs us with principles for decision making (which is what this book is about), it directs us along other lines as explained in this chapter and the ones that follow. The theoretical possibility of special guidance concerns us less than the concrete, practical guidance already supplied. So when Peter writes that "[God's] divine power has given us *everything we need* for life and godliness through our knowledge of him who called us by his own glory and goodness" (2 Peter 1:3, NIV, italics added), I take that to include the moral will of God fully revealed in the Bible.

A more extended discussion of special revelation is presented in chapter 15, "Special Guidance and Decision Making."

---

1. John Murray, *The Epistle to the Romans, The New International Commentary on the New Testament* (Grand Rapids, MI: Wm. B. Eerdmans Publishing Co., 1959), 2:82; Charles Hodge, *A Commentary on Romans* (Carlisle, PA: The Banner of Truth Trust, 1972), 61.
2. J. I. Packer, *Keep in Step with the Spirit* (Old Tappan, NJ: Fleming H. Revell Co., 1984), 10.
3. Philip Gulley, *Home to Harmony* (New York: HarperCollins Publishers, Inc., 2002), 173.
4. R. N. Frost, *Discovering the Power of the Bible* (Eugene, OR: Harvest House Publishers, 2000). The genius of this book lies in its challenge to treat Scripture reading like an Olympic event rather than intramurals or a spectator sport.
5. A set of guidelines for a Bible Marathon is included in appendix 3.
6. When the Pentateuch course is over, some of my students ask if I have chapter titles for other books of the Bible. The answer is yes, and maybe some day I'll publish a volume with chapter titles for every book of the Bible. But don't hold your breath. Until then, see my website: http://www.gfriesen.net.

chapter nine

GOD-GIVEN FREEDOM (AND RESPONSIBILITY) TO CHOOSE

"Love God and do whatever you please."

Augustine, the author of this startling quote, got it right. Predating by several centuries the understanding of decision making that has become the traditional view, he boldly articulated the second principle of the wisdom view: *Where there is no command, God gives us freedom (and responsibility) to choose.*

Augustine can be misunderstood, so we must be careful with his statement. "Do as you please" must not be separated from "love God." And "love God" must be biblically defined. As I explained in the previous chapter, the person who truly loves God will keep all of His commandments (John 14:15, 21, 23; 1 John 2:5; 5:2–3; 2 John 1:6). Obedience to the command to "love God" will always be expressed by keeping all of the moral will of God. But the second half of Augustine's dictum must not be denied. When you have kept all of the commands, then you are free to do "whatever you please" without displeasing God. Within the moral will of God, there is an area of freedom. You *cannot* go wrong if you are obeying all of the moral will of God, and the one who loves God will obey His moral will.

It is at this point that the way of wisdom most dramatically parts company with the traditional view. In the place of a dot, which is thought to represent God's individual will, the Bible reveals an area of freedom (and responsibility) within the safety of God's commands.

TRADITIONAL VIEW OF GOD'S INDIVIDUAL WILL

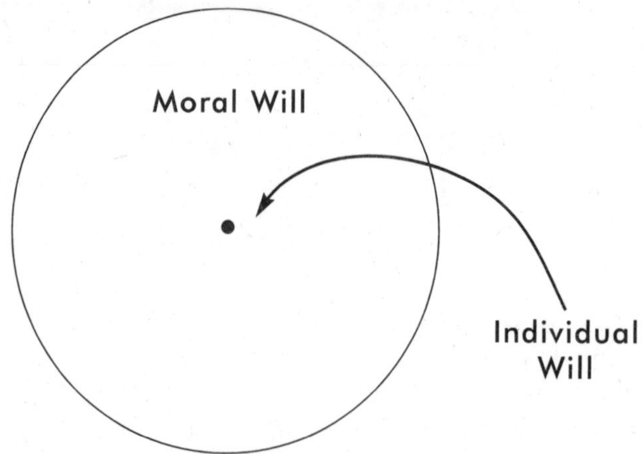

BIBLICAL VIEW OF FREEDOM WITHIN GOD'S MORAL WILL

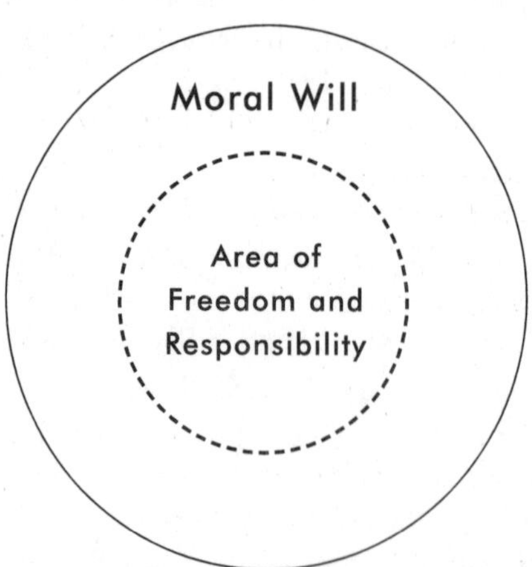

Where did I get this idea? I first encountered it in the beginning, in the Garden of Eden. If I may be permitted a few lighthearted paragraphs, I hereby submit an imaginative rendition of…

"THE FIRST SUPPER"

(with apologies to Moses ben Amram[1])

Adam was hungry. He had had a long, challenging day naming animals. His afternoon nap had been refreshing, and his postsiesta introduction to Eve was exhilarating, to say the least. But as the sun began to set on their first day, Adam discovered that he had worked up an appetite.

"I think we should eat," he said to Eve. "Let's call the evening meal 'supper.'"

"Oh, you're so decisive, Adam," Eve said. "I like that in a man. I guess all the excitement of being created has made me hungry, too."

As they discussed how they should proceed, they decided that Adam would gather fruit from the garden, and Eve would prepare it for their meal. Adam set about his task and soon returned with a basket full of ripe fruit. He gave it to Eve and went to soak his feet in the soothing current of the Pishon River until supper was ready. He had been reviewing the animals' names for about five minutes when he heard his wife's troubled voice.

"Adam, could you help me for a moment?"

"What seems to be the problem, dear?"

"I'm not sure which of these lovely fruits I should prepare for supper. I've prayed for guidance from the Lord, but I'm not really sure what He wants me to do. I certainly don't want to miss His will on my very first decision. Would you go to the Lord and ask Him what I should do about supper?"

Adam's hunger was intensifying, but he understood Eve's dilemma. So he left her to go speak with the Lord. Shortly, he returned. He appeared perplexed.

"Well?" Eve said.

"He didn't really answer your question."

"What do you mean? Didn't He say anything?"

"Not much. He just repeated what He said earlier today during the garden tour: 'From any tree of the garden you may eat freely; but from the tree of the knowledge of good and evil you shall not eat.' I assure you, Eve, I steered clear of the forbidden tree."

"I appreciate that, but that doesn't solve my problem," Eve said. "What fruit should I prepare for tonight?"

From the rumbling in his stomach, Adam discovered that lions and tigers were not the only things that growl. So he said, "I've never seen such crisp, juicy apples. I feel a sense of peace about them. Why don't you prepare them for supper?"

"All right, Adam. I guess you've had more experience at making decisions than I have. I appreciate your leadership. I'll call you when supper's ready."

Adam was only halfway back to the river when he heard Eve's call. He jogged back to the clearing where she was working, but his anticipation evaporated when he saw her face. "More problems?" he asked.

"Adam, I just can't decide how I should fix these apples. I could slice them, dice them, mash them, bake them in a pie, a cobbler, fritters, or dumplings. I really want to be your helper, but I also want to be certain of the Lord's will on this decision. Would you be a dear and go just one more time to the Lord with my problem?"

Adam was not keen on bothering the Lord again, but after Eve said some very nice things about him, he agreed to go. When he returned, he said, "I got the same answer as before: 'From any tree of the garden you may eat freely; but from the tree of the knowledge of good and evil you shall not eat.'"

Adam and Eve were both silent for a moment. Then with light in his eye, Adam said, "You know, Eve, the Lord made that statement as though it fully answered my question. I'm sure He could have told us what to eat and how to eat it; but I think He's given us freedom to make those decisions. It was the same way with the animals today. He told me to name the animals, but He didn't whisper any names in my ear. Assigning those names was my responsibility."

Eve was incredulous. "Do you mean that we could have any of these fruits for supper?" Eve said. "Are you telling me that I can't miss God's will in this decision?"

"The only way you could do that is to pick some fruit from the forbidden tree. But none of these fruits are from that tree. Why, I suppose we are free to eat a little from each one of them." Adam snapped his fingers and exclaimed, "Say, that's a great idea! Let's have fruit salad for supper!"

And so they did.

The pattern of personal freedom and responsibility within revealed limits was part of the Creator's purpose from the very beginning. For it was *explicitly declared in one of the very first recorded commandments.* In a demonstration of God's goodness, He began His first directive with a declaration of the extent of Adam's *freedom* of choice: "From *any* tree of the garden you may eat *freely*." Then He added the single restriction ("the tree of the knowledge of good and evil") with a clear explanation of the consequence of violation ("you will surely die"; Genesis 2:16–17).

In the diagram above, the tree of knowledge of good and evil would be outside the circle of God's will—forbidden. The rest of the trees of Eden would not only be inside the larger circle of God's moral will, they would be within the circle of freedom. (If there had been a tree from which they were required to eat, it would have been inside the moral circle, but not within the smaller circle of freedom.)

This direct commandment conforms perfectly to God's original design for mankind. For when God created human beings, He made them in His own image (Genesis 1:26–27). That image accounts for man's great value to God and distinguishes humans from all other earthly creatures. Only humans were endowed with the features of personality: intellect, emotion, and will. Only man was assigned a position of responsibility requiring the exercise of those attributes of the soul.

If men and women were to make their decisions as a function of instinct, they would be no different than the animals. If they required direct input from the Creator for every choice, they would be no more than programmed robots. By God's design, only the image bearer approaches decisions *in the same manner as the Creator*. Within boundaries prescribed by God's own character, humans analyze, evaluate, judge, and freely determine their choices. No other creature but man was given the competence to make free judgments. And only humans were given the dignity of bearing moral responsibility for the consequences of their choices. The nature of God's image requires that people follow God's commands and act as creators where God gives freedom.

Now, while the concept of freedom within limits is foreign to the traditional view of guidance, it actually makes sense—both in everyday life and in our relationship to God. What I will show in this chapter is that this freedom (and responsibility) is evident from the nature of laws, the nature of sin, and other direct statements of Scripture.

THE PRINCIPLE OF FREEDOM AND THE NATURE OF LAWS

The principle of freedom of choice within revealed limits is applied routinely in everyday situations. For instance, public beaches often have regulations for swimmers. These signs inform everyone of the restrictions that must be observed for the sake of safety. Each swimmer rightly assumes that she is free to do anything else not forbidden. She may build a sand castle, fill a pail with water, do the sidestroke, and so on. She does not have to ask the lifeguard for permission to do things that are not on the list.

Before You Ask, the Answer Is Yes

In my role as a college teacher I often prepare assignments for my students. My instructions usually assume a freedom of choice within the course requirements. Guidelines for a research paper on C. S. Lewis might read as follows: "This paper must be on one of the topics listed in the syllabus; it must be typed, double-spaced, and be eight to ten pages long."

Such an assignment both assumes and restricts freedom. I must present it this way or it would take reams of paper to explain a single assignment. But imagine the student who does not recognize his freedom within the bounds of the instructions. "Prof, the syllabus doesn't say anything about using a computer to write the paper. Can we use one?" The syllabus doesn't say anything for good reasons. So I answer, "You may use one, but you don't have to." He raises his hand again. "Can I do the first topic of the five you listed? I would really like to do that one." I reply, "You may pick that one or any of the five." If he raises his hand once more the other students will groan and say, "Ask the prof after class!" Like

Adam and Eve in our parable, this student needs to recognize what is obvious to his classmates—there is freedom within the parameters of the assignment.

This example illustrates that to be effective, normal lawmaking assumes freedom of choice within the designated limitations. God demonstrated this when He gave ten laws that fit on two transportable stone tablets. He did not try to legislate every conceivable situation. He gave ten commandments and then examples of their application throughout the rest of the law. The law of Moses is concise compared with the detailed ancient Code of Hammurabi or with our modern law codes.

"If a Little Is Good, Then..."

A similar contrast may be seen between the respective approaches of Pharisaic Judaism and Christ. By the time of Jesus' birth, Jewish life was rigidly governed by a minutely detailed body of tradition. The scribes and Pharisees had achieved the ultimate in specific legislation. The requirements for "holy living" had become so complex, common people despaired of even learning them, much less observing them. "Righteousness" became the private property of the legal professionals.

But Jesus repudiated the Pharisaic approach to religion. He rebuked the legalists for burying the law of God beneath a mountain of minutiae. Jesus focused on revealing the spirit of the law, explaining how God had always intended the law to be understood. In so doing, He returned to a normative approach where principles were illustrated by concrete examples (Matthew 5–7).

If a Chariot Was Good Enough for David...

Understanding the nature of laws and their freedom can correct a common error. Some sincere Christians refuse to participate in certain activities or use any human inventions unless they can find specific warrant in the Bible. Of course, the Bible says nothing about eyeglasses, electric appliances, automobiles, computers, the Internet, or any number of things devised since the first century. And so these saints unnecessarily deny themselves many of the products of human progress. Francis Schaeffer corrected this misunderstanding, maintaining that there is freedom within the commands of Scripture :

> [W]e cannot bind men morally except with that which the Scripture clearly commands (beyond that we can only give advice).... [S]imilarly, anything the New Testament does not command in regard to church form is a freedom to be exercised under the leadership of the Holy Spirit for that particular time and place.[2]

FREEDOM IN DECISION MAKING

1. The **nature of effective law making** requires that where there is no command, there is an assumed area of freedom.

THE PRINCIPLE OF FREEDOM AND THE NATURE OF SIN

Biblical explanations of the nature of sin also support the concept of freedom of choice within revealed limitations. Sin is described as breaking God's law: "Everyone who practices sin also practices lawlessness; and sin is lawlessness" (1 John 3:4). The reverse is also true: "Where there is no law, there also is no violation." (Romans 4:15). As a result, the only way a person can sin against God in a decision is to break one of God's commands—that is, make a decision outside the moral will of God. Such an offense could involve a wrong purpose or attitude, as well as a wrong action.

However, if a particular decision is not directly addressed by God's commands, and our goals and attitudes are right, then we cannot sin in making the decision. For instance, the Bible does not command believers to attend any particular college. So a student's choice of a school cannot in itself be sinful. If no biblical principles are violated, such a decision lies within the area of freedom and responsibility.

Nevertheless, some Christians experience feelings of guilt after making a decision not specifically addressed by Scripture. Why? They fear that they have missed God's individual (specific) will. In the absence of clear leading, they went ahead and made a choice. Now they feel guilty because they aren't certain they have done what God wanted them to do. For some, the feelings are compounded by the belief that failure to perceive God's guidance is an indication of spiritual insensitivity or carnality. So they feel guilty on two counts: blocking out God's signals and possibly missing His will. The more sincere and sensitive the believer is, the more likely he is to feel this burden of uncertain guilt.

Such guilt is not intended by God. If His moral will has not been violated, there has been no sin. If there has been no sin, there should be no guilt. It's as simple, and profound, as that. In decisions where God's law does not restrict, the believer has real freedom to decide. Where there is no moral law, there can be no moral sin, and therefore no condemnation.

As I have explained these concepts, both in oral and written presentations, the most common response is relief. As the truth of the principle of freedom within the moral will of God sinks in, sincere believers who have misinterpreted their floating guilt feelings as conviction from God experience a sense of release. They are set free from an unnecessary burden. The inner turmoil can end when the God-given freedom within His moral will is recognized. This eliminates false guilt and answers the slanderous accusations of our enemy (Revelation 12:10).

FREEDOM IN DECISION MAKING

1. The *nature of effective law making* requires that where there is no command, there is an assumed area of freedom.
2. The **nature of sin** requires that where God gives no command, there is freedom.

THE PRINCIPLE OF FREEDOM IN DIRECT STATEMENTS OF SCRIPTURE

The clinching argument for God-given freedom comes from the direct statements of Scripture. I have already demonstrated (at some length) that this was the case with one of the very first commands God gave to Adam (Genesis 2:16–17). And that was only the beginning! There are numerous other instances in which the freedom that is always assumed in the Bible is directly declared.

Any Item from the Approved Menu

The introduction of sin into human nature and experience did not require that the principle of freedom within revealed limits be revoked. It did require a more extensive revelation of God's moral will and character to the fallen heart of man (Jeremiah 17:9). Nevertheless, the principle of freedom remained in force as a feature of the Mosaic law. For example, in Leviticus 11 and Deuteronomy 14, definite limits were placed upon which animals the Israelites could eat and which ones were forbidden. Unclean animals were outside the circle of God's moral will for Israel. But from among the clean animals, the Hebrews could freely choose: "These are the creatures which you may eat from all the animals that are on the earth" (Leviticus 11:2). Israel was to gather for feasts in God's presence. What food should a family buy for the trip? "Whatever your heart desires" (Deuteronomy 14:26). There was freedom of choice as long as they were selecting from the approved menu.

The *freewill offering* (Leviticus 22:18; Numbers 15:3) was different from the required sacrifices and demanded the reality of God-given freedom. If an Israelite asked God, "Do you want me to give a freewill offering today?" how would He answer? If He said yes, then the Israelite would be under obligation to bring it. If He said no, then the Israelite would be prohibited from offering it. Either response from God would prevent the offering from being what it was intended to be—a "freewill" offering. This catch-22 is solved by simply recognizing that God intended this offering to be in the area of freedom as a voluntary way of displaying devotion.[3]

Once a person freely chose to bring this offering, certain stipulations explained what sacrifices were acceptable for such purposes (Leviticus 22:18–25). But even that instruction gave freedom within limits. For while the animal chosen for the burnt offering had to be a male without defect, it could be a bull, a ram, or a goat.

Other examples of Old Testament commands that contain *explicit* statements of freedom within limits are not hard to find.

- An Israelite could voluntarily make a vow before the Lord, but once it was made, the keeping of it was required (Deuteronomy 23:21–23; see Numbers 30:2; Psalm 50:14; Ecclesiastes 5:4–5; Nahum 1:15).
- A former slave was free to live "in the place which he shall choose in one of your towns where it pleases him" (Deuteronomy 23:15–16). The freedom that was assumed for everyone else had to be spelled out in this case.

In the Gospels, Jesus' parable of "The Laborers in the Vineyard" illustrates freedom within moral bounds. Every worker should be treated fairly, but the landowner was free to pay some workers more generously. To the complaining hired hand, the landlord said, "Is it not lawful for me to do what I wish with what is my own?" (Matthew 20:14–15). Jesus concurred with the landowner's freedom of choice since the wages agreed upon were fair.

Freedom Inflation

The freedom found in the instructions of the Old Testament and Jesus continues in the rest of the New Testament, but with one striking difference. In this age of the New Covenant, freedom for the believer *is expanded.* This is clearly seen in the matters of eating, circumcision, and giving.

The subject of food, which was so important in the Garden of Eden as well as in Israel, reappeared as a topic of discussion in the early church. Two questions arose in the predominantly Gentile churches: Is it permissible for Christians to eat meat (as opposed to vegetarianism, Romans 14:2), and is it permissible for Christians to eat meat that was previously offered to idols (1 Corinthians 8:1)? Paul addressed both of these questions.

First, Paul classified the eating of meat as morally neutral in itself. "Food will not commend us to God; we are neither the worse if we do not eat, nor the better if we do eat" (1 Corinthians 8:8). God prohibits hurting a weaker brother by this "liberty" (1 Corinthians 8:9) and He prohibits idolatry (1 Corinthians 10:14), but the meat itself does not affect our status with God. Thus, Paul stated the doctrine of freedom both positively, asserting our "liberty," and negatively, explaining that food won't help us please God. To make sure no one missed the point that believers are truly free to choose their menu, Paul used a variety of expressions. He said this choice was a "liberty," a "right," a "lawful" thing, and a "freedom." Simply stated: "Eat anything" (1 Corinthians 8:9; 9:4; 10:23, 25, 29; 1 Timothy 4:3–5).

You Are Cordially Required to Attend

Next, Paul applied this principle to a specific situation. What should a Christian do if an unbeliever invites him to supper where he suspects "idol meat" might be served? Paul boldly asserted the believer's freedom: "Eat anything that is set before you without asking questions for conscience' sake" (1 Corinthians 10:27). The dinner guest is not to probe the meal's pedigree or recent history. He is free to enjoy the meal with thankfulness (10:30).

Paul understood the value of a blameless conscience (Acts 23:1; 24:16; 1 Timothy 3:9), which should be the goal of every believer. If that is so, why would Paul use such a bold phrase that seems to contradict his earlier teaching? Why would he tell a believer to "eat anything...without asking questions for conscience' sake" (1 Corinthians 10:25, 27)? The context provides the key.

One function of the conscience is to make judgments on moral questions—"Is this activity I'm considering right or wrong?" On valid moral issues, the Christian is to pay heed to his conscience. But if the matter in question is morally neutral, then there is no need for the conscience to rule. Paul had already established that "idol meat" cannot condemn or commend us to God (1 Corinthians 8:8). Since his ruling moved this matter out of the arena of moral concerns, there is no need to even engage our conscience about where the food came from. Thus, in context, the advice to "eat anything...without asking questions for conscience' sake" becomes a striking way of saying that the believer has "freedom" on this issue.

Paul extends the believer's freedom to the dinner invitation itself. At this point Paul might be expected to invoke the directives of the traditional view to seek God's leading, but he doesn't go there. Instead he says, "If one of the unbelievers invites you and *you want to go...*" (1 Corinthians 10:27). In the absence of a biblical command or prohibition, the decision is decided by the believer's own wish. It was this verse that one of my seminary professors used in a chapel service to introduce this concept of freedom. He reasoned, what does "if you want to go" mean, if not that there is freedom within the moral commands?

With the inauguration of the New Covenant, the regulations appropriate to Israel's national life were set aside (Hebrews 7:18; 10:9; see Acts 10:9–16; 11:1–18; 15:5–29; Romans 6:14; 7:6). In Christ there is the freedom to choose from a wider menu than the Mosaic law allowed. The fuller revelation of Christ increased the scope of freedom. When the Lord explained this expanded freedom to Peter (through the Joppa vision), it was hard for him to accept (Acts 10:9–16). And it is hard for some trained in the traditional view to accept. Three times the sheet full of unclean animals descended and each time a horrified Peter was told to get up and eat. To his credit he understood and believed in his God-given freedom before he finished preaching to Cornelius and the formerly unclean Gentiles (Acts 10:28–29).

> In the absence of a biblical command or prohibition, the decision is decided by the believer's own wish.

Like Peter we must learn that when God guides us by giving us freedom, it should be accepted by simple faith. Food is now "clean" (Romans 14:14, 20), and those who forbid it are teaching false doctrines (1 Timothy 4:3–4). That's because the kingdom does not consist of food and drink, but righteousness, peace, and joy—that is, the moral will of God (Romans 14:17).[4]

But What Matters Is...

One of the Bible's clearest expressions of freedom in decision making is found in 1 Corinthians 7:19: "Circumcision is nothing, and uncircumcision is nothing."

How could Paul say that circumcision was "nothing" when it was one of the hottest issues in the early church? The dramatic Jerusalem Council convened to debate the relationship of circumcision to salvation (Acts 15:1–29). Much of the book of Galatians is occupied with the same issue. Paul's point: circumcision is "nothing" because something else matters much more.

"Circumcision is nothing, and uncircumcision is nothing, *but what matters is the keeping of the commandments of God*" (1 Corinthians 7:19). In the Old Testament, circumcision was commanded as a sign of the covenant and an outward sign of faith (Genesis 17; Romans 4:11). But under the New Covenant circumcision is neither commanded nor prohibited. In the moral sense it is now "nothing." But "what matters is the keeping of the commandments of God." Paul gives great significance to the moral commands of God, but when there is no command the believer is free. It no longer mattered whether or not a man chose circumcision (Galatians 5:6; 6:15).[5]

This verse argues strongly for our first two principles: (1) Where God commands, we must obey. (2) Where there is no command, God gives us freedom (and responsibility) to choose.

I Already Gave at the Office

The amount, which is left totally up to the individual to determine, is not as significant as the spirit of the giver.

When an opportunity is presented to give money to some aspect of the Lord's work, or when a Christian brother is in financial need, how should the believer determine how much money to contribute? Should he go to the Lord in prayer and request a divine impression for a specific amount? Should he give 10 percent?

When the Corinthian Christians were gathering funds to send to their impoverished brothers and sisters in Judea, the instruction they received from the apostle Paul was: "Each one must do just as he has purposed in his heart, not grudgingly or under compulsion, for God loves a cheerful giver" (2 Corinthians 9:7). Here is freedom of choice within the moral will of God. In this case, the emphasis of the moral will was not so much on the *act* of giving as it was on the *attitude*. Consequently, the amount, which is left totally up to the individual to determine, is not as significant as the spirit of the giver. What is God's will for our giving? Generosity, enthusiasm, and faith are imperative; a reluctant spirit that forks over money only under pressure is forbidden. The actual amount is a personal decision, freely made.[6]

Whom Should I Marry? Dot?

Should I marry? If yes, whom? The New Testament gives no clue that God's individual will determines these decisions. The marriage decision is probably the classic example of the principle of freedom within the moral will of God. Two full chapters in part 4 (19 and 20) are dedicated to a close look at decision making and marriage.

At this point we will look at only one key verse: "A wife is bound as long as her husband lives; but if her husband is dead, she is free to be married to whom she wishes, only in the Lord" (1 Corinthians 7:39). The moral will of God commands the permanency of marriage by a binding covenant. The widow, however, is "free to marry" any believer "whom she wishes." This verse directly contradicts the teaching of those who insist there is only one right person in the world for someone to marry. (That is, if God tells them to marry!)

"Free to be married" concisely communicates that (1) the widow did not have to marry and (2) she was not prohibited from getting remarried. "Free to be married" says them both. "Only in the Lord" expresses God's moral will restricting the pool of legitimate candidates to believers. But within that circle, God gives freedom in the selection of which person—"to whom she wishes."

A Final "Useful" Example

The beautiful story of Paul and Onesimus (literally, "Useful") in the book of Philemon also gives us an example of freedom when there is no command. While imprisoned in Rome, Paul had converted Philemon's runaway slave, Onesimus. The new convert quickly captured the heart of Paul and became very "useful" to the aged apostle (Philemon 11). Paul desired to keep the runaway with him so that Onesimus could minister to him in Philemon's place (Philemon 12–13).

As an apostle, Paul had the authority to command Philemon to leave Onesimus with him. But Paul decided against this. "[W]ithout your consent I did not want to do anything, so that your goodness would not be, in effect, by compulsion but of your own free will" (Philemon 14). A command from the apostle would necessitate obedience (Philemon 8). Without a command from Paul, Philemon was free to show goodness in the way he saw best.

FREEDOM IN DECISION MAKING

1. The *nature of effective law making* requires that where there is no command, there is an assumed area of freedom.
2. The *nature of sin* requires that where God gives no command, there is freedom.
3. The **direct statements of Scripture** reveal that God gives freedom where He gives no command.

The Scripture verses that speak directly about our freedom to choose are conclusive. If the traditional view were correct, we would not expect to find such explicit expressions of freedom. We would expect directives to "seek the Lord's will" about decisions ranging from the mundane (what to eat) to the strategic (whom should I marry?). But that is not what we find! What we find is freedom within revealed limits. If these verses don't mean freedom, what do they mean? What better explanation of these passages can be offered than simply taking the words at face value? Critics of the wisdom view complain that this freedom implies a lack of guidance. However, they have not given a better interpretation of what the freedom verses mean. Direct statements of Scripture argue for the concept of freedom clearly and strongly.

Being a part of God's design for our lives, this gift of freedom is hardly a defect in His plan. God knows the perfect balance of commands and freedom that people should have. He is the model for missionaries, teachers, supervisors, parents, pastors, and nannies. When one teaches and leads others, the right balance of direction and freedom is crucial. A teacher must give enough instruction to assure that effective learning occurs, but enough freedom to allow motivated students a chance to spread their wings. Salesmen must have boundaries, but also enough freedom for self-starting achievers to fulfill their potential. Children need a different balance of command and freedom at each stage of development. Very young children need much explicit guidance to protect them from unknown dangers, but as the children grow, wise parents expand the area of freedom and responsibility in decision making to prepare them for adulthood.

God has chosen not to *micromanage* our choices within His moral will. Within the protective framework of His laws, He has created room for creativity and development. He has perfectly balanced command and freedom for our growth and His glory.

This freedom principle is key to infiltrating other cultures with the gospel. Evangelism is commanded, but the method can fit the culture being reached. God directs all believers to sing and worship, but the exact words and style of music can be those that most speak to the heart of each culture. The Scripture must not be changed, but we have freedom to translate it into the words of each people group. The commands of Scripture stand in judgment over every culture, but the principle of freedom encourages the great variety of expression in cultures that will one day surround the throne of God.

A statement in 1 Corinthians 10:23 provides a beautiful bridge between the principle of freedom (discussed in this chapter) and the principle of wisdom (presented in the next chapter): "All things are lawful, but not all things are profitable. All things are lawful, but not all things edify." Paul summarizes the area of freedom as "lawful," and then introduces our third principle when he says, "not all things are profitable...not all things edify." Freedom is qualified by the moral command to be wise—to select what is profitable or edifying from the lawful options. But we will look at more of God's wisdom and guidance in the next chapter.

PRINCIPLES OF DECISION MAKING
THE WAY OF WISDOM

1. Where God commands, we must obey (chapter 8).
2. **Where there is no command, God gives us freedom (and responsibility) to choose (chapter 9).**

frequently asked questions

> *Question:* Are you saying that God doesn't care about decisions that aren't specified in the Bible? For instance, does He really not care whom I might choose as a marriage partner?

I avoid saying "God doesn't care" about a noncommanded decision because that terminology implies indifference (though 1 Corinthians 7:19 and 8:8 come very close to that wording). I affirm with Scripture that God cares about every aspect of the life of His child (Matthew 6:25–34; 1 Peter 5:7). But that concern doesn't require Him to dictate our decisions. The positive way to express it is to say that God is *equally pleased* with two options that equally conform to His moral will.

Furthermore, as we shall see, there are at least two ways in which He is actively involved in our decision making—even in the area of freedom. First, He promises to give us wisdom to recognize if one option is more profitable than another (see the next chapter). Second, He sovereignly directs all things (including our freely chosen decisions) so that they work together for good. God cares that we believe Him when He says that we are free, and He cares that we enjoy and use that freedom to His glory. Remember the freedom given to Adam and Eve? It was in God's gracious and perfect guidance that He said, "of every tree of the garden you may freely eat"—not because He did not care.

> *Question:* Are you saying that two options are really equal or that they only seem equal? Wouldn't God know how each would turn out and know that one was really better?

In the ultimate sense, no two options are perfectly equal. If you're shopping for a car and you narrow the choice to two vehicles, one will turn out to be the better value. And, yes, God knows which one that is. But He has not promised to divulge that information and you are not required to know it in order to make an acceptable decision. Furthermore, the choice you make cannot obstruct the outworking of God's sovereign purposes for your life with respect to that car. Indeed, as we shall see, God is sovereignly at work in your decision to accomplish His purposes. At a practical level, then, the ultimate superiority of one of two options is not our concern. If two options are equally moral and wise on the basis of the wisdom God has given us, then He is equally pleased with either choice. He, however, is sovereign and will work out the choice that best fits His sovereign plan for us and for the universe.

> *Question:* How can you speak of the believer's freedom when God is sovereign over every detail of life including our decision making?

I believe in the sovereign will of God. But God's sovereignty versus human responsibility will have to wait until chapters 12 and 13. In this chapter, we have explored passages that clearly teach freedom within revealed limits. *Freedom* is the Bible's word—"From any tree of the garden you may eat *freely*" (Genesis 2:16). I believe that when God said it, He meant it. What better term than *freedom* could we use?

> *Question:* In the first edition of *Decision Making,* you spoke of decisions within the area of freedom as "nonmoral" decisions. You also described the believer's freedom as "moral" freedom. In this edition you have not used this terminology. Why?

I found that I was inadvertently confusing some people with my vocabulary. Most readers recognized what I meant when I spoke of "nonmoral decisions." If the Bible doesn't address a specific decision, such as which car to buy, then the purchase of one vehicle or another is, *in and of itself,* a nonmoral decision. God's command (moral will) cannot be violated. In that sense, "nonmoral decision" is a useful designation.

On the other hand, there is a sense in which *no* decision is "nonmoral." For the moral will of God touches every aspect and moment of life. So while a specific decision may not be directly addressed by Scripture such that there is genuine freedom of choice, our goals, attitudes, actions, and perspective that bear upon this choice *are* governed by the moral will of God. So when we set out to buy a car, we will not find any biblical injunction determining that decision. But all of the passages that address financial stewardship and Christian business ethics (among others) will apply. The moral command to be wise is also applicable—and so important that the next chapter is devoted to it.

So for the sake of consistency, and to reduce the likelihood of misunderstanding, I chose not to use "nonmoral decisions" and "moral freedom" in this edition. Instead, I describe decisions in the area of freedom as "biblically noncommanded."

> *Question:* Isn't your desire for freedom just an irresponsible worldview that does not want to be restricted?

I don't think so. It is certainly possible, even probable, that freedom is misunderstood or misused for selfish ends. The problem with grace is that it is susceptible to abuse. But it is important to remember that not only is this biblical freedom real, it is freedom *within the moral will of God.* His commands prohibit pride or self-will. His commands require love for people and God. They require wisdom to promote the kingdom of God. Freedom is taught in the Scriptures, but always in the context of God showing us how to use that freedom for His glory—not our own selfish ends.

This being the case, the Scriptures that specifically state this freedom prompt us to turn the question around. "If God gives freedom, isn't it a lack of faith not to believe it and enjoy that freedom?" There will be anarchists and pharisees who will distort God's freedom on both sides; but God-given freedom within God's commands is the perfect balance.

> *Question:* In a chapter that explains the believer's freedom in noncommanded decisions, I couldn't help but notice that you occasionally inserted the words "and responsibility" (usually in parentheses) when describing this freedom. The point would be that if we are free to choose in such instances, we're also responsible to choose. But if we're not trying to find the individual will of God, on what basis are we to make our choices? How is our responsibility exercised and evaluated?

This question is posed by a very perceptive reader! And I can't think of a better segue to the next chapter.

---

1. Assuming the Mosaic authorship of Genesis, he would have been the writer of the original narrative.

2. Francis A. Schaeffer, *The Church at the End of the Twentieth Century* (Downers Grove, IL.: InterVarsity Press, 1970), 67. In a footnote he added, "It seems clear to me that the opposite cannot be held, namely that only that which is commanded is allowed. If this were the case, then, for example, to have a church building would be wrong and so would having church bells or a pulpit, using books for singing, following any specific order of service, standing to sing, and many other like things. If consistently held in practice, I doubt if any church could function or worship."
3. Surprisingly, there is one reference to a required freewill offering (Deuteronomy 16:10). It was expected at the Feast of Weeks. The "freewill" part referred to the fact that the worshipper freely chose what and how large the offering would be.
4. The subject of eating meat, or eating meat offered to idols, and the central passages (Romans 14–15; 1 Corinthians 8–10) are developed in greater detail in chapter 25, "Wisdom When Christians Differ."
5. The circumcision issue is discussed further in chapter 10, "Wisdom for Decision Making," under the subtitle, "The Circumcision Schism."
6. The subject of giving and the central passage (2 Corinthians 8–9) are developed in greater detail in chapter 24, "Giving and Wisdom."

chapter ten

WISDOM FOR DECISION MAKING

High school teachers participate in an annual ritual in which the characters change but the script remains the same—graduation. One part of this drama that teachers notice is the attitudes of graduates as they look to the future. Most seem to be filled with excitement. In some, the anticipation of freedom is palpable: "No more teachers, no more parents, no more *anybody* telling me what to do! I'm outta here!" But look in the eyes of other seniors and you'll see that deer-in-the-headlights stare. They, too, may be excited about their impending freedom, but they've seen beyond their release from the confines of home and school. "What am I going to do now?" For the time has come to pay their own way. With freedom comes responsibility.

Something of that sort is often experienced by those who make the transition from the traditional view of guidance to the way of wisdom. If there is initial relief from being delivered from the pressure of finding God's perfect will with certainty, there is a subsequent realization of personal responsibility that also dawns. For if believers are free to choose in noncommanded decisions, they are also *required* to choose. If there is no right choice that automatically determines the decision, then it follows that a believer may not shift the responsibility for the decision onto someone else. And responsibility presupposes accountability—as Paul expressed in a decision-making context: "Each person must be fully convinced in his own mind.... For we will all stand before the judgment seat of God" (Romans 14:5, 10). So there's a lot at stake.

These realities raise an important question: Within the area of freedom, when there is no biblical command, *on what basis is the believer to make decisions?* The question assumes that if God has granted the privilege of choice and the dignity of accountability, He has also given appropriate instructions for the exercise of our responsibility. God has done just that. But to someone steeped in the traditional view, as I was in my youth, that instruction is (if I may be permitted an understatement) surprising.

When I was doing research for the doctoral dissertation that became the basis for the first edition of this book, I repeatedly read through the book of Acts and the Epistles asking specific questions: When the apostles were not responding to direct commands from God, how did they make their decisions? How did they explain their actions, whether in process or in retrospect? Further, when they gave instructions to Christians and churches, what directions did they give for decision making in the area of freedom? Were those instructions consistent with their own practice, or were there procedural differences between apostles and "ordinary" Christians?

The results of that study were eye-opening. I was struck, first of all, by what I did *not* find—the distinctive vocabulary of the traditional view. The apostles gave plenty of reasons for their actions, and gave lots of instruction on making decisions. But they never spoke of "seeking God's will" (or used terminology that was synonymous or expressed ideas similar in meaning) in noncommanded decisions. It just isn't in the text.

But what *is* there is a consistent pattern. While the vocabulary varies, there is an identifiable basis for decision making in the area of freedom. In a word, it is *wisdom*. What the believer is to seek in noncommanded decisions is not a dot, but wisdom; not God's individual will, but God-given wisdom. This concept is perhaps best summed up by the apostle Paul in Ephesians 5:15–16: "Therefore be careful how you walk, not as unwise men but as wise, making the most of your time, because the days are evil." He echoed that sentiment in Colossians 4:5: "Conduct yourselves with wisdom toward outsiders, making the most of the opportunity." And so the third principle in the "Way of wisdom" is: *Where there is no command, God gives us wisdom to choose.*

In my initial research, I turned to the apostles—their practice and instruction—because of the authority they bring to the church. In my Bible reading since then, I have come to realize that the pursuit of wisdom in decision making permeates the entire Bible. The examples and exhortations of godly men and women in the Old Testament as well as the teaching of Jesus Himself are consistent with the pattern of the apostles in pointing to wisdom as the guiding principle for decisions that are beneficial to the individual and pleasing to God.

The pursuit of wisdom in decision making permeates the entire Bible.

In this chapter, we will survey biblical examples and instruction on noncommanded decisions, suggest a definition of practical wisdom, and summarize ways to acquire this valuable guide to decision making.

OLD TESTAMENT WISDOM IN DECISION MAKING

Righteous Moses Becomes Wise Moses

Israel's great leader of the Exodus was the most humble man on the face of the earth (Numbers 12:3). Following the spectacular conquest of Egypt through the ten plagues and the crossing of the Red Sea, Moses was humble enough to learn from a family counselor. Before arriving at Sinai he was reunited with his Midianite family. The next day it was business as usual. When Moses pulled back the flap of his tent, he saw a long line of people coming for legal judgments. "The people stood about Moses from the morning until the evening" (Exodus 18:13).

Jethro, his father-in-law, watched, pondered, and concluded, "The thing that you are doing is not good. You will surely wear out, both yourself and these people who are with you, for the task is too heavy for you; you cannot do it alone" (Exodus 18:17–18). Jethro recommended a two-pronged solution. First, Moses should teach God's statutes to all (18:20); then he should appoint "able men who fear God, men of truth...as leaders of thousands, of hundreds, of fifties and of tens" (18:21). This wisdom would allow Moses to "endure" and the people to "go to their place in peace" (18:23).

Though Moses was a prophet, he did not receive direct revelation on this occasion, but rather wisdom from a family member. Where there is no command, the believer is free and responsible to use wisdom.

Joseph provides another example of wise governance over many people. The cry of the hour was for a man "discerning and wise" to be set over the land of Egypt as an administrator (Genesis 41:33). Joseph fit the description. The specifics of his wise planning are detailed in Genesis 41–48.

Brave David Becomes Wise David

When his son, Absalom, usurped the kingdom, David gathered loyal soldiers around him in the wilderness (2 Samuel 15). David wisely organized his army by putting proven soldiers, Joab, Abishai, and Ittai, in command (2 Samuel 18:1–2). David's rule over Israel was hanging by the thread of a few swords. With the heart of a soldier he told his people, "I myself will surely go out with you also" (2 Samuel 18:2). It did not seem right to David that he should enjoy the security of a walled city while his soldiers were exposed to danger on the field of battle for his sake.

His supporters saw the matter differently. David was a great soldier, but he was only one soldier. Furthermore, David was the only lawful king. Their whole reason for fighting was to return David to his throne. If he died in battle they would have risked their lives for nothing. So they told David, "You should not go out.... You are worth ten thousand of us." It was "better" for David to be securely protected in a city and come to fight only if the need was desperate (2 Samuel 18:3).

David was pulled up short by this application of wisdom. He closed his kingly mouth to further argument and said, "Whatever *seems best* to you I will do" (2 Samuel 18:4). When there is more than one way for a servant of God to serve, wisdom should determine the best way. David illustrates that even the courageous must use wisdom to best serve God (2 Samuel 18:4). On another occasion, David strayed from this wisdom and had to be rescued by Abishai at the last moment. The men of David swore to him, "You shall not go out again with us to battle, so that you do not extinguish the lamp of Israel" (2 Samuel 21:17). Courage was no substitute for wisdom, and David finally learned.

Another of David's sons, Solomon, has come to personify wisdom. He illustrates beautifully the humble attitude that finds wisdom: "O LORD my God, You have made Your servant king…yet I am but a little child" (1 Kings 3:7). He sought God as the ultimate Source of all wisdom and asked for an understanding heart (1 Kings 3:9). The request was pleasing to God. He acknowledged that Solomon's plea for wisdom to judge Israel was superior to a desire for long life, riches, and victory over enemies (1 Kings 3:11). In God's delight over Solomon's request He said, "I have given you a wise and discerning heart, so that there has been no one like you before you, nor shall one like you arise after you" (1 Kings 3:12).

This wisdom was immediately displayed when two harlots claimed to be the mother of one baby. Solomon's wisdom included justice, but also shrewdness. In a dramatic moment he spoke as only an absolute sovereign could. He demanded that the child be cut in half. His acting job was so convincing that it exposed the fraudulent mother and revealed the real one. This was "the wisdom of God" and was recognized by all (1 Kings 3:16–28).

Solomon's wisdom included the moral will of God and astuteness, but it also included wide knowledge about life: proverbs, songs, knowledge of trees, animals, birds, and fish (1 Kings 4:32–34). His ability to answer the difficult questions posed by the queen of Sheba took her breath away (1 Kings 10:1–5).

In contrast to David and Solomon, Rehoboam, Solomon's son, ignored the wise advice of older counselors, and his foolishness was the human reason for the division of Israel (1 Kings 12:1–15). Solomon had asked God for wisdom above all else and brought the golden age of peace to God's people. Rehoboam refused the wisdom God had put at his doorstep and ripped the nation in two.

Hokema and the Hare

For centuries, ordinary people have turned to the writings of sages to tap into the reservoir of their wisdom. In the providence of God, the practical insights of Solomon, David, and others have been preserved for us as part of the divine revelation contained in the Hebrew Scriptures. Scholars describe the contents of Job, Psalms, Proverbs, Ecclesiastes, and Song of Solomon as "Wisdom Literature." These writings underscore the value of wisdom for everyday living and decision making.

Consider the tale of Hokema the woodcutter. To silence the boasting of the town braggart, Hokema accepted his challenge to a race. Each man was given an identical axe and an equal amount of firewood to chop. At the signal to begin, they each attacked their piles with vigor. Almost immediately, both contestants realized that they shared an unexpected handicap—their axes were dull. The challenger responded to this hindrance by exerting more energy. But Hokema stopped chopping long enough to hone the axe blade with a whetstone. When he resumed splitting the logs, Hokema was well behind his nemesis. But with the greater efficiency of his sharpened axe, he soon overtook his tiring and chagrined opponent. By his timely employment of wisdom, Hokema won the contest with relative ease and brought peace to the village.

Is this fable in the Bible? Well, not exactly. But Solomon wrote a shorter version in a proverb: "If the axe is dull and he does not sharpen its edge, then he must exert more strength. Wisdom has the advantage of giving success" (Ecclesiastes 10:10). Since *hokema* is the Hebrew word for wisdom, we could imagine Solomon narrating this Jewish version of "The Tortoise and the Hare." And his point? In wood chopping as in cutting through life, "Wisdom has the advantage." The man who cuts wood for God's temple with a dull axe may be quite dedicated, but the man with a sharpened axe will serve God more skillfully. Is this biblical wisdom or just plain common sense? The answer is, yes. It is both. This is wisdom the world understands, but it is not worldly wisdom.

The book of Proverbs is a great source of wisdom. The one who ignores it is called naive, a fool, or a scoffer (Proverbs 1:22). The wisdom of Proverbs is both moral and practical. Some of it fits under what we have called the moral will of God (Proverbs 14:34). This direction for righteous living truly is wisdom, for it shows the proper way to please God and prepare for eternity. But there is also a practical wisdom that enables us not only to live life morally, but to live it skillfully. It is that functional insight I refer to when I speak of "the way of wisdom."

In making decisions, the book of Proverbs instructs the seeking of wisdom.

> Without consultation, plans are frustrated,
> But with many counselors they succeed. (Proverbs 15:22)

> Where there is no guidance the people fall,
> But in abundance of counselors there is victory. (Proverbs 11:14)
>
> Prepare plans by consultation,
> And make war by wise guidance. (Proverbs 20:18)
>
> For by wise guidance you will wage war,
> And in abundance of counselors there is victory. (Proverbs 24:6)

At the same time Proverbs directs us to drive out foolishness.

> Foolishness is bound up in the heart of a child;
> The rod of discipline will remove it far from him. (Proverbs 22:15)

In Ecclesiastes, Solomon ponders the futility of all things—including wisdom apart from faith and obedience in God. But Solomon learned the value of wisdom. "Wisdom excels folly as light excels darkness" (Ecclesiastes 2:13). The man who has labored with wisdom, knowledge, and skill has a legacy to give (Ecclesiastes 2:21). There is wisdom in teamwork since those who work together gain a "good return for their labor" (Ecclesiastes 4:9).

Wisdom is an "advantage," a "protection," and it "preserves the lives of its possessors" (Ecclesiastes 7:11–12). "A wise heart knows the proper time and procedure" (Ecclesiastes 8:5). Wisdom is "better than strength" or "weapons" (Ecclesiastes 9:16, 18). By implication, Solomon summarizes the decision-making process in three steps: wisdom, planning, and then activity (Ecclesiastes 9:10).

Wise Men and Other Counseling Centers

Jeremiah lists three types of people that were well known in the Old Testament. "Surely the law is not going to be lost to the priest, nor counsel to the sage, nor the divine word to the prophet!" (Jeremiah 18:18). The prophet declared the direct word of the Lord. The priest had the role of studying and teaching the law. The wise man or sage gave counsel on life and the application of the truth to life.

Jesus named a parallel list when He proclaimed to Israel, "I am sending you prophets and wise men and scribes" (Matthew 23:34). This trio embodies the guidance of God. The Word of God was given by prophets, taught by priests and scribes, and applied by wise men. They all ministered the guidance of God. The Christian must take the words of the prophets (Bible), learn them using the help of teachers, and apply them to life with the help of the wise—parents, leaders, and counselors.

WISDOM FOR DECISION MAKING

1. The Old Testament teaches wise decision making by its Wisdom Books and examples of wise men—"Wisdom has the advantage of giving success" (Ecclesiastes 10:10).

WISDOM FOR DECISION MAKING IN THE TEACHING OF JESUS

When the children in our Sunday school sing, "The wise man built his house upon the rock," they are echoing the words of Jesus, the Master Teacher. When He instructed the people of Israel in parables, He was employing the wisdom genre of the Jewish culture. Many of these stories focused on the choices involved in discipleship, and Jesus used them to make a case for following Him. By arguing from analogy, Jesus assumed the validity of applying wisdom to the choices people face in daily living. Just as we seek to be wise in the circumstances of life, Jesus was saying, so we should be wise about eternal issues.

In His parables, Jesus implicitly teaches the necessity of wisdom. The parable of the "Two Foundations" (Matthew 7:24–27) assumes the validity of using wisdom in building a house. This assumption then is transferred to teaching wisdom when deciding a destiny. The one who rejects Christ's teachings is like the foolish man who builds his house upon the sand. Believing Christ's teaching is illustrated by the wisdom of building on a rock foundation.

To encourage His listeners to take the high cost of discipleship seriously, Jesus gave two parables on "Counting the Cost" (Luke 14:25–32). He affirmed that it was necessary to wisely calculate the cost before building a tower or one could end up as the civic fool. If a military commander failed to wisely calculate the strength of his forces compared to those of his enemy, the results could be catastrophic. Jesus assumed the validity of applying wisdom in these decisions and then built upon that foundation to extend the principle of counting the cost of something even more valuable—discipleship.

The parable of the "Ten Virgins" also depends on sensible behavior to make its point (Matthew 25:1–13). The virgins are described in two groups: the "foolish" who didn't bring enough oil, and the "wise" who made proper preparation. Missing a wedding celebration is not as serious as missing entry into the kingdom of God. But the great truth depends upon the validity of the illustration. If prudent preparation for social situations is necessary, how much more should we wisely prepare for eternal life.

Jesus taught the role of wisdom when He answered the difficult question of divorce (Matthew 19:1–12). His view of divorce was strict enough that His disciples said, "If the relationship of the man with his wife is like this, it is better not to marry" (Matthew 19:10). Jesus agreed, but said that the statement was not absolute and could not be applied to everyone. "He who is able to accept this, let him accept it" (Matthew 19:12). Jesus concluded that for some it is better to remain single. Christ's teaching is a summary of what Paul expounds in 1 Corinthians 7 on the advantages of singleness.

In the future reign of Christ over the earth, we have a promise that He will use wisdom. Israel was given a promise that God would raise up a "righteous Branch" from David's lineage, a ruler who "will reign as king and act wisely and do justice and righteousness in the land" (Jeremiah 23:5). In His life and in His future reign, Christ combines perfectly the two aspects of proper decision making: righteousness and wisdom. The moral will of God is perfectly obeyed by Christ's righteousness and wisdom is perfectly expressed in the exercise of His rule.

And Remember, Be Careful Out There

So treacherous was the life of a servant of God that Jesus described it as being like "sheep in the midst of wolves." In light of the difficulties they would encounter, Jesus commanded the apostles, "So be shrewd as serpents and innocent as doves" (Matthew 10:16). Again the moral will of God and wisdom are brought together in this picturesque command of Christ. The moral will of God with all of its commands must be obeyed with the innocence of a dove. Without sacrificing that innocence, followers of Jesus must also be wise, prudent, clever, and as shrewd as serpents. This is the way of wisdom portrayed by two simple images. In the moral will of God be doves; in the area of freedom be serpents. Only the "serpent-and-dove" person is walking according to the way of wisdom.

WISDOM FOR DECISION MAKING

1. The Old Testament teaches wise decision making by its Wisdom Books and examples of wise men—"Wisdom has the advantage of giving success" (Ecclesiastes 10:10).
2. Jesus commanded His servants to be wise—"Be shrewd as serpents" (Matthew 10:16).

APOSTOLIC EXAMPLES OF WISDOM FOR DECISION MAKING

A Serpent on the Mission Field

Luke presents the ministry of Paul in such a way that the reader experiences the wisdom and shrewdness of the apostle. In Philippi, Paul risked his life for the sake of the jailor by not escaping; but then he made the Roman magistrates admit their error by refusing to leave jail until they came and provided an official escort for Paul and Silas (Acts 16:37). Paul was wise in his commendation of the Athenians for being "very religious"—even to the point of erecting an altar to "an unknown god." This observation provided him with a shrewd segue into his proclamation of the true God over all (Acts 17:22–31). In Jerusalem, he got the attention of a riotous mob bent on his destruction by his use of the Aramaic language (Acts 22:2). The next day, he demonstrated the shrewdness of a pit of serpents when he caused the members of the Sanhedrin to turn on one another by a few, well-chosen words (Acts 23:6). He later avoided an ambush by appealing to Caesar as a Roman citizen, thereby obtaining the protection of an armed escort (Acts 25:11).

The Thessalonian Connection

On his second missionary journey, Paul founded a church in Thessalonica, but jealous Jews drove him out (Acts 17:1–8). He moved on to Athens, but he knew that the believers in Thessalonica would be tested by persecution without the aid of experienced leadership (1 Thessalonians 3:4–5). So Paul, Silas, and Timothy agreed on a plan to help them.

> Therefore when we could endure it no longer, we *thought it best* to be left behind at Athens alone, and we sent Timothy, our brother and God's fellow worker in the gospel of Christ, to strengthen and encourage you as to your faith. (1 Thessalonians 3:1–2)

How was their decision made? "We thought it best." They made the decision on the basis of good spiritual reasons. They were concerned to strengthen their converts (3:1, 5). As far as they could tell, sending Timothy was the best means to accomplish that spiritual goal. Can missionaries (and ordinary Christians) make God-pleasing decisions by applying wisdom and saying, "We thought it best"? Yes, they can.

The Case of the Homesick Minister

As Paul awaited his trial before Caesar in Rome, he enjoyed the company of a number of men. One of them, Epaphroditus, had come from Philippi bearing Paul a love gift from the church (Philippians 4:10, 14). In carrying out his mission, Epaphroditus became ill and perilously close to dying. When God preserved his life, Paul decided to send him home and gave this explanation:

> But I *thought it necessary* to send to you Epaphroditus, my brother and fellow worker and fellow soldier, who is also your

> messenger and minister to my need; *because* he was longing for you all and was distressed because you had heard that he was sick. (Philippians 2:25–26)

In this decision, Paul "thought it necessary" to send Epaphroditus back to Philippi, not because he had been directed by God to do so, but because of the exigencies of the situation. Paul wanted to dispel the Philippians' anxiety, thereby reducing his own concern for them (2:28); and Epaphroditus was anxious to get home to let everyone know that he was all right (2:26). Additionally, Epaphroditus would be the messenger of the book we now call Philippians.

On what basis did Paul make this decision? It was the best way to accomplish important spiritual goals. When an apostle or any believer faces a difficult situation, it is acceptable to make a decision and say, "I thought it necessary."

Blest Be the Offering that Binds

The Gentile churches of Greece, Macedonia, and Asia Minor had agreed to collect an offering to send to the Jewish believers in Judea who were in dire straits (Romans 15:25–26). Paul explained his role.

> When I arrive, whomever you may approve, I will send them with letters to carry your gift to Jerusalem; and *if it is fitting* for me to go also, they will go with me. (1 Corinthians 16:3–4)

Would Paul join the messengers bearing the gift? He would "if it was fitting." What did he mean by "fitting"? Paul did not say. Most commentators believe that the issue was the size of the gift.[1] If it turned out to be small, such a gift would hardly warrant the apostolic presence. If, however, the gift was generous, it would be a tangible demonstration of the unity of Jews and Gentiles in Christ (Ephesians 2:11–22). The financial gift might also serve as a sort of down payment on the spiritual debt the Gentiles (and Paul himself) owed to the Jewish Christians (Romans 15:27; 1 Corinthians 15:9, 1 Timothy 1:13).[2]

Whatever Paul meant by his "if," it is clear that "fitting" reflected wisdom. In this case, one as-yet-unknown circumstance would be the deciding factor. And there is no hint that Paul thought of this as a so-called fleece.[3] He was simply calculating how to make best use of his time and energy for the Lord. Similarly, when David was being pursued by Saul, he left his parents safely in Moab "until I know what God will do for me" (1 Samuel 22:3; see Philippians 2:23). To make a decision because it is a fitting way to serve God is biblical and proper.

On the Care and Feeding of Widows

During the earliest days of the Church, one of the first internal problems was a charge of discrimination against the food service. The Hellenistic Jews felt that their widows were being overlooked in the daily distribution of food (Acts 6:1). The matter was dealt with as follows:

> So the twelve summoned the congregation of the disciples and said, "*It is not desirable* for us to neglect the word of God in order to serve tables. Therefore, brethren, select from among you seven men of good reputation, *full of the Spirit and of wisdom*, whom we may put in charge of this task. But we will devote ourselves to prayer and to the ministry of the word." (Acts 6:2–4)

The role that wisdom played in the decision-making process emerges at two points in this narrative. First, wisdom was applied in the manner in which the problem was addressed. The plan that was adopted was designed to alleviate a situation that was "not desirable." The apostles were being distracted from the priorities Christ had given to them. And so something had to be done. They analyzed the problem, reviewed their assignments, and came up with a wise, practical plan that would meet all the relevant needs.

The second application of wisdom appeared in the qualifications set out for the deacons (or protodeacons) who would assume the duties of caregiving. They were to have a reputation for being "full of the Spirit and of wisdom" (Acts 6:3). This short phrase is yet another way of uniting the moral will of God and wisdom. "Full of the Spirit" refers to being full of righteousness, characterized by the fruit of the Spirit—that is, a mature believer. "Full of wisdom" describes someone characterized by wisdom in their decision making and way of life.

At no point did the twelve stop to seek the "individual will of God" either for the solution to the problem or for their choice of men to carry it out. Rather, they established qualifications that were appropriate for a task that would require spiritual insight and personal sensitivity. Then they left the choice of the men to the people. (This mirrors the pattern of delegation followed by Moses who told the people to "choose wise and discerning and experienced men from your tribes, and I will appoint them as your heads" [Deuteronomy 1:13].) The plan that was chosen was wisely formulated to give all concerned the time and opportunity to exercise their gifts and fulfill their responsibilities. Because it accomplished those objectives, it proved to be a good decision.

A similar pattern appears later on in Paul's instructions regarding the appointment of elders or pastors in churches. Most of the qualifications he sets out are moral in nature (1 Timothy 3:1–7; Titus 1:5–9)—summarized as "blameless" (NIV) or "above reproach." In addition church leaders must demonstrate the wisdom that it takes to run a household and be sensible (1 Timothy 3:2, 4; Titus 1:8).[4]

The Circumcision Schism

A second problem encountered during the early years of the Church was more serious. At stake was the doctrine of justification by grace through faith apart from works. The threat to the doctrine came from a Judaistic faction that insisted that all Gentile believers must be circumcised. In essence, they said that Gentiles had to become Jewish proselytes before they could be saved through faith in Christ.

The issue was discussed at a council in Jerusalem (Acts 15:1–29), and there was much debate (15:7). Peter reviewed the work of the Holy Spirit to bring salvation to the Gentiles through the grace of the Lord Jesus (15:7–11). Barnabas and Paul related the confirming ministry of the Holy Spirit who produced supernatural signs and wonders through them as they preached the gospel to the Gentiles (15:12). And James cited relevant Scripture passages stating that God was "taking from among the Gentiles a people for His name" (15:14–18).

By then, the solution to the issue was obvious: Circumcision was not required for salvation. The council decided to draft a letter to the Gentile churches declaring the judgment that had been reached. In it, the

Gentile believers were asked to refrain from practices that would be especially abhorrent to their Jewish brethren. The letter concluded:

> For *it seemed good* to the Holy Spirit and to us to lay upon you no greater burden than these essentials: that you abstain from things sacrificed to idols and from blood and from things strangled and from fornication; if you keep yourselves free from such things, you will do well. Farewell. (Acts 15:28–29)

The expression, "it seemed good" appears three times in Acts 15 (vv. 22, 25, 28). In the third instance only, the Holy Spirit was included as a coauthor of the decision. Does that mean that the conclusions of the council were supernaturally dictated by God? He certainly gave special guidance on other occasions in Acts. But in this case, in the absence of any direct statement to that effect, a better explanation is that the Holy Spirit had *already given* His guidance before the council ever met. That is, He had worked through Peter to bring salvation to Gentiles apart from circumcision (15:7–11); He had miraculously confirmed the evangelistic ministry of Barnabas and Paul among the Gentiles (15:12); and He had inspired the writers of Scripture to foretell the inclusion of Gentiles among the people of God (15:15–18). For these reasons, the church leaders could write that their decision "seemed good" to the Holy Spirit as well as to them.

The decision of the Jerusalem Council was not the result of discovering God's individual will. If they discovered anything, it was God's moral will that had already been revealed. The actual decision-making process involved debate, application of Scripture, and a determination of what "seemed good" to do. The final decision was first described as the "judgment" of James (15:19), and then of the whole group (15:22, 25, 28). The request that the Gentiles exercise restraint with respect to Jewish sensibilities was not the product of divine revelation, but reflected a reasonable desire to promote unity in the Church.

Evidently this decree was temporary. For when it was no longer considered relevant, it faded from use and is not mentioned by Paul (1 Corinthians 8–10).[5] Apparently, the decision came to be seen as the best way to deal with a specific but temporary situation.

WISDOM FOR DECISION MAKING

1. The Old Testament teaches wise decision making by its Wisdom Books and examples of wise men—"Wisdom has the advantage of giving success" (Ecclesiastes 10:10).
2. Jesus commanded His servants to be wise—"Be shrewd as serpents" (Matthew 10:16).
3. The apostles modeled wisdom in their decision making—"We thought it best" (1 Thessalonians 3:1).

The witness of the entire Bible to the importance of wisdom as the basis for decision making in noncommanded decisions is impressive. The lives of Israel's leaders, the message of Old Testament Wisdom Literature, the teaching of Jesus, and the practices of the apostles provide a uniform testimony to the virtue of wisdom. But the clincher—the biblical data that provoked the radical reshaping of my understanding of decision making and the will of God—was the instruction of the apostles. That's what we'll talk about in the next chapter.

---

1. Archibald Robertson and Alfred Plummer, *A Critical and Exegetical Commentary on the First Epistle of Paul to the Corinthians, The International Critical Commentary* (Edinburgh: T&T Clark, 1911), 387.
2. Frank E. Gaebelein, gen. ed., *The Expositor's Bible Commentary*, vol. 10: "2 Corinthians," by Murray J. Harris (Grand Rapids, MI: Zondervan, 1976), 311–12.
3. See our discussion of the role of "fleeces" in decision making in chapter 13, "God's Sovereign Will and Decision Making."
4. The Greek term *sophron* probably emphasizes "sensible" since another word on the list, *egkrate,* means "self-controlled" (Titus 1:8).
5. Charles A. Hodge, *An Exposition of the First Epistle to the Corinthians* (Grand Rapids, MI: Wm. B. Eerdmans Publishing Co., n. d.), 135–36; locality rather than the temporal aspect is another possible explanation. See F. F. Bruce, *The Epistle of Paul to the Romans* (Grand Rapids, MI: Wm. B. Eerdmans Publishing Co., 1963), 248.

chapter eleven

MORE WISDOM FOR DECISION MAKING

We are seeking a biblical answer to the question: In the area of freedom, on what basis should a believer make a decision? The examples of Old Testament leaders, the theme of biblical Wisdom Literature, the instruction of Jesus, and the practice of the apostles all point to *wisdom* as the single controlling factor. As we saw in the previous chapter, the pattern the apostles followed is particularly striking. Not once is it recorded that they attempted to discover God's individual will for such decisions. Their explanations for their plans are couched in phrases such as: "We thought it best," "I thought it necessary," "If it is fitting," "It is not desirable," "It seemed good," and simply, "I have decided" (Titus 3:12). (Luke explained a decision Paul made about an itinerary with the words, "for he was hurrying" [Acts 20:16]!) Clearly these men were exercising their freedom of choice (as well as their responsibility to decide) within God's moral will. And *wisdom* best encapsulates the criteria for these decisions.

Here is the concept stated as a principle: *In the area of freedom, the believer's goal is to make wise decisions on the basis of spiritual usefulness.* Or, when there is no command, God gives freedom and wisdom to make spiritually advantageous decisions.

Some definitions are needed. "Spiritual" means that the ends in view, as well as the means to those ends, are governed by the moral will of God. With decisions in the area of freedom, the Christian's aim is to glorify and please God. In that sense, every goal and procedure is to be "spiritual."

"Usefulness"[1] refers to the quality of being suitable or advantageous to the end in view. Put simply, it means whatever works best to get the job done—within God's moral will, of course. And finally, J. I. Packer's definition of "wisdom" is right on target: "Wisdom is the power to see, and the inclination to choose, the best and highest goal, together with the surest means of attaining it."[2] Wisdom is the ability to figure out what is spiritually profitable in a given situation. In a widely read article, A. W. Tozer described wisdom as "sanctified common sense." He argued that for many decisions that is the goal of the believer, rather than making the one "right" choice.[3]

To be precise, this pursuit of wisdom fits under the first principle of obeying God where He commands. For God has commanded us to be wise (Ephesians 5:15–16) and has included the whole book of Proverbs to make that directive crystal clear. On the flip side of the coin, foolishness is a sin (Mark 7:22). So obedience to the command to obey God includes seeking, praying, and learning wisdom from God. Augustine knew this and so he could rightly combine the two and simply say, "Love God and do whatever you please." For you can't love God without keeping His commands and you can't keep His commands without applying wisdom.

So technically, the requirement to decide wisely could be subsumed under the first principle, "Where God commands, we must obey." Nevertheless, it seemed good to me to spotlight wisdom with its own axiom: "Where there is no (other) command, God gives us (not only freedom but also) wisdom to choose."

As we return now to our survey of passages that provide specific examples of apostolic teaching, we are in a position to appreciate the consistency between how the apostles actually made decisions (as described in the previous chapter) and the instructions they gave to others.

APOSTOLIC EXHORTATIONS TO WISDOM IN DECISION MAKING

A Vacancy on the Bench

In 1 Corinthians 6, Paul declares his conviction that Christians, of all people, ought to be competent to make wise decisions:

> Does any one of you, when he has a case against his neighbor, dare to go to law before the unrighteous and not before the saints? Or do you not know that the saints will judge the world? If the world is judged by you, are you not *competent* to constitute the smallest law courts? Do you not know that we will judge angels? How much more matters of this life? So if you have law courts dealing with matters of this life, do you appoint them as judges who are of no account in the church? I say this to your shame. Is it so, that there is not among you *one wise man* who will be *able to decide* between his brethren, but brother goes to law with brother, and that before unbelievers? (1 Corinthians 6:1–6)

In this rebuke of the Corinthians, Paul maintains that there ought to be at least one man among them who could be trusted to make fair judgments and settle disputes. The administration of justice requires some moral decisions (discernment of right and wrong, guilt and innocence), and some that are wisdom issues rather than moral ones (such as determining the best means to carry out an equitable judgment).

It is noteworthy that in the church, "ordinary" Christians (such as those at Corinth!), who will one day judge the world and fallen angels, are deemed competent to judge the more mundane "matters of this life." Furthermore, those who possess a greater measure of wisdom are recognized as being able to make the better decisions.

Good, Better, Happier

Probably the classic chapter of instruction on decision making within the moral will of God is 1 Corinthians 7. In that chapter, the apostle Paul answered a number of questions about singleness and marriage. For some of the questions, the moral will of God is determinative. For instance, married believers are not to abstain from fulfilling their sexual responsibilities to one another (7:3–5), nor are they to get divorced (7:10–11). Other issues, however, fall within the area of freedom where the decision is left up to the individual believer. To those questions, Paul gave his advice rather than command (7:6), together with reasons showing the wisdom of his counsel.

The two adjectives that most often qualify his advice are "good" and "better." Should a believer get married? There is no command from Scripture one way or the other. So how should we decide? Paul said it is "good" for a man not to touch a woman (7:1). It is "good" for the unmarried to remain single (7:8). It is "good" in view of the present distress for a man to remain in his present state (7:26). Now Paul is not speaking of "good" in contrast to "evil." He is using it in the sense of "advantageous."[4] So what is advantageous about remaining single? Two things: First, in Paul's view, the circumstances of that time brought great stress upon families—pressure that would not be nearly so acute for a single person (7:26, 28); and second, single people are freer to serve the Lord without the distraction of family commitments (7:7, 32–35).

On the other hand, Paul recognized it is "better" to be married than to be consumed with passion (7:9). If a single person lacks self-control or has not been gifted by God to live without a partner (7:7), he will not be able to give "undistracted devotion to the Lord" (7:35). For such a person, marriage is "better." For in spite of whatever problems marriage might bring, the potential for holy living would be greatly enhanced (7:2).

Paul gives similar advice to men who are responsible to decide whether certain women in their charge will get married. (Translators are divided over whether Paul is addressing fathers with respect to their daughters [NASB], or engaged men with respect to their fiancées [NIV]. In either case, the counsel is the same.) Paul first declared that such a decision belonged within the area of freedom: "Let him do what he wishes, he does not sin" (7:36). He did have a practical preference: "So then he who gives her in marriage does well, but he who does not give her in marriage does better" (7:38, NKJV).

In each instance, Paul's counsel reflects a recognition of spiritual priorities. He urges Christians to establish relationships and conditions that are the most conducive to the accomplishment of spiritual goals. It is in this same vein that we find some of Paul's most surprising terminology:

> A wife is bound as long as her husband lives; but if her husband is dead, she is free to be married to whom she wishes, only in the Lord. But in my opinion she is *happier* if she remains as she is; and I think that I also have the Spirit of God. (1 Corinthians 7:39–40)

In his answer to the question about the remarriage of widows, Paul once again establishes the principle of freedom within the revealed will of God. The believing widow is free to be married. The man that she marries must be a Christian ("only in the Lord"). But she may marry *whichever* Christian man she *wishes*. However, for the reasons noted above, Paul believes she will be happier if she does not remarry.[5]

It is a measure of the greatness of God's love that our happiness is permitted as a valid consideration in decision making (1 Corinthians 7:40)! It is not the *only* consideration, nor is it the *primary* factor (cf. Matthew 6:19–33). But our happiness is significant and must not be discounted. For enjoyment in the outworking of a decision promotes an attitude of eagerness and gratitude, and that kind of motivation is pleasing to God (Colossians 3:17, 23). Consequently, when we face a decision in an area of freedom, it is valid to ask, "With which option will I be happiest?" It is not the only question to consider, but it is clearly a biblical one. Unfortunately, some believers justify immoral decisions on the basis that God wants them to be happy. God wants us moral first. He will give joy to those who suffer for doing what is right.

Every Day in Every Way

The principle of wise decision making according to spiritual usefulness is clearly stated in Ephesians 5:15–16, and its parallel Colossians 4:5:

> Therefore be careful how you walk, *not as unwise men, but as wise*, making the most of your time, because the days are evil. (Ephesians 5:15–16)

> *Conduct yourselves with wisdom* toward outsiders, making the most of the opportunity. (Colossians 4:5)

The proper Christian walk or lifestyle is described by the words "wise" and "wisdom." And those words are further qualified by the expression "making the most of your time" or "opportunity." *Wisdom* has a great breadth of meaning in Scripture. In Ephesians 5:17, it is directly related to understanding "what the will of the Lord is." In context, that refers to understanding the truth that God has revealed in His Word. But in both passages, wisdom is also linked to making the most of specific opportunities that come up from time to time. Wisdom, in short, is spiritually opportunistic.

To sum up: The pattern we observed in examples from both Testaments matches the apostolic instructions to the saints. Together, these examples and exhortations form the biblical foundation and validation for this principle: In the area of freedom, God requires and provides wisdom.

WISDOM FOR DECISION MAKING

1. The Old Testament teaches wise decision making by its Wisdom Books and examples of wise men—"Wisdom has the advantage of giving success" (Ecclesiastes 10:10).
2. Jesus commanded His servants to be wise—"Be shrewd as serpents" (Matthew 10:16).
3. The apostles modeled wisdom in their decision making—"We thought it best" (1 Thessalonians 3:1).
4. The apostles commanded believers to use wisdom in decision making—"Conduct yourselves with wisdom" (Colossians 4:5).

ACQUIRE WISDOM

For the sincere Christian committed to glorifying God through wise decisions, one further question begs to be answered: How do we get the requisite wisdom for such decisions? The biblical answer to that question has several parts. But the core truth is, wisdom is gained from God by those who *seek for it.*

> "I [wisdom] love those who love me;
> And those who diligently seek me will find me." (Proverbs 8:17)

For the believer, the question of wisdom's source is hardly difficult. For "wise" is what God is in His essence—every bit as much as He is love or truth or holiness (Job 9:4; 12:13; Isaiah 40:28; Daniel 2:20). In Him alone can wisdom be found in its fullness (Romans 16:27). And so whatever wisdom is to be found is to be obtained from God: "For the LORD gives wisdom" (Proverbs 2:6). But such wisdom is not given to just anyone. It is granted only to those who value it enough to pursue it "as silver and search for her as for hidden treasures" (Proverbs 2:4–5).

Such seeking must be done properly if the treasure is to be uncovered. The "how" of this important endeavor involves the believer's *attitude* and his *approach*.

The Christian's *attitude* is to reflect, first of all, his awareness that no man, himself included, is naturally wise (Proverbs 3:7); if he is to gain wisdom, it must come from some other source. Equally, his attitude must mirror his conviction that the ultimate source of wisdom is God alone. Those who refuse to acknowledge these basic realities are self-deceived fools (Romans 1:21–22).

Accordingly, God grants wisdom to those who manifest certain spiritual characteristics: reverence of God (Proverbs 9:10), humility (Proverbs 11:2; 15:33), teachableness (Proverbs 9:9; 15:31; 19:20), diligence (Proverbs 2:4–5; 8:17), and uprightness (Proverbs 2:7).

Finally the believer must have faith:

> But if any of you lacks wisdom, let him ask of God, who gives to all generously and without reproach, and it will be given to him. But *he must ask in faith* without any doubting. (James 1:5–6)

In the pursuit of wisdom, the believer must have not only the right attitude, but he must adopt the proper *approach*. Scripture points to at least five avenues of investigation opened to the man who would find wisdom.

First, he must *ask God for it* (James 1:5–6; cf. Colossians 1:9–10). The search for wisdom is never impersonal. Even if research, study, inquiry, and reflection are required, the process is not strictly academic. It is true that God *has given* wisdom through His Word, but He also *gives* it through a variety of channels, such as counselors, personal research, and the experiences of life (see below). And so the search for wisdom begins by asking for it.

James's counsel (1:5–6) includes an exhortation and a promise. The promise is that God will generously give wisdom to the one who asks for it in faith. That promise is straightforward, but its implications merit careful thought. James is not promising, for instance, that God will give instant omniscience to the supplicant. Nor is he suggesting that wisdom is divinely injected "intravenously" apart from a regular diet of God's revealed wisdom, the Bible. The trials of real life are not like those portrayed in a television drama where hopelessly complex problems are unraveled and resolved one hour and ten commercials later. James 1:5 is not a promise of instant solutions to every problem. Such interpretations are simply not permitted by the rest of Scripture.

Faith realizes that wisdom, like every other benefit of temporal experience, is given progressively as a component of spiritual growth. Faith is committed to gaining wisdom, not only for the trial at hand, but *through* the present trial—for future application. And faith rests confidently in the assurance that the One who promises wisdom will give it in abundant measure (Matthew 7:7–8; James 4:2–3).

The second source of wisdom is *Scripture*. For in the pages of the Bible, God has spoken. His gift of wisdom has, in large measure, been given. The superlative value of Scripture as the revelation of God's wisdom is the theme of Psalm 119.

> O how I love Your law!
> It is my meditation all the day.
> Your commandments make me wiser than my enemies,
> For they are ever mine.
> I have more insight than all my teachers,
> For Your testimonies are my meditation.
> I understand more than the aged,
> Because I have observed Your precepts.
> (Psalm 119:97–100; see Psalm 19:7; 2 Timothy 2:7; 3:15–17;
> 2 Peter 1:19)

The third avenue provided in the search for wisdom is *outside research,* where appropriate. Nehemiah's surreptitious inspection of Jerusalem's broken walls supplied the necessary data for a plan to rebuild them (Nehemiah 2:11–16). General Joshua's dispatch of two intelligence agents to Jericho is another example of extrabiblical research for making wise decisions (Joshua 2). And Luke "investigated everything carefully from the beginning," in the writing of his gospel and Acts (Luke 1:3).

Many contemporary writers and speakers recognize the importance of research in decision making. They often suggest that it is a good idea to list all of the assets and liabilities connected with each option. That is sound advice, for we cannot make a wise decision without the facts (cf. Luke 14:28–32).

The fourth source of wisdom is *wise counselors.*

> Where there is no guidance the people fall,
> But in abundance of counselors there is victory. (Proverbs 11:14)

> He who walks with wise men will be wise,
> But the companion of fools will suffer harm. (Proverbs 13:20)

> Without consultation, plans are frustrated,
> But with many counselors they succeed. (Proverbs 15:22)

We should seek out two kinds of counselors. Of those who possess *spiritual insight*, the question should be asked: "Are you aware of any biblical principles that touch upon my decision?" To those who have gone through relevant *personal experiences*, the query should be: "When you went through a similar experience, did you gain any insights that would be of value to me?"

The fifth source of wisdom is *life itself.* We should become students of life as well as of Scripture. Agur, author of Proverbs 30, urges us to learn from the "exceedingly wise" ants, badgers, locusts, and lizards (Proverbs 30:24–28; cf. Proverbs 6:6–11). The writer to the Hebrews applies the same principle to our spiritual life. "But solid food is for the *mature*, who *because of practice have their senses trained to discern* good and evil" (Hebrews 5:14).

Maturity, of which wisdom is a part, is gained by application of learned truth. It is the product of in-depth Bible study and conscientious obedience to God's Word. The practice of the truth expands our capacity for a greater depth of wisdom through maturity.

Finally, God sometimes gave wisdom by *direct revelation,* though He has not promised that to believers. The Spirit and an angel directed Philip to join a chariot in the desert to find a man seeking God (Acts 8:29). Peter was told, "Cast the net on the right-hand side of the boat and you will find a catch" (John 21:6). Paul and his missionary companions were given a vision that determined their travel itinerary (Acts 16:9). This is the exception in the Scriptures, but God may reveal wisdom as He did with the prophets and others.[6]

To sum up: The ultimate Source of the wisdom needed in decision making is God. Accordingly, we are to ask Him to provide what we lack. God mediates His wisdom to us through His Word, our personal research, wise counselors, and the applied lessons of life.

WISDOM FOR DECISION MAKING

1. The Old Testament teaches wise decision making by its Wisdom Books and examples of wise men—"Wisdom has the advantage of giving success" (Ecclesiastes 10:10).
2. Jesus commanded His servants to be wise—"Be shrewd as serpents" (Matthew 10:16).
3. The apostles modeled wisdom in their decision making—"We thought it best" (1 Thessalonians 3:1).
4. The apostles commanded believers to use wisdom in decision making—"Conduct yourself with wisdom" (Colossians 4:5).
5. God has promised wisdom through the Bible, prayer, counselors, research, and experience—"If any of you lacks wisdom, let him ask of God" (James 1:5).

In this chapter, we have completed the exposition of the third principle for decision making according to the way of wisdom. First, there is the moral will of God; second, freedom within the moral will of God; and now the command to use wisdom within that area of freedom.

PRINCIPLES OF DECISION MAKING
THE WAY OF WISDOM

1. Where God commands, we must obey (chapter 8).
2. Where there is no command, God gives us freedom (and responsibility) to choose (chapter 9).
3. **Where there is no command, God gives us wisdom to choose (chapters 10 and 11).**

A simple, practical application issues from these three principles. The believer must ask two questions of every option in a given decision: "Is it moral?" and "Is it wise?" Using A.W. Tozer's terminology, "Is this decision in harmony with 'sanctified common sense'?" To help us remember that we are seeking *godly* wisdom we might ask: "How can I best love God and man?" "Which decision will best promote God's kingdom?" "How can I most skillfully serve God and His people?"

frequently asked questions

> *Question:* This all sounds like a matter of semantics to me. Isn't wisdom just another way of talking about God's individual will?

The traditional view does not equate the two. In fact, proponents sometimes strive to show that the individual will of God may appear foolish by the standard of wisdom. Further, wisdom does not always narrow the options down to one choice. Wisdom recognizes equal options, but the traditional view says there is always only one correct decision. The two are similar when wisdom does identify one best choice, but even in this case, the one choice was found by wisdom—not by claiming that God revealed it.

Question: If I conclude that one choice is wiser than another, am I free to choose either option?

No. The moral will of God includes the command to be wise and mature. To knowingly choose a less wise option is a sin. Strictly speaking, the wisdom principle is an example of the commands of God. I separated them into two principles for clarity. "Where God commands, we must obey" includes the command to be wise. But I emphasized wisdom further by the third principle: "Where there is no command, God gives wisdom."

Question: A person could prolong the quest for wisdom indefinitely. How can you ever have enough wisdom?

The believer is not required to make an omniscient decision, just a wise one. She must be satisfied that she knows of no wiser option when she decides. Wisdom must also be employed in how much time is devoted to a given decision. It is foolish to devote a lot of time to trivial matters. On decisions that are momentous or that affect many people, significant time and prayer should be invested in the search for wisdom.

Question: What if I make a decision that I believe to be wise, but then feel no peace afterwards?

How you respond to that circumstance will depend on the reason for the lack of peace. If you made the decision hastily, you may need to rethink or modify it. On the other hand, the lack of peace may be an indication that you don't really believe that the way of wisdom is biblically correct. Or you may have become intellectually convinced that the way of wisdom is valid, but you haven't had time to retrain your conscience. In either of these events, making a decision based on wisdom (rather than the "leading of the Lord into His individual will") would not be "from faith" (Romans 14:23), and that would produce inner conflict.[7] Getting used to a new paradigm for decision making can take some time. If a review of one's theology and the factors involved in the decision expose no violation of God's moral will or of wisdom, it would seem appropriate to follow through on the decision. Christians are to take their feelings into account; but in the end, we are not to be governed by them.

Question: What if two choices seem equally wise?

This will happen a thousand times a day in the small decisions of life. If two options are equally wise, then the believer can choose either with confidence that God is pleased. He will take care of the unknown details through His sovereign working of all things together for good.

Question: Doesn't the traditional view also commend wisdom just like the wisdom view? What's the difference?

The traditional view is not against wisdom and believes that it may be helpful in finding God's individual will. The wisdom view believes that in the area of freedom, wisdom is determinative—we *must* be wise. We must be able to defend decisions by wisdom when no moral command determines the decision. The traditional view will elevate inward impressions over wisdom. The logic is simple. If the impression comes from the Spirit, it must have precedence over any wisdom discerned by man. Proponents will even emphasize how some inward directives from God contradict human wisdom. (If inward impressions equaled revelation, that logic would hold. But they don't; so it doesn't.) The wisdom view argues that impressions do not have God's authority, but the command to be wise does.

---

1. In the first edition, I used the term *expediency* to qualify wisdom. But this word has negative connotations that troubled some readers. Some dictionary definitions of *expedient* indicate that the advantage in view is practical *rather than* moral, which is the opposite of what I wanted to say. Spiritual wisdom is practical *and* moral. I hope that "spiritually useful" gets this across.
2. J. I. Packer, *Knowing God* (Downers Grove, IL: InterVarsity Press, 1973), 80.
3. A. W. Tozer, "How the Lord Leads," *Alliance Weekly,* January 2, 1957.
4. The word "good" is *kalos*. For cross-references where this term has the idea of "beneficial" see Matthew 17:4; 18:8–9; 1 Corinthians 9:15; Charles A. Hodge, *An Exposition of the First Epistle to the Corinthians* (Grand Rapids, MI: Wm. B. Eerdmans Publishing Co., n. d.), 108–9.
5. The subject of marriage and singleness and the central passage (1 Corinthians 7) are developed in greater detail in chapters 19 and 20.
6. See the extended discussion of "Special Guidance and Decision Making" in chapter 15.
7. See the discussion of the role of the conscience in decision making in chapter 26, "Weaker Brothers, Pharisees, and Servants."

chapter twelve

GOD...THE ONLY SOVEREIGN

Most of the biblical teaching about decision making concerns the moral will of God and wisdom. But what of God's sovereign will? What bearing does it have on the activity of decision making? That is the question this chapter, and the next, are devoted to.

THE NATURE OF GOD'S SOVEREIGN WILL

Does God have a sovereign will? Does He have a "predetermined plan for everything that happens in the universe"? Thinkers have always recognized that humans are not the ultimate determiners of what happens. So what is? Blind chance? An impersonal force or fate? A wicked god or goddess? Such questions have challenged the intellects of philosophers and theologians for centuries. But the nature of the mystery is such that, at best, finite minds are limited to speculation.

There is One, though, who is not so limited. He knows the answers, and He has made them known. That One is "the blessed and only Sovereign, the King of kings and Lord of lords" (1 Timothy 6:15). He is the Ultimate Sovereign of everything that happens, and He has a will.

What does Scripture reveal about God's sovereign will? First, it is *certain of fulfillment*. It will not be frustrated by men, angels, or anything else (Daniel 4:35). The sinner who tries to defy God's plan may shake his fist to the heavens, but God will determine how many times he shakes it and whether that person will live to shake a fist tomorrow (James 4:15). Satan is God's strongest enemy, but God sets the limits on the extent to which the devil may express his evil intents (Job 1:12).

The Ultimate Test Case

The ultimate proof of the certainty of God's sovereign will was presented at Calvary. Far from frustrating God's plan, the most wicked act ever committed—the willful murder of God's Son and Israel's Messiah—actually accomplished the central requirement in God's glorious plan of redemption! The crucifixion did not force God into Plan B. A Savior was foreknown before the foundation of the world (1 Peter 1:20) and promised while the forbidden fruit was still in Adam's mouth (Genesis 3:15). The crucifixion was prophetically described in detail (Psalm 22) and the death of Messiah divinely interpreted as an offering for guilt some six hundred years before the event (Isaiah 53:3–12). Judas's betrayal was prophesied (Matthew 26:24; Acts 1:16) and foretold by Jesus at the Last Supper (Luke 22:21). The time when the Messiah would be "cut off" was predicted by Daniel (Daniel 9:26).

In his Pentecost sermon, Peter declared that the very criminals who carried out the farcical trials accomplished God's "predetermined plan" (Acts 2:23). Herod, Pontius Pilate, the Gentiles, and Israel gathered against Jesus "to do whatever [God's] hand and...purpose predestined to occur" (Acts 4:27–28).

The final verdict is in. No one can frustrate the sovereign will and plan of God. To Paul's challenging question: "Who resists His will?" (Romans 9:19), we are humbly compelled to agree, "No one!" (Romans 9:6–29). God's sovereign will is indeed certain.

GOD'S SOVEREIGN WILL IS...

Certain—it will be fulfilled

God Determines Who Lands on Park Place

The second thing the Bible indicates about God's plan is that it is *detailed*—exhaustively so. It includes the germ as well as the galaxies. God's sovereign will ultimately determines which of our plans find fulfillment (James 4:13–15), the existence of creation (Revelation 4:11), the ruler's personal plans (Proverbs 21:1), the result of the tumbling dice (Proverbs 16:33), the believer's suffering (1 Peter 3:17), and our personal salvation (Romans 8:29–30; 2 Thessalonians 2:13–14). In a word, the sovereign God "works *all things* after the counsel of His will" (Ephesians 1:11).

God's detailed sovereignty is worked out in daily providence whether we see it or not. C. S. Lewis dramatized this in his children's story, *The Horse and His Boy*. The great Lion, Aslan, is sovereignly working behind the scenes to guide and protect Shasta, but he does not realize it at first. The first hint comes when Shasta and Aravis reach the Hermit of Southern March. Aravis remarks to him how lucky they have been. The Hermit wisely replies, "Daughter, I have now lived a hundred and nine winters in this world and have never yet met any such thing as Luck."[1]

The Bible uses the imagery of a book to demonstrate that the details of our lives are encompassed in God's sovereignty:

> Your eyes have seen my unformed substance;
> And in Your book were all written
> The days that were ordained for me,
> When as yet there was not one of them. (Psalm 139:16)

The traditional view sometimes uses this verse to support the idea of an individual will, but the reference is to God's sovereign plan over our whole lives. God's providence and sovereign guidance are "ordained" by God. From the womb to the tomb, we live out the days of our lives under His sovereign knowledge and control (see Psalm 139).

> **GOD'S SOVEREIGN WILL IS...**
>
> **Certain**—it will be fulfilled
> **Detailed**—includes all things

The third thing we learn about God's plan is that it is *hidden*. Older theologians often referred to God's sovereign will as His "secret will," in contrast to His revealed will in the Bible. God hides His sovereign will until it happens. Curl up with a good history book on a rainy day and you are reading God's sovereign will for the past. Would you like to know God's sovereign will for next Tuesday? Wait until next Wednesday. Only God knows what will happen in advance, and He's not telling (Deuteronomy 29:29; Psalm 115:3; Romans 11:33–34; James 4:15).

Nor is God telling us all the *whys* of His sovereign work. It is futile to try to read God's providence.[2] A missionary goes out in faith to a dangerous field. Three months later he contracts malaria. He sadly concludes, "I must have missed God's will for me. God would not have sent me here only to get sick." To his malaria is added an additional misery—guilt!

This missionary is suffering for the gospel and should be honored. His suffering is not proof of missing God's individual will. Only God knows why He allows such things. Missionary speakers sometimes proclaim, "You are safer in the darkest jungle if you're in God's will than you are anywhere else outside of God's individual will." Since when has obedience been equated with safety? It would be more biblical to say that going to a perilous field may entail suffering for the gospel—like the esteemed Epaphroditus who risked his life for the gospel (Philippians 2:29–30), or Paul and Barnabas who "risked their lives for the name of our Lord Jesus Christ" (Acts 15:26).

No Exceptions Except...

There are two exceptions to the secrecy of God's plan. One of them is prophecy (Amos 3:7). For instance, God foretold that Christ is coming back (Matthew 24:30), and that there will be wars on earth right up to the end (Matthew 24:6–7).

The other thing God has revealed about the future is the ultimate destiny of the saved and the lost. If you are trusting in Jesus Christ as your Savior, you have been given everlasting life and you will spend eternity with Christ in heaven (John 3:16; 14:3). If you reject Christ and the salvation He has provided, you can be certain of your reservation in the burning fire of hell (John 3:16; Revelation 20:11–15; 21:8).

> **GOD'S SOVEREIGN WILL IS...**
>
> **Certain**—it will be fulfilled
> **Detailed**—includes all things
> **Hidden**—except when revealed by prophecy

To the thoughtful person these truths raise some important questions. For instance, if God has determined in advance everything that happens, doesn't that make God responsible for sin? The Bible does not accept that logic. It rather affirms the absolute holiness of God (Isaiah 6:3) and declares:

> The LORD is righteous in all His ways
> And kind in all His deeds. (Psalm 145:17)

God is truly sovereign, even over sinful acts of men (Acts 2:23), but He is not Himself a sinner (James 1:13).

No full explanation of this mystery is given in Scripture, even when the issue is raised by one of God's prophets (Habakkuk 1:3). God's justice is often brought into question (Romans 3:5; 9:14), but Paul ruled such objections out of court: How dare you impugn the righteous character of your Creator, is the apostle's incredulous reply (Romans 3:4–6; 9:14, 20–21).

How can God sovereignly control sin, yet be perfectly righteous in all He does? This is probably one of the "secret things" (Deuteronomy 29:29) that may simply be beyond the grasp of finite minds. Still, I am helped by an illustration suggested by Jonathan Edwards.

The Sun Turned Me Cold

Imagine a planet that by nature is a cold and desolate sphere. Yet, it is warm because of its proximity to the sun. Now suppose that, for reasons of its own, the sun decided to move away from that planet toward another. The consequences for the first planet would be devastating. The former climate so conducive to life would give way to frozen desolation.

Now, did the sun make the planet cold? The answer is yes *and* no. Yes, the sun ultimately determined the frigid condition of that planet by moving and leaving that orb to its own nature. But no, the sun was not morally guilty for the coldness of the planet. The sun did not produce the frozen atmosphere of the planet. In a similar way, God ultimately determines all things, including sinful acts. Yet He cannot be called the author of sin.

A second question commonly raised is this: If God sovereignly determines everything that happens, how can human decisions have any meaning? Isn't fatalism the natural, logical conclusion of sovereignty?

The Devil Made Me Do It

Once again, the Bible does not concur with such thinking. Scripture presents humans as moral agents who make real decisions for which we are responsible. God is not a cosmic puppeteer, and we are not marionettes that jump when He jerks our strings. No one can say of his actions, "God made me do it," or "the devil made me do it" or even "my mother-in-law drove me to it." A person's decision constitutes a real cause, produces genuine effects, and brings accountability. God is the ultimate determiner, but humans produce real secondary causes with their decisions and actions.

How God works this out is another mystery, but I have found this line of thought helpful. God does not usurp our responsibility because He doesn't work contrary to our nature, nor force our wills. As we decide, He works within our wills and in harmony with our nature to bring about His determined end. If God did force us, we would not be responsible.

Consider two biblical examples. The first is an instance when God did overrule the evil intentions of an individual. King Saul wanted to kill David, but God blocked his efforts by turning Saul (temporarily) into a prophet (1 Samuel 19:23–24). Saul could not take credit for preserving David's life nor for his prophesying. His behavior was *inconsistent* with his nature and intent because it was not Saul's decision—God made him do it. (This is the exception that proves the rule.)

Judas, on the other hand, accomplished God's plan in a manner perfectly consistent with his greedy, fallen human nature. God was sovereign over the betrayal of Jesus (Matthew 26:24; Luke 22:22); the traitor's act was certain from eternity past. But Judas was not coerced. God worked within circumstances and within Judas' will to determine exactly how Judas would express his evil desires. It was possible that Judas could have bailed out earlier when he saw that his days of pilfering the petty cash were over. He could have gone home, yelled at his wife, and kicked the dog. God, however, determined that Judas would willingly act, according to his own nature, by betraying Christ for thirty pieces of silver. It was certain, but Judas was certainly responsible.

Some theologians have couched this mystery in terms of God's "permissive" will (though not in the misleading way the traditional view sometimes uses the term).[3] The idea is that God sovereignly permitted sin without being its direct agent or author. This is a helpful distinction and accords with biblical statements, as when Jesus gave permission for demonic activity and God "permitted all the nations to go their own ways" (Mark 5:13; Acts 14:16).

Only Your Wife Knows for Sure

I have always appreciated an illustration given by one of my favorite professors. Prior to his marriage, he assumed he was acting voluntarily in courting his wife. The decision to propose to her was his own. He acted freely in accordance with his nature and desires. He was certain that he was in control of the whole situation as the initiator.

After they were married, however, his wife informed him that he only thought he was in control. Actually, she had considerable influence over his actions and decisions. She desired his courtship and willed his proposal of marriage. So she moved to make him willing. She did not hold a gun to his head, but acted in more subtle ways—ways she claims a man would not understand—to mold his will. As a result (she claims), she was the one who determined they would marry. As they say, he chased her until she caught him.

Who is right? I trust they both are. If so, the illustration shows in a limited way that while a man is not a puppet, God does ultimately write the script.

A similar illustration is suggested by an image that appears frequently in the Old Testament. The prophets repeatedly told God's people, "If you seek Him, He will let you find Him" (1 Chronicles 28:9; 2 Chronicles 15:2, 4, 15). Man really seeks, but God is in control of the finding. I have played "hide and seek" with young children like my nieces Brittany and Erica. Picture a typical game. I begin with a knowledge of how capable my nieces are of ferreting out a hidden uncle. I can choose a hiding place too difficult for them, or I can be a good uncle and pick a spot that is not beyond their ability and patience. I hide in a closet easily accessible to them. They call out, "Here we come, ready or not." The children search diligently and then finally find legs attached to the shoes in the closet. "Uncle Garry, we found you!"

Did they find me, or did I determine that I would be found? Aren't both true?

Though these illustrations are simple, they show that it is reasonable that an all-knowing God could determine the end without forcing the human agents. For instance, God's knowledge of Pharaoh's heart was part of the means He used to bring about the end. Pharaoh chose to pursue Israel after they had departed. But God had Israel look like they were "wandering aimlessly." This was a catalyst that motivated Pharaoh to pursue them (Exodus 14:1–8).

Causality is more complex than a whodunit mystery. Who was the cause of Job's troubles? Was it Satan who moved against Job (Job 1:12)? Was it the Sabeans and Chaldeans who attacked his servants (Job 1:15, 17)? Or was Job right when he said, "The LORD gave and the LORD has taken away" (Job 1:21)? All three are correct. God is the ultimate determiner, but He acts without taking away the causal roles of either humans or Satan.

God's sovereignty and man's responsibility are asserted side by side in Scripture (Acts 2:23; 4:27–28). Whether or not we can put them together in our minds, we must accept both truths.[4] And so we acknowledge a fourth characteristic of God's sovereign will: it is the *supreme* determiner of all things—without violating human responsibility or making God the author of sin.

The story is told of two soldiers who experienced a lull in the fighting several days after their D-day landing at Normandy. As they approached the plaza of a city, they found a statue of Christ that had been toppled. On the intact base someone had scrawled the words, "His reign is over." It can seem that way in the carnage of battle, but these soldiers knew better. They quietly replaced the statue and added three words to the base. Now it read, "His reign is over…heaven and earth."

Believers know God reigns despite their theological arguments about it. J. I. Packer contends that in prayer all believers really do believe that God is sovereign. "On our feet we may have arguments about it, but on our knees we are all agreed."[5]

> ## GOD'S SOVEREIGN WILL IS…
>
> **Certain**—it will be fulfilled
> **Detailed**—includes all things
> **Hidden**—except when revealed by prophecy
> **Supreme**—without violating human responsibility
> or making God the author of sin

There is one final characteristic of God's sovereign will to consider. God's sovereign will is *perfect*. It is perfect in that it will ultimately lead to God's greatest glory. No other plan could be as perfect. In fact, there never was another plan (Ephesians 1:4).

I and a group of other doctoral candidates tried to guess what the professors might ask during our theology oral exams. I was certain that I would be asked, "Why would a perfect God create a world where sin could enter?" After much soul searching, I decided that if asked, I would answer, "Because it was the best of all possible plans."

But wouldn't a plan that excluded sin be better? Apparently not. God's glory is not always immediate, but it is certain. He will be glorified for His holiness, for His defeat of Satan, for His righteous judgment, and for His grace to redeemed sinners (Revelation 5). This glory must have a backdrop of sin to be fully realized. The Cross is followed by Resurrection, and His victory over the grave brings Him glory (John 12:32–33). The first sin is followed by the promise of a Redeemer, and God is glorified for His grace (Genesis 3:15; Romans 5:20). The temporary rejection of the Savior by sinning Israel results in the reconciliation of the world, and God is glorified for His wisdom (Romans 11:15, 30–33).

C. S. Lewis reminds us that God took the risk of creating beings who could choose to sin.[6] God in His wisdom chose to make people rather than robots. Robots are efficient and they cannot sin. But when God created man and woman, "behold, it was very good" (Genesis 1:31).

All Is Not Good that Ends Well

We often quote Romans 8:28 and receive comfort from the truth that "God causes all things to work together for good to those who love God." The basis for the truth of that statement is the sovereign will of God, as indicated in the verses that follow. We must be careful to note that God does not say that all things are good, for they are not. Rather, all things *work together* for good. They work together to make us conformed to Christ (Romans 8:29) and thus glorify God through His people. Even a flat tire, a crying child, or a disabled washing machine "work together for good" to conform us to Christ's quality of endurance (James 1:2–4).

We know that God's plan is perfect because God is perfect. Our knowledge of that fact is grounded in faith, not sight. According to the human eye, the world often seems chaotic, controlled by the sovereign rule of Satan. The person who walks by sight will not be equipped to cope with tragedy when it comes to him. Such a person sees circumstances from the same perspective as an unbeliever and is inclined to curse his bad luck or become bitter toward God. But the Christian who trusts in God's sovereign plan is spiritually prepared for anything. She may not fully understand why she had to endure some difficulty, but she will know that her experience was part of the sovereign plan of an all-wise and loving God. In tragedy, we can never unscrew the inscrutable and explain why something happened. All our "why" questions ultimately must have the same answer—our loving God in His sovereign wisdom willed it so. His plan is perfect. Os Guinness has wisely observed: "As believers we cannot always know why, but *we can always know why we trust God who knows why*, and this makes all the difference."[7]

GOD'S SOVEREIGN WILL IS...

Certain—it will be fulfilled
Detailed—includes all things
Hidden—except when revealed by prophecy
Supreme—without violating human responsibility or making God the author of sin
Perfect—working all things together for God's glory and our good

God's sovereign control was secretly working things together for my good late one night as I returned from leading a high school rally for Youth for Christ. About midnight I stopped on the quiet Arkansas road in front of Maysville Bible Church where I ministered and tried to determine if I had enough strength to safely drive the remaining thirty miles back to John Brown University.

I prayed for a few minutes and then decided to drive on. Only God knew what was happening up the road in those moments when I paused. I soon came over a hill and saw a dim light swinging back and forth. I began to slow down and then jammed on the brake. I barely avoided slamming into a mess on the road. The mess included a car stalled sideways in the middle of the highway, a dead cow, and a dazed teenager swinging a lantern. I recognized the boy from my Sunday school class.

Later we pieced together the events of our unlikely rendezvous. His car had struck a wandering cow, smashing the headlights, disabling the engine, and precariously blocking the road. He wandered off for help and got a lantern to warn any drivers coming over the hill. My short pause for prayer gave him enough time to get back to the highway to warn me. Then I was able to help him get to the hospital. I never made it to John Brown, but ended up sleeping in my student's bed and teaching my Sunday school class in the morning.

(This exercise of God's sovereign purpose affects you, too. If I had not paused to pray, you might not be reading this book.)

Ruth, the Moabite widow, had a similar experience. Her faith in God was rewarded when she entered Boaz's field, though she was unaware of God's sovereign guidance. There was no voice behind her saying, "This is the field. Walk ye in it." In fact the text says she "happened to come" upon the field (Ruth 2:3)! Humanly speaking, she had no specific reason for choosing the field, but God perfectly, secretly, in detail, guided her within His sovereign will.

Learning about God's sovereignty often leads to consternation. It is beyond our full understanding. Sadly, it can result in needless arguments between believers. What it should do is expand our view of God. Lucy, from the Narnia chronicles of C. S. Lewis, is our guide. In *Prince Caspian*, the children were lost in the woods trying to come to the aid of Prince Caspian and his bedraggled army. In the middle of the night Lucy woke up and unexpectedly met the person she most wanted to see—Aslan the Lion. She gazed up into the large wise face.

"Welcome, child," he said.

"Aslan," said Lucy, "you're bigger."

"That is because you are older, little one," answered he.

"Not because you are?"

"I am not. But every year you grow, you will find me bigger."[8]

frequently asked questions

> *Question:* You argued against the concept of a dot, but isn't there a sovereign dot? Wouldn't you agree that God's sovereign will applies to individuals as well as every individual thing that happens? How can you say there is no individual will of God?

I addressed this issue in endnote 2 of chapter 3, "Does God Have Three Wills?" but it naturally surfaces here as well. And I acknowledge that the point is well taken. God's sovereign will is, in fact, individual. I affirmed that in this chapter by explaining that the sovereign will is detailed or exhaustive. In the end, for each decision made by a human being, there is one divinely appointed alternative—sovereignly chosen.

So when I say there is no "individual will of God," I mean there is no individual will *in the sense intended by the traditional view*. You see, I have also established that the sovereign will of God is hidden or secret. It cannot be discovered in advance. But that is just what the traditional view claims we can and must do. So, yes, there is an individual will encompassed by the sovereign will. But since that is not what the traditional view means by that terminology, I have refrained from saying so (until now) in order to avoid confusion.

> *Question:* If God has a sovereign will that is perfect, doesn't it follow that God has a perfect plan for each believer?

Yes. But again, this is true only in the sovereign sense. This perfect plan cannot be discovered in advance and it cannot be missed. And it includes the bad things that happen to us and the bad things that we do, all of which God "works together for good." Thus, believers can be assured of

God working sovereignly for their good, but they do not have to discern this plan.

From a different perspective, and in a more general sense, God's moral will can also be viewed as a perfect plan.

> *Question:* God's sovereign will seems so cold and impersonal to me.

The implied question seems to be, "If the decisions of my life are determined by some eternal plan I cannot know in advance, in what sense is God personally involved in guiding my life?"

I devote a whole chapter to this question (chapter 18, "Practicing the Presence"). One of the reasons the traditional view appeals to many is that they do not recognize God's personal hand in His sovereign will.

For now, the short answer. Some people mistakenly equate God's sovereign will with something akin to fate. That *would* be impersonal. But if you factor in a loving God dynamically "working all things together for good," then it is very personal. That is what the Bible teaches. The traditional view may feel better to some because they imagine God whispering directions for their decisions. But it is better (and more reliable) to learn to recognize His involvement in our lives in the ways He has told us He is guiding us—through His moral and sovereign wills.

> *Question:* 1 Corinthians 7:17 and 20 speak of God's "calling" and "assigning." How does this fit with the thesis of your book?

First Corinthians 7:17–24 is a "sovereignty paragraph." The call in this passage refers to the grace that brought a person to salvation (7:22). The assignment was that person's life situation or condition (7:20) at the time of conversion. For instance, some were slaves; some were free. That circumstance had been sovereignly determined, and the fact that they had responded to God's call to saving faith did not require them to try to change their situation. On the other hand, their state at salvation was not a *directive* from God. So if the slave had an opportunity for freedom (sovereignly provided!), he or she was free to take it (7:21). Until then, each person should serve God right where he had been placed in God's sovereign will.[9]

1. C. S. Lewis, *The Horse and His Boy* (New York: MacMillan Publishing Co., Inc., 1954), 125.
2. The futility of "reading providence" is addressed in greater detail in the next chapter, "God's Sovereign Will and Decision Making."
3. In some constructions of the traditional view, "permissive will" is used to describe a decision made within God's moral will, but which misses God's individual will. For example, let's say that it is God's individual will for Jim to marry Marjory. Jim knows it is God's moral will for him to marry a believer. But he misses the "signs" pointing to Marjory and marries Suzanne (who is also a Christian) instead. In this version of the traditional view, Jim's marriage decision would place him within God's "permissive will" (a.k.a. "second best"). Because of the permanence of the marriage covenant (moral will), this condition is irreversible.
4. Kenneth Boa's book, *Unraveling the Big Questions About God* (Grand Rapids, MI: Zondervan, 1988; previously titled, *God, I Don't Understand*), provides an excellent treatment of the tension between truths that are both biblically necessary but appear mutually contradictory. He and other theologians call these mysteries "antinomies."
5. J. I. Packer, *Evangelism and the Sovereignty of God* (Downers Grove, IL: InterVarsity Press, 1961), 17.
6. C. S. Lewis, *Mere Christianity* (New York: Simon and Schuster, 1996), 53.
7. Os Guinness, *In Two Minds: The Dilemma of Doubt and How to Resolve It* (Downers Grove, IL: InterVarsity Press, 1976), 255 (italics his).
8. C. S. Lewis, *Prince Caspian* (New York: MacMillan Publishing Co., Inc., 1951), 117.
9. First Corinthians 7 is discussed at length in chapter 19, "Singleness, Marriage, and Wisdom."

chapter thirteen

GOD'S SOVEREIGN WILL AND DECISION MAKING

Now that we've surveyed the biblical data on the nature of God's sovereign will, we may consider the ways sovereignty affects the believer's decision-making process. We will see how God's sovereignty relates to such important considerations as planning, circumstances, open doors, and fleeces.

SOVEREIGNTY AND PLANNING

If God controls everything that happens, what point is there in making any plans? It's a logical question, and James 4:13–16 expounds the biblical viewpoint.

> Come now, you who say, "Today or tomorrow we will go to such and such a city, and spend a year there and engage in business and make a profit." Yet you do not know what your life will be like tomorrow. You are just a vapor that appears for a little while and then vanishes away. Instead, you ought to say, "*If the Lord wills*, we will live and also do this or that." But as it is, you boast in your arrogance; all such boasting is evil. (James 4:13–16)

James portrays a group of successful, confident, self-made Jewish merchants. They are hovering over a map discussing plans. One of their coterie points to a city on the map and declares, "That's the place to go. If we do business in 'Such a City' for a year, we're certain of substantial profit. Let's leave with our merchandise today, or tomorrow at the latest."

James, however, interrupts the business meeting with a stern rebuke. He condemns arrogant, self-confident planning, which does not recognize God or His sovereignty. James attacks their boastful presumptuousness for "all such boasting is evil" (4:16). His "Come now" (4:13) is sarcastic because the merchants are displaying a foolish self-confidence. Each added detail of the plan underscores the attitude of arrogance. Like the rich fool of Jesus' parable (Luke 12:16–21), their omission of God highlights their self-trust.

The Best Laid Plans of Mice and Merchants

Such boasting is absurd, for life is like a vapor (4:14). No man can say what his life will be like tomorrow. The high-pressure life insurance salesman has a point when he says, "If you don't want to buy a policy now, think about it tonight and call me in the morning—if you wake up." Life is uncertain and short. The life-span line on a tombstone, 1905–1970, puts it starkly: life is just a hyphen, just a vapor.

But while James condemns presumption, he never reproves planning itself. He apparently accepts their short-range planning ("today or tomorrow"), their long-range planning ("spend a year"), their site selection ("such a city"), and their formulation of a goal ("make a profit"). Like the Hebrew Proverbs (21:5), James approves planning. It's the godless, self-assured attitude he deplores.

"If"—the Motto of the Humble

In verse 15, James submits his corrective. He commands that believers adopt a humble attitude in planning, an attitude that properly recognizes God's sovereignty. The Christian's life is also vaporlike and his planning is always iffy. The most ungodly, immoral, foolhardy plan always has an "if" attached to it. The same is true of the plan that is godly, moral, and wise.

The believer is to express his humility in planning not only with an "if," but further with "if the Lord wills." Proper planning recognizes that God's sovereign will is the final determiner of the outcome. It is a mystery why God allows certain godly plans to fail while allowing other wicked plans to find fruition. However, no plan, whether good or bad, comes to pass unless God sovereignly wills it.

Finally, James says that when all contingencies have been duly acknowledged, *planning is appropriate:* "we will...do this or that" (4:15). God's sovereign determination of all things in no way diminishes the need or importance of wise planning. Christians should simply express their intentions in using the future tense of resolve—"we will do this or that...." A good plan should probably include all of the elements noted before: a starting time, a location, a goal, and a target date for completion (4:13).

To sum up, James condemns arrogant planning, which does not recognize God or His sovereignty. He commends planning that submits in advance to the outworking of God's sovereign will.

What James taught the apostle Paul modeled. He humbly made both short-range (Acts 20:16; 1 Corinthians 4:19) and long-range plans (Acts 18:21; 19:21; 1 Corinthians 16:5–7). He did not always use the phrase "if God wills," which indicates that a slavish repetition of the phrase is not necessary, but only the continual humility that recognizes God's sovereignty. The expression is most useful to avoid the appearance of arrogance when a strong resolve is expressed, such as Paul's intent to come to Corinth to confront a prideful faction in the church (1 Corinthians 4:18–19).

A variety of synonymous expressions found in Scripture appropriately express the proper attitude in planning. "By the will of God" emphasizes the role of divine sovereignty in bringing plans to fulfillment (Romans 1:10; 15:32). "If the Lord permits" acknowledges that God puts limits or boundaries on the plans of men (1 Corinthians 16:7).

In the end, most of Paul's plans did come to pass (Acts 18:21; 1 Timothy 1:3), just as most of our well-laid plans are accomplished. Each time a carefully devised plan is successful, two truths are reinforced: the importance of wise, orderly planning (Proverbs 24:6); and the effectiveness of God's sovereign will in accomplishing the plans of men and God (Romans 1:10; 15:32).

The failure of a plan should prompt the believer to reevaluate the strategy and to correct it if appropriate (Proverbs 20:5). A lack of success should also remind us that God is working in all things, even our uncompleted or aborted plans, to accomplish His divine purposes for good (Romans 8:28; 1 Thessalonians 2:18).

After reading this section on planning in the first edition, a lay leader from Arkansas called with a pressing question. He had sacrificed for five years to start a Bible church in a needy area, but it failed. His friends inadvertently rubbed the salt of guilt into his wound of disappointment. "The failure shows that it was not God's will in the first place," they said. "You should have known that." He wondered if his failure might simply be explained by God's sovereignty. I told him that God would reward his faithful efforts, not just his "successes."

King David was denied in his bid to build the temple, but received God's commendation. God told David, "Because it was in your heart to build a house for My name, you did well that it was in your heart. Nevertheless you shall not build the house" (1 Kings 8:18–19). Godly ideas, plans, and efforts are a delight to God even when His sovereign plans do not allow their completion. The believer must pursue actions that glorify God and then leave the results to Him. We act and then "let Him do what seems good to Him" (1 Samuel 3:18; 2 Samuel 10:12; 15:26; 1 Chronicles 19:13).

My caller was relieved by this perspective and even encouraged. Near the end of the conversation he said, "We still don't have a good Bible-teaching church in the area. Do you think it would be all right if I tried again?"

"If a church is needed and you have the heart to try to start it," I replied, "I don't see why not—as long as you remember that God doesn't promise success, as we define it."

Paul attempted many times to go to Rome for ministry. He did not regard sovereign roadblocks as indicators that something was wrong with the attempt (Romans 1:13). All kinds of worthwhile projects have been accomplished (according to God's sovereign will) on the second, third, or fourth effort.[1]

GOD'S SOVEREIGN WILL AND DECISION MAKING

1. God's sovereignty does not exclude the need for planning; it does require humble submission to His will.

SOVEREIGNTY AND CIRCUMSTANCES

Some proponents of the traditional view teach that the believer should "read providence" as a means of determining direction from God. It is not uncommon to hear Christians say, "The Lord led me to do thus and such." When asked about the means and details of this leading, they list a series of circumstances that pointed the way to God's will. However, nothing in Scripture authorizes interpreting circumstances in that way.

If there is no individual will of God, as we have established, such an approach to decision making is flawed. Circumstances do not lead; they are not even intended to give hints about God's future sovereign will or His moral will. His sovereign will is hidden, and His moral will is already revealed in its entirety in the Bible.

Telegram from the Blue

The only time that circumstances can be read is when a divine interpretation is placed upon them by supernatural revelation. Apart from such revelation, circumstances may be taken to mean almost anything. Just listen to this imaginary but believable discussion about the message God was trying to convey when lightning struck a church steeple.

"God is telling us to relocate in the suburbs."

"Oh no, I think it's quite obvious He's saying 'no' to our expansion plans."

"Maybe the Lord is telling us that there is sin holding back the work in our church."

Solomon made it clear that reading providence makes life confusing at best and futile at worst (Ecclesiastes 1:1–11). It often appears that God favors the wicked rich and resists the downtrodden righteous (Psalm 37:1).

Accordingly, biblical characters who attempted to interpret providence failed in their efforts. When a viper clamped onto Paul's hand, the Malta natives concluded he was a murderer and waited for him to swell up or drop dead (Acts 28:4). When he was unaffected by the venom, they determined that he must be a god (Acts 28:6). They were sincere, but wrong both times.

Jesus declared that the disciples were incorrect in attributing a certain man's blindness to sin (John 9:2–3). Popular opinion erred in thinking that a group of Galileans killed by Pilate were greater sinners than others (Luke 13:1–3). Nor was there any special guilt in the eighteen who perished when the tower of Siloam unexpectedly collapsed (Luke 13:4–5). From the human perspective, some things should simply be viewed as happening by chance, just as the Bible does (1 Samuel 6:9; 2 Samuel 1:6; Luke 10:31; see also Ruth 2:3; 1 Kings 22:34). Such events are determined by God, to be sure, but they are not to be viewed as signs to be read.

In his essay, "Historicism," C. S. Lewis refuted those who try to read messages into providence and see an "inner meaning in the historical process." The attempt may be just a waste of time or "positively mischievous." "It encourages a Mussolini to say that 'History took him by the throat' when what really took him by the throat was desire."[2]

Counselors know that the most ingenious stories of interpreted providence come from those who have fallen in love. Every detail is further confirmation to them of God's approval of their relationship. They ask, "What is the chance that out of a hundred people, we would sit next to each other and both be wearing blue?" Don't answer them. You will only get them going. But they are reading their own hearts, not providence.

Even Hindsight Isn't 20/20

God has His wise and sovereign reasons for each event, but He does not regularly give us a running commentary of His reasons. Paul did not pontificate on the sovereign reasons behind the escape of Philemon's servant, Onesimus, even though the flight resulted in the man's salvation. He only suggested, "*Perhaps* he was for this reason separated from you for a while" (Philemon 15–16). Mordecai believed in God's providential care for Israel, but could only guess Esther's part in it: "Relief and deliverance will arise for the Jews.... *And who knows* whether you have not attained royalty for such a time as this?" (Esther 4:14). In the short run, Gamaliel's view that success in ministry is an indicator of God's approval is not correct (Acts 5:38–39).

Wisdom must take account of "chance" happenings and include a safety net for some endeavors. Solomon explains: "You do not know the activity of God who makes all things. Sow your seed in the morning and do not be idle in the evening, for you do not know whether morning or evening sowing will succeed, or whether both of them alike will be good" (Ecclesiastes 11:5–6).

Job's "comforters," Eliphaz, Bildad, and Zophar, tried to turn the interpretation of providence into an art form, but they were most helpful when they sat silently (Job 2:13). For nine chapters they expounded on providence (Job 4–5, 8, 11, 15, 18, 20, 22, 25). They were interrupted only by Job's depressed denial. In their interpretations of Job's situation, they were wrong nine chapters out of nine! Only God really knew what was going on, and Job never did receive the divine interpretation of his troubles. During his earthly life, the most he could say was, "The LORD gave and the LORD has taken away. Blessed be the name of the LORD" (Job 1:21).

Fathoming Famines

An event cannot communicate a message apart from divine revelation. Israel's crop failures and plagues were often the result of God's judgment—judgment the Lord's prophets announced in advance (Deuteronomy 11:17; Amos 4:6–8). The prophet Joel declared that an invasion of locusts was not chance tragedy (Joel 2:1–10), but an act of divine discipline designed to bring Israel to repentance (Joel 2:11–17). Without such divine commentary, locusts are just locusts. There was a reason for a famine in David's time (2 Samuel 21:1), but without divine explanation, a famine is just a famine. Even Agabus did not explain the reason for the famine he predicted, but only spoke to warn the people to prepare (Acts 11:27–30).

Another kind of event that Scripture indicates is capable of communicating truth is the divinely wrought miracle. The miracles of Christ attested that He was from God (John 5:36) and manifested His glory (John 2:11). A miracle clearly indicates supernatural intervention by Satan or God, and God gives revelation to distinguish the source (Deuteronomy 13:1–5; 18:20–22).

Apart from these two exceptions, attempts to read messages from God in circumstances are invalid. For God's sovereign plan presently includes both good and evil. It permits Gabriel and Lucifer, Jesus and Judas to exist side by side. However, in the day of judgment, God will judge all evil and reward all good. Then we will be able to read God's goodness and justice in His providence. Then the prayer, "Your will be done, on earth as it is in heaven" (Matthew 6:10), will be answered.

Circumstances *do* have a role to play in decision making. They frame the context we now live in. Wisdom will not try to read messages in the circumstances, but will judge the wisdom of a course of action in light of the current situation. Some actions are wise because of the present context. Others are foolish for the same reason. If you lack money for college, it is probably foolish to register this year. But why not pray for a change of circumstances—more money or a scholarship? If the prayer is answered, then it will become wise to enroll now.

GOD'S SOVEREIGN WILL AND DECISION MAKING

1. God's sovereignty does not exclude the need for *planning*; it does require humble submission to His will.
2. **Circumstances** define the context of the decision and must be weighed by wisdom, not read to find God's individual will.

SOVEREIGNTY AND OPEN DOORS

But doesn't Scripture speak of "open doors"? What are they if not circumstantial indications from the Lord about a direction He wants us to take?

The term "open door" is a natural figure for free access or an opportunity to do something. For example, one summer I was engaged in church-planting efforts doing door-to-door evangelism in Texas. On 100-plus degree days, my zeal to enter a cool home increased remarkably. As I knocked, I literally prayed, "Lord, give me an open door." I was praying both for access into the air-conditioned house as well as for an opportunity to evangelize.

In the scriptural expression "open door," the nature of the access or opportunity is determined by the context. In Acts 14:27, Paul and Barnabas reported how God "had opened a door of faith to the Gentiles," meaning that the Gentiles had been given an opportunity to hear the gospel and believe. Most occurrences relate to some opportunity for gospel ministry.

Understanding open doors is important for guidance, for their very existence implies that a decision must be made. Does an open door constitute direction from the Lord that must be obeyed? Or is it an opportunity that should be judged by wisdom? The answer emerges from the key passages: 1 Corinthians 16:8–9, 2 Corinthians 2:12–13, and Colossians 4:3.[3]

Opportunity and Opposition

> But I will remain in Ephesus until Pentecost; for *a wide door* for effective service *has opened* to me, and there are many adversaries. (1 Corinthians 16:8–9)

At the time of this writing, Paul's short-range plans called for him to remain in Ephesus for approximately two months. After that, he intended to travel through Macedonia and spend some extended time in Corinth, something Paul was hoping the Lord would permit (1 Corinthians 16:7).

More significantly for Paul, "a wide door for effective service" had been opened for him and there were "many adversaries" trying to close that door. In short, Paul stayed to utilize the opportunity and neutralize the opposition.

Now the "door" in this case was an opportunity for effective and widespread gospel ministry. The adversaries in question were seeking to hinder the potentially large harvest. It is instructive to see how

Paul regarded this situation. He did not, on the one hand, look upon the door as a sign commanding him to stay in Ephesus. The door was not a revealed command, but an opening for the spiritually opportunistic. Nor did Paul view the adversaries as a semaphore from God signaling him to move on to more productive fields of service. To Paul, the excellent soldier (2 Timothy 4:7), the presence of opposition indicated the need for reinforcements. The combination of opportunity and opposition provided him with good spiritual reasons for an extended ministry in Ephesus. He was making the most of his time and his opportunities (Ephesians 5:16) while combating the enemy with the shrewdness of a serpent (Matthew 10:16).

The door was not a revealed command, but an opening for the spiritually opportunistic.

Get Me a Soapbox

> Praying at the same time for us as well, that God will *open up* to us a *door* for the word, so that we may speak forth the mystery of Christ, for which I have also been imprisoned. (Colossians 4:3)

The one who seeks opportunities to minister for Christ is motivated to pray for them and to seek partners in such prayer. That is what Paul was doing—recruiting the Colossian believers as prayer partners. Since he wrote from prison, this verse could be an expression of Paul's hope that he would be released after his hearing before the Roman tribunal. Such a release would open his prison door and allow him to resume preaching with complete freedom. It is even more likely that the prayer was simply a request for abundant opportunities to share the gospel, a request that was subsequently answered in a wonderful way (Philippians 1:12–18). In Acts, the apostles prayed for opportunity to minister the Word and it resulted in the opening of figurative and literal doors (Acts 5:19; 12:6–11; 16:26).

Paul's prayer was not a prayer for guidance, but rather for opportunity. He needed no providential sign to encourage him to preach. He always looked for an empty pulpit and filled pews.

The Door Not Taken

> Now when I came to Troas for the gospel of Christ and when *a door was opened* for me in the Lord, I had no rest for my spirit, not finding Titus my brother; but taking my leave of them, I went on to Macedonia. (2 Corinthians 2:12–13)

Behold, here is an "open door" the apostle walked away from! The reason for his decision can be understood only in light of the historical context. Apparently, Paul had written a "sorrowful letter" to the Christians at Corinth, and had sent Titus to deliver it (2 Corinthians 2:4; 7:8). At a later time, Paul was to leave Ephesus (1 Corinthians 16:8) and stop in Troas (2 Corinthians 2:12–13) en route to Corinth. He planned to meet Titus in Troas and get a report from him about the Corinthians' response to his letter. The situation was so serious that the future of the church might depend on their response.

Once in Troas, Paul waited anxiously for Titus to arrive with the verdict. While he waited, he became aware of an open door for gospel ministry. However, he was so concerned about the situation in Corinth that he left Troas, open door and all, and went looking for Titus.[4] It was a search fraught with fear and conflict (2 Corinthians 7:5). But it ended happily with the rendezvous in Macedonia with Titus and the report that the Corinthians had responded to his letter with sorrow and repentance (2 Corinthians 7:6–12). From Macedonia, Paul joyfully penned another epistle (2 Corinthians) to acknowledge his receipt of Titus's report and to prepare further for his personal arrival in Corinth.

Why did Paul leave an open door? If an open door constitutes a sign commanding the believer to enter, then Paul's action is inexplicable. But if an open door is an opportunity to be judged by wisdom, then the explanation is not difficult. Normally, Paul would take advantage of an open door for ministry (1 Corinthians 16:9; Colossians 4:3). He would pass up such potential only if something more important demanded his attention. And that was precisely the situation in this case. Rather than build a new church (Troas) with available land and materials, Paul ran to put out the flames that threatened the existence of a church (Corinth) he had already built. Some Bible scholars think that he did, in fact, return and establish a church in Troas when he later visited (Acts 20:6).

Paul again applied wisdom in bypassing opportunities when he twice refused to go through the open door of the Philippian jail in Acts 16. An earthquake opened the jail doors, but Paul stayed put to keep the jailor from committing suicide (Acts 16:27–28). Later the officials realized that Paul was a Roman citizen and tried to secretly release him. Paul refused again until they came and recognized their miscarriage of justice (Acts 16:35–37). Normally, one would seize the chance to get out of jail. But higher priorities prompted Paul to remain until he received a proper release.

Evaluating Doors

On the basis of these passages, we can make the following conclusions about the place of open doors in guidance and decision making: (1) the term *door* refers to an opportunity, usually related to the effective ministry of the Word; (2) opportunities, like everything else, come through God's sovereignty; (3) most of the time open doors should be utilized as part of wise, resourceful living for the Lord (Ephesians 5:15–16); (4) if a greater opportunity or more pressing work is at hand, it is proper to pass by the open door; and (5) an open door is not a providential command from God. Doors facilitate entrance. It is foolish to climb through a back window or tear down a wall when the front door is open.

A final word on so-called "closed doors." The need for open doors certainly implies the existence of closed doors, though Scripture never uses the term. Paul did not have a "closed door" mentality. If he was sovereignly prevented from pursuing a sound plan, he simply waited and tried again later. He did not view a blocked endeavor as a "closed door" sign from God that his plan was faulty. He accepted the fact that he could not pursue that plan at that time. Yet he continued to desire, pray, and plan for the eventual accomplishment of the goal. This approach is clearly demonstrated in Paul's attempts to visit Rome (Romans 1:10–13), which will be discussed in the next chapter.

GOD'S SOVEREIGN WILL AND DECISION MAKING

1. God's sovereignty does not exclude the need for *planning*; it does require humble submission to His will.
2. *Circumstances* define the context of the decision and must be weighed by wisdom, not read to find God's individual will.
3. **Open doors** are not divine commands but God-given opportunities to be evaluated by wisdom.

SOVEREIGNTY AND FLEECES

> Then Gideon said to God, "If You will deliver Israel through me, as You have spoken, behold, I will put a fleece of wool on the threshing floor. If there is dew on the fleece only, and it is dry on all the ground, then I will know that You will deliver Israel through me, as You have spoken." And it was so. When he arose early the next morning and squeezed the fleece, he drained the dew from the fleece, a bowl full of water. Then Gideon said to God, "Do not let Your anger burn against me that I may speak once more; please let me make a test once more with the fleece, let it now be dry only on the fleece, and let there be dew on all the ground." God did so that night; for it was dry only on the fleece, and dew was on all the ground. (Judges 6:36–40)

For many in the traditional view, "putting out a fleece" is a method of determining God's individual will in a specific situation by asking God to guide through a circumstantial sign. Here is a good description of the method.

> Gideon's fleece has become the basis of a practice among some Christians which is called "putting out a fleece." In essence, when you put out a fleece you say to God, "If you really want me to carry out plan A, then please make the telephone ring at

9:10 p.m., then I will know that plan A is what you want." (You can make the "fleece" anything you wish, just so long as it can serve as a "sign" to you.)[5]

The Fleece that Wasn't a Fleece

At a number of points, the event described in Judges fails to authenticate the contemporary practice of "putting out a fleece." First, Gideon's fleece was not simply a circumstantial sign, but rather a miraculous display of divine power. The reversal of the fleece sign further confirms its miraculous nature.

Second, Gideon was not employing the fleece to ascertain guidance, but to gain confirmation of guidance *already given* by direct revelation. Gideon's own words confirm this: "then I will know that You will deliver Israel through me, as *You have spoken*" (Judges 6:37).

Third, Gideon's demand for a further sign is an example of doubt, not model decision making. God's instructions to Gideon were clear (6:37). Apparently, God graciously acceded to Gideon's lack of faith because of the severe circumstances that tested him. For God's attitude toward those who demand signs is expressed in Christ's rebuke of the scribes and Pharisees (Matthew 12:38–39) and demonstrated in the silencing of the priest Zacharias (Luke 1:11–20). Gideon's apologetic tone in asking for the second fleece sign shows that even to him "it looked so like a peevish...distrust of God and dissatisfaction with the many assurances he had already given him."[6]

For these three reasons "putting out a fleece" cannot be authenticated by the passage on which it is based. Even some proponents of the traditional view do not approve of fleeces, and the New Testament gives no support for them either.[7]

Neither does the traditional view argue for "casting of lots" to make decisions. This is curious because this practice appears to be the most defensible method for putting out a fleece. Why create your own circumstantial sign before a decision when you can pull out dice (or lots)? It's quicker, cleaner, and has biblical precedent—lots were used to select Achan (Joshua 7:14–26), Jonathan (1 Samuel 14:40–42), Jonah (Jonah 1:7) and the replacement apostle, Matthias (Acts 1:24–26).

On the other hand, imagine a leader who announces: "We should be led by God. So I will not make decisions, but every issue will be decided by casting lots." Would that approach instill confidence in his followers? Most would probably suspect that this was not leadership, but decision making by random chance.

There is no direction for the use of lots in the New Testament. The only instance in the New Testament where lots were used for decision making is the selection of Matthias to replace Judas (Acts 1:24–26), which occurred before the coming of the Spirit inaugurating the church age.[8] More important is that when the use of lots was valid, the outcome was confirmed miraculously.[9]

Wisdom in Sheep's Clothing

So if putting out a fleece is improper, why does it sometimes seem to work? The answer is that on some occasions the fleece that is chosen is really wisdom in disguise.

The distinguishing feature of this whole process is that *the decision maker chooses the circumstantial sign.* Now the person who chooses a bizarre fleece or a sign unrelated to the decision risks being fleeced. Here are two examples: "I will know God is telling me to change jobs if I see a 1957 automobile run a stop sign today"; "I will know God wants me to go to Bible school if the Detroit Tigers baseball team wins today." These fleeces range from improbable to a 50-50 chance of fulfillment. But a flip of a coin has the same degree of reliability. Decisions made on the basis of such circumstances are determined by chance.

But some fleeces often lead to good decisions in spite of themselves. These are the fleeces that reflect wisdom. Let's say, by way of illustration, that a church is considering a building project. The leadership puts out a fleece: "If 90 percent of the membership wants to build and is willing to sacrifice for the project, then God is telling us to build." All other things being equal, this is really wisdom under the guise of a fleece. It is wise and usually necessary for a church to postpone building until the members are united and consider it important enough to sacrifice.

Here is another fleece that would lead to a good decision. A man is thinking of selling his car and has determined that $2,000 would be a good, fair selling price. If the owner follows the traditional view, he might set up this fleece: "If someone offers me $2,000 or more for my car, I will take that as a positive sign that God wants me to sell it." If someone subsequently offered $2,000 for the car, he would sell it and the result would be a good decision. The reason that particular fleece might work is not because the practice itself is valid, but because the man was applying wisdom to his decision—even if he didn't think of it that way.

Let's look at that same situation from the perspective of the wisdom view. In this case the owner might say to himself: "I would like to sell my car. If I can't get at least $2,000 for it, I would be better off keeping it. So if someone offers me at least $2,000, I will sell it." Then he would pray for a buyer and advertise his car. This believer would be consciously seeking to manifest wisdom and good stewardship in his decision. But he would be under no illusions that he was getting a "sign" from God. If the car sold, he would thank God for giving him the wisdom to set a good price and for the provision of a buyer. Furthermore, if someone offered him $1,999, he would be able to accept the payment as "close enough" since the $2,000 figure was not a sign.

GOD'S SOVEREIGN WILL AND DECISION MAKING

1. God's sovereignty does not exclude the need for *planning*; it does require humble submission to His will.
2. *Circumstances* define the context of the decision and must be weighed by wisdom—not "read" to find God's individual will.
3. *Open doors* are God-given opportunities to be evaluated by wisdom—not divine commands.
4. "Putting out a fleece" is an invalid practice that occasionally works out well when it is really wisdom in disguise.

The Difference Is in the Attitude

In conclusion, the question we have been concerned with in this chapter is: What bearing does the sovereign will of God have on decision making? The answer has three parts:

1. Believers should make plans humbly, remembering that God is the final sovereign determiner of every plan.
2. Believers should trust the sovereign God to always work things together for good even though He does not reveal His sovereign plan ahead of time.
3. God is sovereign over open doors and the circumstances surrounding every decision. He requires us only to be moral and wise. He will secretly guide in everything else.

PRINCIPLES OF DECISION MAKING
THE WAY OF WISDOM

1. Where God commands, we must obey (chapter 8)
2. Where there is no command, God gives us freedom (and responsibility) to choose (chapter 9).
3. Where there is no command, God gives us wisdom to choose (chapters 10–11).
4. **When we have chosen what is moral and wise, we must trust the sovereign God to work all the details together for good (chapters 12–13).**

---

1. This approach is radically different from that taken by advocates of the traditional view. They assume that prior knowledge of God's individual will must inevitably result in success. So they caution against "running ahead of the Lord" in decision making. And, as we have noted, lack of success is interpreted as failure to discern God's will in the first place. But this is neither the paradigm nor the perspective adopted by the apostles. See my extended exposition of Paul's ministry plans in Romans 1 and 15 in chapter 14, "Guidance: A Biblical Model."
2. C. S. Lewis, *Christian Reflections* (Grand Rapids, MI: Wm. B. Eerdmans Publishing Co, 1967), 100, 110.
3. The meaning of "open door" in Revelation 3:8 is not clear. The verse speaks of an open door that the risen Lord placed before the Philadelphian church. It may refer to entrance into the messianic kingdom (see "the key of David" in 3:7). It may also refer to an open opportunity for effective missionary work.

4. In 2 Corinthians 2:13, Paul said, "I had no rest for my spirit…" The traditional view might argue that this was an instance where "lack of peace" was an indicator that it wasn't God's will to remain there. The passage itself neither says nor implies that conclusion. It wasn't a "lack of peace" that prompted Paul's decision as much as the circumstance of Titus's absence. In that situation, reconnecting with Titus and resolving the problem in Corinth was a higher priority than launching a new work in Troas. Paul's restlessness of spirit was produced by the difficulty of the circumstances, not an absence of leading from God (see the subheading "Disturbing the Peace" in chapter 7, "The Leading of the Holy Spirit").
5. John White, *The Fight* (Downers Grove, IL: InterVarsity Press, 1976), 165. White does not advocate putting out a fleece. In fact, his very next statement is, "Forget about fleeces. If you've never used them, don't start. If you have, then quit."
6. Matthew Henry, *An Exposition of the Old and New Testaments*, vol. 2, *Joshua to Esther* (London: James Nisbet, and Co., 1884), 163.
7. Two other Old Testament passages tell of believers employing circumstantial signs to determine God's specific leading. I discuss the first of these, Genesis 24, in detail in chapter 20, "Marriage and Wisdom." The process by which Abraham's servant selected a bride for Isaac was not normative then, and offers no support for utilizing fleeces now.

   The second passage is 1 Samuel 14:6–15. Though not normally cited by the traditional view in support of using fleeces, it appears to be an example of the method. In the narrative, Jonathan determined that if the Philistines invited him up to their battle site, he would take that as a sign that he should go up and fight them. They did and he did. The result was a great victory in which Jonathan killed twenty of the enemy (14:14) and an earthquake sent the Philistine army running. When the Israelites perceived the fear of the Philistines, they attacked and were victorious (14:15–30).

   As was the case with the selection of Isaac's bride, the explanation for this unusual incident lies in the nature of God's covenant with Israel. Israel's conflict with the Philistines is categorized as "holy war." In a holy war, God was fighting *His* enemies through the army of Israel: For such warfare, God customarily provided supernatural guidance for His earthly king through revelatory dreams, the Urim and Thummim, or a prophet (1 Samuel 28:6). When the army obeyed God's commands, victory was certain. In such cases, supernatural guidance was normative—as when Saul sought specific battle plans through the Urim and Thummim found in the ephod (14:36–37). Saul later employed lots—just as Joshua did to implicate Achan (Joshua 7:13–21)—to identify those who disobeyed his command to fast (1 Samuel 14:41–42).

   In this instance, however, Israel's king, Saul, was in a disobedient posture with God. By contrast, his son, Jonathan, loved and obeyed the Lord. In view of his father's disobedience, Jonathan went out with only his armor bearer to secretly fight for God. In this undertaking, Jonathan was cut off from the normal sources of supernatural guidance, for he had no prophet with him, and the Urim and Thummim in the ephod were with Saul (14:3). And if God revealed a plan to Saul through a dream, Jonathan had no way of learning it.

   Though cut off from the usual channels of divine guidance, Jonathan nevertheless thought that "perhaps" the Lord would work through him (14:6). In contrast to Gideon, Jonathan was motivated by courage, faith, and the desire to preserve God's honor. The great victory is evidence that the Lord consented to go along with Jonathan's unorthodox approach.
8. Because this incident occurred prior to the outpouring of the Spirit, and no further instruction appears in the Epistles validating the practice, most commentators agree that casting lots is not a valid means of discerning God's will. Some scholars debate whether

the choice of Matthias by that means was approved by God. In the first edition of this book, I sided with those who doubted the legitimacy of that action. Jesus had declared that in the Kingdom, the apostles would judge from "twelve thrones" (Matthew 19:28). While Matthias is never mentioned again as carrying out the apostolic office, Paul's claim to apostleship is well established.

But I have changed my view. I now agree that Matthias's selection by lot was legitimate. Luke's own evaluation is evident from his statement written years later that Matthias "was added to the eleven apostles" (Acts 1:26). When "many wonders and signs were taking place through the apostles" (Acts 2:43), there is no indication that Matthias was not included among them. These "signs of a true apostle" (2 Corinthians 12:12) prove his authenticity. And while it is true that Paul was added to the original apostles, he did not meet the requirements set out by Peter to be included among the original witnesses. Paul himself said that his apostleship was distinctive, as "one untimely born" (1 Corinthians 15:8). Only twelve thrones are mentioned by Christ (Matthew 19:28) and twelve foundation stones represent the twelve apostles in Revelation (21:14), but Paul might have been like the Levites. They were the thirteenth tribe without land. (See John R. W. Stott, *The Spirit, the Church, and the World: The Message of Acts* (Downers Grove, IL: InterVarsity Press, 1990), 57–59; Frank E. Gaebelein, gen. ed., *The Expositor's Bible Commentary,* vol. 9: "Acts," by Richard N. Longenecker (Grand Rapids, MI: Zondervan, 1981), 265–67).

9. I discuss casting of lots at greater length at the end of chapter 15, "Special Guidance and Decision Making."

chapter fourteen

GUIDANCE: A BIBLICAL MODEL

So far we have seen that Scripture uses "God's will" in two ways: God's *sovereign will* is His secret plan that works all things together for good. His *moral will* refers to all the commands in the Bible. On the other hand, we have set aside as scripturally invalid a third, commonly accepted concept—the *individual will* of God. As a result, we have discarded the idea that where the Bible does not command we must find another "will of God." Instead, we have shown that where there is no command, God provides freedom and wisdom to decide.

BIBLICAL GUIDANCE DEFINED

God truly guides, but finding an "individual will" outside of the Bible is not the means. *How then does the Holy Spirit lead or guide God's people?*

(This book needs an audio dimension—a drumroll! I have just

asked the question that this volume was written to answer. And this is the chapter where it all comes together. Cue the drumroll!)

God guides in the four specific ways defined below.

FOUR DISTINCTIVE WAYS GOD GUIDES

Moral Guidance: In moral areas God guides by scriptural commands.
Wisdom Guidance: Where there is no command, God gives freedom and wisdom sufficient for every decision.
Sovereign Guidance: God secretly guides by working all events together for the believer's good.
Special Guidance: In rare cases God may supernaturally reveal (by voice, angel, or dream) a divine command to a specific person.

When viewed from this perspective, God's guidance is abundant indeed! There is no decision which is not touched by His directing hand. Moral decisions are guided by biblical commands. When He gives no command, God gives wisdom. When there are facts or details that we cannot know, He secretly works by His sovereign superintendence.

Observing the four kinds of guidance produces a few further insights.

1. Faith in God's guidance is both active and passive. Seeking God's moral will and wisdom is active. Trusting God to be sovereign and to give special guidance when needed is passive.
2. God shows His personal care by guiding in every detail, but guides differently than the traditional view expects. God does not promise to tell us all the right decisions. He guides us as sons and daughters, not as robots.
3. The first three types of guidance are God's promised norms to be believed and expected. But special guidance is a maybe, not a promise. God knows when special guidance is called for. If it is not given, we should trust that it is not needed and move confidently ahead.

BIBLICAL GUIDANCE DESCRIBED

Sometimes concepts are better understood if they can be visualized. The following diagram represents one attempt to illustrate the relationships between the various aspects of God's will.[1] The circles (from the outside in) represent the sovereign will of God, the moral will of God, and the area of freedom within the moral will of God. The numbers represent distinct classes of action, attitude, or motive within those various spheres.

RELATIONSHIPS BETWEEN THE VARIOUS ASPECTS OF GOD'S WILL

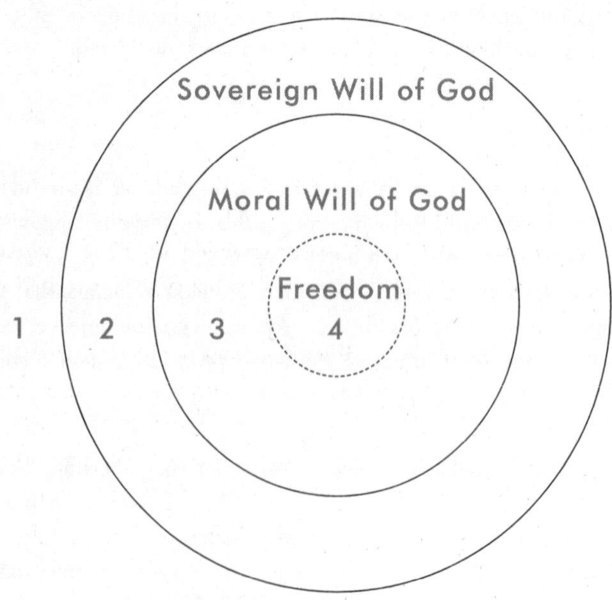

The largest circle represents the sovereign will of God. Outside of it (#1) are all events (whether sinful, moral, or free/noncommanded acts) that have not happened or will not happen. Inside of it (#2, 3, 4) are all events that have happened or will happen (Ephesians 1:11).

Category 1 includes potentially good actions that don't actually happen, such as the repentance that God desires of all men (2 Peter 3:9). It also includes potentially evil actions that don't happen, such as Abimelech's intention to take Sarah into his harem (Genesis 20:6). God's sovereign plan encompasses what actually takes place, though God knows the other possibilities that do not happen (1 Samuel 23:11–12; Matthew 11:21–24).

The circle inside the sovereign circle represents the moral will of God. All actions outside of that circle are sinful; all decisions within the circle are moral. So Category 2 includes all actual sinful actions. They are outside of God's moral will, but permitted within His sovereign will. The crucifixion of Christ was a heinous violation of God's moral will, but fulfilled God's sovereign plan (Matthew 26:24; Acts 2:23; 4:27–28).

Category 3 identifies any moral action that actually takes place. God's Word commanded it, and someone obeyed it (Joshua 11:15). An obedient response to special guidance also fits here. For instance, Philip obeyed a supernatural command from an angel (Acts 8:26–27).

The third, broken-lined circle marks out the area of freedom, which includes actions that are neither commanded nor forbidden by God (1 Corinthians 8:8). Sinful acts are excluded since the area of freedom is within the moral circle.

Category 4 indicates all decisions made with God-given freedom. They are within the moral will of God but are not commanded by God. Believers are free to marry, but not commanded to do so. When a believer does marry, it is a freely chosen act that happens as part of God's sovereign will.

When we consider the practical ramifications of the various types of guidance, we see that the believer's decision-making process is affected by each circle.

First, one asks, what bearing does God's sovereign will have on my decision? Negatively, we are reminded that God's sovereign will is *hidden*—it cannot be known in advance. It does not tell you what to do. Believers should read the Bible but not try to read providence. An open door is an opportunity, not a command from God.

God sovereignly superintends every circumstance showing that He cares personally for every detail and decision in your life (Luke 12:6–7). So, on the positive side, sovereign guidance should give a calm sense of security and peace that God is working all the details together for good. He helps us make choices that are moral and wise. And when circumstances are beyond our knowledge or control, we can confidently place them in His hands, knowing that they are under His control.

Second, the moral will of God has the most perceivable direct effect on our decisions. Every command that pleases God is included. Every goal, motive, attitude, and means is governed by God's moral will. Even when a decision falls within the area of freedom—such as the decision to marry—our motives, attitudes, and means must be pure.

Third, in noncommanded decisions made with God-given freedom, the goal of the believer is to choose the alternative that will best expedite and promote the revealed will and purposes of God. To accomplish that objective, we should seek for wisdom through the channels God has provided: prayer, Bible study, research, counselors, past experience, and personal reflection. The amount of time and energy invested in such a search should be in proportion to the importance of the decision (Ephesians 5:15–16). If one option is recognized as the most spiritually advantageous, it should be chosen. If two alternatives appear equally prudent, either may be selected.

We should be able to explain and defend our final decision on the basis of moral guidance ("God's Word says…") and wisdom guidance ("It seemed best…"). The decision should be in harmony with the moral will of God in all its details. Then the decision maker should demonstrate that the decision is spiritually advantageous for promoting God's moral will.

Finally, special guidance need not be sought, but must not be refused if it is given. Special guidance has not been promised and is infrequently provided. But if God sends an angel to give direct revelation for evangelism (as he did for Philip, Act 8:26), it would not be wise to tell God He can't do that anymore!

BIBLICAL GUIDANCE DEMONSTRATED

A significant and thorough application of these guidelines appears in Paul's Epistle to the Romans. This great theological treatise is so freighted with mind-boggling concepts, the present-day reader is apt to overlook the wealth of insight in the seemingly incidental comments at the letter's beginning and end. But if the Roman believers had been wondering about such practical matters as principles for decision making, this letter would have provided welcome instruction. That instruction was contained in Paul's explanation of his plans to visit them.

(If a writer is entitled to only one drumroll, then the narrative that follows deserves a fanfare. If the apostle Paul had deliberately set out to illustrate the principles elucidated in this book, he could not have done a better job. What you are about to read is nothing short of spine tingling. Cue the fanfare!)

> First, I thank my God through Jesus Christ for you all, because your faith is being proclaimed throughout the whole world. For God, whom I serve in my spirit in the preaching of the gospel of His Son, is my witness as to how unceasingly I make mention of you, always in my prayers making request, if perhaps now at last by the will of God I may succeed in coming to you. For I long to see you so that I may impart some spiritual gift to you, that you may be established; that is, that I may be encouraged together with you while among you, each of us by the other's faith, both yours and mine. I do not want you to be unaware, brethren, that often I have planned to come to you (and have been prevented so far) so that I may obtain some fruit among you also, even as among the rest of the Gentiles. (Romans 1:8–13)

Paul the Planner

The first thing the Romans would have noticed from Paul's explanation is the *appropriateness of making plans* (1:13). In contrast to the assumptions of the traditional view, Paul did not seek out the individual will of God. He did not consider it presumptuous to say, "often *I* have planned to come to you." His Roman readers may have known that on two or three occasions Paul had received special guidance about his geographic field of ministry (Acts 16:6–10); but no such revelation is mentioned here. God neither commanded Paul to go to Rome nor forbade such a journey.[2]

Second, Paul *prayed* about his plans (1:8–10). He asked that they might be accomplished. Apparently, Paul had made several plans to go to Rome (1:13), and he was asking the Lord to bring this one to pass, hopefully soon (1:10).

Third, through his prayers, Paul *submitted* himself and his plans to *God's sovereign will.* The wording of his petition reveals his conviction that if he ever made it to Rome, it would be "by the will of God" (1:10). To that point he had been "prevented" (1:13). And though he did not yet indicate the direct cause of the hindrance, it was clear that, as far as Paul was concerned, the ultimate cause was God's sovereign will. Accordingly, he was able to accept delay without undue frustration.

Ready...Aim...

The fourth thing the Romans would have noted is that Paul's plans were *based on spiritual goals.* Though not stated first, the goals were certainly established first. For the plans were formulated as means to achieve the goals.

And what were Paul's goals?

1. To provide spiritual ministry to the Roman believers (1:11)
2. To further establish and encourage the church in Rome (1:11–12)
3. To receive encouragement from them (1:12)
4. To win unbelievers to Christ (1:13–15)

Some believers in the Roman church might have wondered why Paul was planning to come to Rome rather than some other worthy destination where the same goals might be accomplished. If so, they had to wait until almost the end of the epistle to find out.

> And thus I aspired to preach the gospel, not where Christ was already named, so that I would not build on another man's foundation; but as it is written, "THEY WHO HAD NO NEWS OF HIM SHALL SEE, AND THEY WHO HAVE NOT HEARD SHALL UNDERSTAND." For this reason I have often been prevented from coming to you; but now, with no further place for me in these regions, and since I have had for many years a longing to come to you whenever I go to Spain—for I hope to see you in passing, and to be helped on my way there by you, when I have first enjoyed your company for a while—but now, I am going to Jerusalem serving the saints. For Macedonia and Achaia have been pleased to make a contribution for the poor among the saints in Jerusalem. Yes, they were pleased to do so, and they are indebted to them. For if the Gentiles have shared in their spiri-

> tual things, they are indebted to minister to them also in material things. Therefore, when I have finished this, and have put my seal on this fruit of theirs, I will go on by way of you to Spain. I know that when I come to you, I will come in the fullness of the blessing of Christ. (Romans 15:20–29)

"We're Number Four, We're Number Four"

Our Multnomah Bible College basketball team is used to winning the conference tournament. One year we lost in the semifinals and went to the consolation game. When we won that game handily, a group of students chanted, "We're number three! We're number three!" It was even worse for the Romans.

If Paul's initial explanation of his plans in chapter 1 generated a sense of excitement among the Roman Christians, these later details may have initially had the opposite effect. For what the Romans learned is that they were not at the top of Paul's priority list. Nor were they second. They weren't even third. They were fourth!

Paul had goals that were even broader and more ambitious than the ones he had stated earlier. While he had specific objectives for a visit to Rome, they were subordinate to the greater strategy of which they were but a part.

The fifth point that should not be lost on observers of Paul's decision making process is that Paul *arranged his spiritual goals according to priorities*. Since he did not know how much time he had, he determined which things needed to be accomplished first, and which projects could wait.

Paul, Your Priorities Are Showing

The immediate priority was to complete the task of evangelizing Greece. Ever since Jesus Christ commissioned Paul as "an apostle of Gentiles" (Romans 11:13), Paul followed a policy of taking the gospel to regions where people had never heard of Christ (2 Corinthians 10:16). In explaining this to the Romans (Romans 15:20–21), Paul mentioned again the hindrance that prevented his coming to them (15:22). In all likelihood, it was his unfinished work in Greece that had prevented his coming before now (15:23). It was just taking longer than he had expected to establish reproducing churches in that region. And Paul recognized the wisdom of finishing one job before moving on to another.

But now, it looked as if he would soon be able to move on to his second priority—a trip to Jerusalem (15:25).

"Wait a minute," thought the Romans readers, "Jerusalem is in the opposite direction!"

True. But it was number two on the list. Paul wanted to accompany the financial gift that the churches of Greece, Macedonia, and Asia Minor were sending to the beleaguered saints in Judea.[3] It is apparent from a number of New Testament references that Paul considered this gift to be highly significant. In Romans 15:27, he explained the gift from two perspectives: it was a gift of love ("they were pleased to do so"), and it was the down payment on a spiritual debt ("they are indebted to them").

Paul arranged his spiritual goals according to priorities.

But for Paul, the most important factor, the one that warranted his presence in Jerusalem, was that the gift symbolized the truth he had been declaring and defending: the unity of Jewish believers and Gentile believers in one body, the church (Ephesians 2:11–22). Paul could have found some burly deacons to assure that the money made it to Jerusalem safely. But he went himself because he anticipated that moment when he would deliver the money and say, "My fellow Jews, this generous gift comes to you with love from our Gentile brothers because we are all *one body*—aren't we." This wonderful "mystery" (Ephesians 3:1–10) would be experienced as well as taught.

Pit Stop—Rome

That accomplished, Paul would head west. To Rome? Well, yes. But ultimately to Spain. As Paul envisioned it, Rome was going to be a sort of pit stop on his journey to "the uttermost part of the earth." Paul now made it clear that he was hoping to raise his support for Spain while he was in Rome (Romans 15:24).

Was Spain more important to Paul than Rome? Probably. For Paul was the consummate missionary. Rome had the gospel; Spain did not. It was as simple as that. Did God command Paul to go to Spain? No, not specifically. He had told Paul that his primary ministry would be to the Gentiles (Acts 9:15; 26:17), and He had announced that He would send Paul "far away" to reach lost people (Acts 22:21). But it was Paul who made it his life goal to reach "all the Gentiles" (Romans 1:5; 2 Timothy 4:17). His plans were calculated, apart from special revelation, to reach the world in his lifetime.

Thus did Paul spell out his priorities: Greece, Jerusalem, Spain, and, in passing, Rome.

Paul knew that being transparent about his priorities might offend some shortsighted Roman believers. He valued mature believers and modeled decision making. But Paul withheld the full declaration of his plans until near the end of his epistle, after he had given his most complete exposition of the gospel and its far-reaching ramifications. It seems likely that, having learned of the glories of the gospel, the Roman church would have been eager to assist in the spread of this good news in any way possible.

The postscript to this discussion is that Paul did eventually make it to Jerusalem, Rome, and possibly even Spain, in that order. He did have to modify his plans somewhat along the way. For the two-year stopover in the Caesarean jail and the shipwreck at Malta had not been included in Paul's original projections. Nor did Paul just visit the Romans "in passing." His confinement under house arrest delayed his plans for westward advancement for at least two years.

On the plus side, Paul's transportation from Palestine to Rome was provided courtesy of Caesar, who also furnished a military escort for his protection. And Paul used the period of imprisonment to pen a major portion of what was to become the New Testament.

Because he responded properly to God's guidance in its various forms, Paul became a model of one who engaged in *long-range planning* on the one hand, and *snatched up present opportunities* on the other. Interruptions became occasions for personal growth and ministry. It is just such a balance that believers today should seek to maintain.

STEPS IN PAUL'S DECISION-MAKING PROCESS

- **Purposes:** Paul adopted spiritual goals that were based on divine revelation.
- **Priorities:** He arranged his goals into wise priorities determining what should be done first, second, third, and so on.
- **Plans:** Next, he devised a strategy for accomplishing his objectives.
- **Prayer:** Through prayer, he submitted himself and his plans to the sovereign will of God. (No doubt, he also prayed for wisdom in the formulation of his plans, though not mentioned in this context.)
- **Perseverance:** When providentially hindered from accomplishing his plans, he assumed that the delay was God's sovereign will. This conviction freed him from discouragement. Since his plans were sound, the only thing he adjusted was the timetable.
- **Presentation:** Paul explained his decisions on the basis of God's moral will and his personal application of wisdom.

frequently asked question

> *Question:* Our pastor recently presented his ministry plans. He has resigned to accept a position in another church. His explanation to the congregation sounded spiritual, but vague: "God is leading me to another ministry." I wonder what his real reasons were.

The brief, cryptic explanation has some advantages—to the minister. The biggest one is the implication that this was not a personal choice. "God is responsible, so direct any further questions to Him, not me."

But if you hide under the refreshment table at a pastors' conference, you will hear no such euphemisms. This same pastor will share with fellow shepherds the specific reasons not spelled out in the resignation letter. Most of what the eavesdropper will hear is not bitter complaint, but ministry wisdom—wisdom that is shared freely with other shepherds, but not the sheep.

Paul did not tell everything he knew, but he did reveal the spiritual reasons for his priorities. And so the Romans were given the privilege of watching mature decision making in action. With wisdom and care, spiritual leaders should do the same today.

---

1. This diagram is simpler than the one in the first edition. What I have discovered (after spending considerable time playing around with circles) is that, while it is technically possible to represent all of the permutations I could think of, the resulting diagram ends up resembling Ezekiel's vision of "the wheel in the middle of the wheel"—and is too complicated to be useful. Since this isn't divine revelation, I've opted for simplicity and clarity. (The reader is welcome to make his or her improvements on my diagram.)
2. Later, God did guarantee Paul's safe arrival in Rome, but that was well after the plans had been made and Paul was en route (Acts 23:11; 27:23–24). From the outset, the idea and the plan were Paul's (Acts 19:21, where "spirit" is best understood as human spirit; Romans 1:13; 15:22–29).
3. Some commentators conclude that Paul's decision to go to Jerusalem was an act of disobedience to the clear guidance of God. The main reason for this position is Acts 21:4: "And after looking up the disciples, we stayed there seven days; and they kept telling Paul through the Spirit not to set foot in Jerusalem." This verse describes what happened in Tyre on Paul's journey to Jerusalem. Was Paul disobedient to continue?

   There is no hint of any disobedience in Romans 1 or 15. Nor is there any other comment in the book of Acts that shows Paul in defiance of divine guidance. Apart from Acts 21:4, Luke seems favorable in his comments.

   It is best to consider the Jerusalem trip as free of disobedience but full of risk to Paul. The trip itself was the result of Paul's planning after leaving Ephesus on his third journey. He "purposed in the [s]pirit to go to Jerusalem" (Acts 19:21). This is best understood as Paul's human spirit since the text gives no evidence of direct revelation from the Holy Spirit, and Romans 1 and 15 describe it as Paul's spiritual planning. The NIV captures this meaning when it says "Paul *decided* to go to Jerusalem." At the end of the third journey, Paul hurried past Ephesus to try to get to Jerusalem by Pentecost (Acts 20:16). In his human spirit he had made a firm decision that he would make this trip (Acts 20:22).

   However, all along the way to Jerusalem the Spirit spoke through prophets revealing that "bonds and afflictions" awaited him in Jerusalem (Acts 20:23). This happened in

Tyre (Acts 21:4–5) as well as Caesarea (Acts 21:10–14). The fullest account of how the warnings came to Paul comes in Caesarea with the prophet Agabus. He took Paul's belt, bound his own feet and hands, and said, "This is what the Holy Spirit says: 'In this way the Jews at Jerusalem will bind the man who owns this belt and deliver him into the hands of the Gentiles'"(Acts 21:11).

At this prophecy Paul's companions and local residents urged him to cancel his trip to Jerusalem. Paul answered them and their fears by saying, "What are you doing, weeping and breaking my heart? For I am ready not only to be bound, but even to die at Jerusalem for the name of the Lord Jesus" (Acts 21:13). When further persuasion failed to dissuade Paul, they committed the matter to the sovereign God and quietly said, "The will of the Lord be done!" (Acts 21:14).

Soon after Paul arrived in Jerusalem the prophecy was fulfilled. God's word to Paul after his arrest and the uproar before the Jewish council was, "Take courage; for as you have solemnly witnessed to My cause at Jerusalem, so you must witness at Rome also" (Acts 23:11).

The majority of the evidence supports the view that Paul was not disobedient to God's guidance. The trip itself was neither commanded nor forbidden. Paul could make the trip within the moral will of God if he considered it spiritually advantageous. Paul had good reason for going since he desired to accompany the Gentile gift to needy Jewish believers. Furthermore, Paul wanted to testify once more to his unbelieving countrymen.

The prophecies were warnings of what would happen if he went, not commands prohibiting the trip. This is best seen in the most complete description of the warnings at Caesarea through Agabus. The prophecy predicted but did not forbid. Paul's decision was courageous, not sinful. The efforts of his friends to dissuade him were loving, not sinful. This turned out to be a conflict of values. His friends were concerned for his safety; Paul's priority was mission.

This interpretation is even stronger if "spirit" in Acts 19:21 and 20:22 is translated [Holy] Spirit rather than Paul's human spirit (as in NIV and elsewhere). If the Holy Spirit is meant, then God gave Paul direct revelation to go, in addition to revealing that he would be bound when he arrived. However, if the Holy Spirit was directing Paul to Jerusalem (20:22), why would the people object (21:12)? And why didn't Paul counter that his trip was by divine command (21:13)? It appears more likely that Paul's human spirit is in view because the decision is described in human terms in Romans 1:10–15 and 15:22–29.

That said, I would add that this conclusion is not required by the wisdom view. A proponent of the wisdom view of guidance could conclude that Paul was being disobedient and still be consistent. And a proponent of the traditional view may also hold to either view of the Jerusalem trip and be consistent with his view of guidance.

chapter fifteen

SPECIAL GUIDANCE AND DECISION MAKING

Since the initial publication of *Decision Making and the Will of God*, a significant percentage of reader inquiries have probed the subject of special guidance. In response, this entire chapter is devoted to these frequently asked questions.

> *Question:* In your principles of decision making according to the way of wisdom, you describe how the believer should respond to God's moral guidance, wisdom guidance, and sovereign guidance. Why is there no similar principle for God's *special* guidance?

There is debate among evangelical leaders whether God gives supernatural guidance today in the same ways that He occasionally did during the biblical era. I see nothing in Scripture that would prevent Him from doing so. And so, as I indicated earlier, it is inappropriate for the believer to be closed off to such guidance out of hand. But even in the biblical record, special guidance is rare. Since principles of decision making attempt to summarize the believer's normative experience, I see no guidelines emerging from the text that ought to be applied in the routine business of decision making.

Having said that, any comprehensive theology of guidance must respond to the fact that God has provided special direction to specific people from time to time. And readers' questions call for a more thorough analysis of the Bible's teaching on this subject.

Pillar and Prophets

Perhaps the place to begin is with some examples. In the Old Testament, the *pillar of cloud* gave supernatural guidance that was perfectly clear (Numbers 9:15–23). It told the Israelites when to move, which direction to go, and where to stop. It led one generation from Egypt to Canaan. But when the faithful generation entered the promised land, that guidance ceased. God chose when it was needed and removed it when its purpose was accomplished.

The *prophets* of the Old Testament received direct revelation, and they are prefigured in Moses. God gave him divine directions through the burning bush (Exodus 3). The unquenched flame was miraculous and the divine voice from the bush was undistorted, but Moses wondered how the Israelites would know that God had sent him. They did not see the bush or hear the voice. God gave Moses three miraculous signs so the people would know that the command to leave Egypt with Moses was truly divine: the ability to change his rod into a serpent (and back), to make his hand leprous (and whole again), and to turn the water of the Nile to blood (Exodus 4:1–9). God's instructions for His people, supernaturally confirmed, were clear to Moses and equally clear to those who heard him (Exodus 4:30–31).

The pattern displayed in Moses was spelled out in the tests for true prophets. How would Israel know if a self-proclaimed prophet truly spoke for Yahweh? He must come in the name of the Lord, his message must harmonize with God's earlier revelation about Himself, and the message must be confirmed by fulfilled prophecy or other miraculous sign (Deuteronomy 13:1–5; 18:20–22). A prophet without a miraculous sign could not even begin to compete with false prophets from Satan who were often endowed with impressive abilities (Exodus 7:11–12).

But possessing such power by itself was insufficient; for Satan could deceive people with counterfeit supernatural power. So the second test of true doctrine was needed. Satan does not give a true miracle and a message of the true gospel to his prophets. This would only divide and ruin his kingdom (Matthew 12:26).

We find in the New Testament that God again gave prophets to His people (Ephesians 4:11). Our best example is Agabus who is called a prophet because of his predictive accuracy (Acts 11:28). He speaks like a prophet with divine authority, "This is what the Holy Spirit says" (Acts 21:11), and his prophecy is fulfilled accurately in the life of Paul (Acts 21:31–36). The example of Agabus confirms that when New Testament writers used the word *prophet,* they intended to convey a continuity with their Old Testament counterparts (the same Greek word for prophet is used for Agabus as is used of Old Testament prophets when they are mentioned in the New Testament).

Angelic Voices

Other instances of supernatural guidance are recorded in the book of Acts. In chapter 5 the apostles were jailed by the jealous high priest (5:17). During the night an *angel* of the Lord opened the prison gates and led them out (5:19). He told them to go to the temple and speak "the whole message of this Life" (5:20). This was not a frivolous miracle. The eyewitnesses of the resurrection were enabled to carry out part of the great commission by miraculous help and direction. This miracle reminds us that the purpose behind most of the miracles was to further the gospel. I don't believe every secondhand "missionary legend" I hear of miraculous episodes today. But it makes sense that when God does such miracles, it will advance the progress of the gospel.

Philip, too, received special guidance from a heavenly messenger. He had been preaching the gospel in "many villages" (Acts 8:25) when he was directed from the beaten to the unbeaten path. An "angel of the Lord" told Philip to go south to a desert road (Acts 8:26), where he met a true seeker who had come from Ethiopia to worship in Jerusalem. This was supernatural guidance and again it was for the great commission.

God's guidance through His Scriptures and wisdom is normally fully sufficient. If more is ever needed for guiding the believer, He will take the initiative and give further direct miraculous guidance.

The Macedonian Call

Another means of special guidance is the revelatory *vision* such as the one Paul received directing him to Macedonia (Acts 16:9–10). The divine nature of this vision should not be downplayed. It was not merely a good and wise idea. It was not a committee's "vision statement." It was not a figurative way of saying that a Macedonian brother came and asked for Paul's help. It was not an impression in Paul's heart. It was a miraculous revelation from God that had His authority and had to be obeyed: "When he had seen the vision, immediately we sought to go into Macedonia, concluding that God had called us to preach the gospel to them" (Acts 16:10).

As a Bible teacher, I am often asked, "How often does supernatural guidance occur?" The answer is simple, sort of: God gives supernatural guidance as often as He sovereignly decides to do it. If you tell God He can't do it today, you're going beyond what is written. If you tell Him He must speak often, that also goes beyond what is written. What we can say is that bona fide instances of special guidance have been rare—even for the apostles. The Macedonian vision, for instance, was an anomaly within the context of Paul's second missionary journey. Unlike the first venture, which was mandated by the Holy Spirit (Acts 13:2), this one was initiated by Paul: "Let us return and visit the brethren in every city in which we proclaimed the word of the Lord, and see how they are" (Acts 15:36). It was an appropriate decision based on obedience to the Great Commission plus wisdom. Modern-day missionaries do not need a Macedonian call to take the gospel out. Like Paul, they have the Great Commission. Like Paul, they can say of a mission plan, "We thought it best" (1 Thessalonians 3:1). If further guidance is needed, God can sovereignly break in at His initiative, just as He did with Paul. But if He does, there will be no doubt about it.

In all of these instances of special guidance, the area of freedom was reduced for the recipient and the moral will of God was expanded: where God commands, we must obey. When the Spirit gave direct supernatural guidance to the church of Antioch, it became the moral will of God for them. Restricting the ministry of Saul and Barnabas to Antioch would have been disobedience (Acts 13:1–2). Until the angel appeared to Philip, he was free to preach the gospel wherever there was opportunity. The angelic directive replaced that freedom with an assignment. Likewise, the Macedonian vision reduced Paul's options for travel to a single destination (Acts 16:10). Asia or Bithynia were placed outside of God's moral will (Acts 16:6–7).

But such special guidance does not constitute an addition to the Scriptures. God's superintendence of the canon determined what revelation is normative for all generations of believers. Paul had other revelations (2 Corinthians 12:1–3) that are not included in the canon. Only a few words of Agabus's prophecies are included in Luke's account, but the rest were true prophecy. We have no record of the words of the prophets who were in Rome (Romans 12:6), Ephesus (Ephesians 4:11), or Corinth (1 Corinthians 14). The coming witnesses or prophets in Revelation 11 will not open the canon even though they are true prophets and speak with divine authority (Revelation 11:1–13). If God does give supernatural revelation and guidance today, it will be authoritative only for those to whom it was given, but will not be part of the canon as authoritative revelation for all believers.

To summarize, this survey of special guidance in the Bible shows us the following truths.

SPECIAL OR SUPERNATURAL GUIDANCE

1. God's moral, wisdom, and sovereign guidance are normally sufficient. God does not promise, but may give special revelation for guidance when He sovereignly chooses.
2. Revelation is God supernaturally transferring His thoughts accurately to another.
3. Revelation has divine authority and must be believed and obeyed.
4. Special guidance by revelation is self-evident because it is supernaturally confirmed and in harmony with the Scriptures.
5. Most often, special guidance is given to enhance evangelism.
6. If God gives special guidance, the recipient's freedom is reduced and God's moral will is enlarged for that individual.
7. Supernatural guidance will not add to the canon of Scripture, which was closed with the passing of the apostles.

> *Question:* God gave special guidance through prophets in both the Old and New Testaments. So when men and women claim to issue prophetic pronouncements today, what are we to make of that?

One novel suggestion involves a redefinition of the word *prophet.*[1] This view maintains that in the New Testament, only an apostle received the same level of supernatural revelation as an Old Testament prophet. God's communication to and through other prophets was (and is) less precise and hence fallible. So a modern-day "prophet" cannot declare, "Thus saith the Lord." Instead, he or she should say, "I sense that God may be revealing something to me. Listen and see if you perceive that this is God's revelation to you." (Interestingly, Agabus is cited as an example of a "fallible" prophet whose predictions fell short of being perfectly accurate.)[2]

But the argument for this position is unconvincing. One purpose of predictive prophecy is to inform people about something that is going to happen *before* it happens. But it is hard to see how this is accomplished by a fallible prophecy. How could you know ahead of time if such a message "sensed" by a prophet is from God? You can't. If it comes true, it will be said that it was from God. If it proves false, it will be chalked up to human error. I call that "nonauthoritative prophecy." But who isn't a prophet in that watered-down sense? Everyone has received an impression that might be true or might be false, but we don't know ahead of time. But it is unacceptable to say your impression was from God when you are proved right and excusable as human error when you are wrong. A prophecy that isn't certain before it happens is singularly unhelpful. It is, by definition, not a prophecy at all.

On the other hand, many who make prophetic pronouncements maintain that their message has the status of revelation from God. A Christian man in Portland, Oregon, said God had given him a divine message. He predicted a terrible earthquake in Portland on a particular date. He claimed God had directed believers to leave the city to spare their lives and then return to help the injured. Those who knew this believer said he was godly and sincere. On the eve of the predicted catastrophe, I went to bed and slept like a baby. The next morning Portland still had too much rain for my tastes, but everything else was intact.

Why did I not take this sincere man's prediction seriously? Neither he nor his "prophecy" were heretical. But the pronouncement lacked the requisite confirming sign. His prediction did not contradict the Bible, but he never gave evidence of supernatural connections. Moses did not say, "I saw a burning bush and that should be good enough for you." God gave him signs so that there was no question (Exodus 4:1–9).

Let me boldly state the obvious: If you are not sure whether you heard directly from God, you didn't. If you had, it would not only be crystal clear to you, but God would also supernaturally supply you with ways to confirm that message to others.[3] Both tests are necessary. If the miraculous sign is absent, you will always be uncertain. The test of harmony with Scripture is necessary, but it is not enough. The scriptural test will keep you from heresy, but it will not keep you from stupidity.

Let me boldly state the obvious: If you are not sure whether you heard directly from God, you didn't.

A man I know from the signs and wonders movement pressed me on this. He argued that if you felt an impression might be from God, you had better obey it so that you would not risk missing God's word to you. Do you see the problem? You don't know for sure if impression "A" is from God, but it might be. You can't ignore it because if it is from God, you will be guilty of not acting on God's word to you. The answer to this dilemma is simple. God makes sure this situation cannot occur. God's supernatural voice is not uncertain. It is not a guessing game. If you think some impressions are God's revelation and some are not, you will be left guessing forever. The supernatural element of true revelation plus the test of true doctrine will always make it miraculously clear.

> *Question:* So how do you respond in a private conversation when a friend says, "God told me to do thus and such," or "I felt led by the Spirit to do thus and such"?

Such statements can put me in an awkward situation. It's not my job to be continually "correcting" everyone else's theology. So if the thing my friend feels led to do appears harmless or is really wisdom in disguise, I usually don't say anything about their "leading." If, on the other hand, the perceived guidance appears foolish, I might raise questions to provoke reconsideration of the plan and a better understanding of how God guides.

I do think we need to use our terminology carefully. *The traditional view has inadvertently invented a new category of revelation and authority.* Special guidance, if it occurs, is supernatural revelation and has authority over the believer. The moral will of God is likewise supernatural revelation and we must obey it. The moral will of God includes the command to be wise. *But inner impressions are not supernatural revelation, nor are they authoritative.* They may be insightful and valuable, but they do not rise to the level of divine authority.

So it is inappropriate to apply the vocabulary of revelation (whether scriptural guidance or special guidance) to inner impressions. The use of phrases such as "from the Holy Spirit," "God told me," "God showed/revealed to me," "impression from the Spirit," and "I must obey God" is (unintentionally) misleading. This is not just a matter of imprecision. It causes confusion in the minds of believers and creates the expectation that all Christians should be receiving these messages.

So when someone says, "God told me in my heart," if it seems appropriate, I will ask him precisely what he means. "Did you receive supernatural revelation? Do you mean that you are applying God's moral will to your situation?" If he means neither of these, he is assuming a third category that is self-contradictory. "Authoritative nonrevelation" is an oxymoron.

Impressions can be very useful—a point I develop at length in the following chapter ("Making a Good Thing Better"). They often reflect godly and wise ideas and motivations. But their valuable character can be tapped only when they are recognized as not being revelation and not having authority. Once this is understood, we are free to test impressions by legitimate authority and ask, "Is the impression moral and is it wise?" These questions show there is an authority over impressions that can help us discern which ones are most valuable for best serving God.

Question: Is it ever appropriate to "cast lots" to make a decision?

It may surprise some readers that my answer to this question is a qualified yes. Again, we need to look at the biblical material. But first a brief definition. The Bible speaks of casting lots when an impartial, random means is used to decide something. In our culture, we would flip a coin, toss dice, or draw straws. The results indicate a "yes" or "no" answer.

The biblical examples of casting lots fall into two categories. The first is the use of lots to make an *impartial choice* when more than one candidate was qualified. Lots were cast to select those who would supply wood (Nehemiah 10:34), to identify those who would populate Jerusalem (Nehemiah 11:1), to divide up the land (Joshua 14:2), and to determine who would offer the incense when there were more than enough priests (Luke 1:9). Even when the lot method was used for fairness, God was sovereignly in control of the outcome (Proverbs 16:33). But this was never taken to mean that God was indicating that only one choice was right. Lots were used because multiple options were equally valid (Proverbs 18:18) and an impartial choice needed to be made.

The second category is the use of lots to obtain *supernatural guidance*. The lot tossed by the pagan sailors fell upon Jonah identifying him as the guilty one (Jonah 1:7). The lot exposed Achan as the one who violated the ban on Jericho, and the stolen booty was found in his tent (Joshua 7:14–26). The lot fell on Jonathan, and through him Saul's foolish oath was canceled (1 Samuel 14:41–42). The lot selected Saul to be king (1 Samuel 10:20–21)—a choice confirmed by God's direct word to find him hiding in the baggage (10:22–24).

In the New Testament, the apostles cast lots to ascertain the Lord's choice between two candidates deemed qualified to replace Judas the defector (Acts 1:24–26). For a variety of reasons, I believe that God approved this action and that Matthias served as a legitimate apostle alongside the other eleven.[4] But I also agree with those scholars who claim this was the last valid use of lots to obtain special guidance from God.

The inappropriateness of this practice is well illustrated by author George Eliot's hapless weaver, Silas Marner. When his church drew lots to determine the thief of the congregation's funds, his guilt was wrongly substantiated, with disastrous consequences: He was excommunicated from the group and he renounced his faith.

One summer while teaching at Singapore Bible College, I found myself kneeling in a busy street with a young boy and his missionary father. We were about to enter the pagan temple of Kuan Yin, and the father wanted to emphasize that we were about to enter enemy territory. This so-called goddess claims to give divine answers to worshippers' questions. Inside we saw people bow down and secretly ask Kuan Yin a question. After prayer they took a canister filled with foot-long thin sticks. They rocked the canister and lowered its opening until one stick worked its way out. Then a block of wood with a *yes* and *no* side was flipped. If it landed on *yes* they had the right stick. No miracle, no voice, nothing but a stick with a number on it. The stick was taken to a booth and exchanged for a numbered message, and supposedly Kuan Yin had answered their question. The indecisive inquirer now knew exactly what to do!

Biblical lots were never like this. They had miraculous confirmation. Without such corroboration one is deciding by chance. There is no reason to try to read divine messages into providential happenings.

To return to the question, then, the first category of using lots remains valid. If you are looking for an impartial way to choose between two equal options or to avoid dispute, flipping a coin still seems appropriate wisdom (Proverbs 18:18). But there is no evidence that we can use lots today to discern supernatural guidance. There are no examples or instruction advocating this practice after Pentecost, nor are lots confirmed by supernatural evidence as they were in the Old Testament episodes.

I knew a couple who could not agree on whether to have another child. They were both firm in their differing views of what God wanted. They decided to cast a lot (actually flip a coin) and take the result as God's answer for what He wanted them to do. "Heads, we add to the quiver. Tails, we have had our last child." They flipped. It was tails—no baby.

Uncertain of the validity of this leading from God, they asked me what I thought. (They were not substituting me for the Almighty, but I had written a book on the subject.) Did their coin flip convey God's answer for them? I ruined their tranquillity. My answer was a definite *maybe*. I think it is valid to settle a difference by flipping a coin and sticking with the result. I also think God is sovereign over coin tosses (Proverbs 16:33) and will work things together for good. On the other hand, if they thought God had made His divine moral desire known through the back side of a coin, I disagreed. God was not saying another child was "against His will" by the way the coin landed. Nor does a coin have any inherent wisdom by the way it lands. Such methods should be used only to help settle differences in an impartial manner where truth and wisdom show that the choices are equal.

1. Wayne Grudem, "Why Christians Can Still Prophesy," *Christianity Today*, September 16, 1988; Wayne Grudem, *The Gift of Prophecy in 1 Corinthians* (Lanham, MD: University Press of America, 1982).
2. Grudem argues that Agabus erred when he said that the Jews would bind Paul, when it was actually the Romans who did it (Acts 21:30–36). Plausible explanations for this apparent discrepancy have been around for a long time. Peter said that the Jews killed Jesus (Acts 3:15; 4:10), but it was really the Romans, wasn't it (Acts 2:23)? Both Peter and Agabus were pointing to the catalyst behind the action and the Jews were the reason that the Romans killed Jesus and bound Paul. In addition, it is also possible that the Jews did actually bind Paul before he was rescued by the Romans and arrested.
3. Once a prophet has been supernaturally confirmed, he does not need to do a miracle each time he prophesies. But apart from that initial authentication, he would never be considered a prophet. Moses was given three signs, but did not perform a confirming miracle every time he came down from the mountain.
4. See the discussion of this incident in endnote 8 of chapter 13, "God's Sovereign Will and Decision Making."

chapter sixteen

MAKING A GOOD THING BETTER

In a formal debate, the two sides—affirmative and negative—are arrayed against each other. The assignment of both teams is to make their case by pressing the merits of their position while exposing the weaknesses of the opposition. Because the thesis of this book has been set out as "an alternative to the traditional view," I have often found myself in a kind of attack mode. In the quest for an accurate understanding and application of biblical truth, I have had to be thorough in my critique of the interpretive foundations and practical consequences of the traditional view.

Having completed that task, I am now in the position to acknowledge a real-world fact: the traditional view has served many believers well in making decisions that are pleasing to God. This is so for a couple of reasons. First, the traditional view rightly insists that all decisions must conform to the moral will of God. The Lord has promised to bless obedience to His Word. So decisions that promote such obedience are profitable.

The second factor behind many of the practical successes of the traditional framework is the maturity and wisdom of those applying it.

When wise people search for God's ideal will, what they usually find and apply is wisdom. Wisdom by any other name still makes good decisions.

As good as the traditional view is, *it is not good enough*. The flaws I've highlighted in this book produce predictable problems that range from frustration to heartache. The way of wisdom not only exposes the weaknesses of the traditional view, but brings needed correction, both in doctrinal accuracy and practical application. In part 2, "The Case of the Missing Dot," we critiqued the biblical and experiential deficiencies of the traditional view. In this chapter we will revisit those weaknesses and see how the way of wisdom provides the needed correctives.

RESOLVING INTERPRETIVE DIFFICULTIES

As we observed in chapter 3, "Does God Have Three Wills?" the traditional view encounters a major problem when it appeals to *biblical examples* for evidence of an individual will of God. For the historical illustrations say too much, and the statements of doctrine say too little.

Historical examples, such as Paul's "Macedonian call," are instances of supernatural revelation. This goes beyond what the traditional view promises in guidance. And while the general statements in the Epistles speak of being led by the Holy Spirit, they say nothing about God revealing His will to the heart of the believer on each decision. These promises are more general than what the traditional view promises.

The way of wisdom is not compelled to either water down or spice up the biblical record. The incidents of divine revelation are recognized as being supernatural provisions in exceptional circumstances. And the general promises of guidance into God's moral will are accepted and appreciated for what they are—provisions of guidance mediated through God's revealed Word.

The same situation exists with *biblical teaching*. In chapter 4, "Does Scripture Teach the Dot?" we saw that the concept of an individual will is not required by the text. In most instances, God's moral will is clearly intended. The traditional view lacks a single, definitive proof text. The wisdom view, on the other hand, emerges out of a thorough, natural interpretation of the biblical record.

RESOLVING APPLICATIONAL DIFFICULTIES

In chapters 5 and 6, we identified four experiential flaws in the traditional view. The way of wisdom resolves each of these difficulties.

APPLICATIONAL DIFFICULTIES OF THE TRADITIONAL VIEW

1. *Ordinary Decisions:* The traditional view must be abandoned in making the minor decisions of life.
2. *Equal Options:* The traditional view must deny equal options, generating anxiety over missing the dot.
3. *Immaturity:* The logic of the traditional view promotes immature approaches to decision making.
4. *Subjectivity:* Certainty of God's individual will is impossible without an objective source of knowledge.

An Unneeded Dichotomy Dissolved

In practice, those who follow the traditional view find they simply don't have time to conscientiously seek God's will for every decision. If they tried, it would take all day just to get dressed. And so they reserve the prescribed decision-making process for "significant" matters. In ordinary decisions, they try to exercise good judgment, without wasting time.

This pragmatic necessity results in an experiential dichotomy between the "big" and "little" decisions of life. The traditional view consistently maintains that God's individual will applies to every detail of our lives. But in practice, the theology is selectively discarded, being too cumbersome for the demands of real life.

The wisdom view teaches what the traditional view is forced to practice for ordinary decisions—good judgment. But it also takes the same approach to the more important matters. Whatever the decision, the criteria are the same: What is moral and what is wise? Those factors are equally relevant to my choice of a menu and my choice of a spouse.

Wisdom does not deny that some decisions are more significant than others. On the contrary, wisdom recognizes that the more important a decision is, the more time and energy should be devoted to it. Insignificant decisions should be made quickly. Such an approach makes good use of time, an important element in walking in wisdom (Ephesians 5:15–17).

APPLICATIONAL SOLUTIONS OF THE WISDOM VIEW

	Traditional View	Way of Wisdom
Ordinary Decisions:	The decision-making process must be abandoned in the minor decisions of life.	**We should exercise good judgment and not waste time.**

Equal=Equal

As long as the traditional view has to find the dot, the center of God's will, it must maintain that in any given decision, there can be only one correct choice. That rules out the possibility of equal options. When you are able to recognize the superiority of one alternative among several, there is no problem. But when two or more possibilities show the same degree of promise, and no clear winner emerges, the anxiety level begins to climb.

The wisdom view eliminates that tension. In noncommanded decisions, we can say, "six of one, half dozen of the other." And we have the theology to back it up. It really doesn't matter which shoe you put on first. If you're ambidextrous, use either hand.

In the area of freedom, equal options are more likely than not. Realizing that enables us to be grateful when God, in His sovereign grace, opens two or more doors of opportunity. The choice may not be any easier (a decision still must be made), but we don't have to worry about "missing the dot." When alternatives that are equally wise appear within the moral will of God, that is a no-lose situation. The believer can make his choice with the full confidence that God will work out His purposes through whichever decision he makes!

APPLICATIONAL SOLUTIONS OF THE WISDOM VIEW		
	Traditional View	Way of Wisdom
Ordinary Decisions:	The decision-making process must be abandoned in the minor decisions of life.	We should exercise good judgment and not waste time.
Equal Options:	Insistence upon only one correct choice generates anxiety over "missing the dot" rather than gratitude for more than one fine opportunity.	**We should thank God for the opportunity to select from equally acceptable alternatives, and choose our personal preference.**

Immaturity Exposed

The traditional view is unable to account for the fact that immature Christians tend to make immature decisions while more mature believers usually show greater wisdom in their decisions. The traditional position maintains that God's individual will is perfect; it also holds that this perfect will is fully available to each Christian regardless of his level of growth.

The wisdom view better corresponds to reality. It recognizes that wisdom is gained progressively. God has not promised to whisper perfect plans or omniscience into the mind of any believer who asks. Accordingly, the apostles counseled that when a decision is required, those who are "full of…wisdom" (Acts 6:3) and "prudent" (1 Timothy 3:2) will do the best job. The church has not been told to choose as leaders those who are best at picking up and decoding inner impressions, but those who are mature and wise (1 Corinthians 6:5).

Not only is the traditional view unable to account for an "immature will of God," it actually tends to promote immature approaches to decision making in certain circumstances. In chapter 5, "More Doubts About the Dot," we identified six ways this happens.

THE TRADITIONAL VIEW PROMOTES IMMATURE DECISIONS

1. By permitting justification of unwise decisions on grounds that "God told me"
2. By fostering costly delays because of uncertainty of God's individual will
3. By influencing the rejection of personal preferences when facing equal options
4. By encouraging putting out a fleece and letting circumstances dictate
5. By giving young believers confidence that they can make perfect decisions (apart from mature counsel) if they are sincere
6. By inadvertently moving believers to misuse their Bibles to get needed guidance

The way of wisdom provides the needed corrective to each of these improper approaches.

First, since the way of wisdom requires the believer to defend his decisions with sound reasons, he is not permitted to hide his motives behind a vague "the Lord led me." If the decision in question is reckless or foolhardy, a more mature believer has a basis for counseling his brother. By gently exposing the fallacies in the foolish plan, he can direct the less mature believer away from potentially harmful consequences. He can do that because he is not intimidated by any "final word" that supposedly came from the Lord.

Furthermore, a mature Christian's explanation of the reasons behind a decision can become an occasion of training and growth for others. For when younger believers watch a godly person work through a complex problem, the process of seeking wisdom is modeled for them. That's one reason I am so thankful for the numerous explanations the apostle Paul gave for his decisions.

Second, where the follower of the traditional view might waste valuable time seeking an unmistakable message from the Lord, the wisdom view encourages decisiveness. For one of the prime characteristics of a wise decision is good use of time, as we have already established. The decision maker should allow adequate time to gather facts and acquire wisdom, but there is no need to wait for some inner signal to proceed.

Third, where a person using the traditional view might choose the less appealing of two equal options (to guard against self-centeredness), the one who follows the way of wisdom will probably do just the opposite. For he understands that, all other things being equal, he is perfectly free to choose the alternative he prefers (1 Corinthians 7:39–40). In fact, wisdom recognizes that following our personal inclinations will make it easier to carry out the decision with eagerness and gratitude, attitudes that are part of God's moral will (Colossians 3:17, 23).

> One of the prime characteristics of a wise decision is good use of time.

Fourth, rather than putting out a fleece and expecting God to reveal His plan circumstantially, the believer using the way of wisdom carefully evaluates possible outcomes and considers their potential side effects on the decision. The decision maker who is seeking wisdom determines which circumstances would render a given option wise and which ones would make it unwise. But he would not view those circumstances as a message from the Lord.

Fifth, while the theology of the traditional view might give immature believers undue confidence that they can find God's will by listening to the inner impressions of their heart, the way of wisdom counsels them to seek the advice of mature believers on important decisions.

Finally, the way of wisdom challenges any inclination (inadvertently encouraged by the traditional view) for an immature Christian to use his Bible as a "divining rod" to determine God's individual will. The "close your eyes and point to a verse" approach is corrected by an insistence that God's moral will is learned by applying accepted principles of interpretation to biblical passages in their context.

APPLICATIONAL SOLUTIONS OF THE WISDOM VIEW		
	Traditional View	**Way of Wisdom**
Ordinary Decisions:	The decision-making process must be abandoned in the minor decisions of life.	We should exercise good judgment and not waste time.
Equal Options:	Insistence upon only one correct choice generates anxiety over "missing the dot" rather than gratitude for more than one fine opportunity.	We should thank God for the opportunity to select from equally acceptable alternatives, and choose our personal preference.
Immaturity:	In some instances, the logic of the traditional view tends to promote immature approaches to decision making.	**We should apply maturity by gathering and evaluating data, devoting sufficient time to the process, giving personal desires their proper place, seeking mature counsel, rightly using Scripture, and basing the decision on sound reasons.**

The Goliath of Subjectivity

The way of wisdom also eliminates the major applicational difficulty of the traditional view—subjectivity. In chapter 6, "Impressions Are Impressions," we saw how subjectivity permeates the traditional approach. The decision maker has to: (1) evaluate the signs to determine whether they are indicating some direction from God; (2) discern what the message is; (3) decide whether it is confirmed by other signs; and (4) determine whether the leading is clear enough to be considered authoritative. And he must do all of that without having directions from the Bible on how to do it. Scripture is helpful in that it sets the moral limits on the options, but it is not specific enough to point to God's individual will for a particular decision. God could break through with supernatural revelation, but that kind of direction is not to be sought or expected. Without an objective source of knowledge, the decider is denied the certainty that he needs in order to obey God's individual will. As a result, while the traditional view requires the believer to know God's will in order to make correct decisions, it does not offer an objective source of truth to discover it.

Certainty at Last

In the wisdom view, there is no individual will of God that must be discovered and no ambiguous system for sorting it out. Christian decision making is grounded on the objective truth of God's *moral* will. According to the Bible, the only aspect of God's will that must be known, the only aspect that can be known, is God's *moral* will. And 100 percent of God's moral will—not 80 percent, not 90 percent, but 100 percent—has been revealed in the Bible. The believer already has at his disposal everything that God is going to tell him about his decision. There will be no further hints, clues, nudges, or hunches to try to decipher. They just aren't needed.

The moral will of God is objective, complete, and adequate. If we needed more revelation, God would give us more. But the Bible says that what God has told His children is sufficient for every area of life. Paul wrote: "All Scripture is inspired by God and profitable for teaching, for reproof, for correction, for training in righteousness; so that the man of God may be adequate, equipped for every good work" (2 Timothy

3:16–17). And Peter added that God's "divine power has granted to us everything pertaining to life and godliness" (2 Peter 1:3).

Not only does the Bible contain all of God's moral will, it also instructs us about the application of God's will to decision making. God's Word does not tell us *what* to decide in every situation; it teaches *how* to come to a decision that is acceptable to God. It is from Scripture that we learn the necessity of determining those choices that are both *moral* and *wise.* It is the Bible that tells us to acquire wisdom and apply it to our decisions. It is the Bible that tells us where wisdom is to be found. It is the Bible that tells us of God's involvement in giving us wisdom. It is the Bible that establishes the objective standard by which we may define and recognize what is moral and wise.

Furthermore, it is assumed in Scripture that knowledge of God's moral will and the necessary wisdom for good decision making are attainable. Whether the passages contain a promise (Romans 10:9; James 1:5), a command (Ephesians 5:17; Colossians 4:5), a statement of purpose (Romans 12:2; Proverbs 6:6), or a prayer (Colossians 1:9; James 1:5–7), the goal is always viewed as reachable.

The Reality of Growth Incorporated

The wisdom view acknowledges growth in the process. The Bible indicates that our depth of wisdom and knowledge of God's moral will increases over time. God never requires of us either absolute knowledge of His moral will or perfect wisdom (omniscience). Nor does He promise it. The believer is expected to study the Word to become personally convinced of its meaning (2 Timothy 2:15). On the basis of that understanding, she is to develop spiritual convictions (Romans 14:5). If the decisions she makes are consistent with the commands of Scripture (1 Thessalonians 4:1–3) and her own carefully derived convictions, they are acceptable to God (Romans 14:3, 22). As she grows in spiritual insight and understanding of God's Word, her convictions will be appropriately revised, her judgment will mature, and her decisions will reflect greater wisdom. But at any given point, the believer can acquire a sufficient knowledge of God's moral will and an adequate level of wisdom to make a decision that meets God's approval. And the Bible tells her how.

Less Than Unanimous Is Okay

The way of wisdom also resolves the tensions a group of Christians may experience when it tries to make a unified decision. From the traditional viewpoint, we would expect God to reveal His "perfect will" to the group in such a manner that there would be unanimity. But this does not always happen. And, as we noted in chapter 6, "Impressions Are Impressions," that fact has been disturbing to some individuals seeking to maintain consistency between their doctrine and practice. Most believers, however, accept differences of opinion as a fact of life. And so churches with congregational forms of government usually make decisions based on a majority or two-thirds vote.

The wisdom view resolves the conflict between principle and practice. When the goal of a group or committee is a wise decision, it is expected first of all that several opinions will be expressed in the process of gathering wisdom. Wisdom also anticipates that some within the group will recognize the merits of one option while others may be more convinced of the advantages of another. That's because people have different perspectives, and most alternatives have their strengths and weaknesses. When, at last, a decision must be made, a less than unanimous vote is no cause for alarm. For the goal is not a "perfect will" but a wise decision.

Once a matter has been thoroughly discussed and the decision is made, each member is obliged to put away his personal preferences and join in wholehearted support of the plan selected. For that is how unity is maintained. That unity, which Christ so desired for His Church, is not the product of uniformity of thought that determines an ideal will; it comes through the submission of each member to the authority of the local church by accepting and supporting the wisdom of the group.

The goal of the traditional view (certain knowledge of God's individual will) is unreachable, while the goal of the wisdom view (adequate knowledge of God's moral will and wisdom) is attainable. The traditional approach cannot reach its goal because there is no individual will of God to be found and the method for finding it always yields uncertainty. The way of wisdom can reach its goal because the moral will of God has been objectively and completely revealed, and the means of acquiring wisdom is spelled out. Furthermore, God is personally involved in guiding believers into His moral will, increasing their knowledge of His moral will, and increasing their store of wisdom.

APPLICATIONAL SOLUTIONS OF THE WISDOM VIEW

	Traditional View	Way of Wisdom
Ordinary Decisions:	The decision-making process must be abandoned in the minor decisions of life.	We should exercise good judgment and not waste time.
Equal Options:	Insistence upon only one correct choice generates anxiety over "missing the dot" rather than gratitude for more than one fine opportunity.	We should thank God for the opportunity to select from equally acceptable alternatives, and choose our personal preference.
Immaturity:	In some instances, the logic of the traditional view tends to promote immature approaches to decision making.	We should apply maturity by gathering and evaluating data, devoting sufficient time to the process, giving personal desires their proper place, seeking mature counsel, rightly using Scripture, and basing the decision on sound reasons.
Subjectivity:	Certainty that we have found God's individual will is impossible apart from an objective source of knowledge.	**Since God's moral will has been completely revealed and the means of acquiring wisdom has been explained, we can fully attain the knowledge required for decision making.**

chapter seventeen

A NEW WAY OF SEEING

A father and his teenage son were driving home in the family car. The boy, having recently acquired his driver's license, was at the wheel. And he was in a hurry to get home. The after-work traffic was heavier than usual, but if he could get through one more signal light, it would be clear sailing for the last mile. He stepped on the accelerator hoping to negotiate a left-hand turn before the light turned yellow. There was only one car ahead of them—but it was moving so slowly that he had to suddenly apply the brakes to avoid a rear-end collision. Stubbornly maintaining a snail's pace, the obstructing vehicle took so long to make its turn, the young man was forced to stop as the light turned from yellow to red. It would be a full ninety seconds before the lights cycled through again! He squeezed the steering wheel in frustration.

"There ought to be a law against people driving so slow," he complained.

"Slowly," his father corrected.

"Whatever. Why would anybody take so long to make a simple turn?"

"Well, that's a good question," his father said. "We have a few moments to think about it. What do you think?"

"I think the driver saw me coming in his rearview mirror and slowed down on purpose so I wouldn't be able to make that light."

"That's a possibility," the father admitted. "Any other ideas?"

The boy shrugged. "Probably he's just somebody who always drives slooowly and is clueless about being in the way of other people who need to get somewhere."

"That could be."

Pause.

"I can't think of anything else," the boy said.

"What if those folks just bought a houseplant that they're transporting in the back of their car, and they're trying to keep it from tipping over and making a big mess?"

Silence.

"Or maybe there's someone who doesn't feel well lying down in the backseat, and the driver's trying to provide a gentle ride so they won't get carsick."

The boy took a deep breath and relaxed his grip on the steering wheel. "I guess it's possible that they had a good reason for taking that corner so slowly." The light turned green and he drove the car through the intersection with all four tires firmly on the ground.

The way we see things governs how we respond to them. And additional information or fresh insight will change not only our perception, it can transform our attitude.

One of the benefits of conversion is the gift of spiritual sight (2 Corinthians 4:4–6). The Spirit enables the believer to begin to see things from God's point of view. As C. S. Lewis wrote: "I believe in Christianity as I believe that the Sun has risen, not only because I see it, but because *by it I see everything else*." [1]

But learning to "walk by faith, not by [physical] sight" (2 Corinthians 5:7) takes some getting used to. The main resource God provides is the Bible. In a way, studying the Bible is like putting on a pair of glasses that brings our spiritual vision into focus. And some of what we see is startling because heaven's perspective often reverses the viewpoint of the world: trials are to be received with an attitude of joy because of the opportunity they present for character growth (James 1:2–4); personal weakness can be an advantage when it demonstrates God's strength and teaches us the sufficiency of God's grace (2 Corinthians 12:9–10); success is not measured by achievement but by faithfulness to our assignments (1 Corinthians 4:2); and so on.

But our metaphor lacks precision. For we don't look at the world through the glasses of the Bible itself, but rather our *understanding* (or interpretation) of the Bible. And if we misread one part or another, our "prescription" will be out of kilter and our vision will be blurred.

We see this problem in the Gospels. The leaders of Israel had formulated a religion that was based, they said, on the law and the prophets. Much of it was on target. But some elements—notably their rules and regulations for keeping the law, their definition of *neighbor*, and their expectations of God's coming Messiah—were distorted. Their theology and, correspondingly, the lifestyle that issued from their faulty vision, needed correction. So Jesus provided a new prescription: "You have heard that it was said…but I say to you…" (see Matthew 5).

Again, in Acts, Jesus told His disciples, "You shall be my witnesses…even to the remotest part of the earth" (1:8). But it took a threefold adjustment in Peter's vision for him to see the Gentiles as worthy recipients of the gospel of grace (Acts 10–11).

ROAD SIGNS OR WISDOM SIGNS

Corrected theology is a normal aspect of Christian growth (1 Corinthians 13:11; Hebrews 5:11–6:1), and that is what I have experienced in my developing understanding of divine guidance. When I was young, I "heard that it was said" that I needed to find God's individual will by following the road signs the Spirit provided. Subsequent study of the Bible has convinced me that that interpretation is faulty. As the principles of the way of wisdom have emerged, they have brought needed correction in the way I view the data considered for making decisions.

Whether we apply the traditional view or the way of wisdom, the factors under consideration are the same. What differs is the *meaning* and significance assigned to the variables. Rather than seeking out road signs pointing to the individual will of God, I have learned to look for wisdom signs—sources to be consulted in the acquisition of wisdom. The difference in perspective will be evident as we compare the two approaches to the "road signs" of common sense, spiritual counsel, personal desires, circumstances, results, the Bible, and inward impressions.

Horse Sense Bridled

No one is against good ol' *common sense*. The traditional view commends its use as a pointer to God's individual will—usually. But specific biblical illustrations where God's individual will ran counter to common sense requires the traditional view to hedge. God must be given the freedom to lead in an uncommon way, as He did with Noah, Abraham, Joshua, Gideon, and Naaman. So in most cases, the traditional view utilizes common sense as an indicator of God's individual will—but not always.

With the wisdom view, the believer may confidently apply common sense to every single decision. For common sense is regarded as one form of wisdom that is part of God's gracious endowment to men. The opposite of common sense is naïveté, foolishness, or stupidity.

The only time common sense is to be set aside is when it contradicts God's revealed (moral) will. Man's perspective must always give way to God's moral will when the two come into conflict.

That principle accounts for Noah's ark, Abraham's sacrifice, and the military strategies of Joshua and Gideon. In every case, God revealed His moral will by divine revelation. In the same way, believers today must test and submit their common sense to the "divine sense" of God revealed in the Bible. For common sense that opposes the wisdom of God is no longer sensible.

So important is common sense that Scripture commands that church elders must be "sensible" (Titus 1:8), and that older men, young women, and young men should learn to be "sensible" (Titus 2:2, 5–6). Much of the wisdom in the book of Proverbs is just good common sense. This is evidenced by the fact that many of those proverbs have parallels in other cultures, as well as in our own.

So rather than being a road sign that we try to read in order to find God's individual will, common sense is a source of wisdom that we are expected to follow as long as it harmonizes with the moral will of God. If that qualification is maintained, the source of the common sense does not matter. In fact, there are situations where unbelievers can be a valuable source of counsel for the Christian (cf. Luke 16:8). A local mechanic or a consumer magazine may offer valuable common sense that can help us make a wise decision.

Expanding the Frame of Reference

The traditional view takes seriously the scriptural admonitions to seek guidance from *spiritual counselors* (Proverbs 11:14; 24:6). But it has to add some words of caution. For the advice of counselors might conflict at some points, obscuring rather than clarifying the Lord's leading. Furthermore, since only the individual can ultimately discern the Lord's ideal will for his decision, he must realize that the counsel of others must be carefully evaluated rather than simply adopted. As a result, the believer must exercise great care in reading this road sign. For some counsel could point down the wrong path.

The advisory nature of counsel creates no problems for the wisdom view. Counselors are viewed as one source of wisdom. They can supply facts and insight not otherwise available to the decision maker. But they are not omniscient, nor is their counsel the final word. The searcher of wisdom asks not only for a counselor's opinion, but the reasons behind the viewpoint expressed so he is better able to judge the merits of the advice. In particular, there are two good questions that could be put to a godly advisor: "Do you know of any scriptural or biblical principles that apply to the decision I am making? Have you gained practical insight through your experience in making a similar decision that would be of value to me?"

Avoid Lemons with a Fruit Inspector

Wisdom seeks for competent advice where it is most needed. I am a dunce about anything under the hood of a car. So I do not shop for a car by myself. Most of the cars I have owned were located and recommended to me by my father or some other mechanic friend. It is an application of wisdom for me to call my father and say, "This is your auto-ignorant son. I'm in the market for a car. I need something that will get at least twenty miles per gallon and cost no more than seven thousand dollars. Would you look for one for me?" I have yet to buy a lemon, and I don't think it has just been luck.

Counselors have real value in uncovering blind spots often overlooked under the pressure of a difficult situation. I regularly talk with students who are under great stress because they are unable to do all their school work. Often I learn that those students missed a week of classes because they caught some bug that was going around. I can say, "Is your goal to be faithful to God, or to get a certain grade in this course?" When they say, "I want to be faithful to God," the light begins to break through. I'm able to point out that God expects them to be faithful in their use of whatever time is available to them—even if that results in a lower grade. If they are faithful with what they have to work with, God is pleased.

Under the pressure of grades, the students had substituted an unreachable, human goal for the attainable objective established by God. By getting fresh insight from a counselor, the tension was eliminated, enabling them to function again.

That is a major value of good counsel. It can put matters into a proper and manageable perspective. And that kind of perspective is necessary if we are to make sound decisions.

Putting Desires in Their Place

The traditional view teaches that our *personal desires* can be a road sign pointing to God's individual will. But once again, there is some difficulty in reading the sign. For believers have godly desires, sinful desires, foolish desires, proud desires, and any number that are hard to identify. Christians continually ask, "How can I distinguish a desire given by the Holy Spirit from one that springs from my own heart that would be satisfied with less than God's best?"

The wisdom view is not left with introspective guesswork. To begin with, it does not view any desire as authoritative. All desires must be judged by God's moral will and wisdom. Morally acceptable desires are approved by God and sinful ones are not—and the Bible explains which are which. Personal desires must also be judged by wisdom. Sometimes I feel like leaving my office to work out in the gym on campus. As I look at the work on my desk, I am forced to admit that it would be wiser to finish grading the Bible exams. If any time remains after that, I can run over to the gym for some exercise. My desire to continue as a faculty member overrides my desire to shoot a few baskets.

Personal desires that God's moral will and wisdom have declared acceptable can be an excellent source of wisdom. For the Scripture says that we are to serve God eagerly with all our hearts. We can more easily obey this command if our decisions are in harmony with our personal inclinations. If third-grade girls give you the hives, and you are motivated by the challenge of giving some direction to junior high boys, accept the eighth-grade boys Sunday school class. If the options are genuinely equal, wisdom chooses the one that would be most enjoyable to carry out.

Spiritual growth will make a significant impact on our desires. For as we mature, we will have an increasing desire to live a life that manifests wisdom. As growth takes place, our personal desires will more and more reflect what is wise.

It All Depends

Since God controls all *circumstances*, the traditional view concludes that He reveals His individual will through them to the believer who has learned to "read providence." In addition, the traditional approach looks for open and closed doors, which it considers "yes" and "no" road signs indicating God's leading. The problem is determining the message that the circumstances are supposed to communicate. And, as we saw in chapter 13, it is impossible to make a biblical case for reading providence as a means of gaining guidance for a personal decision.

That does not mean that circumstances are unimportant to the wisdom view. Quite the contrary. Since circumstances provide the context in which a decision is made, they are a key source of wisdom for the decision maker. They must be evaluated, not to determine some clue from God, but to help decide the advisability of a course of action. *Circumstances* covers a multitude of factors: cost, people available, time, mechanical problems, opportunities, and so on. Wisdom recognizes that every option has its advantages and disadvantages. Circumstances indicate many of the pros and cons, but they carry no "yes" or "no" tags.

What About Jeremiah?

The traditional view often speaks of a decision being confirmed as God's will by the *results* that followed. But again, this road sign requires a tricky interpretation of circumstances. For we must answer the question:

Which results equal confirmation? And no one is exactly sure. Human success is not an automatic proof, or Jeremiah never was in God's will. When Paul and Silas obeyed the Macedonian call, they were beaten and thrown in jail. Many of God's servants have been faithful in their ministries and have encountered nothing but difficulties and obstacles. Are they to be labeled as failures? Was their lack of productivity due to being out of God's will? That's not the teaching of Scripture (read Hebrews 11). But the traditional view has no other basis for defining confirmation.

The way of wisdom views results from a different perspective. It is wise to gain wisdom from the results of previous decisions, whether those of others or our own. For those results may reveal factors we had not previously taken into consideration. And the results of past decisions may indicate the potential outcome of a current decision. So it is good to ask questions of others who have been down similar paths: "How long did it take you to get to the church camp via Highway 30?"; "Was Bob effective as a teacher in Vacation Bible School?"; "How many miles to the gallon are you getting with your SUV?"

Results can reveal wisdom to the careful observer, but they must be viewed within the framework of God's sovereignty. Situations change and the impact of different factors varies. So the results that followed from a decision in the past do not guarantee the same results for an issue currently under consideration. Christian businessmen do well to analyze cause-and-effect relationships between marketing plans and actual sales. But they know that an unforeseen strike, a downturn in the nation's economy, or a sudden shift in consumer buying habits can make a shambles of a "proven" strategy. And so the believing businessman gains what wisdom he can from past successes and failures, sets his plans in motion, and leaves the outcome to the sovereign disposition of God.

The Bible Says

We have already discussed the two positions' perspectives on *the Word of God.* The traditional view places a great emphasis on understanding the Bible, for a great deal of God's will for the individual has already been spelled out. The wisdom view goes further and says that 100 percent of God's will has been revealed. God has said what He is going to say about how to make our personal decisions. That makes understanding God's Word the most important aspect of effective decision making.

Benefiting from Impressions

Next to the road sign of the Bible, the traditional view regards *inner impressions* as the most direct link between the believer and God. Through these impressions God is said to point the way to His ideal will for a given decision.

The wisdom view acknowledges the reality of inner impressions. In making decisions, everyone experiences internal hunches that point to some specific conclusion. What the wisdom view disavows is the significance the traditional view attaches to those inward impulses. The reasons for this were explained in chapter 6, "Impressions Are Impressions." They may be summarized as follows: (1) there is no indication in *Scripture* that the Holy Spirit leads believers through inner impressions; (2) it is impossible to determine with certainty the *source* of the impressions; (3) it is impossible to judge with certainty the *message* of the impressions; (4) the need for corroborative *verification* from the other signs discredits the genuineness of the inner voice; and (5) since inner impressions are not revelation from God, they lack the necessary *authority* to compel obedience.

Some have inferred from this critique that the wisdom view places no value on inner impressions. The reality is that, properly evaluated, impressions can be an excellent source of wisdom.

What constitutes a proper evaluation? First, wisdom recognizes that the origins of impressions are multiple and mixed rather than single and simple. When a traditionalist gets a strong impression, the first question he may ask is, "Was it from God or from Satan?" But that is the wrong question. For if it were 100 percent from God, it would be direct revelation (with both the clarity and supernatural confirmation to authenticate it). If it were 100 percent from Satan, it would be divination—raising issues much graver than the comparatively innocuous interpretation of an inner impression!

As we noted in chapter 6, people intuitively recognize that impressions can be generated from all sorts of sources: a Bible passage, commercials, meditation, medication, hormonal imbalance, insomnia, stream of consciousness, suppressed memories, subliminal influences, and so on ad infinitum. Sometimes we are able to trace the dominant source, but many seem to come from out of the blue. Given the complexities of the interactions of body, soul, and mind, it is likely that a given impression arises from multiple sources that are each influenced by factors or agents that are good and evil to varying degrees. Our persons are the arena for an ongoing conflict between God and righteousness on the one hand and the world, the flesh, and the devil on the other. Most impressions will reflect this mixture of influences, with none being perfectly good or perfectly evil. So wisdom doesn't waste time wondering about the source.

It is likely that a given impression arises from multiple sources that are each influenced by factors or agents that are good and evil to varying degrees.

Second, since we understand that impressions lack the authority to function as divine guidance, we are free to evaluate them for whatever help they might be to us.

Third, the basis for this evaluation is to be the moral will of God and wisdom. There are numerous occasions when an idea pops into a person's head apparently out of thin air. Subsequent reflection brings the individual to the conclusion that that impression is a first-rate plan. It promotes the accomplishment of one's goals and does so in an effective way. That impulse ought to be followed, not as an indicator of God's ideal will, but as a wise way to serve God. On the other hand, those impressions that are either sinful or foolish ought to be ignored. Ideas that violate common sense, distract us from accomplishing other important tasks, or otherwise result in a waste of time can be confidently rejected.

I once prayed that God would help me with some creative ideas for a campaign to run for student body president. I also racked my mind and picked the brains of my friends. In the middle of the night, I awoke with all sorts of ideas bubbling up into my groggy consciousness. I feverishly wrote down as many thoughts as I could capture and went back to sleep.

What was I to make of those ideas? Were they from the Holy Spirit? That was the wrong question. Did God work in my heart and mind to answer my prayer for help with my campaign? Yes, but those ideas were not revelation. They didn't have authority. God wasn't telling me what to do. I had to sort through them to find the most effective ones for my purposes. Of twenty ideas, five formed the basis for my campaign. The rest were discarded. Soon thereafter, my fellow students were asking each other about those signs all over campus displaying the number 32 and a small degree symbol. It was a simple, creative way of reminding voters of the freezing point of water—and my last name. Don't laugh. It worked.

God was involved in that intangible, indescribable process called creativity. He helped me separate the ideas that were morally acceptable from any that were dubious, and the effective concepts from the foolish ones. I don't know how the thoughts were formed during my sleep. I do know that God answers prayer and that He helps us apply wisdom.

Not all of these impressions work out like we expect them to. Traditionalists tend to call attention to the ones that lead to good results and to explain them as the Lord's leading. But when a "Spirit-directed" plan doesn't succeed, the person involved may be confused or have feelings of spiritual failure.

God was involved in that intangible, indescribable process called creativity.

The way of wisdom sees things differently. Since the impression was not regarded as the voice of God, it doesn't carry the requirement of inevitable success. And, as we noted in chapter 13, an idea doesn't have to be accomplished to be pleasing to God. King David wanted to build a temple for God, and for that he received commendation: "You did well that it was in your heart" (2 Chronicles 6:8). But David's dream was reserved for his son to fulfill.

A friend of mine received a strong impression that she and her husband should invite me to spend some time with them so I could get some needed rest. She was sure it was from God. When she told me about it, I was pleased that her heart was concerned for my needs. I was fatigued, and normally I would have jumped at the opportunity. However, I had a ministry commitment that took clear precedence and enough energy to fulfill it. When I told her of my obligations, she agreed that I should honor them.

And what should we make of my friend's impression? "It was good that it was in your heart." It wasn't revelation, so it didn't have to work out. But I was certainly encouraged and strengthened by the support I felt from someone who cared about me and my ministry, who was not only praying for me but was actively seeking ways to help.

"I Just Don't Have Peace About It"

One aspect of inward impressions is the presence or absence of *peace*. We have shown that the way of wisdom doesn't consider peace or lack of peace as direct guidance into the individual will of God. This does not mean, however, that the way of wisdom is oblivious to the importance of a believer's emotional state. Lack of Galatians 5:22 peace is a matter of sin, which should be corrected by dependence upon the Spirit. Other times lack of peace may indicate immaturity, concern about the wisdom of a course of action, or simple uncertainty.

The way of wisdom does not give the feeling of peace or anxiety an authoritative role as the voice of God. It rather asks, "Why do I feel peaceful or anxious?" The answer to that question is the real guidance from God. Wisdom considers the emotional maturity of the person making the decision. Immaturity may indicate that a believer is not yet spiritually ready to pursue a difficult but significant ministry.

In the final analysis, every good thing comes from God (James 1:17). So any thought, impression, or feeling that is both moral and wise has its ultimate origin in Him. We should thank God for whatever wisdom He imparts through whatever means. But we should always recognize wisdom for what it is—the perception of an effective way to accomplish spiritual goals. Wisdom must be followed; but a particular piece of wisdom is not a command from God; nor is wisdom a guarantee of success.

To sum up: Everyone utilizes essentially the same sources of information in decision making. So whether we follow the traditional view or the wisdom view, we will study input from common sense, spiritual counsel, personal desires, circumstances, results, the Bible, and inner impressions. The two views do not look at the data in the same way, but since the sources are the same, it is not surprising that the conclusions reached are often the same.

The differences are noteworthy, starting with the way each view perceives the sources of input. To the traditional view, they are road signs pointing to the individual will of God when interpreted properly. In the wisdom view, Scripture reveals the moral will of God and the other sources are wisdom signs pointing to a moral and wise decision. The two approaches also differ in what they seek. The traditional view is looking for the individual will of God while the wisdom view is pursuing a wise decision within the moral will of God.

frequently asked question

Question: Isn't it true that some recent writers have elevated the role of personal desires in decision making based on Psalm 37:4?

Yes. Psalm 37:4 reads: "Delight yourself in the LORD; and He will give you the desires of your heart." The line of thought is that as the believer grows in his delight of the Lord, God will transform that person's desires so that they conform to His. Bruce Waltke writes: "When God is in control of your life, He is also in control of your desires. The things you long for in your heart will be put there by the Holy Spirit."[2] John MacArthur says that if you are Spirit-filled, "Do whatever you want!... God does not say He will fulfill all the desires that are there. He says He will put the desires there! If you are living a godly life, He will give you the right desires, His desires."[3]

For the traditionalist, the equation of personal desires with God's desires becomes a means for determining His individual will. On the other hand, the wisdom view sees such personal desires as simply agreeing with Augustine: "Love God and do what you please."

But this appears to be another exercise in inferring conclusions that go beyond the statement of the text. The passage does not say anything about God giving desires to anyone. In the context, the believer is disturbed because the wicked are prospering and the righteous are being victimized (Psalm 37:1, 7). So he pleads his case to God in prayer. In response, God assures him that the godly will receive the land as an inheritance (37:11). Their prayers will be answered and the wicked will fail. In this setting, the promise of verse 4 points to the expectation of *answered prayer*. Allen Ross summarizes the meaning: "Rather one should trust in the Lord who can answer prayers of the heart (vv. 3–4)."[4] Delitzsch shows a parallel example where delight in the Lord is connected with God hearing prayer (Job 20:26–27). He says that delight in God means desiring the right things which God will not "refuse."[5] The desires in question, then, are those of the believer who appeals to God in prayer—not desires transplanted by God.

In heaven our desires will be perfect. But until then we will need to judge our desires by the Word of God. But when our desires are in harmony with all of God's moral will, they can be followed with confidence.

This is not a novel way of finding God's individual will, but simply loving God and thus being able to do what we please. This is the way of wisdom.

---

1. C. S. Lewis, "Is Theology Poetry?" *The Weight of Glory and Other Essays* (New York: Simon and Schuster, 1996), 106 (italics mine).
2. Bruce Waltke, *Finding the Will of God: A Pagan Notion?* (Grand Rapids, MI: Wm. B. Eerdmans Publishing Co., 2002), 100. See my review of this book in appendix 1.
3. John MacArthur, *God's Will Is Not Lost* (Wheaton, IL: Victor Books, 1973), 31. See my review of this book, now titled *Found: God's Will,* in appendix 1.
4. Allen P. Ross, "Psalms," *The Bible Knowledge Commentary* (Wheaton, IL: Victor Books, 1985), 822.
5. C. F. Keil and F. Delitzsch, *Psalms* (Grand Rapids, MI: Wm. B. Eerdmans Publishing Co, 1976), 2:12.

chapter eighteen

PRACTICING THE PRESENCE

Without question the number one complaint about the way of wisdom is that, in noncommanded decisions, it often seems that God is excluded from the process. That it is not necessary for the believer to consult with God on many mundane decisions can lead us to neglect to seek His involvement in *any* decisions in the area of freedom. Christians can become virtual deists, "leaning" too heavily on their "own understanding," in defiance of Proverbs 3:5.

Conversely, one of the attractions of the traditional view is the sense that God's leading is personal and direct. There is a great sense of security in believing that God is really making our decisions and telling us in detail what to do.

My contention is that equating our inner impressions with the voice of God is a misinterpretation of our experience. And the idea that the way of wisdom excludes God from our decision making is a caricature of what the Scriptures plainly teach. The abuse of freedom does not nullify the reality of freedom. If a believer who purports to follow the way of wisdom drifts into the habit of making choices without any reference to God, the problem is not with the principles but with the practice.

Making decisions has become disconnected from the core of a vital, daily walk with Christ.

Hands-On Guidance

The problem, then, is not that God is not personally involved in our decision making. We have already identified several significant ways that God is engaged with us as we make decisions that are pleasing to Him. To summarize:

First, He has *provided the resources* for making decisions that are acceptable to Him. He has revealed His moral will in its totality. He has instructed us in His Word to seek wisdom for making decisions and has informed us how to do it. Further, He has given us a new nature that makes obedience of His moral will possible. As a loving Father, He has equipped us with everything we need to make decisions that are pleasing to Him.

Second, as we work through the process of arriving at a decision, God is *continually present and working within us.* The words of Paul remind us that "it is God who is at work in you, both to will and to work for His good pleasure" (Philippians 2:13). Specifically, His grace enables us to trust in Him (Acts 18:27). He gives us the desire to obey His will. By His Spirit, He enables us to keep His commandments. So every single act of obedience is proof of God's personal involvement in our lives (cf. Romans 8:5–8).

Third, it is God who *sovereignly opens doors of opportunity* for us. When we ask for wisdom, He gives it through the channels He has established for our benefit. He also answers our prayers about our decisions. And He brings to successful completion those of our plans that are within His sovereign will.

Fourth, along the way, He utilizes the circumstances and the very process of decision making to *change our character and bring us to maturity.* As we depend on Him, He blesses our obedience to His moral will and produces His spiritual fruit in our lives.

Finally, He works through our decisions *to accomplish His purposes*—not only in us, but through us.

No, the problem is not the lack of God's involvement in our decision making. The problem lies in our failure to properly integrate the Bible's instruction on decision making with the larger framework of its teaching on a personal relationship with God. Making decisions is but a slice of our walk with God. If we are to properly interpret the details of our lives, we need to have a more complete understanding of what it means to "walk by faith, not by sight" (2 Corinthians 5:7).

Making the Transition

What happens when a believer who has been following the traditional view becomes convinced of the validity of the way of wisdom? What is it like when a person who has interpreted her inner impressions as the voice of God recognizes those perceptions to be fallacious? For some, it may seem that the God who "walks with me and talks with me" has become abruptly silent. True, the frustrations that attend the practice of the traditional view may be replaced by a profound sense of relief as the believer embraces her God-given freedom to make her own decisions. But when the sense of God's presence is lost in the process, the trade-off is disorienting to say the least.

Let's say, for the sake of argument, that the way of wisdom as set forth in this book is an accurate expression of the teaching of Scripture. And let's assume that a major change in paradigm—of how we perceive God's role in our decision making—requires some getting used to. How would we go about making the transition from the traditional view to the way of wisdom in a way that avoids unhealthy pendulum swings?

First, of course, it will not do to *assume* that the way of wisdom is correct. It must become a matter of conviction. And the only way that is going to happen is through a combination of careful study and the illumination of God's Spirit. The number two complaint about this book is that it is too long. But one of the major factors in its length is my insistence on careful exegesis of the relevant passages, of which there are many! Few books on guidance address the biblical text with such thoroughness. This lack is one of the reasons for ongoing confusion about God's will. The way of wisdom is constructed from my understanding of the teaching of God's Word. The reader will have to decide whether or not I have gotten it right.

Second, it ought to be clear by now that the way of wisdom requires the believer to let go of the idea that inner impressions equal the authoritative voice of God. When the Creator said to Adam, "From any tree of the garden you may eat freely" (Genesis 2:16), He fully intended for the man to make his own choices. In noncommanded decisions, our freedom and responsibility are real.

Third, it is invalid to conclude that just because God is not telling us what to do in every decision that He has withdrawn from our lives or that His involvement with us is in any sense less personal. What we need is a corrected understanding of the nature of that personal relationship with God. In other words, we are not now asking whether the way of wisdom is true; we're trying to figure out how it works.

Seeing the Invisible

Every child of God must come to terms with an undeniable and uncomfortable fact: the God to whom we long to relate is *invisible*. A. W. Tozer made this striking observation:

> The real Christian is an odd number anyway. He feels supreme love for One whom he has never seen, talks familiarly every day to Someone he cannot see, expects to go to heaven on the virtue of Another, empties himself in order to be full, admits he is wrong so he can be declared right, goes down in order to get up, is strongest when he is weakest, richest when he is poorest, and happiest when he feels worst. He dies so he can live, forsakes in order to have, gives away so he can keep, sees the invisible, hears the inaudible, and knows that which passeth knowledge.[1]

While God is a person, He is not in His essence a human being. He is spirit. So while there are similarities between the ways that we relate to a human friend or relative and the ways we relate to God, there are also profound differences. And the one thing we long for the most—to know God as He is, face to face—is denied us in this life (Psalm 27:8–9; Exodus 33:18–23). "No one has seen God at any time," says John (1:18). One day we shall see Him as He is (1 John 3:2). But in the meantime, "now we see in a mirror dimly, but then face to face; now I know in part, but then I will know fully just as I also have been fully known" (1 Corinthians 13:12).

And so "we walk by faith, not by sight" (2 Corinthians 5:7). And yet that faith opens out into knowledge that is meaningfully personal. So we say with Paul, "I know whom I have believed" (2 Timothy 1:12). We affirm Peter's assessment that "though you have not seen Him, you love Him, and though you do not see Him now, but believe in Him, you greatly rejoice with joy inexpressible and full of glory" (1 Peter 1:8).

A Personal Relationship

But what do we mean by such statements? What is the nature of a personal relationship with an invisible God? Perhaps we could begin with these affirmations:

1. Because God is a person, I can know Him personally (John 17:3).
2. Because I am a person, I can know God personally (1 Corinthians 13:12).
3. Knowing about God is indispensable to knowing God (Colossians 1:9–10; 1 John 1:1, 3).
4. The supreme revelation of God is in His Son, Jesus Christ (John 1:1–18; Colossians 1:15–20; Hebrews 1:1–3). He is, as J. B. Phillips put it, God-in-focus. As I come to know Him through the Gospels, I come to know God (John 14:9–10; 2 Corinthians 4:5–6).
5. The Holy Spirit transforms the objective truth about God into a subjective experience of God that evokes faith and spiritual life (John 3:5–8; 16:12–14; Romans 8:15–16; 1 Corinthians 2:9–10, 13–14).
6. As the Spirit makes me aware of Jesus, I respond to a person. Dependence, trust, obedience, and love are appropriate expressions of that relationship (Romans 8:15; 2 Corinthians 5:9; Colossians 1:10; 1 Peter 1:8).
7. As I respond to what I know of God, He changes me from within. That change is the product of a living relationship (Romans 12:1–2; 2 Corinthians 3:18).
8. This knowledge of God can grow during my lifetime on earth (Ephesians 3:16–19; Colossians 1:10; 2 Peter 3:18).

These statements (especially when read with the referenced passages) provide a helpful framework for thinking about a personal relationship with God. For the purposes of the subject at hand, some of them need to be fleshed out.

Less Is Better

When I reflect on the ways that God relates to me, I note (again) that He is not continually telling me what to do. Could He do that if He wanted to? Yes. In fact, there was a forty-year period when the guidance He gave His people was extremely detailed and specific. When the children of Israel came out of Egypt, God met with them at Mount Sinai. He gave them not only the Ten Commandments but guidelines for living that regulated such matters as: which persons were to be their spiritual leaders; when they were required to go to the worship center; which foods they could and could not eat; when they were to go to battle as a nation; when they must bathe; which cities their spiritual leaders must live in; the amount of a minimum offering; the exact location and dimensions of the "church building"; the precise words their prophets were to deliver; how they were to celebrate the new year; who would inherit a man's land; how long land was available for sale; which years the people must work and which ones they must rest; how punishment was to be meted out to the convicted thief, murderer, homosexual, idolater, and rebellious child; what uniforms the religious leaders must wear; when all male Israelites must be circumcised; how interest rates were to be regulated; and even how the corner of each garment was to be adorned! (For a more complete list, start with Exodus and Leviticus.) And through His presence in the pillar of fire, God even indicated exactly where they were to camp and how far they were to travel each day.

But He doesn't do that with His people today. In fact, most of the regulations that constituted God's moral will for the Israelites have been moved into the "area of freedom" for Christians. We are free and responsible to decide what to eat, what to wear, where we will live, which church we will attend, and so on. Has God withdrawn from us, become less personal? The New Testament writers indicate that the provisions of the New Covenant are better and our relationship with God is more intimate. How can this be?

We get a clue from an analogy Paul developed in Galatians 4:1–7. In His wisdom, God saw fit to guide Old Testament saints as "immature children" who had a limited understanding of His nature and will. But those who have the benefit of receiving the revelation of Jesus Christ and the empowerment of His Spirit, God treats as "grown-up children." New Testament believers are equipped to relate to their Father on an "adult" level without requiring the detailed parental supervision appropriate to childhood.[2]

In his insightful book, *Reaching for the Invisible God,* Philip Yancey notes, "Somehow we must learn to distinguish between appropriate *childlike* behavior, a prerequisite for the kingdom of heaven, and inappropriate *childish* behavior, a mark of stunted growth." One indication of stunted growth is "a pattern of unhealthy dependence." Yancey continues:

> I know a man who at age seventy still lives with his mother, asks her permission before going out, and turns over his money to her each week.... I know other adults who continue to act like children because of smothering parents who never learned to let go. They defy a basic principle of nature: the goal of parenthood is to produce healthy adults, not dependent children.[3]

My parents did it right. As I was growing up, they were training me so that I could learn to make decisions as an adult. They taught me to distinguish right from wrong; they taught me biblical values and principles that I could apply to specific decisions. The older I got, the less they told me what to do.

When it came time for me to choose which college I would attend, my parents were very helpful. As we discussed the options together, their loving concern was evident. But they refrained from suggesting what I should do. As I agonized over that decision, there were times when I wished they would tell me which school to choose. But they would not. Instead, they assured me that I was mature enough to come to a good decision myself. And I was encouraged by the knowledge that they were praying for me.

God's refusal to tell us what to do in every situation is actually for our benefit.

Were my parents withholding guidance? No. For nearly twenty years they had provided guidance that I could appropriate for this decision. Were they unloving, disinterested, or impersonal? Quite the contrary. Their insistence that I come to my own conclusion was evidence of their love. In making their wisdom available to me, they were personally involved. In a similar manner, our Heavenly Father personally guides His children.[4]

God's refusal to tell us what to do in every situation (for which the way of wisdom is criticized) is *actually for our benefit.* For as we learn to apply biblical principles to the decisions of everyday life, each of us grows toward becoming the person God created us to be.

God in Three Persons, Blessed Trinity

That explanation surely makes sense as far as it goes. But it doesn't explain how the Christian's relationship with God is more intimate than that of Old Testament saints. The New Testament's development of that theme is trinitarian.

First, through Christ, the Christian has come to know of God as his "Father in heaven." In the Israelite paradigm, YHWH was the holy King—mysterious, distant, separate. But with the advent of Christ, and the revelation of God through Him, an entirely new order of relationship between God and the believer was opened up. J. I. Packer gives this superb explanation:

> If you want to judge how well a person understands Christianity, find out how much he makes of the thought of being God's child, and having God as his Father. If this is not the thought that prompts and controls his worship and prayers and his whole outlook on life, it means that he does not understand Christianity very well at all. For everything that Christ taught, everything that makes the New Testament new, and better than the Old, everything that is distinctively Christian as opposed to merely Jewish, is summed up in the knowledge of the Fatherhood of God. "Father" is the Christian name for God....
>
> [T]he stress in the New Testament is not on the difficulty and danger of drawing near to the holy God, but on the boldness and confidence with which believers may approach Him.[5]

Accordingly, says Paul, as children of God, "we cry out, 'Abba! [Daddy!] Father!'" (Romans 8:15).

Second, while it remains true that "no one has seen God at any time," Jesus, "the only begotten God who is in the bosom of the Father, He has explained Him" (John 1:18). As the enfleshed revelation of God, Jesus gives the Father a face (2 Corinthians 4:6). As we read the Gospels, we participate vicariously in His interactions with His disciples, and we come to know Him (1 John 1:1–3). Jesus' words to the befuddled Philip, "He who has seen Me has seen the Father," (John 14:9) become true for us as well.

And third, that is so because of the ministry of the indwelling Holy Spirit. Of this one who "comes alongside," Jesus said, "He will glorify Me, for He will take of Mine and will disclose it to you" (John 16:14). Dr. Packer sees that statement as the essence of the Spirit's mission:

> The distinctive, constant, basic ministry of the Holy Spirit under the new covenant is so to mediate Christ's presence to believers—that is, to give them such knowledge of his presence with them as their Savior, Lord, and God—that three things keep happening.
>
> *First, personal* fellowship *with Jesus*...becomes a reality of experience, even though Jesus is now not here on earth in bodily form, but is enthroned in heaven's glory....
>
> *Second, personal* transformation *of character into Jesus' likeness* starts to take place as, looking to Jesus, their model, for strength, believers worship and adore him and learn to lay out and, indeed, lay down their lives for him and for others....
>
> *Third, the Spirit-given* certainty *of being loved, redeemed, and adopted* through Christ into the Father's family...makes gratitude, delight, hope, and confidence...blossom in believers' hearts.[6]

As the Holy Spirit brings us into experiential fellowship with Jesus, we are drawn into a relationship with God that is indeed personal and intimate. There are times when "the experiential side of Christianity" has great intensity.

> [D]irect perceptions of God—perceptions of his greatness and goodness, his eternity and infinity, his truth, his love, and his glory, all as related to Christ and through Christ to us...are given through the Spirit to the loving and obedient disciple....The

> perceptions themselves...bring great joy because they communicate God's great love. They belong to the inner life, as distinct from that of the outward senses by which we know men and things.[7]

On the other hand, our sense of closeness to God is not always so vivid. In a healthy marriage, romance ebbs and flows, but the relationship is sustained by a deep, undergirding commitment. Similarly, the intensity of our awareness of God's presence is variable and not under our control. "[Direct perceptions of God]...can neither be demanded nor predicted; they simply happen as God wills."[8] Most of the time, God's involvement with us is not so remarkable as to be perceptibly noticed. He is the environment in which we live, His active presence assumed as a matter of faith.

The assurance that we have is that, whether our awareness of God is heightened or He seems to be maintaining a low profile, He *is* with us (Matthew 1:23; 28:20; Hebrews 13:5–6). Our role is to be with Him. A good deal of New Testament teaching on the life of faith is summed up in the picturesque vocabulary of Brother Lawrence—we are to "practice the presence of God."[9] That is the context in which Christians are to make their decisions.

Here Am I, Send Fred

To say, then, that God does not customarily tell us what to do as we make our decisions does not mean that He is not involved with us or that we don't have communion with Him in our inner life. It only means that the Spirit works in other ways to nurture our spiritual life and deepen our sense of Christ's presence with us. Those other ways may be multifaceted, but we will highlight two of them.

One means the Spirit uses to connect us existentially with God is His ministry of illumination by which the objective truth of Scripture is clarified in the mind and applied to the heart. An experience that Robin had as a young adult illustrates this.

> During my junior year at Wheaton College, I decided to apply for summer placement with the Student Mission Project (SMP). The process was quite rigorous, requiring a sophisticated written application followed by a personal interview with a screening committee. As I looked

forward to the adventure of ministry in a foreign country, I had only one reservation. I didn't feel confident about my ability to proclaim the gospel effectively in a Muslim country. What if the screening committee wanted me to go to Saudi Arabia?

Through a period of intense introspection, I wrestled with my motivations, questioned my abilities, and grappled with my willingness to submit to and trust God's will. Striving for openness with the screening committee, which consisted mostly of SMP veterans (fellow students), I let them listen in on my private debate as I worked through the application process. In the end, I concluded that I was prepared to go anywhere I was sent—even Saudi Arabia. The struggle had been intense, but I came to a peaceful and settled resolution.

On the day the summer assignments were posted, I was full of anticipation as I went to the college post office to see where I would be spending my summer. The first time I scanned the thirty-three names on the list, I missed my posting. I went down the list a second time, more slowly. The names were listed in alphabetical order. It shouldn't be that hard to… And then reality sank in. It wasn't there. Not just my assignment—my name. I hadn't been chosen to participate in the Student Mission Project at all!

I read through the list one more time, taking note of who *had* been selected. "Unbelievable! They approved that guy and not me? *She*'s going to France? That's where I wanted to go." Dazed and confused, I made my way back to my room. What in the world had gone wrong? Was I being penalized for my honesty? Was there any appeal? I had agonized over my availability only to be told it was all for naught. It was the first time I had aspired to an opportunity or challenge where I fell short. I had opened myself up to my peers. They weighed my assets and my flaws and gave their stamp of disapproval—"rejected."

In my plans and in my prayers I had anticipated every eventuality but this one. I had echoed Jesus' words of submission: "Your will be done." I had made myself available to serve anyplace on the planet. And He was sending me—where? Home? Through tears of confusion and frustration, lying in the top bunk in my dorm room, I vented my anger at the patent unfairness of the treatment I had received. And as I came to grips with the undeniable reality that such clueless students had become the administrators of God's will in my life, I complained about His complicity in their collective stupidity.

But the anger surrendered to a deeper commitment to the lordship of Christ. Coming to my senses, yet still deeply hurt and confused, I asked, "What are You trying to teach me?"

Then I "heard" the words of Jesus: "What is that to you? You follow Me" (John 21:22). He had spoken those words to Simon Peter some two thousand years previously. They were recorded in the concluding verses of John's Gospel. In an analogous situation, Peter had been questioning the fairness of Jesus' intentions for John compared to His plans for Peter. But as I heard His reply in my mind, Jesus may as well have been standing in my room. And the words were clearly being addressed to me.

Now this may sound like I'm describing the same "inner impression" or "inner voice" espoused by the traditional view. But there are important differences. In this instance, the message was the verbatim, recorded words of Jesus being applied to me in the same way they had originally been applied to Peter. And there was no purported guidance into the individual will of God, only the moral will of God: "Follow Me."

The impact of those two sentences was immediate and overwhelming. I was being told that the Lord of the harvest knows what He's doing. Thirty-three students were being deployed around the world. He had other plans for me. I was not to compare myself with anyone else. I was not to fret about the opinions of others; my worth and security rest in the Lord. While not knowing what I would be doing with my summer, I was to trust in Him. If this door was closed, another would open.

Two sentences spoken by Jesus brought clarity, hope, and peace.

But where had they come from? Well, from the Bible, to be sure. But earlier in the semester, during Spiritual Emphasis Week, Dr. Vernon Grounds had spoken in chapel from John 21. Jesus' correction of Peter had been the theme of one of his messages. I had appreciated the theoretical application of those words to my life at the time. Now the Spirit of God was drawing those words from my memory and driving them home to my heart. The effect on me was profound. (I even wrote a song about the passage and my experience—"What Is That to You?"—that has encouraged half-dozens of people.)

There are two parts to "the rest of the story." Part 1 is that my home church offered me a position to lead the Christian education ministry for the summer. It was an open door that I chose to accept. I got to benefit from the mentoring of my own father who was senior pastor of the church. The experience was extraordinarily fruitful. And four years later,

I was granted an assignment through the summer mission program of Dallas Theological Seminary. Four additional years of growth and training expanded not only the value of the three months I spent in Nigeria, but also my ability to contribute to the work of SIM. I got to teach at a training school for pastors, and a correspondence course that I wrote to assist the follow-up ministry of a prolific Nigerian evangelist was distributed all over the country.

When I applied for the Student Mission Project assignment in college, I had thought that God said, "No." Instead, it turned out He intended for me to wait—and prepare. As with Paul's plans to visit Rome (Romans 15), it wasn't a matter of *whether* but *when*. And while the delay was initially frustrating, hindsight has demonstrated that my earlier rejection proved to be spiritually valuable to me and others in a host of ways. That encounter with Jesus and His Word assured me of His personal interest in me and gave me confidence that He was indeed working out His purposes in my life.

Chicago, We Have a Problem

Another way that the Spirit can convey the reality of God's presence is through His sovereign and circumstantial response to a difficult situation in our lives. This may take the form of an answer to prayer, or it may be a provision to a need we didn't even know we had. Again, the illustration comes from Robin's experience.

On the second Sunday in January, 1996, my wife, Louise, and I took our eighteen-year-old daughter, Rachel, to Reno, Nevada, to put her on a plane back to school. We had just completed Christmas vacation and it was time for our firstborn to return for the second half of her freshman year at Wheaton College. We arrived at the airport a full hour ahead of the scheduled departure time for her flight. It probably should have struck me as odd that there wasn't a longer line of people given that her plane was bound for Chicago. But, in fact, we were the only ones there.

My first clue that something was amiss was the perplexed look on the ticket agent's face as she looked from Rachel's ticket to the computer monitor in front of her. What she held in her hand was a ticket with a confirmed reservation. What was missing from the monitor was any indication of that particular flight. The agent turned to her supervisor and said, "We don't have a 12:15 flight today, do we?"

The answer was no. Reno Air had canceled that flight. I had purchased the ticket some four months previously from a travel agent in Portland, Oregon, so there had been no way for Reno Air to notify us of the cancellation. There was good news. There was another flight scheduled for 6:15 that evening, and there was still a seat available on it. It wouldn't arrive until 12:30 a.m., but Rachel wouldn't be stranded forever in Reno.

Plan B was not without its problems. Before she left Wheaton, Rachel had purchased a round-trip ticket for a shuttle service at a cost of fifteen dollars each way. The shuttle was a van usually shared by several students for the half-hour drive from campus to the airport. But at 11 p.m., the van stopped running and was replaced by a limousine that cost forty-three dollars one way. She would have to cough up the additional twenty-eight dollars, a substantial sum to a college student. And the loss was all the more galling because the delay was not her fault.

Actually, it was my fault. At first I had been angry at Reno Air (a common emotion in airports), but it eventually sank in that they had had no way to inform us of the change. I had purchased the ticket, and it was my responsibility to confirm the flight a few days in advance. But I had forgotten to do that. So I was too busy kicking myself to give Rachel the extra fare for the limo.

We hung out at Barnes & Noble for the afternoon. Then we put Rachel on the 6:15 flight and she was off to Chicago, right on schedule.

Louise and I made the five-hour drive back to our home in Southern Oregon. As we're driving along in the dark, we're wondering how everything is going to work out. And we're praying about it. My emotional involvement is heightened because this incident has surfaced a couple of issues. One of them has to do with my identity, because a big chunk of who I am is Rachel's dad. And part of my new assignment is to release the care of my daughter into God's hands. But I'm not feeling too good about this situation for a couple of reasons. First, my neglect was responsible for this whole mess. And what I was experiencing was a failure in fatherhood, of not taking care of her.

And now, thanks to me, she's about to get off an airplane two thousand miles away and get into a limousine driven by God-knows-who. I'm wondering, where do they get their drivers? My eighteen-year-old daughter is about to get into a car in Chicago with a strange man at 12:30 in the morning for a half-hour drive to the suburbs—and I'm having serious second thoughts about the wisdom of this whole plan. Because she is totally unprotected in the Big City. And there isn't anything I can do about it. So that's why I'm praying.

Rachel gets to O'Hare, finds her luggage, and calls the limo. The driver pulls up in a station wagon. As she climbs into the car, she's crying because she's worn out and frustrated and things just seem out of control. The limo driver notices that she's upset and asks her what's wrong. She says, "I just need to get to school." And he asks, "Is the additional cost you're having to pay the problem?" And she admits that's part of it. And he replies, "Well, why don't you just pay the fifteen dollars you planned on in the first place, *and we'll let Jesus take care of the rest.*"

I'm worried that the devil himself is going to pick her up, and God sent a brother. (I hope, somehow, he gets to read this.)

God was actively engaged with us, teaching us some important things. Rachel learned that even when she feels like she's all alone, she isn't. And I learned, again, that God can be trusted to be my daughter's Father. God was using an anxiety-filled situation to strengthen both of us in areas that needed growth. And in the process, He encouraged all of us by giving us a glimpse of His involvement in our lives.

Pay Attention, Sherlock

I have since come to label such interventions as the "fingerprints of God." Here's a formal definition: A fingerprint is a noteworthy event or provision or change of circumstance that draws my attention to God in a way that provokes awe, thanksgiving, love, and trust, and encourages me to endure in faithfulness to Him. I don't have a biblical reference that obligates God to leave such pointers to His activity on my behalf. But He has promised to meet my needs and to provide sufficient grace for my weaknesses. And fingerprints are one way He fulfills those promises in my life and the lives of others.

The thing about fingerprints is that they are subtle. What we would like is a finger pointing the way we should go. What we get, sometimes, is a tangible clue that wherever we go, He is with us. We would like to see God face-to-face. But in this life, where we walk by faith, we may occasionally catch traces of Him in our peripheral vision, so to speak.

And when that happens, though it is only a foretaste of what is to come, it takes our breath away.

Even though God is not giving specific guidance through inner impressions, that does not mean He is absent from our lives. The Spirit of God has His ways of mediating the presence of Jesus to our hearts. In the two instances just narrated, the perception of God's involvement occurred *after* the decision was made. In the first case, a decision that did not initially work out the way Robin had hoped became the occasion for a "message" from Jesus: "What is that to you? You follow Me." In the second case, a faulty decision by Robin provided the opportunity for God to teach important lessons while demonstrating His faithfulness and grace. It was with hindsight that Joseph said to his brothers, "As for you, you meant evil against me, but God meant it for good in order to bring about this present result, to preserve many people alive" (Genesis 50:20).

This pattern substantiates the notion that God is more concerned about who we are than what we do; He focuses more on our character than our conduct. We want to know what God wants us to do; God wants us to know Him. So instead of telling us how to choose in advance, He confirms (often later) that as we decide, He is actively involved with us, working out His purposes in our lives through our decisions. (And that is true even when we mess up.)

We want to know what God wants us to do; God wants us to know Him.

So how are we to respond to this personal guidance? "We walk by faith, not by sight" (2 Corinthians 5:7). Philip Yancey put it well:

> I now hear the phrase "practicing the presence of God" in a different way. Previously I sought an emotional confirmation that God is actually there. Sometimes I have that sense, sometimes I do not. I have changed the emphasis, though, to one of putting myself in God's presence. I assume that God is present all around me, though undetectable by my senses, and I strive to conduct my daily life in a way appropriate to God's presence.[9]

Oh, and watch out for fingerprints.

1. A. W. Tozer, *The Root of the Righteous* (Camp Hill, PA: Christian Publications, Incorporated, 1986), cited by Charles R. Swindoll, *The Tale of the Tardy Oxcart and 1,501 Other Stories* (Nashville, TN: Word Publishing, 1998), 77.
2. James Montgomery Boice gives the following explanation of the imagery in the first paragraph of Galatians 4:

   "The English reader will miss the flavor of these verses unless he realizes that the moment of growing up was a very definite one in antiquity and that it involved matters of great religious and legal importance....

   "Under Roman law there was...a time for the coming of age of a son. But the age when this took place may not have been as fixed as is often assumed (cf. Lightfoot), with the result that the father may have had discretion in setting the time of his son's maturity.... A Roman child became an adult at the sacred family festival known as the *Liberalia,* held annually on the seventeenth of March. At this time the child was formally adopted by the father as his acknowledged son and heir and received the *toga virilis* in place of the *toga praetexta* which he had previously worn....

   "This is the general background...of Paul's words in these verses.

   "When the child was a minor in the eyes of the law—it is this word that Paul actually uses—his status is no different from that of a slave, even though he was the future owner of a vast estate. He could make no decisions; he had no freedom. On the other hand, at the time set by his father the child entered into his responsibility and freedom. The application of the illustration is obvious as Paul applies it to the inferior condition of a person under law, both a 'minor' and a 'slave,' and to the new freedom and responsibility that come to him in Christ." (Frank E. Gaebelein, gen. ed., *The Expositor's Bible Commentary*, vol. 10: "Galatians," by James Montgomery Boice [Grand Rapids, MI: Zondervan, 1976], 471.)
3. Philip Yancey, *Reaching for the Invisible God* (Grand Rapids, MI: Zondervan, 2000), 214, 217.
4. J. I. Packer makes this intriguing observation: "God...is very gentle with very young Christians, just as mothers are with very young babies. Often the start of their Christian career is marked by great emotional joy, striking providences, remarkable answers to prayer, and immediate fruitfulness in their first acts of witness; thus God encourages them, and establishes them in 'the life.' But as they grow stronger, and are able to bear more, He exercises them in a tougher school. He exposes them to as much testing by the pressure of opposed and discouraging influences as they are able to bear—not more (see the promise of 1 Corinthians 10:13), but equally not less (see the admonition, Acts 14:22). Thus He builds our character, strengthens our faith, and prepares us to help others." J. I. Packer, *Knowing God* (Downers Grove, IL: InterVarsity Press, 1973), 223–24.
5. Ibid., 182, 184.
6. J. I. Packer, *Keep in Step with the Spirit* (Old Tappan, NJ: Fleming H. Revell Company, 1984), 49.
7. Ibid., 72–73.
8. Ibid., 72.
9. Yancey, *Reaching for the Invisible God,* 207.

part four

deciding the BIG ONES

The Wisdom View Applied

chapter nineteen

SINGLENESS, MARRIAGE, AND WISDOM

Before we stroll down the pathway to marital (or celibate) bliss, let's shinny up a flagpole for a better glimpse of the terrain.

In part 4 we move from our development of general principles to a consideration of specific applications. The way of wisdom will now be applied to decisions pertaining to singleness and marriage, vocational choices, giving to the Lord's work, and matters where Christians disagree.

The specific topics addressed in part 4 have three common elements: (1) they are of *universal interest,* (2) they involve *important decisions*, and (3) there is significant *biblical teaching* directed to each issue.

Part 4 will shed the light of God's Word on specific, important decisions and further validate the way of wisdom through consistent application of the guidance principles we have established.

Marital (or Celibate) Bliss

Without question, Ted Bradford and Annette Miller qualify as the great matchup of the year at Faith Bible College. They are highly committed to Christ, and both are strongly considering vocational service to the Lord. They are perfect for each other.

Well, almost perfect. If it weren't for the Africa business... If Ted had a clearer call to the ministry... If only they could, in good conscience, follow the "almost perfect" will of God. It is unsettling when the pieces of the decision-making jigsaw refuse to match. When the issues are life shaping, the anxiety can be acute.

Indeed, if the counsel sincerely offered by Pastor Thompson is correct, the implications for Ted's marriage decision are sobering. There is either no person or only one person who is eligible to be his wife. If God wants him to be single, any marriage is wrong. If he marries the wrong person, he is out of God's will. If either he or the woman God has chosen marry out of God's will, there is nothing they can do to return to the center of His will. They are permanently stranded in the barren terrain of God's "second (third, fourth...) best."

When the stakes are that high, most people would rather not gamble on anything less than a sure thing—but getting to the sure thing is precisely the problem.

The sad part is that so much of the trauma Ted and Annette experience is unnecessary. Though the marriage choice is significant, the obligation imposed by the traditional view to discover the one and only acceptable candidate among a field of millions has added unnecessary stress.

There is a better way. It may not be simple, but it is more biblical. The way of wisdom teaches that since believers are given no imperatives commanding or forbidding marriage, these decisions fall within the area of freedom. From that perspective, the goal of all Christians is to make wise decisions—decisions that will best enable them to obey God's commands to the fullest.

In the Bible there are passages that explicitly address singleness and marriage. This chapter will apply that scriptural wisdom to the decision of whether to marry. The next chapter will consider the selection of a mate.

THE TEACHING OF JESUS

Celibates for Jesus

> Some Pharisees came to Jesus, testing Him and asking, "Is it lawful for a man to divorce his wife for any reason at all?" (Matthew 19:3)

This was a loaded question. Some Jews followed the stricter school of Shammai in holding that sexual immorality was the only legitimate grounds for divorce. But many agreed with the more liberal rabbi, Hillel, that a man could divorce his wife if she displeased him "for any reason at all."

Rather than becoming embroiled in that dispute, Jesus reaffirmed God's original purpose—marriage was designed to join one man and one woman permanently. "What therefore God has joined together," He concluded, "let no man separate" (Matthew 19:6). It was a brilliant answer, undercutting all of the pious debate over what was merely permissible.

"Why then," they countered, "did Moses command to give her a certificate of divorce and send her away?" (19:7). Jesus' reply was complete:

> Because of your hardness of heart Moses permitted you to divorce your wives; but from the beginning it has not been this way. And I say to you, whoever divorces his wife, except for immorality, and marries another woman commits adultery. (Matthew 19:8–9)

That answer, which simultaneously refuted the position of Hillel and silenced the Pharisees, planted a serious question in the minds of His disciples. "If the relationship of the man with his wife is like this, it is better not to marry" (19:10). It was conceivable, they reasoned, for a man to unwittingly marry a contentious woman who could make life miserable for him (Proverbs 21:9). If divorce was ruled out except for immorality, the man would be permanently locked into an intolerable situation.

The Pharisees must have been delighted with the disciples' reaction. If Jesus agreed with His disciples, He would be contradicting the Old

Testament teaching of the blessedness of marriage and the reward of a quiver full of children (Genesis 2:18; Psalm 127:3–5). But if He could not accept the ramifications articulated by His disciples, He would have to adopt a more liberal stance on divorce.

Jesus did not agree or disagree with the disciples. Instead He said, "Not all men can accept this statement, but only those to whom it has been given." He then went on to list three categories of men who, in fact, do not marry: (1) those who are unable to do so by reason of birth defect; (2) those who are rendered incapable of marriage by the hands of others; and (3) those who choose to remain single in order to more effectively serve the kingdom of heaven (Matthew 19:11–12).[1]

In effect, Jesus was agreeing that for some men singleness is preferable to marriage. This was true not just because of the negative risks inherent in the bonds of marriage, but because of the positive potentials of service to God. On the other hand, His warning, "He who is able to accept this, let him accept it" (19:12), was a reminder that not all men can handle celibacy. For them, a wise marriage is better.

In short, Jesus taught that singleness and marriage are both acceptable to God. Neither marriage nor singleness is commanded by God, even for the sake of the kingdom of God. For some, as the disciples had said, "it is better not to marry." But others could find celibacy too hard to take. For them, the ability to function most effectively as a single person had not been given (19:11).

THE TEACHING OF PAUL

What Jesus declared in capsule form, Paul amplified and developed in 1 Corinthians 7. Answering the Corinthians' questions about the appropriateness of marriage, he penned the central passage in the Bible on singleness.

If ever there was a place where we could expect biblical substantiation of the traditional view, that place is 1 Corinthians 7. Should a Christian marry? One would expect the apostle to direct believers to discover God's individual will for such a crucial decision. But Paul did not hold that view. Probably for this reason few contemporary books on God's will give much attention to this passage despite its in-depth treatment of the issue. For while Paul has a lot to say about the pros and cons of celibacy and marriage, he makes no comment whatsoever about God's individual will.

Paul's discussion has three parts. In 1 Corinthians 7:1–7, he establishes the general principles as a foundation for the whole chapter. In verses 8–24, he focuses on the problems of the married. And in verses 25–40, he discusses the problems of the unmarried.[2]

Regulated Freedom

> Now concerning the things about which you wrote, it is good for a man not to touch a woman. But because of immoralities, each man is to have his own wife, and each woman is to have her own husband. The husband must fulfill his duty to his wife, and likewise also the wife to her husband. The wife does not have authority over her own body, but the husband does; and likewise also the husband does not have authority over his own body, but the wife does. Stop depriving one another, except by agreement for a time, so that you may devote yourselves to prayer, and come together again so that Satan will not tempt you because of your lack of self-control. But this I say by way of concession, not of command. Yet I wish that all men were even as I myself am. However, each man has his own gift from God, one in this manner, and another in that. (1 Corinthians 7:1–7)

Paul's opening statement reveals his preference for the celibate state. ("Touch a woman," being a euphemism for sexual intercourse, is a practical equivalent for "marry.")[3] Those who are single are most vulnerable to sexual sin. For that reason, marriage provides the surest protection from temptation. Again, neither celibacy nor marriage is commanded (7:6). Each person has to choose what is best in their situation (7:7).[4] So Robertson and Plummer summarize Paul's thought: "Celibacy is good, but marriage is natural."[5]

Those who choose marriage incur certain obligations. These obligations prohibit intimate relations outside of marriage (7:2) or sexual fraud within marriage (7:3–5). The one who marries is thereby bound to fulfill his or her conjugal duties.

At the outset, Paul established an important principle: One's decision about marriage is *regulated* by the moral will of God, but *not determined* by it. If a believer marries, he or she may marry only another believer (Paul assumes here what he states later; see 7:39). That is God's moral will and it must be obeyed. Second, if one marries, the biblical obligations to one's spouse must be met.

One's decision about marriage is regulated by the moral will of God, but not determined by it.

But the choice of whether to marry or remain single lies within the area of freedom. Paul clearly preferred celibacy and "wished" all others could so choose. But he knew he could not give his desire the force of a command. For not everyone "has the gift." God graces each believer differently. It is likely that Paul's meaning is that some are gifted to enjoy singleness while others are gifted to enjoy marriage with its extra responsibilities (7:7). One's own makeup must be taken into consideration, but the choice is a personal one (7:6).

The principle that the marriage decision is regulated but not determined by God's moral will is reaffirmed throughout the chapter. Freedom to choose is declared in each of the following verses:

> *1 Corinthians 7:25*: Now concerning virgins I have *no command* of the Lord....

> *1 Corinthians 7:28*: But if you marry, you *have not sinned*; and if a virgin marries, she *has not sinned.*

> *1 Corinthians 7:36*: But if any man thinks he is behaving improperly toward his virgin, if she is past the flower of youth, and thus it must be, *let him do what he wishes. He does not sin;* let them marry (NKJV).

> *1 Corinthians 7:39*: A wife is bound as long as her husband lives; but if her husband is dead, she is *free* to be married *to whom she wishes*, only in the Lord.

Again, all of those expressions of freedom of choice are circumscribed by the moral will of God. In addition to the imperatives already noted from the first seven verses, God's moral will prohibits: (1) divorce for two married believers (7:10); (2) remarriage of either a Christian wife or a Christian husband if they separate (7:11); (3) divorce by a believer of an unbeliever who is willing to continue the marriage (7:13–15); (4) marriage to an unbeliever (7:39; 9:5; 2 Corinthians 6:14).

Weighing the Factors

Nowhere does Paul suggest that the marriage decision is determined either by God's moral will or by His individual will. It lies in the area of freedom and believers are responsible for their choices. Now if God's moral will and so-called individual will are not the basis for such a decision, *there must be some other criteria.* Since this is a noncommanded decision, on what basis is it to be made?

Paul enumerates some of the advantages and disadvantages of both states. His emphasis is upon the advantages of singleness. His reasons for this preference are as follows: to avoid unnecessary worry (7:20–21); to avoid needless troubles (7:28); to make better use of limited time (7:29–31); to be free from concern (7:32); to be able to give undistracted attention to "the things of the Lord" (7:32); to promote personal happiness (7:40). Paul sums up the reasons for his recommendation of celibacy in 1 Corinthians 7:35: "This I say for your *own benefit;* not to put a restraint upon you, but to *promote* what is *appropriate,* and to secure *undistracted devotion to the Lord.*" That is practical wisdom.

To appreciate Paul's perspective, I suggest a simple exercise. Find a couple whose marriage you respect and ask them, "Does it take hard work to make a marriage work?" Then listen to the wisdom flow.

I Don't Think I Have the Gift!

On the other hand, there are advantages to marriage that make it preferable for most. The temptation to sexual sin is greatly reduced by marriage (7:2–5). Contentment with celibacy requires a "gift" from God not all possess (7:7). If an individual lacking this gift were to try to serve the Lord as a single person, it is likely that there would be continual distractions from sensuous enticements (7:9). For the person lacking in self-control, the choice is between potential distraction (marriage) or potential destruction (sexual sin).

On the positive side, marriage offers opportunities for ministry, especially to one's family (7:14–16). Furthermore, it always pleases God when His children obey His commandments (7:19). And so the fulfillment of one's marital obligations conforms to the moral will of God (7:2–5). In short, marriage permits people to channel their God-given drives away from illicit behavior and toward God's original design for mutual fulfillment and completion. That, too, is practical wisdom.

A Mutual Appreciation Society

Writing the first edition of this book provided an illustration of these contrasts between singleness and marriage. I am single and Robin is married. And, for the record, we both enjoy our respective states. In working so closely together, we came to appreciate in a fresh way both the advantages of the other's status and the blessings of our own.

Garry: "I stayed in the home of Robin and Louise Maxson for five weeks while Robin and I began our work on this book. At the beginning of the project, my pump was primed. I was away from my office, my classroom, and, above all, my telephone. As far as I was concerned, Klamath Falls, Oregon, was at the end of the world and I was delighted to be there. I was able to work all day without interruptions, get some exercise, eat supper, and put in another two or three hours at the typewriter before going to bed."

Robin: "I was excited to be involved in such a project, and I think my enthusiasm matched Garry's. It wasn't long, though, before I began to notice a difference in the level of our productivity. Garry was able to devote more time to the project than I could, since, in addition to my wife (who could have easily become a 'book widow'), we had an eleven-month-old baby girl who needed some attention from Daddy. From time to time, some of that attention was demanded in the middle of the night. And so there would be mornings when, as Garry left for the office bright-eyed and bushy-tailed, I was still recovering from my early morning visits with Rachel Beth. When he headed back to the office after supper, I stayed home to spend some time with my family.

"Both Garry and I understood that my responsibilities to my family took precedence over my work on the book. And normally that is a priority I find great delight in. But in that situation, I had to consciously deal with the feelings of resentment that began to creep in because of my inability to match Garry's output on the manuscript."

Garry: "My apartment in Portland was a house, but not really a home. I felt the difference with the Maxson family. Meals were occasions for fellowship, not just eating. I began to appreciate the value of companionship between husband and wife through the thick and thin of everyday living.

"Then there was my new love—Rachel Beth. She was just shy of being one year old, and barely shy of being able to walk. As she began to take her first steps, I saw a glimpse of the miracle of watching a young life develop. It was nice being 'Uncle Garry' instead of 'Dr. Friesen' for five weeks. Each day I looked forward to getting 'home' from writing to play 'Where's Rachel?'—a variation on the peekaboo theme.

"Then, Michael Benjamin arrived. He looked like elder material, though it was a bit early to tell. I'm an uncle twice! I'm content in my single state, but you won't hear me knocking marriage. God made it beautiful, just like Paul said in Ephesians 5."

Robin: "The frustration I experienced over not being able to match Garry's pace was new to me. We had worked on projects together before and our contribution had been about equal. But that was when we were in seminary and I was single, too!

"Did this experience make me long for the days when I was footloose and fancy-free? Sure it did...for about five seconds. That's how long it took my good sense to return. The Lord has gifted me with a beautiful family and the ability to enjoy each one thoroughly. Yet I marvel afresh at God's wisdom in equipping some to live alone. I am a beneficiary of what such individuals are able to accomplish in their 'undistracted devotion to the Lord.' And I am grateful."

Bloom Where You Are Planted

In 1 Corinthians 7:17–24, Paul sets forth an overriding principle that applies to all Christians. To the married, the single, the divorced, the widowed, the circumcised, the uncircumcised, the enslaved, the free, Paul says: "Each one is to remain with God in that condition in which he was called" (7:24). Rather than being preoccupied with a change of status, we should each seek to serve God as effectively as possible in our present state. The poster says it well: "Bloom where you are planted!"

Paul was not forbidding marriage for single people or freedom for slaves. If the opportunity comes along and it is beneficial to take it, do so (7:21).[6] His point was that people tend to concentrate on the wrong things. They pour their energies into changing their condition rather than changing the world for Christ's sake.

So, how should we decide about marriage? Weigh all the factors and make a wise decision. And what constitutes a wise decision? A wise decision:

1. Is good (in the sense of profitable, 7:1, 8, 26)
2. Is better (7:9, 38)
3. Leads to peace (7:15)
4. Best helps me keep the commands of God (7:19)
5. Causes the least trouble (7:28)
6. Makes the best use of time (7:29)
7. Is most free of external concerns (7:33)
8. Is beneficial (7:35)
9. Promotes what is appropriate (7:35)
10. Leads to undistracted devotion to the Lord (7:35)
11. Is necessary (7:36)
12. Promotes personal happiness (7:40)

The decision about our choice of singleness or marriage must be made according to spiritual advantage or benefit. Paul's detailed discussion urges us to carefully consider the advantages and disadvantages of each state for serving God. The believer is then free and responsible to choose the state that, in his judgment, will bring the greatest benefit to the Lord's kingdom. For some, singleness is better than marriage; but for others, the natural state of marriage is better. The objective for the believer is not to find the decision God has already made (as in the traditional view), but to make a wise decision.

---

1. "Eunuch" may be taken in a literal or figurative sense. It is best to take the first two cases in Matthew 19:12 as literal and the final case as figurative "of those who abstain fr. marriage, without being impotent." William F. Arndt and F. Wilbur Gingrich, trans., *A Greek-English Lexicon of the New Testament and Other Early Christian Literature*, 2nd. ed. (Chicago: The University of Chicago Press, 1979), s.vv. εὐνουχίζω and εὐνοῦχος.

2. S. Lewis Johnson Jr. "1 Corinthians," in *The New Testament and Wycliffe Bible Commentary* (New York: The Iverson-Norman Associates, 1971), 607.
3. Accordingly, the New International Version renders the statement: "It is good for a man not to marry." "To marry" is probably not the best translation, but it is clearly Paul's meaning since sexual relations are proper only within marriage. "Touch" is equal to sexual intercourse in Genesis 20:6. Arndt and Gingrich, *A Greek-English Lexicon*, s.v. ἅπτω.
4. Some people have construed Paul's remarks here as a deprecation of marriage. Ephesians 5:22–33, written by the same man, proves that is not the case. If a person were to read only Ephesians 5 with its obvious message that marriage is beautiful, he might conclude that Paul considered the celibate state to be second-class. If that same person were to read only 1 Corinthians 7 with its assertion that singleness has advantages, he might conclude that Paul considered the married state to be second-class. Reading both passages reveals Paul's true perspective: Marriage is beautiful, but singleness has advantages. One must weigh the advantages and disadvantages of each state, and choose.
5. Archibald Robertson and Alfred Plummer, *A Critical and Exegetical Commentary on the First Epistle of St. Paul to the Corinthians, The International Critical Commentary* (Edinburgh: T&T Clark, 1911), 130.
6. The NIV translates, "although if you can gain your freedom, do so." Some commentators take this phrase in an opposite sense to mean even if you can gain your freedom, rather use your slavery position and turn the freedom down. Such an interpretation is possible, but has weaker contextual support. Reasons for the view taken here are enumerated by Robertson and Plummer, *First Epistle of St. Paul to the Corinthians*, 147–48; Frank E. Gaebelein, gen. ed., *The Expositor's Bible Commentary*, vol. 10: "1 Corinthians," by W. Harold Mare (Grand Rapids, MI: Zondervan, 1976), 235.

chapter twenty

MARRIAGE AND WISDOM

It is better to live in a corner of a roof
Than in a house shared with a contentious woman.
(Proverbs 21:9)

It is better to live in a desert land
Than with a contentious and vexing woman. (Proverbs 21:19)

A constant dripping on a day of steady rain
And a contentious woman are alike;
He who would restrain her restrains the wind,
And grasps oil with his right hand. (Proverbs 27:15–16)

Reflecting on verses such as these prompted Pastor Bill Hybels to write:

> The first time I read the book of Proverbs, I was a little surprised by its straightforward manner in addressing the subject of marriage. After many years of study and analysis, I have concluded that the wisdom of Proverbs regarding the selection of a marriage partner is: Don't mess it up.[1]

Indeed! Nobody's going to argue with that sentiment. But the divorce rate in our culture proves that it's easier said than done. So how does one avoid a huge mistake in the selection of a suitable spouse?

The traditional view says there is only one way to not mess it up: Find the individual will of God for this decision. Follow His leading, they say, to the one person He has already chosen for you. And proponents of the traditional view often refer to two beautiful stories in Genesis to support their approach. For in both instances, God chose the bride.

GOD'S WILL FOR ADAM AND EVE

A Matter of Limited Options

Genesis 2 describes the creation of Adam (v. 7) and Eve (v. 22) and their subsequent wedding.

> The LORD God fashioned into a woman the rib which He had taken from the man, and brought her to the man. The man said, "This is now bone of my bones, and flesh of my flesh; she shall be called Woman, because she was taken out of Man." (Genesis 2:22–23)

Some writers take this passage to indicate that for each man, God has prepared one woman perfectly suited to be his wife. Now Genesis 2 *does* set forth several normative principles for marriage. We know this because they are stated, and *declared to be normative,* in verse 24: "For this reason a man shall leave his father and his mother, and be joined to his wife; and they shall become one flesh."

However, nothing whatever is said about mate selection. No promise is made that God will similarly prepare and introduce men and women He has chosen to be joined in marriage. Eve was part of God's *revealed* will for Adam because He created her and brought her to Adam to be his wife. The whole scenario was an extraordinary event never again repeated. There could be only one first man and one first woman. That's what it took to start the human race.

GOD'S WILL FOR ISAAC AND REBEKAH

One Hump or Two?

The most frequently cited biblical support for the traditional view's concept of a divinely chosen spouse is Genesis 24. Abraham sent his trusted servant to the city of Nahor in Mesopotamia to seek out a wife for his son Isaac from among Abraham's relatives. When he arrived at his destination, the servant stopped by a well and made this request of God:

> O LORD, the God of my master Abraham, please grant me success today, and show lovingkindness to my master Abraham. Behold, I am standing by the spring, and the daughters of the men of the city are coming out to draw water; now may it be that the girl to whom I say, 'Please let down your jar so that I may drink,' and who answers, 'Drink, and I will water your camels also'—may she be the one whom You have appointed for Your servant Isaac; and by this I will know that You have shown lovingkindness to my master. (Genesis 24:12–14)

Soon thereafter, Rebekah came to the well and fulfilled the sign completely. The servant visited her family, Rebekah agreed to become Isaac's wife, and the servant was able to take her back to Canaan. Mission accomplished!

This passage provides apparent support for three specific aspects of the traditional view: (1) the granting of detailed guidance beyond the moral will of God, (2) the validity of using a circumstantial fleece to discover God's will, and (3) the notion that God's individual will includes the specific person a believer is supposed to marry.

The problem with arguing these points from Genesis 24 is that the experience of Abraham's servant is *not normative.* Virtually no one is inclined to take it that way. Who would be willing to send out a servant to seek a wife for a son, and then accept that servant's choice on the basis of a drink of water for man and beasts?

But Does She Do Windows?

Of course, it could be done. Making cultural allowances, a father could hire a Christian dating agency. He could then send its agent on a search to find a wife for his son. The agent could drive into a service station, offer a prayer, and sign up the first woman who meets his request for a drink by filling his water jug and checking his radiator! The idea sounds preposterous, because Genesis 24 is not normative for several reasons.

First, the Bible does not promise that every believer will have a mate. But Isaac *had* to have one, because God had promised Abraham that he would have innumerable descendants (Genesis 15:5; 24:7). That promise required both a wife and the birth of a son. Therefore, Genesis 24 does not depict the normal father using the normal method to pick a normal wife for his normal son. Rather, the account concerns Abraham, the recipient of God's covenant oath and the consequent promise of a great seed. "Isaac was not regarded as a merely pious candidate for matrimony, but as heir of the promise."[2] For this reason, the servant based his request on God's character as One who is faithful to His promises (Genesis 24:7, 14, 27). And the wife that would fulfill the divine promise was appropriately described as the one "appointed" (Genesis 24:14)—appointed, not because God has selected a mate in His individual will for each person, but because God promised a wife for Isaac.

Furthermore, God had promised special guidance for the servant to guarantee the success of his venture. Specifically, an angel went ahead of the servant to make sure that the goal was accomplished (24:7, 40). Such a guarantee and such angelic assistance go beyond the normal promises of God's guidance.

When in Doubt, Check Things Out

From the behavior of Abraham's servant, it is clear that the circumstantial fleece was not the usual method of guidance even then. Having no other ideas on how to proceed, but being fully assured of God's guidance, the servant asked God to give the needed guidance through this method (24:12). He did not know for sure that the Lord would do what he asked; he simply asked, and then watched to see what would happen. Even when the sign was quickly fulfilled, he was still not sure that God was using his sign (24:21).[3] Even when the woman's background was discovered to be acceptable (24:23–24), the matter was not concluded in the servant's mind until Rebekah indicated a willingness to return with him (24:58). If her family would not let her go, he would look elsewhere for a wife (24:49). By his careful investigation following the fulfillment of the sign, the servant showed his awareness that such a procedure was highly unorthodox, and not to be fully trusted until all other conditions were met.

Genesis 24 does not contain a promise of specific guidance, nor approval for providential signs, nor any indication that God will choose and reveal one's perfect mate. From the text it is clear that events unfolded as they did because of the existence of a special covenant, the promise of angelic assistance guaranteeing success, and God's willingness to use a nonnormative method in response to the servant's prayer. This account of special guidance was recorded in detail not because it describes how God normally leads, but because it was an important step in the fulfillment of God's promise to Abraham. God proved to be faithful to each part of the covenant, including the promise of a great seed—a promise that is central to the theme of the book of Genesis.

GOD'S WILL FOR BELIEVERS WHO MARRY

God's normal guidance for choosing a spouse is revealed in 1 Corinthians 7. We have already identified the basic principle expounded by Paul: The believer's decision about marriage is *regulated* by the moral will of God, but *not determined* by it. And this is true not only in the choice between singleness and marriage, but in our choice of a spouse. That is, God's moral will does not tell us who to marry, but it establishes the parameters for making that selection.

In Paul's day, the cultural situation in Corinth was much different from our own. We expect important decisions to be left up to the individuals involved. But 1 Corinthians 7:36–38 reflects a custom where the men made the arrangements for marriage and unwed women had little or no say in the matter.[4] Nevertheless, in any culture the choice of a marriage partner must be made, and the decision is extremely important: "Don't mess it up."

On what basis is it to be made?

"Only in the Lord"

The first test question a believer should ask is: Are there any commands of Scripture that relate to this decision? The answer is yes. Believers may marry only believers. This restriction is assumed throughout 1 Corinthians 7. It is implicit in verses 12–16, which deal with "mixed marriages" where one partner has become a Christian after the marriage. But the imperative is explicitly stated in 1 Corinthians 7:39: "A wife is bound as long as her husband lives; but if her husband is dead, she is free to be married to whom she wishes, *only in the Lord*." The phrase "only in the Lord" means that the marriage partner must be "in the Lord," that is, a believer (see verse 22 where "in the Lord" is used in the sense of becoming a Christian).[5]

Pulling in Opposite Directions

The best cross-reference is 2 Corinthians 6:14–16:

> Do not be bound together with unbelievers; for what partnership have righteousness and lawlessness, or what fellowship has light with darkness? Or what harmony has Christ with Belial, or what has a believer in common with an unbeliever? Or what agreement has the temple of God with idols? For we are the temple of the living God.

In 2 Corinthians 6:14, Paul employed an agricultural metaphor of an ox and a donkey (Deuteronomy 22:10) harnessed together in a double yoke.[6] No believer is to be so "mismated" with an unbeliever. The reasons are set forth in five vivid contrasts: righteousness versus lawlessness, light versus darkness, Christ versus Belial (Satan), a believer versus an unbeliever, and the temple of God versus idols. Not only are the believer's values, goals, motivations, and enablement for living incompatible with those of an unbeliever; they are diametrically opposed! They are serving two different lords that are archenemies of one another.

This passage applies to marriage since its "double yoke" is so tight that the two become "one flesh" (Genesis 2:24; Matthew 19:5; Ephesians 5:31). In biblical terms, marriage is more than a contract; it is a covenant—the most intimate relationship two human beings can enter into. For a Christian to marry a non-Christian is to sow the seeds of conflict and to rule out the possibility of that marriage fully accomplishing its design. For a believer and an unbeliever are fundamentally different at the very core of their lives.[7]

Who Is Lord?

Even more important than the success of the marriage is *obedience.* Christians are not left on earth to promote our own happiness on our own terms; we are on assignment for the kingdom of God. To disobey a direct order from the King is to capitulate to the authority of the other side. Alice Fryling puts it well, "The Christian is mocking God by reneging on his or her commitment to Him. A Christian is committing idolatry by falling down before someone other than God...blatantly disobeying God, who said we are to marry only within the faith."[8] On this point I am in total agreement with the traditional view. The only acceptable mate for a believer is another believer.

As in other noncommanded decisions, then, the choice of a spouse lies inside the area of freedom within the moral will of God: "she is free to be married to whom she wishes, only in the Lord" (1 Corinthians 7:39). So does that mean that anyone who professes faith in Christ is fair game? Or is there more to it than that? Are there any other ways that God's moral will regulates our choice of a spouse so that we "don't mess it up"? There is more: The means of selection must be *moral* and the choice itself must be *wise.*

WISDOM SOURCES FOR MARRIAGE

The story of the courtship of Boaz and Ruth is beautifully narrated in the Old Testament book of Ruth. When Boaz declared his intentions to Ruth, he explained, "for all my people in the city know that you are a *woman of excellence* (Ruth 3:11). Ruth was Boaz's real-life answer to the rhetorical question posed by Proverbs 31: *"An excellent wife,* who can find? For her worth is far above jewels" (Proverbs 31:10).

When Proverbs was written, the cultural norms assigned virtually all of the decision-making authority to men, so much of Proverbs consists of a training manual for young men in preparation for leadership.[9] Though a woman might not have much say in the choice of a husband, she would have great influence on his quality of life. In giving counsel to unmarried men, then, the writers of the proverbs described women at opposite ends of the continuum (Proverbs 21:19; 31:10). One's wife could be "contentious and vexing" (NASB), "quarrelsome and ill-tempered" (NIV), "crabby and complaining" (NLT); or she could be "excellent" (NASB), "of noble character" (NIV), "virtuous and capable" (NLT). Don't mess it up! Accordingly, the first "woman" a believing man should court is Wisdom herself! (Proverbs 2:1–6).

God's provisions for wisdom in the choice of a mate are the same ones I have already described. The experiential starting point may be personal desires and inner impressions, but wisdom begins with the Word of God. For the Bible most completely answers the question: "What am I getting myself into?"

As I have pointed out repeatedly, God's Word reveals many significant obligations that are God's job description for husbands and wives. Once a person marries, the list of imperatives that form God's moral will grows considerably. It is crucial that the unmarried Christian discover what those requirements are. Some of the most important questions are:

1. What are the purposes of marriage?
2. What instructions has God given so that Christian husbands and wives can fulfill God's purposes in their marriages?
3. What are the responsibilities of the husband?
4. What are the responsibilities of the wife?
5. What are the biblical responsibilities for raising children?

In Pursuit of Excellence

The relevance of such questions for mate selection is easy to see. A man would be wise, for instance, to select a woman for whom he could most easily and completely fulfill his commitments as a husband. And he would want to choose a woman whose first marital priority is the fulfillment of her God-given functions as a wife. A woman, observing that Scripture requires her to submit to her husband, should ask in advance, "To what kind of man would submission come easily?" and so on. A man should ask whether the woman he is considering will struggle between her loyalty to him and her pursuit of a career.

From a biblical perspective, the goal of the Christian who chooses to marry is to establish a godly marriage. Thus, the Christian should be looking for a counterpart who is qualified and committed to fulfilling that goal. Who fits that description? In the most general terms, the most spiritually mature person willing to be joined in marriage. So, while the moral will of God specifies that a Christian must marry only a believer, wisdom adds spiritual qualifications and limits the choice to a committed and growing believer. When Christians are thinking through the qualities they seek in a spouse, moral and spiritual characteristics should head the list.

This process is wonderfully illustrated in the book of Ruth, which gives a glimpse into what Boaz and Ruth saw in each other. From observing her in the harvest fields, Boaz knew that Ruth was a hard worker. That was relevant because most of life involves work. They both saw each other getting the yield of the ground from the sweat of their brows (Ruth 2; Proverbs 31:13–16). Further, Boaz witnessed Ruth's devotion to her mother-in-law, Naomi—a woman who described herself as "bitter" (Ruth 1:20; 2:11). Boaz concluded that if Ruth could love an embittered mother-in-law, she could love him, warts and all. As she worked in the fields, Ruth noted that Boaz cared for his workers and they respected him as their foreman. Boaz and Ruth impressed each other with their diligence and their caring spirit. Finally, both were growing in faith. Boaz blessed Ruth for her faith (Ruth 2:12; Proverbs 31:28–29), and his workers blessed Boaz for his faith (Ruth 2:4).

This triad of excellence (worker, lover, grower) is a great place to start.

Some women at Multnomah Bible College created a sweatshirt that proclaimed on the front that the wearer purposed to be a "Proverbs 31 woman." On the back it said, "If you want a Proverbs 31 Woman, you have to be a Proverbs 1–30 Man." The best way to attract a worker, lover, and grower is to be one. Ruths attract Boazes. Boazes attract Ruths.

But how can you know if a prospective partner will love for a lifetime? There are no guarantees, but emulating Boaz and Ruth can give a reliable indication. How does the person you are romantically interested in relate to her sisters, brothers, mother, and father? If she can love those closest to her through the slings and arrows of daily life, she has the real thing. The foolish man says, "She hates her sisters and resents her parents, but she really knows how to love me." Put an unloving woman in a white gown and shower her with rice; and when the honeymoon is over, what you get is a vexing wife (Proverbs 21:19). The foolish woman says, "I'm not marrying him for what he is, but for what he will become."

Put a slothful man in a tux, have him recite his vows, and what you get is a lazy husband.

Getting a Second Opinion

The second wisdom source that should be consulted is *spiritual counselors,* and most of us are blessed with an abundance of this kind of wisdom. Even those who do not have personal access to Christian counselors who specialize in marriage preparation do have access to their wisdom in books, cassette tapes, and seminars.

In a series of messages on Proverbs, Robin presented three talks on "Choosing a Mate." The first of these sermons was titled, "Nine Simple Steps to a Miserable Marriage." Adapting insights from Dr. Neil Clark Warren in *Finding the Love of Your Life*[10] and Pastor Bill Hybels in *Making Life Work: Putting God's Wisdom into Action,*[11] Robin came up with the following list:

Step 1: *Marry an unbeliever.* Though the moral will of God is crystal clear in its prohibition, you are the exception to God's command; you know better.

Step 2: *Marry too quickly.* That is, don't spend enough time in courtship.

Step 3: *Marry too young.* That is, marry before you know who you are (and who your partner is) as an adult.

Step 4: *Marry too eagerly.* That is, expect marriage to be the wonderful solution to all your problems.

Step 5: *Marry to please your (mother, peers, fiancé[e]).* That is, make life-shaping decisions in order to make other people happy.

Step 6: *Make assumptions about marriage expectations.* That is, don't bother to identify and explore your very different and unexpressed expectations.

Step 7: *Base your decision on a narrow range of experiences.* That is, routine dating should provide enough information for a lifelong union.

Step 8: Better yet, *test your potential compatibility by living together first.* How will you gauge long-term success without a trial run?

Step 9: *Ignore unaddressed personality or behavioral issues.* That is, assume that your love will resolve your partner's problems and change him or her.

No one wants a miserable marriage. But couples blindly pursue to their sorrow the foolishness embodied in these nine steps. You would think that the choice of a life partner is significant enough to warrant paying attention to the wisdom of experts in the art of marriage. When Robin gave his talk, several married people joked, "Where were you twenty-five years ago?" Only they weren't all joking. Fortunately, the wisdom of spiritual counselors is readily available today in written and recorded media.

There is no substitute, however, for personal counsel, especially when you are thinking about marrying a specific individual. Anyone in love should give great weight to words of caution coming from mature counselors. The book of Proverbs emphasizes the counsel of parents, and those who reject such wisdom do so to their great peril.

Don't Confuse Me with the Facts

A third wisdom source, and one of the most valuable, is *common sense.* During a romance this is usually a scarce commodity. Ted Bradford and Annette Miller are remarkable exceptions to that rule, but we made them up! Ironically, romance's rout of common sense is plainly observable to all but the participants. This is especially true in the Western culture where romance is emphasized.[12]

Common sense recognizes the value of basic compatibility. Bill Hybels writes:

> Researchers in the area of marital success have concluded that what is most likely to make relationships work over the long haul is similarity. That's right—multiple core similarities. How many times have you heard it said that opposites attract? It may be true that they attract, but research shows that often the very things that initially attract two people later push them apart.[13]

So common sense would advocate constructing a list of areas where compatibility is desirable. This list would include areas such as age, finances, employment, education, personal goals, personality traits, birth control, principles of child rearing, health, hobbies, family background, socioeconomic background, and possessions. Further, the items on this list would be prioritized, making a distinction between essential "core similarities" and less important "bonus affinities."[14]

Beware of Football Nuts and Loose Shrews

In most decisions, *personal desires* are valuable indicators of the ease with which a person will fulfill his obligations. But even more than other wisdom sources, personal desires must be judged by the Word of God and wisdom. For when it comes to marriage, many of our personal desires have been molded by our environment (Romans 12:2). The world rather than the Word can profoundly influence our notions of love, attractiveness, and ways of finding happiness.

> What is most likely to make relationships work over the long haul is similarity. That's right—multiple core similarities.

Desires can enter into a constructive partnership with common sense. Take Fred and Sally. Fred loves football. If he marries someone who hates football, he has added a bit of stress to the marriage. It shouldn't spell doom for the marriage, but every football season, she will have to put up with something she hates or he will do without something he loves.

Sally loves Shakespeare. If she marries someone who is bored by drama and chafes in formal wear, there will be added stress. Someone will have to go to the theater alone, or someone will be bored for three hours.

It is simple wisdom for Fred Football to look for a wife who can at least tolerate an occasional gridiron classic. And Sally Shakespeare would be wise to look for a man who does not think the Elizabethan arts are much ado about nothing. Common sense says that the fewer potholes there are in the pathway of adjustment, the smoother will be the journey to marital unity.

A Dangerous Liaison

So the objective is to apply wisdom in identifying an excellent spouse. But now we must address a key aspect of that process: The method employed in finding a mate must be moral.

This principle used to go without saying. In fact I didn't mention it in the first edition of *Decision Making.* But in the intervening decades, there has been a dramatic increase in the number of single adults whose preparation for marriage includes living together. In 1980 (when this book was first published), the number of cohabiting couples (sexual partners not married to each other) was 1.5 million; by 2000, that number ballooned to 4.75 million. "When blushing brides walk down the aisle at the beginning of the new millennium, well over half have already lived together with a boyfriend."[15] At any given time, 30–40 percent of college students are cohabiting. This arrangement is actually taught and encouraged in some university classes.[16]

That trend is not restricted to non-Christian couples. Increasingly, pastors are being put in the awkward position of responding to wedding requests from cohabiting adults connected to the church.

Christians need to know two things about cohabitation. First, and most important, it is morally wrong. All sexual activity outside of marriage is forbidden—for our good (1 Corinthians 6:13; 10:8; Galatians 5:19; Colossians 3:5). God's standards protect us from harm and provide for our well-being. So unmarried people are called to restraint and chastity (1 Thessalonians 4:3–8; Hebrews 13:4). Rather than accommodate sensual desires, single persons are to resist sexual temptation (Genesis 39:5–10; Job 31:1; 1 Corinthians 6:18; Ephesians 5:1–3; 2 Timothy 2:22).

Second, as a trial run for marriage, cohabitation does not work. A massive array of sociological research confirms that cohabitation actually serves to undermine the success or even survival of a future marriage.[17] The National Marriage Project, located at Rutgers University, reports:

> A careful review of the available social science evidence suggests that living together is not a good way to prepare for marriage or to avoid divorce.... Cohabiting unions tend to weaken the institution of marriage and pose special risks for women and children. Specifically, the research indicates that:
>
> - Living together before marriage increases the risk of breaking up after marriage.
> - Living together outside of marriage increases the risk of domestic violence for women, and the risk of physical and sexual abuse for children.
> - Unmarried couples have lower levels of happiness and well-being than married couples.

The actual statistics cited by this report are more alarming than the academic summaries quoted above. For instance, one study found that cohabitors who marry are estimated to have a 46 percent higher chance of marital breakup than noncohabitors.[18]

So while there may be a logic to cohabitation as a means of evaluating a potential marriage partner, that practice is actually counterproductive and destructive. And the reason is not hard to understand—it violates God's design. It is a corrupted hybrid of the two sanctioned states: singleness and marriage. It cannot provide a valid test for compatibility in marriage because it cannot replicate the defining characteristics of marriage. As G. J. Jenkins notes, "It is ironic that many people opt for cohabitation as a trial for marriage because the one thing that you cannot have a trial for is a *permanent* relationship such as marriage."[19] If your goal in the choice of a marriage partner is "don't mess it up," steer clear of cohabitation.

Sound Guidelines for an Important Decision

This chapter and the previous one can be summed up in the following points:

1. The Christian has to make two decisions: whether to get married, and whom to marry.
2. Scripture teaches that both of these decisions fall within the area of freedom. That decision is not determined either by God's moral will or a so-called individual will.
3. There are identifiable advantages and disadvantages with either marriage or celibacy (1 Corinthians 7).
4. Whatever our state, the primary objective is not to strive for a change in status but to learn to serve God effectively in our present condition.
5. While our decision about marriage is not determined by God's moral will, it is regulated by it.
6. The moral will of God determines three aspects of the marriage issue:

    - A Christian may marry only a Christian.
    - The methodology of choosing a spouse must be moral.
    - The choice of a spouse must be governed by wisdom.

7. The sources of wisdom provided by God are both abundant and adequate for making wise decisions in this area.

Permission Granted

In its sincere attempt to provide perfect matches for single Christians, the traditional view sometimes prevents any match at all. Since marriage is such a significant decision, the traditional view expects 100 percent certainty on the choice of a spouse. Inadvertently, the traditional view encourages godly couples to hold off on marriage until God confirms their union with a clear sign.

One weekend, three different couples sought me out at a large church in California. They all wanted to tell me, "We got married because of your book." Writing the book did not have that effect on me, so I naturally asked, "How did that happen?" Their stories were very similar. After a long dating period, they considered marriage and were encouraged in that direction by friends and family. But they wondered if *God* was telling them to get married. They prayed for a sign to make it 100 percent clear. But no sign materialized to nudge them over the edge. Instead a book did—*Decision Making and the Will of God.* The principles contained in these chapters freed them to believe that they did not need a sign to proceed to the altar to begin a wise, godly marriage.

I got the impression they were pleased about that.

---

1. Bill Hybels, *Making Life Work: Putting God's Wisdom into Action* (Downers Grove, IL: InterVarsity Press, 1998), 114.
2. C. F. Keil and F. Delitzsch, *Biblical Commentary on the Old Testament*, vol. 1, *The Pentateuch* (Grand Rapids, MI: Wm. B. Eerdmans Publishing Co., 1951), 258, quoting Hengstenberg, *Dissertations*, 1:350.
3. H. C. Leupold, *Exposition of Genesis*, 2 vols. (Grand Rapids, MI: Baker Book House, 1942), 2:669.
4. It is very difficult to sort out whether the "he" of 7:36 refers to the unmarried woman's father or fiancé, which is why the editors of the NIV include an extended marginal reading. The grammatical and interpretive issues are complex, and commentators are divided. Two who support the "father" view are F. W. Grosheide, *The First Epistle to the Corinthians, The New International Commentary on the New Testament* (Grand Rapids, MI: Wm. B. Eerdmans Publishing Co., 1953), 182–84, and David K. Lowery, *The*

Bible Knowledge Commentary, "1 Corinthians" (Wheaton, IL: Victor Books, 1983), 520. Two commentators favoring the fiancé view are Craig Blomberg, *NIV Application Commentary: 1 Corinthians* (Grand Rapids, MI: Zondervan, 1995), 152–53, and Frank E. Gaebelein, gen. ed., *The Expositor's Bible Commentary*, vol. 10: "1 Corinthians," by W. Harold Mare (Grand Rapids, MI: Zondervan, 1976), 236–37. For our purposes, it doesn't matter which view is taken; the principles remain the same.

5. "But when he dies, she is free to marry anyone she chooses, so long as he is a Christian." Gaebelein, *Expositor's Bible Commentary,* vol. 10: "1 Corinthians," by W. Harold Mare, 237. Cf. also S. Lewis Johnson Jr. "1 Corinthians," *The New Testament and Wycliffe Bible Commentary* (New York: The Iverson-Norman Associates, 1971), 611; Norman Hillyer, "1 and 2 Corinthians," *The New Bible Commentary* (Grand Rapids, MI: Wm. B. Eerdmans Publishing Co., 1970), 1062.
6. Frank E. Gaebelein, gen. ed., *The Expositor's Bible Commentary*, vol. 10: "2 Corinthians," by Murray J. Harris (Grand Rapids, MI: Zondervan, 1976), 359.
7. A thorough treatment of the principle, "marry only a believer," would require exposition of these relevant passages: Deuteronomy 7:1–6; 1 Kings 11:1–8; Nehemiah 13:23–27; Malachi 2:11; 1 Corinthians 9:5. The strong sanctions in the Old Testament against intermarriage with unbelievers were given for two primary reasons: (1) intermarriage would compromise God's holiness (Deuteronomy 7:6); and (2) it would inevitably destroy the experiential holiness of God's people (Deuteronomy 7:4).
8. Alice Fryling, *An Unequal Yoke in Dating and Marriage* (Downers Grove, IL: InterVarsity Press, 1979), 14.
9. David Atkinson, *The Message of Proverbs: Wisdom for Life* (Downers Grove, IL: InterVarsity Press, 1996), 23.
10. Neil Clark Warren, *Finding the Love of Your Life* (Wheaton, IL: Tyndale House Publishers, Inc., 1992), 7–25.
11. Hybels, *Making Life Work,* 114–33.
12. On the dangers of marrying solely for romantic reasons, Dr. James Peterson has written: "First, romance results in such distortions of personality that after marriage the two people can never fulfill the roles that they expect of each other. Second, romance so idealizes marriage and even sex that when the day-to-day experiences of marriage are encountered there must be disillusionment involved. Third, the romantic complex is so short-sighted that the premarital relationship is conducted almost entirely on the emotional level and consequently such problems as temperamental or value differences, religious or cultural differences, financial, occupational, or health problems are never considered. Fourth, romance develops such a false ecstasy that there is implied in courtship a promise of a kind of happiness which could never be maintained during the realities of married life. Fifth, romance is such an escape from the negative aspects of personality to the extent that their repression obscures the real person. Later in marriage these negative factors to marital adjustment are bound to appear, and they were not evident earlier. Sixth, people engrossed in romance seem to be prohibited from wise planning for the basic needs of the future even to the point of failing to discuss the significant problems of early marriage." Lyle B. Gangsei, ed., *Manual for Group Premarital Counseling* (New York: Association, 1971), 56–57.
13. Hybels, *Making Life Work,* 123.
14. Neil Clark Warren writes, "Over the years I have become deeply convinced of this: *For couples, similarities are like money in the bank, and differences are like debts they owe*" (italics his). He devotes the third chapter of his book, *Finding the Love of Your Life,* to this point and supplies the research support (pp. 47–61). He concludes the chapter with a "50-Item List of Helpful Marriage Similarities."

15. David Popenoe and Barbara Dafoe Whitehead, "Should We Live Together? What Young Adults Need to Know about Cohabitation before Marriage: A Comprehensive Review of Recent Research" (Second Edition), The National Marriage Project, Rutgers, The State University of New Jersey, 2002, http://marriage.rutgers.edu/publicat.htm (accessed April 27, 2004). The authors are codirectors of the National Marriage Project, a nonpartisan, nonsectarian, and interdisciplinary initiative located at Rutgers, the State University of New Jersey.
16. "All About Cohabiting Before Marriage," http://members.aol.com/cohabiting/ (accessed April 27, 2004). Compiled and updated by an association of Nazarene churches in Lansing, Michigan, this website contains a huge quantity of substantiating information on the dangers of cohabitation.
17. Popenoe and Whitehead, "Should We Live Together?"
18. Ibid.
19. G. J. Jenkins, *New Dictionary of Christian Ethics and Pastoral Theology* (Downers Grove, IL: InterVarsity Press, 1995), s.v. "Cohabitation" (italics his). See also R. Paul Stevens, *The Complete Book of Everyday Christianity* (Downers Grove, IL: InterVarsity Press, 1997), s.v. "Cohabiting."

chapter twenty-one

THE MINISTRY AND WISDOM

Ted Bradford was at a crossroad. His dilemma was complex and the choices that confronted him were interrelated.

1. Should I marry?
2. If so, should I marry Annette Miller?
3. If so, when?
4. Is God calling me to full-time vocational Christian service?
5. Is God calling me to become a foreign missionary?
6. Should I attend seminary?

According to the traditional view, Ted was looking for six specific dots—the center of God's will for each of the six questions. Each decision would have significant impact. Since they were interrelated, missing one dot could result in missing all of them.

If Ted followed the way of wisdom, what difference would it make? His questions would still be important and still be interrelated. The main difference is that he would be freed from having to find six dots. Under the wisdom view he would weigh the factors and make decisions that would best promote the moral will of God in and through his life.

Which of these two approaches is taught in Scripture? We have already answered that question as it pertains to marriage (chapters 19 and 20). But what about my vocation, my career? Does the Bible direct me to discover the occupation God has already chosen? Or does this decision lie within the area of freedom?

THE CALL TO THE MINISTRY

In discussions about one's lifework, the traditional view employs a distinctive, biblical term: "called." Citing numerous instances in Scripture where God called a specific person to a specific task, the traditional view teaches that the call of God is the indispensable factor in determining my vocation. And that is said to be true even if I do not become a pastor or a missionary.

Since a personal call is the distinctive element in the traditional view on this subject, we begin with a study of the term as it is used in Scripture. The verb "to call" (*kaleo*), appears 148 times in the New Testament, indicating that it is a significant concept.[1]

You Are Cordially Invited...

There are three usages of the word that are theological in character. First, in the Gospels, the term is often used by Jesus in the sense of "summon" or "invite."[2] The invitation was to come to repentance, faith, salvation, and service.[3] It was issued by Christ, not to the righteous, but to sinners (Matthew 9:13). It was a call or summons to enter the kingdom of God—an invitation that could be accepted or rejected (Matthew 22:2–14; Luke 14:16–24).

The second, more restricted doctrinal use of the term is found primarily in the writings of Paul. He employed the word "call" to describe God's gracious work within a sinner to effectively bring that person to faith and salvation. (Theologians speak of this work as "effective grace" or "efficacious grace." This is in contrast to "common grace," which is given to all men, but rejected by many.) God not only invites sinners to repent, but acts to secure a positive response to His summons.[4] "Call" was an important term for Paul's development of the doctrine of sovereign grace and election (Romans 8:28–30).[5] Thus, Christians are frequently designated as "the called" (Romans 1:6–7; 8:28; 1 Peter 1:15; Jude 1; Revelation 17:14). That is, they are sinners who have not only heard God's invitation through the gospel but have responded to it in faith.

C. S. Lewis gives a beautiful illustration of the call of effective grace. Jill Pole enters Aslan's country with Eustace Scrubb in *The Silver Chair*. She meets Aslan, the Lion, who explains why He called them to Narnia. Jill is puzzled and finally says, "I was wondering—I mean—could there be some mistake? Because nobody called me and Scrubb, you know. Scrubb said we were to call to [Aslan]...and perhaps [He] would let us in. And we did, and then we found the door open." Aslan does not contradict Jill, but adds a deeper perspective. "You would not have called on me unless I had been calling to you."[6]

Obviously, neither of these two senses of the term is meant when the traditional view speaks of "being called." It is rather the third usage that is relevant to this discussion: the call to a specific function or office.

In the New Testament, there are three instances of this kind of call: (1) God's call of Paul to be an apostle (Romans 1:1; 1 Corinthians 1:1); (2) God's call of Barnabas and Saul to be the Church's first missionaries (Acts 13:2); and (3) God's call to Paul and his companions to take the gospel to Macedonia (Acts 16:9–10). However, careful examination of these examples, along with the rest of the New Testament, reveals that they are the exception rather than the rule.[7]

In the first place, in each case the *means of communication* was some form of *supernatural revelation*. When Saul of Tarsus received his call to apostleship, he heard the audible voice of Christ (Acts 26:14–20).[8] Next, the command in Acts 13:2 to "Set apart for Me Barnabas and Saul for the work to which I have called them" is attributed to the Holy Spirit. How did the saints at Antioch receive this message? Either God spoke in an audible voice that could be heard by all (as in Luke 9:35); or, more likely, He spoke through one of the prophets in the church mentioned in Acts 13:1. Finally, the "Macedonian call" was communicated to Paul through a vision (Acts 16:9–10). In none of these cases was the call communicated through any sort of inward impression.

Few Are Called

Second, each vocational call was issued only to certain individuals at certain times. The book of Acts makes it clear that the Holy Spirit was carefully superintending the opening stages of the Church's growth. Only at decisive moments and in decisive ways did God intervene supernaturally to commission a worker, chart a particular course, or point in a specific direction. The rest of the time, He accomplished His purposes through saints obeying the moral will of God.

The isolated, infrequent character of the Spirit's overt interventions is consistent with God's activity of "vocational calling" in the Old Testament. The only individuals in Israel who received such commissions from God were those who were called to a specialized, spiritual ministry: the high priest (Hebrews 5:4); judges (1 Samuel 3:4–10); prophets (Isaiah 6:1–8; Jeremiah 1:4–10); kings (1 Samuel 16:11–13); and certain artisans supernaturally endowed to build the tabernacle (Exodus 31:1–6). In neither Testament is such a call promised or required as part of God's provision for all believers.

> In neither Testament is a call promised or required as part of God's provision for all believers.

Third, in every instance the special call of God was *unsought* and *unexpected.* God could give a vocational call to each believer, but there is no instruction directing Christians to seek such a leading. The examples in which God interrupted the normal flow of life to reveal His will emphasize the sovereign origin of those revelations.

Fourth, while "the call of God" is a prominent concept in the New Testament, the vocational sense of the term occupies only a *minor place.*[9] And when it occurs, it is never presented as pertaining to all believers.

To sum up: The idea of a vocational call is consistent with the theological framework of the traditional view, and there are instances in Scripture where God did call certain men to special tasks. But those two facts are not sufficient to establish a vocational call for all believers. God could make such choices and reveal them as He has selectively done in the past. But God did not normally lead that way in Bible times, nor should we expect Him to do so today.[10]

BIBLICAL QUALIFICATIONS FOR CHURCH LEADERS

The traditional view of guidance so permeates evangelical thinking that the validity of a vocational call is not only assumed for all believers, it is actually required for full-time ministers.[11] When a candidate is examined for ordination into the gospel ministry, the council usually questions him in three key areas: (1) his conversion experience, (2) his call to the ministry, and (3) his doctrinal positions.

The Ordination Ordeal

The appropriateness of testing a man in those three areas is obvious. But as I prepared for my own ordination exam, I knew I had a problem. I didn't anticipate any difficulty with the first or third questions. But what would I say about my call to the ministry?

From my study of the Bible, I had come to the conclusion that God does not require of pastors today the same kind of bright light and voice that arrested Saul of Tarsus on the Damascus Road. Furthermore, I was convinced that Scripture does not require some kind of mystical experience whereby I "hear" God's "inward call." I did not anticipate that the ordination council would expect me to relate some "Damascus Road" experience; but I was fairly sure they would expect me to say something about a strong impression in my heart that God had told me to go into full-time ministry.

So on the evening before the examination, alone in my room, I did two things. First, I carefully reviewed the reasons for my desire to spend the rest of my life in Christian ministry. I would tell the council the truth. If they wanted to reject my reasons, they would do so with a clear understanding of what they were. Second, I spent the evening rereading the key biblical passages that set forth the qualifications for leaders in the church. If the Bible required either a bright light or a mystical call, I didn't want to overlook it.

The Case of the Missing Call

Those passages confirmed for me that the Head of the Church has declared what kind of people should be set apart as spiritual leaders (1 Timothy 3:1–7, Titus 1:5–9, and 1 Peter 5:1–4).[12] Here is a summary of those qualifications.[13]

First, leaders in the church must be *Christians.* If someone is going to "shepherd the church of God" (Acts 20:28), he must first be part of the Church of God.

Second, leaders in the church must be *men.* God's order in the church requires this (1 Timothy 2:12–14). Accordingly, the stipulations "husband of one wife" and "one who manages his own household well" (1 Timothy 3:2, 4) assume male leadership. (The requirement of male leadership is debated in evangelical circles.[14] Some argue that Scripture does not exclude women from pastoral leadership. The wisdom view does not require uniformity of interpretation on all points.)[15]

Third, leaders in the church must have the *ability* to *lead* and to *teach.* To determine if a man can lead, the church is told to observe his family. "He must be one who manages his own household well, keeping his children under control with all dignity" (1 Timothy 3:4; see Titus 1:6). The ability to teach cuts two ways. "Holding fast the faithful word which is in accordance with the teaching, so that he will be able both to *exhort in sound doctrine* [positive thrust], and to *refute those who contradict* [negative thrust]" (Titus 1:9; see 1 Timothy 3:2).

Fourth, leaders in the church must be characterized by a *godly desire.* Paul wrote: "It is a trustworthy statement: if any man aspires to the office of overseer, it is a fine work he desires to do" (1 Timothy 3:1). Likewise, Peter warned against placing men in a position of oversight "under compulsion." Rather, the undershepherd is to be characterized by eagerness, serving voluntarily to accomplish God's will (1 Peter 5:2). Rather than waiting for some kind of inward voice, a man should cultivate an inward godly heart to serve God in the fullest manner possible. Certainly God will stimulate that desire, but the aspiration and desire are said to belong to the man himself.

Fifth, leaders in the church must manifest *spiritual maturity.* This qualification is emphasized in three ways. One is the negative requirement: "Not a new convert" (1 Timothy 3:6). The second is the official designation "elder."[16] This title applied to the office of church leader emphasizes a man's character—i.e., he is to be spiritually mature. Third, maturity is underlined by the nature of the qualifications Paul lists. The leader is to be "above reproach…temperate, prudent, respectable, hospitable…not addicted to wine or pugnacious, but gentle, peaceable, free from the love of money," and so on (1 Timothy 3:2–3). These qualities must be confirmed not only by those in the church, but he "must have a good reputation with those outside the church" as well (1 Timothy 3:7).

To sum up: According to the New Testament, a church leader must be a *spiritually mature Christian man* who *desires* a position of leadership in the church and is *able to lead* God's people and *teach* God's Word.

Examining the Examination

Since God Himself has established these qualifications, they should have a direct application to our process of recognizing (ordaining) men for the ministry. And they do, up to a point. For these passages affirm the validity of examining a man's conversion (he must be a Christian) and his knowledge of Bible doctrine (he must be able to teach). It is ironic, however, that while Scripture emphasizes qualifications that many ordaining councils overlook, those councils stress a requirement (his call to the ministry) not mentioned by Scripture.

> Our ordaining procedures should produce evidence of a man's spiritual maturity and his ability to lead.

Our ordaining procedures ought to reflect the pattern of the apostles. Paul selected workers who were "well spoken of by the brethren" (Acts 16:2) and who had been "tested and found diligent in many things" (2 Corinthians 8:22). Similarly, our tests should produce evidence of a man's spiritual maturity and his ability to lead. Prior to the ordination examination, Christian and non-Christian business associates, employers, roommates, family members, and friends could be interviewed.[17]

Such scrutiny may occasionally require godly men to give hard counsel. A promising young candidate might need to be told, "From our conversations with those who know you best, it is apparent that you have a problem with your temper. You need time to develop greater patience and self-control before accepting the stresses of caring for the flock of God."

If the ordination process were adjusted to include evaluation of a man's character and ability to lead, it would be equally appropriate to bring the question about the call into alignment with Scripture. Instead of a "call," the New Testament speaks of a "desire" or an "aspiration" for the pastoral office. A better question might be, "Why do you desire to be set apart for the gospel ministry?"

Meanwhile, Back in the Coliseum

How did my own ordination testing end? About thirty pastors and church representatives sat on the examining council. As I prepared to face their questioning, one of the godly pastors of the association offered me these words of encouragement, "Just remember, son, it's the call of God that matters, the call of God." Just what I needed to hear! The actual examination began well and the pastors were supportive. I enjoyed narrating again how I came to faith in Christ and the blessings of my life with Him.

Then came the inevitable Question Number Two: "Would you now describe your call to the ministry?" I began by explaining that I had never seen any bright lights nor heard any voices as the apostle Paul did. They assured me that was not expected. Trying to reflect a submissive attitude, I asked if they would give me a definition of a call, and indicate where Scripture required it for ministers.

What followed was a very interesting discussion. Several descriptions of the inward call were offered. Expressions like "inward compulsion" and "strong inner feeling" were proposed. Two things became clear: A precise definition was hard to nail down, and the requirement of the inward call could not be found. Still, everyone was convinced that a call was needed. After one pastor defined the call as a strong feeling or compulsion, another pastor added, "If my ministry depended on my feelings, I would probably drop out about every two weeks." He elicited laughter and understanding nods.

Eventually the members of the council remembered that they were supposed to be questioning me. The issues I had raised made it apparent that I had questions about the concept of a call to the ministry. So they reworded the question. "If you don't feel that you have had one of these calls to the ministry, why do you want to be a minister?"

That, I thought, was the right question. My explanation was essentially a paraphrase of 1 Timothy 3:1: "I want to serve the Lord in the best and fullest way possible. God says that the office of pastor provides a good means for serving Him, so I have consciously aspired to become qualified for that position. The characteristics listed in 1 Timothy 3, Titus 1, and 1 Peter 5 have been my personal goals." That was an honest and candid answer.

Then I added, "It's possible that I experienced some kind of mystical impulse at some campfire service when I was younger. But if I did, I don't remember it very well. And even if I could recall it clearly, such an experience would not be the basis for my desire to enter Christian ministry."

The council showed balance in their reply to me. They agreed that my reasons for desiring ordination were good ones, but they also exhorted me to give careful, further consideration to my sense of a call. This I agreed to do. One of the men did warn that unless a man had more of a call than I had, he would quickly drop out of the ministry.

As we left the sanctuary, my pastor pulled me aside and said, "If the council does not vote to ordain you, our church will." He knew that a positive vote was not a foregone conclusion. But, in the end, I was ordained.

DECISION MAKING AND THE MINISTRY

Hang in There, or Hang It Up?

The ordination council's warning about dropping out of the ministry reflects the genuine concern of many who follow the traditional view of the call. I share that concern. Those who enter the ministry do experience extraordinary strains and pressures. And, as the one pastor noted in jest, the temptation to bail out comes up for review at least every two weeks.

But it seems to me that one's sense of a call, which is dubious scripturally and highly subjective at best, lacks sufficient weight to function as the ultimate anchor in the heavy seas of Christian ministry. I can't help but wonder how many Christian workers have given up precisely because the force of an inward feeling faded with the passing of time.

I also wonder how many otherwise qualified people have refrained from pursuing a ministry because they haven't heard "the call." I know of at least one. After a teaching session, a young youth worker approached me with this question: "I have always wanted to serve Christ and share the gospel in a part of the world where people have never heard of Jesus. However, teachers and missionaries have told me to be certain that I have a call from God before I go. I've never really understood what they meant by a call, but after listening to them, I am quite sure I haven't had one. Do you think I could go to the mission field without one of those calls?"

I asked her where the Bible required an inward mystical call to obey the great commission. She knew of none. I told her if she was qualified for the missionary work she wanted to do, that God did not require a mystical call despite popular teaching. God does lay down qualifications for leaders for effective ministry, but she would look in vain for the one qualification that was holding her back.

The Call That Binds

How many Christians are plagued by guilt because they believe that God called them to some ministry at some time in the past, but they chose a secular vocation instead? How many pastors have responded to a supposed call only to experience frustration or even rejection because they lacked the revealed biblical qualifications? How many full-time Christian workers have discovered from painful experience that they just aren't suited for such a vocation, but won't change because they believe they would be disobeying God's call? For how many of God's men has a sense of failure been compounded by feelings of guilt because they were forced to leave the ministry they were "called" to?

If the circumstances of life have required you to serve God through a secular vocation, or if you have chosen such an occupation after evaluating your aptitudes, abilities, and opportunities, rest assured that *your work is pleasing to God* if you do it "heartily, as for the Lord" (Colossians 3:23). But more on that later.

Requiring a call does not solve the problem of attrition from the ministerial ranks. If anything, it complicates it. And it actually creates more problems than it purports to solve. Instead, believers should enter full-time Christian service for the reasons and with the qualifications established by the Bible. And we should make decisions as to whether to continue or change jobs on biblical grounds as well.[18]

frequently asked question

Question: The wisdom view maintains that pastors are not required to have a mystical call to be qualified. How does this square with Acts 20:28, which says that the elders of the Ephesian church were "appointed" (NLT) by the Holy Spirit?

In this passage Paul says that the Holy Spirit made these men overseers (or pastors or elders). The verse says, "Be on guard for yourselves and for all the flock, among which the Holy Spirit has made you overseers, to shepherd the church of God" (Acts 20:28).

While it is clear that the Holy Spirit in some way placed these men in their position of elder, the methodology is not spelled out. The word "made" is a common word that can mean "appoint," "put," or "place" in a position. Various means were employed in the New Testament: Matthias was appointed by prayer and casting lots (Acts 1:23–26); the first deacons were chosen by the Jerusalem church and presented to the apostles (Acts 6:2–6); Paul and Barnabas were called from the Antioch church by special revelation from the Holy Spirit (Acts 13:1–2); and finally elders were appointed by Paul, Barnabas (Acts 14:23), and Titus (Titus 1:5).

These verses illustrate at least three ways that pastors were properly appointed. Advocating only one of these ways could lead to an insistence on apostolic succession, divine revelation, or local church ordination—to the exclusion of the others. In the case of the Ephesian elders, we don't know how they were appointed. But because they met Spirit-inspired requirements that were recognized by the church, Paul concluded they had been appointed by the Holy Spirit. God can do this directly through prophecy, or by a church-planting founder appointing leaders, or by an established church using God's biblical guidelines.

A clear example of God putting a person in a position without a prophetic or mystical call is governing authorities. God says that such authorities are established and appointed by Him (Romans 13:1). The ruler is called the "minister" and "servant" of God (Romans 13:4, 6). All rulers fit this description of being put into office by God.

If God considers secular government officials as having been appointed by Him to be His "ministers," then it is certainly appropriate to regard a pastor as Spirit appointed because: (1) The Spirit qualified him by his spiritual gifting (1 Corinthians 12:11; see 12:28 where the same verb "appointed" is used); (2) He produced the required maturity and fruit of the Spirit in the man (1 Timothy 3:1–7; Titus 1:6–9); and (3) He worked through His church recognizing divinely specified qualifications to appoint him. F. F. Bruce supports this sense of Spirit-appointment in Acts 20:28.

> Probably the reference to the Holy Spirit here does not mean that their appointment to this sacred ministry had been commanded by prophetic utterance in the church, but rather that they were so appointed and recognized because they were manifestly men on whom the Holy Spirit had bestowed the requisite qualifications for the work.... Cf. 1 Corinthians 12:4ff.[19]

Every man, then, who has the necessary gifting of the Holy Spirit, possesses the required character the Holy Spirit produces, and is recognized by the Holy Spirit's Church and placed in the position of pastor is a Holy Spirit–appointed pastor.

---

1. There are an additional seventy occurrences of related terms from the same root. Colin Brown, ed., *The New International Dictionary of New Testament Theology* (Grand Rapids, MI: Zondervan, 1975), s.v. "Call."
2. "We meet the meaning 'invite' for *kaleo* principally in the parables of the great banquet (Luke 14:16–25), where it occurs 9 times." Brown, *Dictionary of NT Theology*, 1:274.
3. Everett F. Harrison, ed., *Baker's Dictionary of Theology* (Grand Rapids, MI: Baker Book House, 1960), s.v. "Call, Called, Calling."
4. Ibid.
5. See also 1 Corinthians 1:9; Galatians 1:15; 2 Thessalonians 2:13–15; 2 Timothy 1:9; Hebrews 9:15; 1 Peter 2:9; and 2 Peter 1:3.
6. C. S. Lewis, *The Silver Chair* (New York: Macmillan Publishing Co., Inc., 1953), 18–19.
7. Charles R. Smith correctly observes, "One of the most frequent causes of confusion with regard to God's will is the common failure to recognize the distinctiveness of God's dealings with those to whom and by whom He chose to reveal Himself in the sacred Scriptures. You are not a Moses! Nor are you a Joshua, an Abraham, Ezekiel, Daniel, Matthew, John or Paul! You are not to expect the kind of revelation they received. God's methods in dealing with them have not been His normal methods of dealing with believers in any age." Charles R. Smith, *Can You Know God's Will for Your Life?* (Winona Lake, IN: B. M. H. Books, 1977), 2.
8. The apostle Paul did not see his calling as providing a pattern for other ministers. Quite the contrary, in 1 Corinthians 9:16–18, he stresses the distinctiveness of his calling: He had been drafted into the Lord's service, while others were volunteers. A vivid contrast appears between Paul's situation and Peter's exhortation for elders. Whereas other undershepherds are to serve "not under compulsion, but voluntarily" (1 Peter 5:2), Paul wrote that he preached "under compulsion" and "against my will" (1 Corinthians 9:16–17). For a fuller treatment of this passage and its relevance to this discussion, see Garry Lee Friesen, "God's Will As It Relates to Decision Making" (PhD diss., Dallas Theological Seminary, 1978), 255–62.

9. J. I. Packer uses the word "subordinate" to describe the vocational use of the term "call." Harrison, *Dictionary of Theology*, 108–9.
10. For the reasons cited, I am inclined to agree with the suggestion of Charles Smith: "In view of the fact that young people are often confused by this terminology, and led to expect some supernatural revelation regarding their vocation, perhaps it would be wise to drop the term 'call' as a reference to such a conviction regarding our life-work." Smith, *Can You Know God's Will?* 3.
11. I realize that all Christians are to be "full-time ministers" in the biblical sense of the term. But we must have some means of distinguishing between vocations where believers earn their living through their ministry (such as pastors and missionaries) and those jobs where people are not paid for such Christian service. For that purpose, throughout the remainder of this chapter, I will use terminology that recognizes a distinction between sacred and secular vocations.
12. That Paul intended his lists in 1 Timothy and Titus to be definitive is clearly indicated in the near-identical introductory words: "An overseer, then, must be…" (1 Timothy 3:2; Titus 1:7). Surely we can expect to find the normative qualifications for church leaders in such passages.
13. For an excellent treatment of leadership in the New Testament church, see Gene A. Getz, *Sharpening the Focus of the Church* (Chicago: Moody Press, 1974), 84–129, and Gene A. Getz, *The Measure of a Man* (Glendale, CA: G/L Publications, 1974). Also see Alexander Strauch, *Biblical Eldership* (Littleton, CO: Lewis and Roth Publishers, 1986); Joseph M. Stowell, *Shepherding the Church into the 21st Century* (Wheaton, IL: Victor Books, 1994); Aubrey Malphurs, *The Dynamics of Church Leadership* (Grand Rapids, MI: Baker Book House, 1999).
14. One can hold the wisdom view and not conclude that church elders must be men. I have come to that conclusion, but evangelicals hold differing views on whether women should be ordained to be pastors. Good materials can be found for both the egalitarian and the complementarian views. The egalitarian view is reflected in the organization Christians for Biblical Equality and the complementarian perspective by the Council for Biblical Manhood and Womanhood.

    Books that present multiple views: Bonnidell Clouse and Robert G. Clouse, editors, *Women in Ministry: Four Views* (Downers Grove, IL: InterVarsity Press, 1989); Craig Blomberg and Thomas R. Schreiner, eds., *Two Views on Women in Ministry*, Counterpoint Series (Grand Rapids, MI:, Zondervan, 2001).

    Egalitarian books: Gilbert G. Bilezikian, *Beyond Sex Roles: A Guide for the Study of Female Roles in the Bible* (Grand Rapids, MI: Baker Book House, 1985); Stanley J. Grenz and Denise Muir Kjesbo, *Women in the Church* (Downers Grove, IL: InterVarsity Press, 1995); Rebecca Merrill Groothuis, *Good News for Women: A Biblical Picture of Gender Equality* (Grand Rapids, MI., Baker Book House, 1997).

    Complementarian books: Wayne Grudem, *Evangelical Feminism and Biblical Truth* (Sisters, OR: Multnomah Publishers, 2004); John Piper and Wayne Grudem, eds., *Recovering Biblical Manhood and Womanhood* (Wheaton, IL: Crossway Books, 1991); James B. Hurley, *Man and Woman in Biblical Perspective* (Grand Rapids, MI: Zondervan, 1981); George W. Knight III, *The Role Relationships of Men and Women: New Testament Teaching*, rev. ed. (Chicago: Moody Press, 1985); Alexander Strauch, *Biblical Eldership* (Littleton, CO.: Lewis and Roth Publishers, 1995).
15. See chapters 25 and 26 of this book, "Wisdom When Christians Differ," and "Weaker Brothers, Pharisees, and Servants."
16. The two principal titles for church leaders in the New Testament are "overseer" (or "bishop," which occurs six times in the New Testament in that sense) and "elder"

(appearing fourteen times with that meaning). The two terms are interchangeable (see, for example, Titus 1:5 and 7). "Overseer" emphasizes the leader's responsibility, while "elder" stresses his character.

17. Many evangelical seminaries now require more extensive internship experiences for their students, which gives opportunity for both practical training and evaluation of potential for pastoral ministry.
18. During the post-Resurrection period of confusion for the disciples, the risen Lord held a vocational counseling session for Simon Peter, His fisherman-turned-shepherd (John 21:1–22). Even though Peter's original call to discipleship seems to be reaffirmed through the actions of Jesus, it is never specifically mentioned. Rather, the thrice-repeated question, "Do you love Me?" points to the decisive factor in the staying power of the shepherd—i.e., the disciple's day-to-day response to the injunction, "Follow Me." It is a biblical principle that persistence in faithfulness to any aspect of one's stewardship is the product of spiritual maturity (1 Corinthians 4:2; 15:58; Galatians 5:22–23; 6:9; Hebrews 12:1–13). In the face of difficulties, what the minister needs in order to continue is the grace of God (2 Corinthians 12:9–10) and the conviction that he is doing something that God wants done—His moral will.
19. F. F. Bruce, *The Book of the Acts, The New International Commentary on the New Testament* (Grand Rapids, MI: Wm. B. Eerdmans Publishing Co., 1980), 416.

chapter twenty-two

MISSIONS AND WISDOM

For Ted Bradford, the vocational issue was not only whether he had been called to the ministry in general, but to the mission field in particular. Much of what was written about ministry in the last chapter applies here, but if a call from God is required for any job, it must be that of a missionary.

There are at least two compelling reasons for this common assumption, one biblical and one practical. The biblical argument is that the very first missionaries in the church, Barnabas and Saul, were explicitly called by God (Acts 13:1–3). The practical reason is that missionary service is even more difficult than at-home ministry since the missionary has to be able to adapt to a foreign culture and often learn a different language. Since God alone knows who can effectively handle these challenges, it is said that He handpicks the laborers for foreign fields.

MISSIONARY DECISIONS IN THE EARLY CHURCH

In the case of Barnabas and Saul, we noted earlier[1] that they were called precisely because they were to be the *first missionaries*. Their call came through supernatural means—either the voice of God or the voice of a prophet (Acts 13:1–2). With no other confirming passages, we should not construe from this unique event that all missionaries must be similarly called. To be consistent, if a mission call is required, we should also insist that it come via special revelation.

That is not to say that Acts 13 is irrelevant to our decisions about missions. We should not require or expect some dramatic call, but we should emulate the wisdom displayed by the Holy Spirit in His choice of missionaries and the timing of their commissioning.

Note God's wisdom from Acts 13: (1) The men selected were qualified to do spiritual work, including evangelism and church planting (Acts 11:19–30); (2) their ability to work together had already been proven at Antioch; (3) their ability to work effectively among the Gentiles, their primary target group (Acts 14:27), was already demonstrated; (4) the sending church had capable leaders to fill the place of these two who were sent out (Acts 13:1).

Sequels to this dramatic start show examples of missions-related decision making that are more directly applicable today. The saga of John Mark is a case in point.

The Case of the Deserting Disciple

John Mark, cousin of Barnabas, was being discipled by Barnabas and Saul at the time of their call (Acts 12:25). So, they took him along as a helper, although he had not been named by the Holy Spirit (Acts 13:2, 5). Mark's service was apparently satisfactory through the first stage of the mission. But before the team began the arduous trek from Perga to Pisidian Antioch, Mark abandoned the project and returned home to Jerusalem (Acts 13:13). After a profitable tour of central Asia Minor, Paul and Barnabas returned to Antioch (Acts 14:27–28).

Some time later, Paul proposed a second missionary journey to Barnabas. "Let us return and visit the brethren in every city in which we proclaimed the word of the Lord, and see how they are" (Acts 15:36).

The text does not attribute this idea to the Holy Spirit, as was the case with the first journey (Acts 13:2). It was apparently generated by Paul's desire to fulfill Christ's commission and see believers brought to maturity. Here is initiative taken by a spiritually mature man to accomplish God's moral will in a wise manner.

There was apparently no discussion as to whether God had called them to make this trip. What was discussed, with great intensity, was whether they should take along John Mark. Barnabas, who wasn't one to give up on people, wanted to take him. Paul, who placed a premium on loyalty, perseverance, and proven competence, wasn't willing to risk another desertion. The issue, once again, was not John Mark's call or lack thereof. The issue was his demonstrated qualifications (Acts 15:37–38).

In the absence of agreement or any direct word from God, Paul and Barnabas decided to separate and form two new teams (Acts 15:39). Barnabas took Mark and headed for Cyprus. "Paul chose Silas" (Acts 15:40), a proven leader with the prophetic gift (Acts 15:32), and with the blessings of the church headed for Asia Minor.

Mark Him Well

Though Barnabas and Mark drop out of sight in Acts, Mark surfaces again in the Epistles. During Paul's first Roman imprisonment, Mark was one of several helpers who stood by him (Philemon 24). From the pen of Paul, we learn that Barnabas's confidence in Mark bore fruit.

> Aristarchus, my fellow prisoner, sends you his greetings; and also Barnabas' cousin Mark (about whom you received instructions; if he comes to you, welcome him);...they have proved to be an encouragement to me. (Colossians 4:10–11)

A few years later, during Paul's final imprisonment in Rome, he sent this word to Timothy: "Pick up Mark and bring him with you, for he is useful to me for service" (2 Timothy 4:11). For Paul, the issue was always personal qualifications. When Mark later proved his worth, Paul did not hesitate to make him a member of his team.

When at First You Don't Succeed...

Returning now to Paul's second journey (Acts 16), we find that Paul and Silas still did not have a helper. When they came to Lystra, Paul was impressed by a young disciple named Timothy. He was chosen to become John Mark's replacement (Acts 16:3). He was a disciple who "was well spoken of by the brethren" (Acts 16:1–2). Again, demonstrated spiritual qualifications, rather than a call, proved to be decisive in the choice.

The wisdom of choosing Timothy for this role was to be confirmed over and over again. We know more of this apostolic assistant than any other of Paul's fellow workers. Timothy was given significant responsibilities for ministry and he consistently fulfilled his assignments (1 Thessalonians 3:1–2, 6). Paul gave him high praise: "But you know of his proven worth that he served with me in the furtherance of the gospel like a child serving his father. Therefore I hope to send him" (Philippians 2:22–23).

Once the Holy Spirit set missionary outreach in motion in Acts 13, all subsequent missions-related decisions were made on the basis of applied wisdom.

As with John Mark and Timothy, Paul explained the sending of all of his fellow workers to various churches on the basis of their proven character and ability to minister: Epaphroditus (Philippians 2:25–30), sister Phoebe (Romans 16:1–2), Stephanas, Fortunatus, and Achaicus (1 Corinthians 16:17–18), Tychicus (Ephesians 6:21–22), Epaphras (Colossians 1:7–8; 4:12–13), an unnamed brother (2 Corinthians 8:22), and even the converted runaway slave, Onesimus (Colossians 4:9; Philemon 10–13).

This review of missionary activity in the New Testament shows that once the Holy Spirit set missionary outreach in motion in Acts 13, all subsequent missions-related decisions were made on the basis of applied wisdom. (The one exception was the Macedonian call in Acts 16:6–10, which we discussed earlier.)[2] In the actual practice of the church, decisions about timing, destinations, and personnel were all made by believers intent on obeying God's moral will in the most effective manner possible. There is a remarkable absence of any reference to the call of God beyond Acts 16.

DECIDING WHO SHOULD GO

What kind of people are mission agencies seeking? What qualifications are they looking for? Our query of a dozen agencies revealed that, while most consider a sense of call important, other qualities and qualifications are far more determinative in the actual selection process. Some missionary leaders even admit to being wary about someone's claim to a call from God. Michael C. Griffiths, former general director of the Overseas Missionary Fellowship, gives this candid explanation:

> [Mission societies] often seem to have a healthy skepticism about our guidance.... Missions are not eager to saddle themselves with impractical romantics who want to join the Mission and see the world. You may be wary about approaching a mission, but you will find them equally cautious about you. They will try to size you up very carefully. If they don't, you should become more wary still![3]

At least one mission agency, SIM, is willing to consider candidates who cannot pinpoint a decisive call to the mission field. General Director Emeritus Raymond J. Davis and (then) General Director Ian M. Hay were asked, "How does SIM react to a person who expresses an interest in foreign service, but who can't honestly say he has had a missionary call?" Hay replied,

> SIM reacts with understanding. We want those people who are first of all committed in their lives to the lordship of Christ, people who understand that their basic responsibility is to do the will of God as outlined in the Scriptures...whether he understands what a "call" is or not. Actually, the use of that word bothers me. There's a lot of misunderstanding regarding a "call." The word has assumed overtones that I think we can do without.

Davis added, "The concept of a 'call' as a necessary introductory experience for serving God cannot be scripturally substantiated. Some, like Paul, did have such an experience, but many others didn't. We've built up the idea of a 'call' into something which simply was not known in the days of the early church."[4]

There are missions leaders at the other end of the spectrum for whom a sense of divine call is considered indispensable. At the pragmatic level, however, most agencies leave the genuineness of a call to the individual and evaluate the candidate according to very practical standards. In the final analysis, if the mission agency concludes that the applicant is unsuited to be a missionary, it will have no part in sending him, whether he claims a call or not. As Griffiths observes: "Most missions have had plenty of experience with people who have been hard to live with or hard to live down. They are not going to rush taking you on."[5]

Significantly, there is essential agreement among mission boards as to the basic requirements—both qualities and qualifications—for missionaries. A list of qualities creates the following profile: patient, mature, emotionally stable, teachable, reliable, goal oriented, person oriented, assertive, servant minded, self-reliant, energetic, steadfast, tactful, serious, loyal, immovable, flexible, gentle, disciplined, generous, wholehearted, humble, practical, friendly, holy, discerning, motivated, and able to leap tall buildings in a single bound. Michael Griffiths puts the list in proper perspective when he notes, "It is the fruit of the Spirit we need more than anything else."[6]

Missions educator George Peters gives a summary of missionary qualifications. "In general, the preparation and qualifications of a missionary candidate are measured by several standards: Spiritual qualifications, doctrinal qualifications, academic qualifications, physical qualifications, personality qualifications, and social qualifications."[7]

These essentials have been forged on the anvil of hard experience by the application of spiritual wisdom. In practice, whether the traditional view of guidance is maintained or not, the contemporary Church is applying the same principles of wisdom in decision making as the first-century Church.[8]

The Bottom Line

Yes, the missionary task is difficult, but rather than waiting for some kind of mystical call from God, every believer should respond to the revealed will of God by giving serious consideration to becoming a cross-cultural missionary. There are at least three reasons to consider personal involvement.

1. The Command. Christ's great commission to "make disciples of all the nations" was given to the Church and remains in effect "even to the end of the age" (Matthew 28:19–20). For the believer, personal involvement in the cause of world missions *is not optional.* We don't need a call—we've already been commissioned. Every single Christian is to be making some contribution to world evangelization and discipleship. Every believer must develop an obedient "great commission" heart and then honestly ask, "How can I best contribute to the commission?"

2. The Need. Of the 6.3 billion people living on the planet at the time of this writing, about one-third (2.1 billion) identify themselves as Christians. About 680 million of those are evangelical. Of 24,000 people groups (defined by language, ethnicity, region, social group, and religion), 10,000 are considered "unreached." That is, there is no *indigenous* community of believing Christians with adequate numbers and resources to evangelize their own people. This is the situation for over 2.2 billion people in the world today.[9]

3. The Provision. The Head of the Church has given to some of His people the personal strength, resources, and gifts to do the job. Obedience to the command to be faithful stewards requires all believers to evaluate whether they have the God-given capability to best fulfill the great commission by personally taking the gospel to unreached peoples. Those who do should go. Those who don't should send.

THE ROAD TO THE MISSION FIELD

Here Am I—Now What?

If you are prepared to respond to the challenge of the great commission, I suggest embarking upon a personal project that, if pursued to culmination in a missionary vocation, entails at least seven steps.

1. Commitment. The first is availability, and that step ought to be settled by grateful submission to the Lordship of Christ (Luke 9:23–26; 14:25–35). One reason there aren't more missionaries is not that God hasn't called more; it's that more people haven't responded to the clear commission already given (Luke 9:59–62).

2. Investigation. An important means for gaining wisdom is the gathering of facts. What do missionaries do? What does it take to become a missionary? What does it cost?[10]

3. Involvement. Every believer who reads this book can participate in Christ's worldwide mission right now. The first means is bearing witness to Christ right in your own "Jerusalem." This ongoing ministry represents obedience to God's moral will and equips for broader ministry, perhaps cross-cultural, in the future.

Further, the responsibility every Christian has to contribute to global outreach can be fulfilled in a variety of ways. These include the indispensable support roles of intercessory prayer and financial investment. Perhaps you can find opportunities to promote the challenge of world missions in your local church. If you're a Sunday school teacher with a heart for missions, God may use you to launch your students on a journey that ends on a foreign field.

Every believer who reads this book can participate in Christ's worldwide mission right now.

4. Evaluation. You should take a personal inventory, evaluating your potential by the standard of missionary qualities and qualifications. In some cases, wisdom will indicate that you can make more of a contribution to missions through a vocation at home. Or you may discover in yourself the raw material from which missionaries are made. If so, you should set out on a course whereby the Potter can shape that raw material into a finished vessel, suitable for service on a foreign field.

5. Consultation. Personal evaluation should not be carried out in a vacuum. The New Testament records the involvement of local churches in recognizing, choosing, and sending those best suited for international outreach. You should be actively involved in ministry in your church so that those in leadership will have opportunity to assess your gifting.

6. Preparation. As long as the light remains green, you should take those steps that will lead to the foreign field. The most important of these steps is to enroll in the school of spiritual growth, whose motto is: "Discipline yourself for the purpose of godliness" (1 Timothy 4:7). Second, your involvement in world missions while still at home provides excellent preparation for serving abroad. And third, you must seek to meet mission agency requirements. Usually, these include adequate education (usually a college degree), some formal Bible training, experience in Christian ministry, cross-cultural exposure, facility in witnessing, commitment to a mission agency, language acquisition, and specialized skills as needed for a particular assignment.

7. Prayer. Pray for wisdom, strength, and open doors of opportunity. And submit, in advance, to the sovereign will of the Lord of the harvest (Luke 10:2). Then proceed, as you pray, to obey His moral will—with the confidence that He is at work in you "both to will and to work for His good pleasure" (Philippians 2:13).

frequently asked questions

> *Question:* This chapter focuses on the decision each believer must make about his or her involvement in missions. But who should send missionaries? It seems as if mission agencies have taken over this function from local churches. Is there any way to restore the role of the local church as the sending agency?

The New Testament establishes an important precedent: Missionaries should be sent by and accountable to local churches. Yet with the complexities of the modern world, mission agencies provide a valuable function in the deployment of missionaries worldwide. Over the years, however, systems have developed that have eroded the strong connection that should exist between missionary and sending church.

In many "faith" missions (those not tied to a denomination), each missionary candidate must go to dozens of churches and individuals for support. At the same time, local churches have tended to proliferate the number of missionaries they support. The end result is that in most cases it is impossible for a local church to be the authority over the missionaries it supports. The mission agencies have no choice but to assume authority over their missionaries. How could they ask twenty churches and fifty individuals to gather and make decisions about a specific missionary? So by necessity, the mission agency becomes the sending and governing authority.

Individual givers often contribute more than local churches to the support of a missionary. Raising financial support from church boards is usually slow and cumbersome compared to contacting individual donors. One missionary told me he could get more support from one week of contacting church members directly than one year of asking the church board. Thus, the local church no longer holds the purse strings.

One sad consequence is that missionaries often spend their home assignment time traveling the country. And when local churches support twenty or more missionaries, they don't have time to allow every missionary to give a detailed report to the church.

One remedy to this situation would require a change of strategy on the part of local churches. Instead of having a budget of $200,000 for fifty missionaries, a church could fund four missionaries full-time. When on home assignment, each missionary would have a position on the pastoral staff of the church. The church could approach a mission agency and say, "We would like to loan one of our staff members to you every three years out of four. We'll cover the bill, but we expect to have final say in all significant decisions affecting this missionary." The church would encourage its members to get to know the four missionaries and sacrifice for them, visit them, and send work teams to help them. And the missionary-in-residence at the church would continually promote the ministry of cross-cultural missions.

> *Question:* The funding of the missionary enterprise is always challenging. How might wisdom be applied to raising financial support for missions?

One untapped method of support is endowments. At Multnomah Bible College we have set up two missions endowments. One is for scholarships for future missionaries and one is to help support short-term mission trips. The concept is simple. Raise money for a protected endowment where the principal is not touched, but earnings are used annually.

The Norm and Muriel Cook Missionary Endowment has raised $135,000. Each year the earnings help faculty, staff, and students finance cross-cultural outreach. A 5 percent annual yield produces over $6,700 yearly in support money.

After the death of Multnomah student Holly Miller in Indonesia, students set up the Holly Miller Missions Endowment. In less than a year they raised $50,000 which has grown to over $60,000. The endowment earns funds every year for scholarships for students with the missionary heart and spirit that Holly had.

1. This passage was discussed in chapter 15, "Special Guidance and Decision Making," and chapter 21, "The Ministry and Wisdom."
2. This passage was discussed in chapter 15, "Special Guidance and Decision Making," and chapter 21, "The Ministry and Wisdom."
3. Michael C. Griffiths, *You and God's Work Overseas* (Downers Grove, IL: InterVarsity Press, 1967), 23–24.
4. "No Voice From Heaven?" *Africa Now,* November–December 1979, 2–5. Mr. Hay became the Director General Emeritus in 1993.
5. Griffiths, *You and God's Work Overseas,* 24–25.
6. Michael C. Griffiths, *Give Up Your Small Ambitions* (Chicago: Moody Press, 1970), 56.
7. George W. Peters, *A Biblical Theology of Missions* (Chicago: Moody Press, 1972), 292.
8. I observed this firsthand when I represented Multnomah Bible College at the InterVarsity Missions Conference at Urbana, Illinois. The mission agencies present did not apologize for their exacting requirements. Students came to us and said, "The missionary agencies tell me that I need at least one year of solid Bible training. What does your school offer along that line?" I was there to inform students that Multnomah has an excellent program set up specifically to meet the requirements of mission boards.
9. Statistics are from the web pages of the U. S. Center for World Mission (http://www.uscwm.org) and Perspectives on the World Christian Movement—Houston Site (http://www.houstonperspectives.org).
10. One way to research this is to survey information from various mission agencies. A good place to start is the website for World Evangelical Alliance, a global network of 7 regional and 121 national evangelical alliances, 104 organizational ministries, and 6 specialized ministries (http://www.worldevangelical.org/). Another valuable resource available on-line is *Send Me! Your Journey to the Nations* by Steve Hoke and Bill Taylor (World Evangelical Fellowship, 1999). This "preparatory global mission workbook…describes the path to cross-cultural service in 10 steps." The individual chapters can be downloaded from urbana.org (http://www.urbana.org/ns.rs.sendme.cfm), or the workbook can be purchased from World Evangelical Alliance.

chapter twenty-three

VOCATION, EDUCATION, AND WISDOM

If men and women of antiquity were dropped into our culture, they would probably be stunned by our variety of choices. Historically, sons usually took up the occupations of their fathers, using the tools passed along from one generation to another.[1] Daughters became wives. Asking a young Israelite if he had discovered God's will for his life's work would probably elicit a blank stare. For young people of our culture, the Big Three among the decisions of life are marriage, vocation, and education. The urgent search by many Christians for vocational guidance is certainly understandable.

Our frantic quest for the vocational dot was no more of an issue to the saints of A.D. 50 than, say, the eating of meat sacrificed to idols is to us today. However, the principles of God's Word remain remarkably contemporary. Though the apostolic world differed greatly from our own, the vocational guidance provided through Scripture is entirely adequate—even for our individualistic age.

GOD'S WILL FOR YOUR WORK

Some of that guidance has already been discussed in chapters 21 and 22. There we discovered that while God has called certain individuals to specific tasks in the past, those divine assignments were the exception to the rule. The idea that God calls each Christian to his life's work fits the traditional view very nicely; it just doesn't correspond to the experience of most of the saints in either Testament.[2]

For those who are not called to some vocation by direct revelation, the choice of a career or job falls in the area of freedom—a decision to be made on the basis of wisdom. For when we read the biblical passages directly related to work, we find the same principle that governs choices about singleness and marriage: The believer's decision about his vocation is *regulated* and affected by the moral will of God, but *not determined* by it.

Worship While You Work

The following principles summarize the moral will of God set forth in the New Testament Epistles for the Christian's work:[3]

1. As there is opportunity, the believer is to find gainful employment (2 Thessalonians 3:10–11). The believer who refuses to work is severely censured.

2. The obligation to provide for his own family is one of the highest priorities a Christian man has (1 Timothy 5:8).

3. The Christian's vocation must be lawful (Ephesians 4:28).

4. The Christian's work is to be characterized by:
   a) Sincerity of heart (Ephesians 6:5; Colossians 3:22–23)
   b) Enthusiasm and diligence (Ephesians 6:6; Colossians 3:23; 2 Thessalonians 3:8; Ecclesiastes 9:10)
   c) Reverence and devotion to Christ (Ephesians 6:5–6; Colossians 3:22–23)
   d) Good will (Ephesians 6:7)
   e) Discipline (2 Thessalonians 3:11)
   f) Quietness (2 Thessalonians 3:12)
   g) Cooperation (Titus 2:9)

h) Honesty (Titus 2:10)
i) Integrity (Ephesians 6:6)
j) Efficiency (Ephesians 5:16)
k) Gratitude (Colossians 3:17)
l) Generosity (Ephesians 4:28)

5. In the exercise of his vocation, the Christian should make it his goal:
   a) To earn his food (2 Thessalonians 3:10)
   b) To provide adequately for his own family (1 Timothy 5:8)
   c) To behave properly toward outsiders and not be in any need (1 Thessalonians 4:11–12)
   d) To avoid being a burden to others (2 Thessalonians 3:8)
   e) To earn enough to meet his own needs and have some left over to contribute to the needs of others (Ephesians 4:28)
   f) To set a good example for others (2 Thessalonians 3:9)
   g) To preserve God's reputation (1 Timothy 6:1)
   h) To adorn the doctrine of God in every respect (Titus 2:10)—that is, to manifest a consistency between profession and practice

6. In his relationship with his employer, the Christian worker must:
   a) Be submissive and obedient, as unto the Lord (Ephesians 6:5; Colossians 3:22; Titus 2:9; 1 Peter 2:18)
   b) Be diligent in his work, since his ultimate superior is the Lord (Ephesians 6:6–8; Colossians 3:23)
   c) Work as hard when no one is watching as he does under direct supervision (Ephesians 6:6)
   d) Regard his employer as worthy of all honor (1 Timothy 6:1) and show respect even to those supervisors who are unreasonable (1 Peter 2:18)
   e) Not take advantage of an employer who is also a believer, but rather serve him all the more out of love (1 Timothy 6:2)

7. In his relationships with his employees, the Christian boss must:
   a) Not abuse his workers (Ephesians 6:9)
   b) Treat his employees with justice and fairness (Colossians 4:1)
   c) Apply the golden rule, treating his workers as he would wish to be treated (Ephesians 6:9)
   d) Be fair and prompt in the payment of wages (James 5:4)
   e) Remember that he is accountable to God, the Master of all, for his treatment of his workers (Colossians 4:1)
8. If it does not otherwise violate the moral will of God, the opportunity for vocational change or advancement may be taken (1 Corinthians 7:21).[4]

Our choice of occupation, then, is to be made on the same basis as every other decision within the moral will of God: wisdom that seeks the greatest spiritual benefit. The question we should ask is: Given my aptitudes, abilities, gifts, desires, and opportunities, which vocation offers the greatest potential for my service to the Lord and my obedience to His moral will?[5]

Spiritual Gift

The believer's spiritual gift is part of his ability and aptitude and so influences his decision making. The best description of spiritual gifts comes from Paul when he describes them as "gifts," "ministries," "effects," and "manifestation of the Spirit" (1 Corinthians 12:4–7). God gives the gift of a spiritual enablement that results in a ministry which is effective for the common good.

The moral will of God requires each believer to use his gift for the common good. "As each one has received a special gift, employ it in serving one another as good stewards of the manifold grace of God" (1 Peter 4:10; cf. 1 Corinthians 12:7; Romans 12:6–8). So a believer's lifestyle must include the use of his spiritual gift. Since believers have received different gifts (1 Corinthians 12:8–11, 29–30), stewardship of those gifts will be expressed differently. The ministry activities of the person with the gift of exhortation will be different from those of the one with the gift of mercy. Yet they will both be obeying the same commandment. The moral will of God requires that a gift must be employed, but does not dictate when and where it must be used.

The gift of teaching, for example, can be exercised in a full-time teaching position or a weekly Bible study. The place that the gift is used could be with junior boys or college women, in Sunday school or one-on-one discipleship, in a local church or at a Bible college. These decisions are determined by spiritual advantage. Where can my gift be most wisely used to effectively serve God?

Wisdom also determines the amount of time devoted to the exercise of my gift. The moral will of God prohibits me from using my gift exclusively while neglecting commands in other passages of Scripture. For instance, fathers are to teach their children (Ephesians 6:4) whether they have the teaching gift or not (Romans 12:7); all believers are to give (1 Corinthians 16:2) though not all have the gift of giving (Romans 12:8); and all believers are to show mercy (Matthew 5:7; Ephesians 4:32), but only some have the gift of mercy (Romans 12:8).

On the other hand, it is wise to invest more time and energy in my area of giftedness. Certainly Billy Graham must show mercy, but wisdom guides him to skip some trips to the nursing home in favor of a citywide evangelistic crusade. Wisdom directs us into those areas where God has gifted us and that will bring the greatest spiritual effect.

We already demonstrated in chapters 21 and 22 that every believer has an obligation to consider full-time vocational Christian service. Because of all the factors involved, most believers who evaluate that option will conclude that they can serve God more effectively through a secular position. A good job allows a believer to provide for his family, bear witness to Christ, and contribute to the proclamation of God's Word through his local church and worldwide missions.

A student who was struggling with this decision once shared with me his dilemma. "Some years ago, I had a secular job that I enjoyed. I shared Christ with my fellow workers, and in time I was given the opportunity to lead Bible studies in our company. The Lord so used those Bible studies in the lives of those people that I began to think I should be teaching the Bible full-time. I became so gripped with the idea that I told my family and my church that I felt God was calling me into the ministry.

"Now, after several years in the pastorate, I've concluded that I was actually more effective for Christ in my secular job than I am in church work. I'd like to go back to what I was doing before, but I can't just withdraw from full-time ministry and return to my previous vocation."

Though I was pretty sure of the reason, I asked, "Why not?"

"Well," he replied, "since I told everyone that I was called into the pastorate, people would think I was disobeying the Lord if I went back to my old job. Also, it would be very humiliating to admit that I had been mistaken about that call."

This brother needed to be assured that no inner feeling had the authority to determine his choices. Once freed from that subjective absolute, he could focus on the right question: "How can I best serve the Lord through my life's work?" To be sure, he had backed himself into a corner by announcing what he had thought was a call from God. That would make it more difficult to reverse his vocational course, even if that is what wisdom indicated. But as far as God was concerned, he was not locked into a less fruitful job for the rest of his life.

More often, in my classes at Multnomah Bible College, I meet men and women who are moving in the opposite direction. Though successful in business or some other secular vocation, many of these students came to recognize that the Lord was using them more outside of their job than in it. Now they are studying the Bible to become better equipped to do full-time ministry. If they continue on this course, they will become Bible teachers, pastors, youth workers, and missionaries. Their change in vocation was brought about by the same question: "How can I best serve the Lord with my gifts and abilities?"

VOCATIONAL DECISION MAKING: A CASE STUDY

Same Song, Second Verse

In seminars that I have conducted on decision making, I have used a personal decision to help translate these precepts into practice. The irony of the illustration is that it closely resembles the decision I described in the introduction to this book. For both decisions required a choice between two colleges. In the first instance, I had to decide where to enroll as a student. In the second, I had to choose where to work as a teacher. In the first case, I experienced great frustration because of my efforts to consistently apply the traditional approach to decision making. In the second, the contrast was striking.

Fifteen years separated the two decisions. During that interim, I had worked through a theology of decision making and the will of God. I had become convinced from the Scriptures that my responsibility before God was not to look for an elusive ideal will, but rather to seek clear guidance that was both objective and available.

As a result, when two Bible colleges invited me to consider a teaching position on their faculties, I genuinely looked forward to the decision-making process. Rather than becoming anxious about missing my vocational dot, I was thankful that I had two excellent opportunities. My prayer for guidance was specific and biblical: I asked for wisdom, believing that God would grant it as He promised.

My new biblical understanding did not magically transform this decision into an easy one. The difference was that I had confidence that the process I was following was scriptural. I knew that I was facing a no-lose situation, so I was able to relax and enjoy the challenge of making a wise decision.

Try this Decision on for Size

In my seminars, I like to hypothetically put students in my shoes just before I had to decide where to teach. Students raise questions that they think I should have asked. I tell them whether I pursued those questions and what I learned when I did. Here is a reconstruction of one of those sessions.

STUDENT: Before you decided where to teach, you had to decide whether to teach. Had that issue already been resolved in your mind?

GARRY: I had concluded from past ministry that God had given me the gift of teaching. It is His moral will that I exercise whatever gift He gives me (Romans 12:6–8; 1 Peter 4:10). So teaching at a Bible college would be an excellent place to exercise that gift.

STUDENT: Where were the colleges located?

GARRY: One was here in Portland. The other was in my hometown in Michigan.

STUDENT: So what's to decide?

(These Oregonians intuitively recognized the wisdom of locating in the beautiful Pacific Northwest.)

GARRY: Actually, the location favored the Michigan college for several reasons. That's where my home church is and most of my family. Accepting a job close to my parents would be a way of honoring them.

STUDENT: What did your parents think? Did you seek their counsel?

GARRY: I was initially concerned that my folks might feel slighted if I turned down a job at home. So I determined that if they would be upset if I chose the Portland offer, I would regard that as a strong reason for accepting the job at home. Life is full of such realities, so I prepared myself for that possibility.

When we actually sat down to discuss my options, my parents demonstrated the same maturity they have always tried to teach me. The first thing they said was, "You know that we love you, and we would love to have you teaching near home. But we want you to know that our greatest desire is for you to make the best possible decision—not just the one that keeps you close to us." My counselors were not only free, but first-rate.

As we analyzed the numerous advantages of the college away from home, Mom jokingly said, "Wait a minute. We're not trying to get rid of him." We could laugh because we knew that was true and because we were not afraid to seek where wisdom would lead us in God's guidance.

STUDENT: Exactly what kind of work did each college want you to do?

GARRY: That's an important question because, in this situation, the openings were not identical. The college in the Northwest was offering me the lowest position on the totem pole. The college in Michigan wanted me to chair the Bible Department as well as teach. In terms of opportunity and responsibility, the two positions were clearly unequal.

STUDENT: But at that point in your teaching career, did you think you could handle the additional pressures of being a department chairman?

GARRY: That's a perceptive observation! There is a business axiom that workers tend to rise to the level of their incompetence. If I had accepted the position of department chairman, the chances were excellent that I would have started out at that level. I did have a desire to serve in a leadership role, but the offer came four or five years too soon. So I concluded that the job descriptions favored the college in the Northwest.

STUDENT: What about the pay scale?

GARRY: At that time, I didn't really care what they paid me and honestly cannot remember what the salary offers were. I know that both colleges offered more than enough for a single person to live on. In the actual decision, however, the prospective pay package was not a factor.

As I have reflected on that part of the process, I have concluded that I should have paid more attention to the salary offers. First, though both salaries were more than adequate for a single person, there was no guarantee that I would continue to be single. Second, the more money I earn, the more money I can give for the Lord's work. In fact, at that very time I was praying that the Lord would enable me to increase my financial support of Ed and Kay Klotz, missionaries in Nigeria. Third, faculty salaries often reflect the stability of a private college.

STUDENT: Did you have an opportunity to teach some classes at each college?

GARRY: Yes, I did. Both colleges had me teach several class sessions. Then, my presentations were evaluated by students and other faculty members.

STUDENT: Did the responses help you in your decision?

GARRY: Yes. The number and type of questions I got from the students, plus the classroom atmosphere, indicated that my teaching had been more helpful to the students in the Northwest college.

Who's in Charge Around Here?

The students in the seminar raised many other excellent questions about doctrinal stance, college reputation, and opportunities for outside ministry—areas in which the two colleges were equally strong. But one question that I hoped would be raised wasn't. "Who would be your direct boss? To whom would you have to submit?"

That is an important question in considering a job. For submission to authority is a biblical imperative for believers. Experience teaches that submission to authority is easiest when the one in charge is reasonable, competent, patient, loving, and compatible in personality. When you take a job, you take a boss. Since God's moral will requires obedience to that boss, the choice should be made wisely. For this reason I studied the two academic deans and felt that I could work with either of them.

But Do They Play Soccer?

At both colleges I asked about a soccer team. Though it may not sound very spiritual, the question about sports was one aspect of my search for wisdom. For Scripture commands us to do all things with zeal and enthusiasm. Being able to play soccer or basketball would help me to obey that imperative in my teaching. The physical exercise would be good for my bodily health, and the fun of playing would help me maintain my emotional health. Our personal happiness is a valid consideration in making a wise decision (1 Corinthians 7:40). To the soccer question, both colleges said I could work out with the team.

Everything You Wanted to Know, But...

From my subsequent experience as a teacher, I have discovered several areas that would have merited careful investigation—areas that I didn't check out because I didn't know to ask the questions. If I had it to do all over again, I would now ask the following:

1. How many different classes will I teach?
2. How much secretarial help will I have for grading assignments and other office work?
3. What type of office equipment and space will be supplied?
4. What will be my responsibilities in publicity and recruitment?
5. How many committee assignments will I be expected to accept?
6. What will be the nature of my relationship to the head of the department?
7. What kind of grading system is used in the college?
8. How often are contracts worked out and signed?

That I did not think of those questions until after the decision was made underscores a couple of corollaries to the principles already stated. First, when we ask for wisdom, God gives wisdom not omniscience. I didn't learn everything I could have learned before making my choice. But the wisdom God gave me was entirely sufficient for a sound decision. Second, the knowledge we acquire through making a decision, as well as the insight acquired as a result of our choice, helps to prepare us for future decisions.

Go West, Young Man

In the end, I accepted the position offered by Multnomah Bible College in Portland, Oregon. The decision was never cut-and-dried, but it has proved to be a great one. God showed Himself to be faithful in this decision. He gave power, wisdom, and motivation enabling me to make a wise choice within His moral will.

My job has been both fulfilling and challenging over the past three decades. Though I have encountered many difficulties, I haven't been second-guessing, quietly worrying, "Could it be that I missed God's perfect will?" Rather, I knew God gave strength to do His moral will and wisdom sufficient for the choice. That knowledge has freed me to concentrate fully on serving God right where I am.

GOD'S WILL FOR YOUR PREPARATION

Three to Get Ready

Upon graduation from high school, many young people enter a time of transition before the commencement of their career. Usually, that period of time is used to prepare for independence from parental support and for full participation in the adult community. For many, deciding which direction to go is the first major decision they've taken full responsibility for.

The basic question is: How can I best prepare to serve the Lord through my life and my vocation?

Because of the differences in time and culture, not many passages of Scripture directly address this decision. And so the decisions a Christian makes about education and training are to be made according to wisdom. The basic question is: How can I best prepare to serve the Lord through my life and my vocation? That question lays out the basic issues: (1) the ultimate goal is to serve the Lord in the most effective way possible; (2) the intermediate objective is appropriate preparation; and (3) that preparation should develop me as a person as well as train me for a vocation.

The options open to a young person in our society are abundant: university, Christian college,[6] Bible college, military service, vocational-technical school, apprenticeship, and so on. Or, the person can immediately go to work and gain valuable exposure and skills through on-the-job experience. The actual possibilities are limited by a number of factors, such as academic aptitude, grades and test scores, openings, financial resources, family circumstances, personal inclinations, individual initiative, and world conditions (peace or war).

The person who has concrete ideas about what he wants to do with his life is in a position to map out a specific course of preparation. The person whose vocational plans remain unclear would do well to consider educational opportunities that are foundational to any career—a liberal arts education or perhaps a tour of duty in the armed forces. Additionally, the Christian young person should weigh the benefits of some formal Bible training to help equip him or her to serve the Lord more effectively through any vocation.

Study to Show Thyself Approved

To the above generalizations, I add a couple of observations. The first is that education or training does not in itself qualify a person for spiritual ministry or a specific vocation. It is only part of the equipping process. For instance, graduation from seminary does not guarantee a man's suitability as a pastor. Seminary can train him so that he is "able to teach" (1 Timothy 3:2). But a seminary education does not insure that a man is able to manage his family well or that he has the spiritual character required of a church leader. A Master of Divinity with an uncontrolled temper is not ready to pastor a church, though the degree looks nice on the wall.

Second, the person himself is the most critical factor in the ultimate success of the preparation. The best university in the world cannot impart much knowledge to a lazy student. On the other hand, an industrious student can gain a good education even from a mediocre school. The self-taught individuals of past generations prove that a disciplined, motivated learner who has access only to a library will be far better educated than a slothful Ivy Leaguer.

---

1. Pat Alexander, ed., *Eerdman's Family Encyclopedia of the Bible* (Grand Rapids, MI: Wm. B. Eerdmans Publishing Co., 1978), 226; Charles F. Pfeiffer, Howard F. Vos, and John Rea, eds., *Wycliffe Bible Encyclopedia,* "Occupations" by Robert H. Belton (Chicago: Moody Press, 1975), 2:1222.

2. In the previous chapter, I refrained from generalizing that God's vocational call has been restricted to those directly engaged in the ministry of the Word. My hesitation stemmed from the fact that, while such a limitation does characterize God's call to special service in the New Testament, there are a handful of exceptions in the Old Testament: Adam (gardener), Noah (boat builder and zookeeper), Bezalel and Oholiab (artisans), Joshua (general), and all the soldiers who fought Israel's holy wars (see Genesis 2:15; 6:14, 19–20; Exodus 31:1–6; Numbers 1:2–3; 27:22–23). And yet, because all of these men were directly involved in carrying forward God's program of redemption, their work cannot be labeled as strictly secular—any more than the work of a missionary pilot. In any event, whether sacred or secular/sacred, every example of a divine vocational call in the Bible came via special revelation from God.
3. The passages these principles are derived from are 1 Corinthians 7:21; Ephesians 4:28; 5:16; 6:5–9; Colossians 3:17–4:1; 1 Thessalonians 4:11–12; 2 Thessalonians 3:7–12; 1 Timothy 5:8; 6:1–2; Titus 2:9–10; James 5:4; and 1 Peter 2:18–25. A number of these references are about relations between slaves and their masters. Most commentators consider that social condition to be roughly analogous to our arrangements between employees and employers. And so the exhortations directed to Christian slaves and masters are directly applicable within the contemporary labor-management context. See, for example, F. F. Bruce, "Commentary on the Epistle to the Colossians," in *Commentary on the Epistles to the Ephesians and the Colossians, The New International Commentary on the New Testament* (Grand Rapids, MI: Wm. B. Eerdmans Publishing Co., 1957), 294–96.
4. The decision whether to change jobs is slightly more complicated than our initial choice of a vocation. That is because, in accepting employment, a worker places himself under certain obligations to his employer. For a Christian to change jobs without violating the moral will of God, he must do so in a manner that will permit him to fulfill his commitments to his present employer. Christian integrity requires the giving of adequate notice so that the employer can secure a replacement.

   Neither does Scripture encourage a believer to change his work just because his working conditions are difficult. (In New Testament times, bailing out was not an option for slaves!) Rather, Christians are to appropriate God's grace to grow through the pressure. One application of this principle is: If the decision rests with you, don't quit your job until in God's sovereignty a better one becomes available.
5. The obvious prerequisite to a wise decision about our vocation is a good understanding of our aptitudes, abilities, gifts, and desires. Such self-knowledge takes time, a variety of life experiences, and diligence. Many people have been helped in their self-assessment by Richard Nelson Bolles's book, *What Color Is Your Parachute? A Practical Guide for Job-Hunters and Career-Changers* (Ten Speed Press). A new edition is published every year and is available at most bookstores. Supplemental information is provided at Bolles's website: http://www.JobHuntersBible.com.
6. The Council for Christian Colleges and Universities (CCCU) has two websites designed to help students explore the option of Christian higher education: http://www.christiancollegesearch.com and http://www.christiancollegementor.com.

chapter twenty-four

GIVING AND WISDOM

Jesus Himself said, "'It is more blessed to give than to receive'" (Acts 20:35). For many Christians, however, the joy of giving to the Lord has been blunted by the pressure to give—pressure generated by the sheer volume of requests for donations. Believers are barraged with appeals from missionaries, Christian schools, parachurch ministries, counseling centers, evangelistic enterprises, and a variety of home missions, including the less spectacular needs of the local church. The effect can be numbing.

By learning and applying biblical principles of giving, we can make a significant contribution to the Lord's work—and enjoy doing it. This chapter sets forth those principles and priorities, but first we will evaluate two common approaches to giving: the tithe and the faith promise.

THE TITHE

10%, 19%, or 22%?

"Will a man rob God? Yet you are robbing Me! But you say, 'How have we robbed You?' In tithes and offerings. You are

> cursed with a curse, for you are robbing Me, the whole nation of you! Bring the whole tithe into the storehouse, so that there may be food in My house, and test Me now in this," says the LORD of hosts, "if I will not open for you the windows of heaven and pour out for you a blessing until it overflows." (Malachi 3:8–10)

More than one Stewardship Sunday sermon has used this text. Tithing, a system of financial support employed in Israel during the age of the Old Testament, is practiced by many Christians today. It has the advantages of simplicity, consistency, and discipline. The believer contributes 10 percent of his income to the church, and the church makes all the decisions on distribution. Tithing follows a biblical pattern and generates considerable revenue in those churches where a high percentage of members practice it. And many believe that personal financial prosperity is conditioned upon faithfulness in tithing.

There is certainly nothing wrong with giving a tenth of our income to the Lord! However, a fuller understanding of the place of tithing in God's overall program will put this practice in its proper perspective.

The much-used text from Malachi deserves attention and comment. Note the following details: (1) failure to bring the designated tithes constituted theft from God; (2) the command was to bring the *whole* tithe; (3) it was to be brought to the temple; (4) the temple was to serve as a storehouse, not only for funds but for food; and (5) as disobedience brought a curse, so obedience would bring material blessing.

Malachi should not have had to bring such a message to Israel. Moses had already done so. It was all contained in Israel's law. The temple-based ministry was to be supported by the tithes of the people.

The word *tithe* literally means "tenth." In the Mosaic law, however, there is evidence that the Hebrews were required to bring not one but probably two or possibly even three tithes![1] The first tithe was 10 percent of all of one's possessions (Leviticus 27:30–33). It was considered to be "the LORD's" and was used for the support of the Levites as well as the temple ministry (Numbers 18:20–21). A second tithe, taken from whatever produce remained after the primary tithe was given, was set apart for a sacred meal in Jerusalem (Deuteronomy 12:17–18). Another tithe was collected every third year for the welfare of the Levites, strangers, orphans, and widows (Deuteronomy 14:28–29). If this third tithe was separate from the second one (which is possible but not certain), each Jewish family was obligated to surrender approximately 22 percent of its annual income for spiritual and social purposes.

Because they were required, the tithes of Israel were more like taxes than gifts. That is why failure to submit the "whole tithe" could be described as robbing God. Furthermore, if one of God's people wanted to express his worship through a voluntary offering, it had to be over and above the 22 percent of his income that was owed (Deuteronomy 12:6, 11; 1 Chronicles 29:6–9, 14).

Planned Obsolescence

We must realize that the tithe, which was foundational to the economic system of the theocratic nation of Israel, is *not* part of the economic system of the church. In the church, there are no taxes, dues, membership fees, or any other prescribed assessments. The ministry of the church is supported as each member gives "as he has purposed in his heart, not grudgingly or under compulsion" (2 Corinthians 9:7). Christians are not under obligation to practice tithing.

Because they were required, the tithes of Israel were more like taxes than gifts.

This is so for several reasons: (1) the local church does not have the same function as the temple "storehouse"; (2) the material blessing that was promised as a reward for faithfulness in the Old Testament is not promised to the saints of this age; (3) according to the apostles, the Mosaic law was no longer binding for Christians; and (4) the command to tithe is not carried over into the New Testament. We will look briefly at each of these facts in turn.

Once it was built in Jerusalem, there was one temple in Israel to which tithes and sacrifices were brought. When Christ died on the cross, the entire sacrificial system was fulfilled and rendered obsolete (Isaiah 53:10; Matthew 5:17; 27:51; Hebrews 10:9). The temple itself was destroyed under the judgment of God in A.D. 70 (Luke 19:41–44).

In the absence of the temple, there is nothing in the New Testament to suggest a physical counterpart in the economy of the church. The only "temple" Christians have a responsibility to is a spiritual one (1 Corinthians

3:16–17). Contemporary church buildings are not "mini-storehouses," for the New Testament knows nothing of our modern edifices. Therefore, without a temple, it is impossible for Christians to comply with the imperatives of Malachi 3.

A second difference between the present age and the Old Testament era is that the promise of material blessing for obedience (Leviticus 26:3–5) is no longer applicable.

> Spiritual blessing (Ephesians 1:3) and the meeting of material needs (Philippians 4:19) are what God promises. Being prospered materially is no necessary sign of deep godliness of faithful tithing; and contrariwise, poverty is no indication of being out of God's will (cf. Paul's own case in Philippians 4:12).[2]

And so the threat of a curse for failing to tithe and the promise of prosperity for those who comply are applicable only to the "sons of Jacob" to whom the words of Malachi were addressed (3:6).

A New Economy for a New Economy

Even if the temple were still standing in Jerusalem, Christians would not be obligated to tithe. For the Mosaic law has been replaced by the "law of Christ" (1 Corinthians 9:20–21), the "law of liberty" (James 1:25; 2:12), and the "royal law" of love (James 2:8; cf. Romans 13:8–10). Under the New Covenant, the law of grace is written on the hearts of believers rather than on tablets of stone (2 Corinthians 3:3–6). And so, as a code of life, the Mosaic law is no longer binding on the children of God (Romans 7:1–6; Galatians 3:19–25; Hebrews 7:11–12).

Now those aspects of the law of Israel that directly reflect the moral character of God and are appropriate to the age of grace (such as the command to love) were repeated in the New Testament (cf. Leviticus 19:18; 1 John 4:8–11). Such imperatives, and those that were added through apostolic revelation, constitute the moral will of God for this age (Ephesians 3:2–11). As far as giving is concerned, two questions must be asked about the New Testament revelation. First, does this new revelation continue the Old Testament practice of tithing? Second, is the Church given new guidelines to regulate giving during the age of grace?

As we have indicated, the answer to the first question is no—tithing is not prescribed for the Church. The tithe is not included in the apostolic teaching except by way of illustration (Hebrews 7:1–10). The answer to the second question is yes—new giving guidelines are established in the New Testament (and will be discussed below).

If It Was Good Enough for Abraham...

But since tithing precedes the Mosaic law, shouldn't it be viewed as a universal principle for every age? This position is based on the correct observation that Abraham (Genesis 14:20) and Jacob (Genesis 28:22) practiced tithing. Ryrie gives a well-stated response.

> Since Abraham and Jacob both tithed, and since their acts antedated the law, does that not relieve tithing of its legal aspects and make it a valid principle to follow today? The answer would be yes, if there were no other guides for giving in the New Testament.... But since the New Testament gives us clear principles to govern our giving, there is no need to go back to two isolated examples in the Old Testament for guidance.... Not even the most ardent tither would say that the Sabbath should be observed today because it was observed before the law (Exodus 16:23–36), yet this is the very reasoning used in promoting tithing today.[3]

In summary, while tithing has some advantages, that approach to giving is not prescribed for Christians. The Old Testament pattern is no longer operational. Believers today couldn't obey Malachi 3:8–10 if they wanted to. In the New Testament, the principle of tithing was replaced by the principle of grace giving.

The Tithe: An Unequal Yoke

An understanding of these truths is important for application. Some Christians need to be set free from the *burden* of tithing, while others need to be released from the *limitations* of giving a "mere tenth." David Hocking illustrates:

> Any study of the percentage of giving in the New Testament must face directly this basic principle: Whatever the percentage, what one sows, he shall reap! The standard of the traditional 10% or the "tithe" might be in some cases to "sow sparingly." In other cases, it would be to "sow bountifully." To illustrate this, here are two men, one who makes $1,000 a year, and one who makes $100,000 a year. The first man gives 10% and he has $900 left to live on; the second man gives 10% and he has $90,000 to live on. That's a far cry from $900! Perhaps the economy only demands $900 to live on; or perhaps $9000 would be more like it. The first man would suffer greatly, while the second would not have a care financially.[4]

Consistent application of the New Testament principle of proportional giving would not only eliminate such inequities, but actually increase the total amount Christians give for the Lord's work.

THE FAITH PROMISE

A second contemporary system of giving is called the "faith promise." While explanations of the approach differ in detail, the following is representative:

> "Faith Promise" is the popular name for a plan that, as one writer says, "helps Christians receive far greater blessing through periodic gifts." It is "trusting God for an amount of money He wants to channel through you for His glory." A Faith Promise is not just a gift, nor just a pledge of future gifts. It is a promise that, as God supplies the money, you will give a certain amount *over and above* your regular giving. It is a promise of money that you do not yet have nor know about; but you believe that God will provide it, to be given to a certain project or ministry. The next step, after deciding to use the Faith Promise approach, is to decide on the amount. How can a person know how much to promise? By asking God what additional amount He wants to channel through you. Then by

means of His Word and a settled peace that comes with prayer, you will come to a conclusion with thanksgiving to Him. Now you can look for the extra amount to arrive, usually from an unexpected source. The extra money, perhaps unexpected overtime pay or a repaid dead loan, should be recognized as God's to be used for His work and not for other purposes.

The distinctive features of the plan are as follows: (1) God is the Supplier of the money; (2) the money given is to be "over and above" all existing giving commitments; (3) the amount to be given is determined by God and revealed subjectively to the heart of the believer in response to faith and prayer; (4) the money is supplied as the Christian continues to trust God for it; (5) the money will come from unexpected sources; and (6) the destination of the gift is already determined—to the organization that explains the approach.

Faith promise giving is a direct application of the traditional view of guidance. The method assumes that God has already determined a certain amount of money He wants the believer to give. Through prayer and inward impressions of the Holy Spirit, God is expected to reveal that specific amount to the believer. The amount thereby derived is believed to be God's individual will for the Christian in his giving.

Nothing Succeeds Like Success

As a system of giving, the faith promise method is quite popular. For not only does it harmonize well with the traditional view of decision making, it also works. Churches have found that a faith promise program increases the amount of money given to missions. Mission organizations are able to raise remarkable amounts of money from a single banquet where the faith promise method of giving is explained. And they are able to do so without siphoning off funds from other essential ministries. One Christian school presented plans for a much-needed building project to the student body of seven hundred students. Following the faith promise format, those students pledged seventy thousand dollars—and that was over and above their present giving commitments!

The faith promise approach is not a biblical plan, but it works, in large measure, because it incorporates two principles that are thoroughly biblical. First, the method greatly encourages *prayer*. Picture the college student who "in faith" concludes that God wants him to give three hundred dollars to the missionary project beyond all his regular giving. This student is motivated to pray for extra money that he can give to missions. The motivation is excellent, and his prayer fulfills the moral will of God. God responds to such prayer whether it is part of a faith promise program or not.

Second, the method encourages great generosity in giving. This, too, is biblical. Picture again that same student with a three-hundred-dollar faith promise. He is now praying regularly for God to supply what to him is an enormous amount of money. He receives an unexpected fifty-dollar refund. Formerly, he might have put five dollars in the offering plate at church, but now the whole check goes to the missions project. That is generosity in action, and it pleases the heart of God whether it is part of a faith promise program or not.

Choose a Number

I almost hesitate to criticize something that is characterized by such good qualities and promotes such fine results. But faith promise giving has some flaws that need correction. The first and foremost is that the method lacks a scriptural basis.[5] The whole system is built upon the traditional model of guidance. The reason the method produces spiritual results is not because the system as a whole is valid, but because people are challenged to pray and give generously.

The first problem is the process for determining the amount to be pledged. As we explained in chapter 6, "Impressions Are Impressions," God does not reveal His individual will for our decisions through inner impressions. All of the problems of subjectivity explored in that chapter apply to the question of determining an amount to give. It is not surprising that for some people a whole jumble of figures come to mind, while others draw a blank and are not "impressed" by any amount at all.

The verses that do address giving correspond perfectly to the principles of decision making explained throughout this book.

> Each one must do [i.e., give] just as he has purposed in his heart, not grudgingly or under compulsion, for God loves a cheerful giver. (2 Corinthians 9:7)

> And in the proportion that any of the disciples had means, each of them determined to send a contribution for the relief of the brethren living in Judea. (Acts 11:29)

In both the exhortation (2 Corinthians 9:7) and the example (Acts 11:29), the individual believer decides whether to give in a specific situation and how much to give. Instead of deciding on the basis of some mystical inner impression, we are to make such decisions based on specific biblical guidelines, which we will discuss more fully in a moment.

Promises, Promises

A second misunderstanding of Scripture that the faith promise format fosters relates to the nature of faith. Christians are encouraged to trust God for something He has not said He will do—namely, come up with a specific amount of money for a specific project within a certain period of time. No verse in the Bible indicates that God will reveal an amount that He wants us to give. Nor is there a verse that obligates Him to provide whatever amount we decide to pledge. If there were such passages, God's faithfulness would be at stake in the fulfillment of the promise. But to hold God to a promise that He hasn't put on the record isn't faith, it is presumption. Genuine faith must be anchored to verifiable promises. That is what characterized Abraham who was "fully assured that what God *had promised,* He was able also to perform" (Romans 4:21). If God doesn't promise, we can't promise. And an inward impression is not a promise.

> To hold God to a promise that He hasn't put on the record isn't faith, it is presumption.

Because of these biblical deficiencies, participants in a faith promise program come to false conclusions based on the results. Those able to meet their pledges are encouraged and conclude that the system is valid. Giving glory to God is entirely appropriate for He is the One who makes all giving possible (2 Corinthians 9:8–10). But the success of the program does not prove its validity. Only Scripture can do that.

On the other hand, many who don't meet their quota, though they are just as prayerful and generous as others, end up wondering if their faith is weak. Not only is that an inappropriate response, but it robs the giver of joy in giving what God did provide and replaces that joy with false guilt.

Those seven hundred students mentioned earlier are a case in point. The seventy thousand dollars they pledged represented an ambitious "step of faith." From the outset of the project, enthusiasm ran high. Students wore buttons reminding them to pray for the successful completion of the goal. But as the deadline drew near, it became increasingly apparent that, barring a miracle, the goal was hopelessly beyond reach.

The amount of money actually given for the project was approximately twelve thousand dollars—a tremendous contribution from financially strapped students. Many had given sacrificially, beyond their means, as the Lord enabled them. But instead of rejoicing over the twelve thousand dollars, the student body was troubled by the missing fifty-eight thousand dollars. And I'm sure that some of those students came out of that experience questioning their faith.

Interestingly enough, there are two other possible explanations for failure to meet one's faith promise: either God didn't come through, or something is wrong with the system. I have concluded that it is the latter, but most people assume the problem lies with them.

Seven Hundred Dollars Short on Faith

What is needed is modification of the faith promise format to bring it into complete alignment with Scripture. In college, I participated in a faith promise project. When the appeal was made, the only figure that came to my mind was one thousand dollars. That was a lot of money. I didn't have that kind of money. If I sold everything I had, I could not raise one thousand dollars. So I prayed and worked. What I was able to contribute, as the target date approached, was three hundred dollars. That was fantastic! I had never given like that in my life. But I was more frustrated than joyful because I was seven hundred dollars short on faith.

So I began asking God to give me a way to raise the remainder of my pledge. What I came up with was an all-school work day. I organized it and many students participated. By the end of that day we had raised seven hundred dollars. But as I reflected on it, I realized that I could not claim that money as the fulfillment of my faith promise. I could say that God answered my prayer for the one thousand dollars, but money earned through the labor of others was *theirs* to contribute, perhaps as part of their own faith promises.

What I needed to learn was that God hadn't promised to give me one thousand dollars. That figure was the product of my own mind. What the Lord did expect me to do was to pray fervently, gratefully accept what He chose to provide, and give generously.

When I went to seminary, I endeavored to apply some of the lessons I had been learning about faith, prayer, and giving. I desired to participate in a church ministry for which the people could not pay me. In order to do that, I needed two thousand dollars per semester from other sources. I didn't have time to work at another (paying) job and do this ministry. So I prayed and asked God to provide the two thousand dollars.

No verse in the Bible said God had to give me that two thousand dollars. There was no passage that exempted me from gainful employment. I was willing to work and would thank the Lord if He chose to provide for my needs in such a manner. But the Lord chose to answer my prayer dramatically. He provided that two thousand dollars per semester through the gifts of other believers, and I was enabled to minister in that church that could not support me. God provided the needed money in that way, not because I had a foolproof system, not because I had more faith than anyone else, not because He was obligated to come up with the amount that came to my mind; but because He is gracious and because He answers prayer.

The two situations I have described are dissimilar, but they share a common bottom line: Money had to be provided if a ministry was to function. And what I learned from the first incident helped me to better approach the second one. In the latter instance, I avoided the mistake of locking God into a box of my own construction. I asked Him to provide an income in some manner that would free me to minister without pay. Then I left the outcome to Him. The figure I asked for was not extracted from thin air, but was based on specific, anticipated needs. Because God is wiser than we are, the way He chooses to provide will be wiser. And by letting Him act with no strings attached, He gets the glory regardless of the outcome.

BIBLICAL PRINCIPLES OF GIVING

Purposeful, Proportionate Giving

Repeatedly in this chapter, I have alluded to biblical principles of giving. The most extended treatment of giving in the New Testament is 2 Corinthians 8–9. You would do well to carefully read those chapters before continuing.

The decisions that each believer must make about giving are numerous. Among them are how much of our income to give and how to distribute what is given. Since we have been discussing various ways of determining the amount to give, we will look first at those passages that address that issue.

In 2 Corinthians 8–9, the phrases that relate to choosing an amount are very instructive: "according to their ability" (8:3); "of their own accord" (8:3); "by your ability" (8:11); "according to what a person has, not according to what he does not have" (8:12).

All of these expressions are consistent with the summary exhortation of 2 Corinthians 9:7: "Each one must do just as he has purposed in his heart, not grudgingly or under compulsion, for God loves a cheerful giver." This verse rules out the "compulsion" of a required tithe. It also speaks against extracting contributions by organizational pressure, guilt trips, or emotional manipulation. The matter is placed squarely on the shoulders of the individual believer who is to give "as he has purposed in his heart." There is no hint of any inward impression to find God's will. Second Corinthians 9:7 *is* God's will for our giving.

The same point is made in different words in 1 Corinthians 16:2: "On the first day of every week each one of you is to put aside and save, *as he may prosper*, so that no collections be made when I come." Under grace, the tithe has been replaced by the principle of proportionate giving.

It is not difficult to compute 10 percent of one's income, but how much is "as he may prosper" or "in keeping with his income" (NIV)? It is neither a specific amount nor a particular percentage. The rich should be "rich in good works" (1 Timothy 6:17–18). Those who have nothing are not expected to give anything (2 Corinthians 8:12). Those who have less than enough are to receive from others who have more than enough (2 Corinthians 8:13–14). Those who have little give the little that they can (2 Corinthians 8:2–3). Increasing prosperity should result not only in an increase in the amount given but in the percentage given. Many

Americans should consider 15, 20, 40, or 60 percent of their income. Their "abundance" (2 Corinthians 8:14) should make them abundant givers.

This principle is well illustrated by an incident that occurred during the early years of the Church:

> Now at this time some prophets came down from Jerusalem to Antioch. One of them named Agabus stood up and began to indicate by the Spirit that there would certainly be a great famine all over the world. And this took place in the reign of Claudius. And *in the proportion that any of the disciples had means, each of them determined to send a contribution* for the relief of the brethren living in Judea. (Acts 11:27–29)

The Rich Young Giver

When I was pastoring in a church, a young man in the congregation came to talk to me about giving. He said, "I used to think that the reason I did not give much was because I did not have much. But now that I have quite a bit of money, I find that I still am not contributing very much of it to the Lord's work. How should I give?"

I explained to him the principles of grace giving. Then I suggested that he select a percentage of his income that he thought would be consistent with how the Lord had blessed him financially. I promised to ask him later if he had chosen a percentage to give.

A week later I checked with him. "Yes," he replied, "I think that 40 percent is about right." I gulped. From next to nothing to 40 percent is a big jump. Nevertheless, I encouraged him to follow his plan for one month and then evaluate. If he felt some adjustment was called for (and I was sure he would need to become more realistic), he could change the amount.

At the end of the month, we again discussed his giving. He was full of joy and said it had been a great period in his Christian life. He had invested significantly in the Lord's work and had derived great satisfaction from it. Moreover, his new commitment to giving was requiring him to more carefully monitor where the rest of his money went. He was amazed at how much he had formerly wasted. When I suggested that he reconsider the percentage of his income that he would give the following month, he readily agreed. "I think 40 percent is too little in view of the way God has been prospering me. This month, I think 60 percent would be more appropriate."

Later, I overheard one of the young people talking about this same brother. "You know, he doesn't spend away his money like he used to. I wonder what's gotten into him?" I knew the answer. He was learning to give rather than waste. Abundant giving and careful spending were his new responses to God's prospering of his life.

God's Grace Giving Guidelines

A complete exposition of New Testament teaching on giving is beyond the scope of this chapter.[6] While not detailed or exhaustive, the following list of principles opens the lid on giving that follows in the steps of the greatest Giver.

1. God Himself is the Model, Motivator, and Equipper of all Christian giving! (2 Corinthians 8:9; 9:8–10, 15).
2. Giving our money to the Lord is an extension of the prior gift of ourselves (Romans 12:1–2; 2 Corinthians 8:5). The donation of a portion of our wealth is made in the recognition that *everything* we have belongs to God (Luke 19:11ff.; 1 Corinthians 4:7; 6:19–20; 1 Chronicles 29:14).
3. The ability and motivation to give to the Lord is a function of grace (2 Corinthians 8:1, 3, 6, 7; 9:8–10). Grace is that work of God in us that gives both the desire and the power to fulfill God's will.
4. In God's eyes, the *attitude* of the giver is more important than the *amount* given (2 Corinthians 9:7). Accordingly, grace giving is to be characterized by: joy (2 Corinthians 8:2); cheerfulness (2 Corinthians 9:7); liberality (2 Corinthians 8:2); sacrifice (2 Corinthians 8:2–3); eagerness (2 Corinthians 8:4, 7–8); willingness (2 Corinthians 8:12; 9:2); perseverance (2 Corinthians 8:10–12); and integrity (2 Corinthians 8:20–21).
5. Giving is a spiritual exercise *all* believers—even poor ones—may participate in (Luke 21:1–4; 2 Corinthians 8:2).
6. The value of a gift is not determined by its amount but by its cost (Luke 21:1–4; 2 Corinthians 8:2). The question should not be,

"How much can I spare?" but rather, "How much can I sacrifice?" Not "How much can I give?" but, "How much can I give up?"

7. We are not expected to give more than we are able. Often, however, we find that we can give more than we thought we could! (2 Corinthians 8:3, 12).
8. The extent of spiritual "treasures" or fruit is either limited or expanded by the extent of the gift (Matthew 6:19–21; 2 Corinthians 9:6).
9. The ability to give is granted by God, who gives even more to those who want to give more (Luke 6:38; 2 Corinthians 9:9–11).
10. The opportunity to give is to be viewed as a privilege, not an obligation (2 Corinthians 8:4; 9:7).
11. The greatest threat to generous giving is not poverty but covetousness (Luke 12:13–34; Acts 5:1–10; 2 Corinthians 9:5).
12. If we promise financial support, we must make every effort to fulfill it (2 Corinthians 8:10–12; 9:5).
13. Our giving is to be regular, individual, systematic, and proportionate (1 Corinthians 16:1–2).
14. The results of grace giving include: a harvest of righteousness (2 Corinthians 9:10; Philippians 4:17); further enrichment of the giver so that he can give more (2 Corinthians 9:11); thanksgiving to God (2 Corinthians 9:11–12); the meeting of needs (2 Corinthians 9:12); the glorifying of God (2 Corinthians 9:13); verification of the message of the gospel (John 13:35; 2 Corinthians 9:13); the offering of reciprocal prayers (2 Corinthians 9:14); and a strengthening of the bonds of fellowship between believers (2 Corinthians 9:14).

BIBLICAL PRIORITIES IN GIVING

Charity Begins at Home

Once we decide how much of our income to give to the Lord, we need to determine where those funds will be distributed. The New Testament gives us guidance for this decision.

Heading the list of priorities is our *own family*. Paul wrote, "But if anyone does not provide for his own, and especially for those of his household, he has denied the faith and is worse than an unbeliever"

(1 Timothy 5:8). Those are strong words—even for Paul! Financial provision for our immediate family is the highest priority, as indicated by the word "especially."

The second sphere of responsibility encompasses our extended family, or *relatives.* In 1 Timothy 5, much of the discussion centers on the proper care of widows. Paul stresses that the primary responsibility for this care falls on the immediate family rather than the church: "but if any widow has children or grandchildren, they must first learn to practice piety in regard to their own family" (1 Timothy 5:4; see 5:16).

Don't Muzzle the Ox—or the Preacher

We also must provide for those who minister the Word to us. "The one who is taught the word is to share all good things with the one who teaches him" (Galatians 6:6). No one should become a pastor to get rich (1 Peter 5:2), but the one who ministers the gospel is entitled to make his living by it (1 Corinthians 9:11, 14; 1 Timothy 5:17–18).

In some situations, however, it is simply not possible for a man to receive a living wage from those he is ministering to. A new and struggling work often cannot fully support a pastor. An evangelist or missionary reaching into a previously unevangelized area cannot expect unbelievers there to take up an offering for him. Thus, we have the opportunity and obligation to provide financial support for those who minister to other people in other places.

Robbing Macedonia to Feed Corinth

Such monetary assistance was probably a part of the church's role in sending out the first two missionaries, Barnabas and Saul (Acts 13:2–3). The new believers in the infant church at Philippi gave to help Paul in his church planting ministry (Philippians 4:15–16). The immaturity of the Christians in Corinth forced Paul to rely on gifts from other churches to sustain his ministry there. Paul later wrote to these Corinthians, "I robbed other churches by taking wages from them to serve you…they fully supplied my need, and in everything I kept myself from being a burden to you" (2 Corinthians 11:8–9).

By Paul's reckoning, the responsibility for his support belonged to the saints he was ministering to—the Corinthians. Because they neglected to provide for him, he "robbed" other churches for his support. On the other hand, he commended the believers from Macedonia for supplying his needs, even though he was not ministering directly to them.

Rescue the Perishing

Giving to meet physical needs is another responsibility that Christ and His apostles emphasized (Galatians 6:10; 1 John 3:17). In fact, all of Paul's exhortation in 2 Corinthians 8–9, from which the church derives many of its principles of giving, was directed toward the collection of relief funds for the impoverished saints in Judea.

The priority established for the relief of the poor is: believers first, unbelievers second. The needy in our spiritual family take precedence over those in the world. We may not neglect the needs of unbelievers by caring exclusively for our own. It is not a case of either/or, but of both/and. Paul said, "So then, while we have opportunity, let us do good to all people, and especially to those who are of the household of the faith" (Galatians 6:10).

To sum up: As we respond to the grace of God by being a good steward of the money He entrusts to us, we determine the distribution of those funds according to biblical priorities. In general, the order of our giving moves outward, with those closest to us having priority: the immediate family, the extended family, the work of the local church, the work of gospel proclamation, and, finally, the relief of needy believers, then unbelievers. This order is part of a sound strategy for outreach. For the long-term support of missionary activity requires a solid base of operations at home.

Passing Out God's Money Is Fun

In recent years, I have adopted the following approach to giving. I have chosen a percentage of my income that I contribute to the Lord's work. A portion of what I give goes to my local church to sustain the ministry of those who share the Word with me. I have also decided that half of what I give will go to ministries where the gospel is proclaimed through evangelism, church planting, and other missionary enterprises. Some of this is channeled through the local church, and some goes directly to the persons or agencies I have a personal interest in.

In the past, I felt overwhelmed when it came to giving money to meet physical needs. There were so many—many more than I could ever hope to meet. I felt guilty every time I heard a moving story or saw a picture of starving people. I found I was being motivated almost entirely by guilt or manipulation, rather than responding to the instructions of Scripture.

So I determined that about 10 percent of the money I give to the Lord will go into a "Need Fund." Every payday, the appropriate amount of money is put aside in that fund. When I learn of a need, if there is money in my "Need Fund," I have the joy of passing it out. And if there is nothing in that fund when I learn of a need, I don't have to feel guilty about not giving. Of course, I'm not restricted to giving only what's in that fund. If the situation warrants it, I can divert money that was earmarked for other purposes to meet an urgent need. Some circumstances call for sacrificial giving.

BIBLICAL GIVING

1. Old Testament tithing has been superceded by New Testament grace giving.
2. The "faith promise" method of giving is unbiblical though it correctly encourages prayer and generous giving.
3. Grace giving is purposeful, proportionate giving as God has prospered you.
4. Giving priorities are immediate family first, then relatives, local church, gospel outreach, relief of believers, relief of unbelievers.

God has entrusted to His children the privilege and responsibility of wisely utilizing this world's goods to attain spiritual fruit. The freedom that Christians have to make decisions about giving can be exploited by some for their own selfish needs. But not for long. For God is not mocked—a man will reap as he sows (Galatians 6:6–10). And those who freely give as they have freely received (Matthew 10:8) will experience great blessing as recipients of God's abundant grace (2 Corinthians 9:6–12).

"Thanks be to God for His indescribable gift!" (2 Corinthians 9:15).

---

1. O. T. Allis, *God Spake By Moses* (Nutley, NJ: The Presbyterian and Reformed Publishing Company, 1975), 143, n. 1; Merrill F. Unger, *Unger's Bible Dictionary* (Chicago: Moody Press, 1957), s.v. "Tithe"; Charles C. Ryrie, *Balancing the Christian Life* (Chicago: Moody Press, 1969), 86; Geoffrey W. Bromily, ed., Eugene E. Carpenter, "Tithe," *The International Standard Bible Encyclopedia* (Grand Rapids, MI: Wm. B. Eerdmans Publishing Co., 1988), vol. 4, 863.
2. Ryrie, *Balancing the Christian Life*, 88.
3. Ibid.
4. David L. Hocking, "Biblical Pattern of Giving" (First Brethren Church, Long Beach, CA, n.d.).
5. The only verse that I have ever heard cited in support of the faith promise plan is 2 Corinthians 9:5: "So I thought it necessary to urge the brethren that they would go on ahead to you and arrange beforehand your previously promised bountiful gift, so that the same would be ready as a bountiful gift and not affected by covetousness." The only point of continuity between this verse and the faith promise method is a "previously promised...gift." Apart from that, none of the distinctive features of faith promise giving is even mentioned.
6. Additional passages on giving: Matthew 6:19–24; 16:1–13; 19:11–27; Romans 12:8; Galatians 6:6–10; Philippians 4:14–19; 1 Timothy 5:8, 17–18; 6:6–19; 2 Timothy 3:1–2; Titus 1:7; Hebrews 13:16; James 1:11; 5:1–6; 1 John 3:17–18.

chapter twenty-five

WISDOM WHEN CHRISTIANS DIFFER

One of the major premises of this book is that in those areas where the Bible gives no command or principle, the believer is free and responsible to make choices. Any decision made within the moral will of God is acceptable to God.

Ironically, with some decisions it is easier to please God than to please our fellow Christians. Given the nature of humanity and the reality of the freedom of choice, it is inevitable that believers are going to come to different conclusions about what is permissible and what is not. That fact has caused no small amount of trouble in the history of the Church.

People are tempted to move toward one of two opposite extremes. On the one hand, there is the Christian who relishes his freedom and appreciates his direct accountability to God. He ignores the opinions of others and lets the chips fall where they may. If others get offended by his enjoyment of Christian liberty, that's their problem. The other extreme is represented by the sensitive saint. Recognizing his accountability to the other members of the body, he bends over backward to keep from violating anyone's convictions. If he bends over far enough, he eventually discovers that he can't move at all.

Neither of these two extremes is appropriate. We cannot ignore our differences; neither can we be immobilized by them. How are we to relate to fellow believers who differ with us regarding decisions in the area of freedom? I attempt to answer that question in this chapter.

Diversity Is More than P. C.

Part of God's design for the church is that it should manifest unity in diversity. It was His intent that people with divergent personalities, nationalities, gifts, abilities, tastes, and backgrounds should become unified in Christ without eliminating personal distinctiveness (1 Corinthians 12:12–27; Colossians 3:11).

Accordingly, God does not view differences of opinion in the area of freedom as a bad thing. Variance of thought is not a flaw in an otherwise beautiful plan. It rather represents one more situation in which the supernatural character of the church, as a living organism, may be manifested before the world (John 13:35; 17:20–21).

What God desires, then, is not uniformity of opinion but unity of relationship (Romans 15:5–7).[1] And so, instead of trying to eliminate differing opinions, the Holy Spirit has given specific instructions to guide our response to them. This teaching is found mainly in Romans 14–15 and 1 Corinthians 8–10.

THE MEAT DEBATE

And in This Corner, the Carnivores

This divine direction was a response to some problems that cropped up in the first-century Church. Believers were lining up on opposite sides of issues about which God had not yet revealed His moral will. The test case that eventually warranted apostolic comment was the propriety of eating meat. There were actually two variations on this one theme. F. F. Bruce gives this excellent explanation of the problem in the church at Rome:

> The question of what kinds of food might and might not be taken agitated the early Church in various ways. One of these

> ways affected Jewish Christians more particularly. The Jewish food-laws, which had been observed by the nation from its earliest days, were one of the principal features distinguishing the Jews from their Gentile neighbors. Not only was the flesh of certain animals absolutely prohibited; the blood of all animals was absolutely prohibited, and "clean" animals slaughtered for food had to be killed in such a way that their blood was completely drained away. Since one could never be sure that meat eaten by non-Jews was free from every suspicion of illegality in one respect or another, it was impossible for an orthodox Jew to share a meal with a Gentile. Indeed, it was difficult enough for a strict Jew to share a meal with a fellow-Jew whom he suspected of laxity in these matters.[2]

The problem in Rome, owing possibly to the sensitivities of Jewish Christians, was whether it was permissible to eat any meat at all. The debate in Corinth differed in one detail. There, believers hotly disputed the spiritual significance of eating meat *previously offered to idols*.

> The buying of butcher-meat in pagan cities such as Corinth and Rome presented some Christians with a conscientious problem. Much of the flesh exposed for sale in the market came from animals which had originally been sacrificed to a pagan deity. The pagan deity received his token portion; the rest of the flesh might be sold by the temple authorities to the retail merchants, and many pagan purchasers might be willing to pay a little more for their meat because it had been "consecrated" to some deity. Among the Christians there were some with a robust conscience who knew that the meat was neither better nor worse for its association with the pagan deity, and were quite happy to eat it; others were not so happy about it, and felt that somehow the meat had become "infected" by its idolatrous association.[3]

Other issues arose as well.[4] But Paul specifically addressed meat eating to establish principles that are to govern the exercise of Christian liberty when opinions differ. Here are those principles, and I will establish the textual support for them from both Romans 14–15 and 1 Corinthians 8–10 as each principle is explained in detail.

DECISION MAKING WHEN CHRISTIANS DIFFER

ROMANS 14:1–15:13

1. Learn to distinguish between matters of command and matters of freedom (14:14, 20).
2. On debatable issues, cultivate your own convictions (14:5).
3. Allow your brother the freedom to determine his own convictions, even when they differ from yours (14:1–12).
4. Let your liberty be limited, when necessary, by love (14:13–15:2).
5. Follow Christ as the model and motivator of servanthood (15:3–13).

DEFINING THE AREA OF FREEDOM

PRINCIPLE 1: *Learn to Distinguish Between Matters of Command and Matters of Freedom.*

Though Paul was discussing eating meat, he placed that issue in a broader category: decisions that fall within the area of freedom. The alternatives (to eat or to refrain from eating) were neither right nor wrong in themselves. Scripture does not command meat eating; neither does it forbid meat eating. And so the question must be answered by each believer on other grounds.

Paul's vocabulary makes it clear that he viewed this as a matter of freedom. In Romans 14:14, 20, the rightness or wrongness of eating meat is declared to be a matter of personal opinion. The terms in 1 Corinthians are even more precise: "This *liberty* of yours" (8:9); "a *right*" (9:4–6); "all things are *lawful*" (10:23); "*freedom*" (10:29).

This distinction between what is commanded and what is left to the choice of each believer is a critical one. For the principles Paul establishes in these chapters govern only those differences that arise in the area of freedom. If a believer departs from a tenet of gospel truth or violates an explicit command of Scripture, different principles governing the response of the church go into effect.[5] On the fundamentals of the faith, there is no room for compromise, no tolerance of diversity of viewpoint.

Unfortunately, gaining a consensus on where to draw the line between matters of command and matters of freedom is not always easy. In Paul's day, to eat meat or not to eat meat—that was the question. But what about today?

The twentieth-century church has managed to divide itself over a whole range of issues. The list below contains ones I have personally encountered. In every case, there are sincere believers who consider the activity in question prohibited by God, while equally sincere brothers and sisters maintain that participation is permitted within the Christian's freedom:

- attending movies
- watching television
- working for pay on Sunday
- mowing the lawn on Sunday
- fishing on Sunday
- drinking wine in moderation
- cooking with wine
- attending the theater for live drama
- participating in sports
- participating in contact sports
- eating food in the church building
- wearing two-piece swimsuits (women)
- mixed swimming
- playing pool
- playing cards
- gambling for recreation
- buying insurance
- smoking
- dancing
- wearing pant suits to church (women)
- using a Bible translation other than King James
- raising tobacco
- playing guitars in church
- listening to rock music
- wearing makeup (women)
- wearing beards (men)
- wearing hair over the ears (men)
- wearing hair cut above the shoulders (women)
- kissing (unmarried couples)
- wearing skirts above the knee
- playing the saxophone in church
- taking sedatives
- speaking in tongues
- going to a psychiatrist

People who read this list tend to react with laughter and incredulity. They chuckle at the items that are "obviously" in the area of freedom, and they can't believe that anyone could feel free before God to do the things that are "obviously" forbidden by principles of Scripture. And yet if we asked ten different believers of various ages and backgrounds to separate those activities into categories of "permissible" and "not permissible," we would likely end up with *ten different lists*.

A primary reason for this is that biblical commands tend to be general in character. They require holiness, love, separation from the world, good stewardship, personal consecration, and the like. Such directives will be obeyed in different ways in different settings. Serious conflict arises when personal or cultural *applications* of divine imperatives are added to the list of universal *absolutes*.[6]

These applications may be valid and therefore binding for those who recognize them. The danger stems from not distinguishing between the scriptural command in its more general expression and the specific manner in which it is obeyed in a given setting. Human traditions—the accumulation of particular applications—tend to harden over time.

In Paul's day, some believers applied the imperatives of holiness and separation from the world to eating meat. The real disagreement was not over the activity itself, but rather the spiritual ramifications of the activity—i.e., whether eating meat would result in spiritual defilement.

This distinction between the activity (which in itself is neutral) and the ramifications (which may have moral implications) characterizes all debated questions. However, in the heat of debate, most people lose sight of that distinction. And all too often, the activity itself is perceived in moral terms of "right" and "wrong." When this happens, the argument becomes highly emotional and the ability to reason objectively is lost. So is any hope of maintaining unity.

Accordingly, part of Paul's objective in Romans and 1 Corinthians was to make his readers aware of the nature of the disagreement: "But food will not commend us to God; we are neither the worse if we do not eat, nor the better if we do eat" (1 Corinthians 8:8). Eating meat is, in itself, neutral. But if a person is convinced that by eating meat he violates God's standard of holiness, then eating meat becomes sinful to him (Romans 14:14; 1 Corinthians 8:7).

Likewise, believers today need to learn to differentiate between biblical principle and specific application. That must be the first step. John

R. W. Stott says it well:

> First, we must distinguish more clearly between tradition and Scripture. Most of us Christian people have a set of cherished beliefs and practices, probably inherited from our parents or learned in childhood from the church. Too many of us have accepted them uncritically en bloc. And evangelical believers are by no means free of this tendency. For example, our "touch not; taste not; handle not" has often been "smoke not, drink not, dance not." I am not expressing an opinion on whether we should or should not engage in these habits. What I am saying is that Scripture contains no explicit pronouncements on them. These prohibitions belong therefore to "the traditions of the evangelical elders"; they are not part of the Word of God.[7]

DECISION MAKING WHEN CHRISTIANS DIFFER

ROMANS 14:1–15:13

1. **Learn to distinguish between matters of command and matters of freedom (14:14, 20).**

DEVELOPING PERSONAL CONVICTIONS

PRINCIPLE 2: *On Debatable Issues, Cultivate Your Own Convictions.* This principle is established in a single statement: "Each person must be fully convinced in his own mind" (Romans 14:5).

Paul refers here to noncommanded issues and underscores the believer's freedom and responsibility. There is freedom because the matter is not dictated one way or the other by God; and there is responsibility because the individual is expected to come to a personal decision based on solid reasons. His decision will be his own application of the general commands he brings to bear on the question. Thus it will be a decision within the moral will of God.

The Examined Life Is Worth Living

The verses that follow Romans 14:5 contain several reasons why each believer needs to come to his own convictions on debated issues. The first of these, suggested in verses 6–8, is that we are to lead a purposeful life. And that central purpose is to please and serve the Lord. This is emphasized by the repetition of the prepositional phrases (italicized) in verses 6 and 8:

> He who observes the day, observes it *for the Lord,* and he who eats, does so *for the Lord,* for he gives thanks *to God;* and he who eats not, *for the Lord* he does not eat, and gives thanks *to God*.... [F]or if we live, we live *for the Lord,* or if we die, we die *for the Lord;* therefore whether we live or die, we are the Lord's. (Romans 14:6, 8)

Whatever we do, our motive should be to serve the Lord, not ourselves. Becoming fully convinced is the process whereby the believer determines his best understanding and makes it his conviction.

Second, we should be fully convinced in our own mind because "each one of us will give an account of himself to God" for the way we exercise our freedom and responsibility (Romans 14:12). Since the reasons for our choices will be evaluated by the Righteous Judge, they better be sound!

A third value of personal convictions stems from the fact that enjoyment of our Christian freedom is one of our spiritual blessings we thank God for: "The faith which you have, have as your own conviction before God. Happy is he who does not condemn himself in what he approves" (Romans 14:22; cf. verse 6). It follows that we cannot enjoy our freedom if we are not sure of it. In fact, if I am unsettled in my mind I can actually sin against my conscience: "But he who doubts is condemned if he eats, because his eating is not from faith; and whatever is not from faith is sin" (Romans 14:23).

Finally, being fully convinced permits us to be responsible for convictions that are truly our own—it keeps us from being held hostage to someone else's views on an issue (1 Corinthians 10:29–30; Colossians 2:16–23).

Convince Thyself

Being convinced that one should be convinced in his own mind about debatable issues, the thoughtful reader of Paul's explanation raises a question: How do we develop our own convictions?[8]

Most of the answer to that question has already been covered elsewhere in this book. (See the discussion on finding wisdom in chapter 10, "Wisdom for Decision Making," and the suggestions for following "wisdom signs" in chapter 17, "A New Way of Seeing.") From Romans and 1 Corinthians, Paul stresses two additional points. First, we must adopt the proper life focus: "we live *for the Lord*" (Romans 14:8). Thinking of our various activities as acts of worship will clarify many issues immediately.

Second, it is important to ask the right questions. Several good ones are suggested by Paul's discussion in 1 Corinthians 10:23–11:1:

- Is there anything wrong with this activity? Is it lawful? (10:23)
- Is it profitable? (10:23)
- Is it edifying? (10:23)
- Is it self-serving at someone else's expense? (10:33; Romans 15:1–2)
- Is this something I can thank God for? (10:30; Romans 14:6)
- Is this something that will glorify God? (10:31)
- Is this worth imitating? (11:1)
- Is this following the example of Christ? (11:1; Romans 15:7–8)

DECISION MAKING WHEN CHRISTIANS DIFFER

Romans 14:1–15:13

1. Learn to distinguish between matters of command and matters of freedom (14:14, 20).
2. **On debatable issues, cultivate your own convictions (14:5).**

ACCEPTANCE AND ACCOUNTABILITY

PRINCIPLE 3: *Allow Your Brother the Freedom to Determine His Own Convictions, Even When They Differ From Yours.*
This principle is implicit in the statement: "Each person must be fully convinced in his own mind" (Romans 14:5), but it is developed in detail through the first twelve verses of Romans 14. In this segment, Paul actually argues for two related principles that, taken together, provide the basis for the summary statement recorded above.

The first of these is the *principle of acceptance:* Though we differ in our opinions, we are to manifest unity in our relationships. "*Now accept* the one who is weak in faith" (Romans 14:1; cf. 15:7). "The one who eats is not to *regard with contempt* the one who does not eat, and the one who does not eat is not to *judge* the one who eats, for God has accepted him" (Romans 14:3; cf. 14:10).

The key verb is "accept." The word literally denotes "to take to oneself or welcome" (cf. Philemon 17). As far as Paul was concerned, different opinions about nonessentials should not be permitted to adversely affect fellowship between believers.

The positive concept of acceptance is clarified by two negative verbs that describe attitudes we are not to have, "regard with contempt" and "judge." To "regard with contempt" is to despise or "look down on" (NIV). It is the attitude of spiritual superiority that characterized the self-righteous Pharisee toward the humble publican in Jesus' parable (Luke 18:9–14). The corresponding negative, "judge," has the sense of "criticize, find fault with, condemn."[9] This harmonizes with the admonition of Jesus, "Do not judge so that you will not be judged" (Matthew 7:1–5; cf. Romans 2:1–3; James 4:11–12).

The tendency of the less strict (who enjoy greater freedom) is to regard the others with contempt, labeling them "legalistic." The more strict (who have more inhibitions) are more vulnerable to the temptation to be judgmental, regarding the strong as "loose" or "unprincipled." Either reaction is evidence of an attitude of spiritual superiority or pride. Both negatives are to be discarded for the positive: "Therefore, accept one another, just as Christ also accepted us to the glory of God" (Romans 15:7).

Let the Judge Judge

To support the concept of acceptance, Paul adds the principle of accountability. All believers are ultimately accountable to God; therefore, we should resist the temptation to judge others and concentrate on making sure our own convictions are sound. Beginning with Romans 14:4, Paul demonstrated the inappropriateness of one believer judging another for his convictions in debatable matters. As a fellow servant, the believer lacks the authority to pass judgment. Further, to criticize another's actions is to focus on the wrong thing. For in matters of debate, motivation is more important than the act itself (14:6).[10]

Instead of worrying about the differing views of a brother, the mature believer accepts him and lets God deal with his opinions. That is God's business. He has assumed responsibility for that brother. He is at work in that brother's life (14:4). And He isn't finished yet. God's evaluation of a man's life comes at the end of the construction project, while fellow Christians tend to critique it at various points along the way. Since these things are true, says Paul, let the Judge do the judging. Unlike you, He knows what He's doing. Again, John Stott provides a concise summary, this time of the second and third principles:

> No Christian can escape the responsibility of trying to think biblically and to decide conscientiously about such ethical questions as these. He then has liberty to refrain or to practice at his discretion. But he has no liberty either to impose his traditions on others or to stand in judgment on others if they disagree with him. We need to say to ourselves again and again, as Christ taught the Pharisees, that "Scripture is obligatory, but tradition optional."[11]

OF MEAT AND MOVIES

The issue of difference between believers in one generation may be eating meat and in another attending movies. But in either case it takes wisdom, maturity, and grace to be convinced and consistent with one's convictions and yet fully loving and accepting of the brother who disagrees. The following narrative helps to illustrate this balance.

"Dad, could I go to the theater tonight to see the Disney movie they're showing? I hear it's really good."

Ryan Timm looked up from the sports page he had been reading. His thirteen-year-old son, Josh, was sitting on the sofa opposite him.

"Don't you already know the answer to that question?" Ryan said, returning to his article.

"Well, I thought maybe you'd change your mind this time."

Ryan put the paper down in his lap and looked at Josh. "Why did you think that, son?"

"Because Mr. Tucker is taking Ty and Michelle to see it. I thought maybe you'd let me go if I went with them."

"Josh, your mother and I have given this matter careful thought and we've decided that our family won't go to movies. We've explained the reasons to you, and those reasons haven't changed."

"But it's not fair!" Josh fought back the tears.

"You don't think it's fair that Ty and Michelle get to go to movies when you're not allowed to?" his father asked.

"That's right." Josh wiped one eye with the back of his hand.

Ryan placed the newspaper on the floor and leaned forward in his chair. "Son, I can see how it wouldn't seem fair to you, right now. So why don't we talk about it awhile? I think you're old enough to understand why we do what we do."

Josh nodded. "Okay. Go ahead."

"The first thing I want you to understand, Josh, is that when we don't permit you to do something, it's not because we don't want you to have fun."

"I know that."

"What we're trying to do is to be faithful to what God has instructed us in His Word." Ryan picked up a Bible from the table next to his chair and opened it. "Do you remember what Romans 12:2 says?"

Again Josh nodded, then quoted: "And do not be conformed to this world, but be transformed by the renewing of your mind."

"That's right," Ryan said. "We're trying to avoid conformity to the world—its values, its goals, its way of thinking, its means of success, and definitions of happiness—and we want our minds to be transformed so that we learn to see life the way God does. We believe that the movies being made today work against those goals, even the films that are rated G or PG. They may not show sensuous or excessively violent behavior, but they still portray many of the world's values that Christians must not adopt."

"But just because they show those things, that doesn't mean that I'll go out and do them," Josh said.

"That's true, son. But the problem is that most of the time we're unaware of the way we've been influenced. Instead of our minds being renewed as we watch movies, they're actually being subtly shaped and molded to conform to the world's perspective. We get brainwashed without even realizing it. Now we realize that we can't block out all of the world's influences on our minds, but we can guard against overexposure. We just don't think it's right to invest time and money in something that can hurt us like that."

"Then how come Mr. Tucker takes his kids to see some movies?"

"He obviously doesn't see things the same way I do."

"But he reads the same Bible and he teaches Sunday school. He's even on the church board, just like you. How do you know that you're right and he's wrong?" Josh said.

"That's not what I said. I said that he doesn't see some things the same way I do."

Josh looked puzzled. "But doesn't that mean that one of you is right and the other one's wrong?"

"Not necessarily." Ryan grinned at his befuddled son. "Josh, very few people fully understand what I'm about to explain to you. If you can grasp it now, as you begin your teenage years, your life will be much more enjoyable and hassle free in the years ahead."

Josh's attention was absolute.

"First, let me ask you a question. Where in the Bible does it say anything about going to movies?"

"In Romans 12:2," Josh said. "We just talked about that."

"I know, but did that verse say anything specifically about *movies?*"

"Well...no, not specifically."

"Do you know of any other verses that talk about movies?"

"No, of course not. Movies hadn't been invented when the Bible was written."

"Right," Ryan said. "So we don't have a verse that says 'Thou shalt not go to movies.' Neither do we have one that says, 'Thou shalt go to movies,' or even one that says, 'It's okay to go to G-rated movies, but no others.' Do you see what I'm getting at?"

"I think so. The Bible doesn't say anything about movies one way or the other."

"Right. You see, while the Bible gives a number of specific commands about many areas of life, it doesn't try to give us rules about every single thing a person might think or do. Instead, God has given us more general principles to apply to specific situations."

"Like Romans 12:2."

"That's right. And each believer is responsible before God to determine how those principles ought to be applied."

"Okay, I understand that," Josh said. "But what happens if two Christians come to different conclusions? Who decides which one's right and which one's wrong?"

"Not 'if,' Josh, 'when.' One of the things I think you're beginning to see is that there are actually many subjects Christians disagree on. Sometimes those disagreements are due to immaturity on the part of one or more of the people involved. But just as often, equally mature Christians come to differing conclusions."

"Like you and Mr. Tucker?"

Ryan laughed. "Well, I don't know how mature we are, but I would say that we're about the same spiritual age. Fortunately, the writers of the Bible knew there'd be disagreements among believers in areas where the Bible doesn't specifically command. In those days, the issue wasn't movies—instead, people debated whether it was all right to eat meat."

"What could be wrong with eating meat?" Josh asked.

"Sometimes it was because the meat had been previously offered in pagan worship to idols. Other times, I think it had to do more with the Old Testament food regulations. But in any case some believers definitely thought it was wrong. In Romans 14, Paul talked about these things. Let me read it aloud and as you listen, imagine that he's talking about movies.

> "Now accept the one who is weak in faith, but not for the purpose of passing judgment on his opinions. One person has faith that he may eat all things, but he who is weak eats vegetables only. The one who eats is not to regard with contempt the one who does not eat, and the one who does not eat is not to judge the one who eats, for God has accepted him. Who are you to judge the servant of another? To his own master he stands or

> falls; and he will stand, for the Lord is able to make him stand. One person regards one day above another, another regards every day alike. Each person must be fully convinced in his own mind....
>
> "But you, why do you judge your brother? Or you again, why do you regard your brother with contempt? For we will all stand before the judgment seat of God. For it is written, "AS I LIVE, SAYS THE LORD, EVERY KNEE SHALL BOW TO ME, AND EVERY TONGUE SHALL GIVE PRAISE TO GOD." So then each one of us shall give an account of himself to God."

Ryan looked up at Josh. "Now what did Paul say we should do about these kinds of disagreements?"

"One thing was that we shouldn't criticize or judge that other person," Josh said.

"And why not?"

"Because that's the Lord's business. Each of us has to answer for our own decisions before God."

"That's right," Ryan said. "In our case, even though Mr. Tucker thinks it's all right to take his children to some movies, and I don't think it's all right for me to do the same, he's not to look down on me for my standards, and I'm not to criticize him for his differing opinion. He isn't accountable to me—he's accountable to the Lord. And I, too, am accountable to the Lord."

Josh was silent for a few moments as he digested what his father was saying. Then he asked, "Is that why you wouldn't say that Mr. Tucker is wrong, even though you're so sure you're right?"

"That's one reason, son. Another reason is that Mr. Tucker might be right in his opinion."

Question marks appeared all over Josh's face. "How could that be?"

"In verse 5 of Romans 14, Paul said, 'Each person must be fully convinced in his own mind.' That means that we're to weigh things very carefully and have good reasons for our opinions. If I concluded that it would be wrong for me to take my family to a movie, but I went ahead and did it anyway, I would be sinning against my conscience. That's why it says in the last verse of Romans 14, 'But he who doubts is condemned if he eats, because his eating is not from faith; and whatever is not from faith is sin.' But if Mr. Tucker decided before God that it was all right for him to attend certain movies, he could do so without offending his conscience. Furthermore, he shouldn't feel guilty because he knows I've come to a different conclusion—not if he's fully convinced in his own mind."

"Do you mean," Josh said, "that the very same thing could be wrong for you, but all right for Mr. Tucker?"

"That's exactly what I believe Paul is saying in Romans 14."

"Wow! I never knew that."

Ryan smiled at his son. "Can you handle one more man-sized idea?"

"I don't know, but I'll try."

"All right, here it is: Not only might the same activity be wrong for one person and all right for another, but the same activity might be wrong for a person at one time in his life, but proper at a later time."

"You'd better give me an example of that one, Dad."

"Okay. Do you remember the old black buggy that we ride in when we visit Grandma and Grandpa back on the farm?"

"Yeah. Last summer, Grandpa let me hold the reins and guide the horse."

"Well, when I was your age we attended a church where the people believed that it was wrong to drive or ride in an automobile."

"Really?"

"That's right. So all the years I was growing up, I felt that cars were sinful. When I was a couple of years older than you are, though, a friend of mine, who was a Christian but didn't belong to my church, bought his very own car. He knew how we believed, but he still talked me into going for a ride with him—he was so proud of that car. It was really fun. But afterwards, I felt very guilty. I had sinned against my conscience. Later, I told my father and he disciplined me for my disobedience. I also confessed my sin to the Lord and the feeling of guilt went away.

"As I grew up and began to study the Bible more for myself, I read Romans 14 and similar passages. I realized that the Bible doesn't say anything about cars one way or the other. I gradually came to see that in many ways, cars are much more suitable for transportation than horse-drawn buggies. I also realized that it wasn't sinful to ride in automobiles."

"What about Grandma and Grandpa?" Josh asked. "They have a car now, don't they?"

"Yes, they do. It took them longer to accept their freedom in this area because the belief was so deeply ingrained in them. There are still some Christians today who feel very strongly that it's wrong to ride in a car. The point I'm making, Josh, is that because of my convictions when I was growing up, at that time it was wrong for me to ride in a car. But later, as I realized that I was free to choose whether or not to ride in cars, I became fully convinced in my own mind that it was all right. From that time on, I could drive a car without sinning."

"I think I understand what you're saying." Josh thought for a moment, then asked, "About this movie business, Dad—have you ever discussed it with Mr. Tucker?"

"Well, we haven't talked about it personally, but we did discuss it once in Sunday school. Several people in the class shared their point of view. I did, and so did Mr. Tucker. Why do you ask?"

Josh was hesitant, but continued. "I was wondering if you could explain to me why he thinks it's all right to attend some movies."

"Well, I don't recall everything he said. I know he thinks that some of the films he's taken his family to see provided decent family entertainment. It's something he feels his family can enjoy together. If he can't take his kids, he doesn't allow them to go alone."

"But what about what you were saying earlier, you know, about not being conformed to the world?"

"Mr. Tucker doesn't believe that the movies he goes to are all that harmful. I think it's fair to say that in his opinion, the values of movie attendance outweigh the dangers. He's very selective, as I've said, about which movies he attends. He also makes a point to discuss the movies with his children afterwards. That way, if he detects that his children might be picking up something they shouldn't, he can correct it and use the situation as an opportunity for instruction."

"That sounds good to me, Dad," Josh said. "What's wrong with Mr. Tucker's ideas? Couldn't you do the same thing with us?"

"I don't think there's anything *wrong* with Mr. Tucker's viewpoint in the sense that it's sinful. I believe he's fully persuaded in his own mind, and that's good enough for me. But I disagree that the values of *any* movie shown in the theater outweigh the dangers, even if they're discussed afterwards. And I think our family can learn the same lessons in other ways without deliberately exposing ourselves to that worldly influence."

The disappointment on Josh's face needed no further elaboration.

"Are you beginning to think you were born into the wrong family, Josh?" Ryan asked.

Josh looked up as though he had been caught with his hand in the cookie jar. "Oh, no! I didn't say that!"

"I know you didn't *say* it, son…" his father said with a smile.

"Wait a minute." Josh sat up straight, his expression reflecting the return of hope. "Didn't you say that in matters where the Bible is silent, *each person* is responsible to make the decision for himself?"

"I was wondering when we were going to get around to this."

Josh looked puzzled momentarily, but continued. "I've been thinking a lot about this whole thing, and I think that I agree with Mr. Tucker."

"You think?"

"Uh, no…I'm, uh, fully convinced in my own mind."

"Sorry, Josh. It was a nice try, but it won't work."

"Why not?"

"Because of another principle of Scripture that I think you'll remember as soon as I tell you the reference."

"Which is?"

"Ephesians 6:1."

Furrows appeared on Josh's forehead as he mentally sorted out his memory verses. Then his face fell.

"What does that verse say, son?"

Reluctantly, Josh quoted, "'Children, obey your parents in the Lord, for this is right.'"

"That's right. Do you recall the fourth verse of that same chapter?"

Josh thought briefly, then recited, "'Fathers, do not provoke your children to anger, but bring them up in the discipline and instruction of the Lord.'"

Ryan asked, "Do you feel that I'm provoking you to anger?"

"Not exactly."

"Good. That shows you're learning how to accept disappointment in a more mature way."

"Yeah, I guess so," Josh murmured.

Ryan waited a moment before continuing. "Josh, I want you to know that I take that verse very seriously. For that matter, so does Mr. Tucker. We believe that God has given us our children as a kind of trust. God has given us the responsibility to bring you kids up in the discipline and instruction of the Lord. We may go at it a little differently, but that's what we're both trying to do to the best of our ability. When I refuse permission for you to do something, it's because I genuinely believe that activity will not be good for you. I do that because I really care about you."

"I know that, Dad," said Josh, beginning to recover.

"My job is to help you grow to manhood. During the next few years, as you earn new privileges by the way you handle increased responsibilities, your mother and I will turn more and more of these decisions over to you. And when you move out on your own, you'll be fully responsible to make all of your own decisions. That's God's design for parents and children. As long as we care for you and support you, you must submit to our authority. And even though that's hard at times, like right now, it will help you in your adult life when you have to submit to the authority of a foreman or a sergeant or a dean or a company president. Your family life is like a laboratory where you learn how to function in the real world. That's how God designed it."

Josh nodded.

"Okay, just one more thing and this sermon is over. It has to do with one more of those principles we've been talking about. In several places in the New Testament, we're told to give thanks in everything. Cultivation of a thankful spirit, even in the face of personal disappointment, is one of the most important goals a man can have. A person can be submissive in his behavior without being submissive in his heart. Do you know what I mean?"

"Sure, Dad. I see it at school all the time."

"God isn't interested in our external behavior alone. He wants us to have submissive attitudes as well. Learning to be thankful in all circumstances and situations will really help to develop the kind of submission that's pleasing to the Lord. It doesn't come easily, but the Lord will help you if you ask Him."

Josh nodded.

"End of sermon."

"Amen!" Josh declared in hallowed tones. "We are dismissed."

Ryan laughed as Josh got up and headed toward the kitchen.

"I wonder what's for supper."

"Say, Josh," Ryan called.

Josh turned back toward his father.

"I was wondering if you'd be free to go to the high school basketball game with me after supper. They're at home tonight against Central."

Josh frowned in mock seriousness. "Well, I was planning to go see this movie, but things didn't work out. Still, I don't know. Are you sure it's, you know, all right?"

"Fully convinced in my own mind, son. Fully convinced."

Ryan illustrates that it is possible to be convinced and consistent with one's convictions and yet fully loving and accepting of the brother who disagrees. Ryan was neither hurt nor indignant about his fellow deacon attending movies. But what happens when a believer who sees nothing wrong with movies hurts his brother or causes him to get mad and upset by his attendance at movies? That's the important topic of the next chapter.

DECISION MAKING WHEN CHRISTIANS DIFFER

ROMANS 14:1–15:13

1. Learn to distinguish between matters of command and matters of freedom (14:14, 20).
2. On debatable issues, cultivate your own convictions (14:5).
3. **Allow your brother the freedom to determine his own convictions, even when they differ from yours (14:1–12).**

---

1. There must, of course, be unity of thought about the fundamentals of the faith. The apostle Paul was vigorous in his opposition to those who taught or practiced doctrine that compromised either truth or holiness, especially where it touched the gospel message of justification by grace through faith (cf. Galatians 1:6–9; 2:1–5, 11–16).
2. F. F. Bruce, *The Epistle of Paul to the Romans: An Introduction and Commentary, Tyndale New Testament Commentaries* (Grand Rapids, MI: Wm. B. Eerdmans Publishing Co., 1963), 247.
3. Ibid., 249.
4. Paul refers to the observance of certain "holy days" in Romans 14:5 and the drinking of wine in Romans 14:21 as other current issues of debate in the first-century Church.
5. Admonition, reproof, and church discipline are the divinely ordered steps that must be taken in the cases of those who depart from the truth by practice or teaching. These responses to rebellion within the church are further discussed in chapter 26.

6. "In Christian circles, we see conviction in many areas, such as doctrine, the prohibition of certain activities, and methods of operating a church. In most cases we call these 'biblical' convictions, but are they?.... We must...remember one key fact—*we are twice removed from the Scriptures* when we make applications to our lives from biblical principles. To discern these principles we must make certain assumptions or generalizations about what the Bible says. This removes us one step. Then we make specific application of the principles, the second step. Frequently at this point we become dogmatic and even insist that this particular application is the right way to function, for everyone. It may be, but we must remember that we have thus moved from direct Bible teaching to principle to application." Jerry White, *Honesty, Morality and Conscience* (Colorado Springs: NavPress, 1979), 222–24.
7. John R.W. Stott, *Christ the Controversialist* (Downers Grove, IL: InterVarsity Press, 1970), 86.
8. See also chapter 12, "How to Develop Biblical Convictions," in White, *Honesty, Morality and Conscience.*
9. William F. Arndt and F. Wilbur Gingrich, trans. *A Greek-English Lexicon of the New Testament and Other Early Christian Literature,* 2nd ed. (Chicago: The University of Chicago Press, 1952), s.v. κρίνω.
10. "The important thing is that one should 'be fully convinced in his own mind' as to the rightfulness of his observance. More important still is the certitude of the individual that his motivation is his desire to honor the Lord in what he is doing." Frank E. Gaebelein, gen. ed., *The Expositor's Bible Commentary,* vol. 10: "Romans" by Everett F. Harrison (Grand Rapids, MI: Zondervan, 1976), 146.
11. Stott, *Christ the Controversialist,* 86.

chapter twenty-six

WEAKER BROTHERS, PHARISEES, AND SERVANTS

Martin Luther began his treatise, "On the Freedom of a Christian Man," with two striking statements. "A Christian man is a most free lord of all, subject to none. A Christian man is a most dutiful servant of all, subject to all."[1]

We could hardly expect to find a more concise summary of the apostle's thought in Romans 14:1 through 15:13. Luther's first sentence captures the essence of the believer's freedom in Christ, the relational ramifications of which are developed in Romans 14:1–12. The chart at the end of the previous chapter (p. 393) summarizes the contents of those verses in Romans 14 and the parallel passage in 1 Corinthians 8–10.

Luther's second observation, that the "free" Christian is by vocation a "dutiful servant," captures the essence of Romans 14:13–15:13. These verses form the central passage for this chapter. Ideally, if everyone followed the first three principles of Romans 14, there would be harmony. But the characters in the drama of real life tend to deviate from the script.

CARING FOR WEAKER BROTHERS

Any person who fails to adopt God's perspective on different opinions in the area of freedom invariably reacts in one of two ways. Either he tries to persuade others to adopt his viewpoint, or he shifts his position to conform to those who differ—in violation of his own judgment.

Both errors are illustrated in Scripture. The Pharisees provide the classic example of those who pressure others to conform to their traditions. But Paul was apparently more concerned for the welfare of those who are too easily influenced by the opinions of others. He called them "weaker brothers," and his message to the church was "Fragile: Handle with Care."

> Therefore let us not judge one another anymore, but rather determine this—not to put an obstacle or a stumbling block in a brother's way. I know and am convinced in the Lord Jesus that nothing is unclean in itself; but to him who thinks anything to be unclean, to him it is unclean. For if because of food your brother is hurt, you are no longer walking according to love. Do not destroy with your food him for whom Christ died. Therefore do not let what is for you a good thing be spoken of as evil; for the kingdom of God is not eating and drinking, but righteousness and peace and joy in the Holy Spirit. For he who in this way serves Christ is acceptable to God and approved by men. So then we pursue the things which make for peace and the building up of one another. Do not tear down the work of God for the sake of food. All things indeed are clean, but they are evil for the man who eats and gives offense. It is good not to eat meat or to drink wine, or to do anything by which your brother stumbles. The faith which you have, have as your own conviction before God. Happy is he who does not condemn himself in what he approves. But he who doubts is condemned if he eats, because his eating is not from faith; and whatever is not from faith is sin.
>
> Now we who are strong ought to bear the weaknesses of those without strength and not just please ourselves. Each of us is to please his neighbor for his good, to his edification. (Romans 14:13–15:2)

PRINCIPLE 4: *Let Your Liberty Be Limited, When Necessary, by Love.* Previously, in a letter to the church of Galatia, Paul had written, "For you were called to freedom, brethren; only do not turn your freedom into an opportunity for the flesh, but through love serve one another" (Galatians 5:13). Sometimes words like "love" and "serve" suffer from ambiguity, but in Romans 14, Paul moves us out of the realm of the theoretical in a hurry. For it is one thing to graciously permit another believer to hold a different viewpoint; it is quite another to actually restrict my freedom because of his differing viewpoint. On the face of it, such a requirement is unfair. But that is the nature of the love that is to characterize the Christian's walk (Romans 14:1). *For agape* love is other centered, and it is sacrificial.

Let us not, however, jump to the rash conclusion that this principle negates Christian freedom completely. It does not. The words "when necessary" are an integral part of the fourth principle. They indicate that the limitation of my freedom is not always required. But they also imply that something is more valuable than my enjoyment of personal liberty. The key to obeying God's will in this regard lies in understanding what that something is.

And so we must begin with some definitions. You can't follow the action unless you know the players. Specifically, we need to carefully identify the *weaker brother (or sister),*[2] the *stronger brother (or sister),* and what constitutes a *stumbling block.*

Those Without Strength

The weaker brother (or sister) is recognized by his weakness in four areas of his life. First, he is weak in *faith* (Romans 14:1, 23). This is not saving faith, but Paul means that "this man's faith is not strong enough to enable him to perceive the full liberty he has in Christ."[3] "'Faith' in this sense is a firm and intelligent conviction before God that one is doing what is right, the antithesis of feeling self-condemned in what one permits oneself to do."[4] The best synonym is "conviction."

One reason he is weak in conviction is that he lacks biblical *knowledge.* "However not all men have this knowledge" (1 Corinthians 8:7). Those to whom Paul refers were ignorant in several respects. They did not know that an idol was a nonentity (1 Corinthians 8:4), so they didn't know that food offered to a "nothing" could not be spiritually contaminated. In short, their faith was weak because it was misinformed.

The weaker brother is also weak in *conscience.* "Their conscience being weak is defiled" (1 Corinthians 8:7; see 8:10, 12). Essentially, that means that his conscience is *overly sensitive,* condemning him for things that Scripture declares are permissible.

Finally, this brother is weak in his *will* because he can be influenced to act contrary to his conscience. "For if someone sees you, who have knowledge, dining in an idol's temple, will not his conscience, if he is weak, be strengthened to eat things sacrificed to idols?" (1 Corinthians 8:10).

Specifically, because he is not fully convinced in his own mind, and because of his respect for the judgment of a more mature Christian, the weaker brother might follow his stronger brother's example and violate his own conscience in the process. He is vulnerable to that kind of sin because his will is weak.

With these facts in view, we can approach our definition of a weaker brother by recognizing, first of all, what he is *not.* He is not just any new or immature believer. He is not any Christian who disagrees with me on some issue. Neither is he simply a brother who disagrees with me and gets upset because he thinks I am wrong. Such people may have weaknesses, but they do not fit Paul's qualifications for "weaker brothers."

A weaker brother (or sister) is a Christian who, because of the weakness of his faith, knowledge, conscience, and will, can be influenced to sin against his conscience by the example of a differing stronger brother.

Stronger Brothers Exercise

Not surprisingly, the stronger brother (or sister) is strong in precisely the same areas where the weaker brother is weak: faith (Romans 14:22), knowledge (1 Corinthians 8:7, 10), conscience (Romans 14:22), and will (1 Corinthians 10:29–30).

Additionally, those who are strong are always pictured as influencing the weak. It is never the other way around. As a result, the responsibility for guarding the integrity of the relationship is given to the strong (Romans 15:1). In these passages, it is also assumed that the strong are correct in their opinion (Romans 14:14; 1 Corinthians 8:4–7). However, the stronger brother is not necessarily strong in love (1 Corinthians 8:1), though he ought to be (Romans 15:1–2).

The stronger brother (or sister) is a Christian who, because of his understanding of Christian freedom and the strength of his conviction, exercises his liberty in good conscience without being improperly influenced by the differing opinions of others.

Thou Shalt Not Kick Thy Brother's Crutch

The third key term requiring careful definition is *stumbling block.* The noun is prominent in Romans 14:13, 20, and 1 Corinthians 8:9. The verb form is found in Romans 14:21 and 1 Corinthians 8:13. Originally, the noun denoted the piece of wood that kept open a trap for animals.[5] Later, it came to stand for the snare itself,[6] and still later, it was used of anything that caused a person to stumble (cf. Leviticus 19:14). In the New Testament, *stumbling block* is used only as a figurative expression.[7] It refers to the tripping up of a person in some moral sense. That is, the individual stumbles into sin or unbelief.[8]

It is significant that *stumbling block* is employed in two different senses throughout the New Testament. When the verb is in the *active* voice, it means "to cause to fall or stumble." For example, Jesus had severe words for anyone who caused a little child who believed in Him to stumble or fall into sin (Matthew 18:6).[9] In such instances, the fault is charged to the one who puts the stumbling block in the way of another.

But when the verb is in the *passive* voice, it signifies "to stumble over, to be offended." In such cases, the blame is placed on the one who stumbles. For instance, when Jesus returned to His hometown of Nazareth, the people "took offense at Him" (Matthew 13:57). Literally, "they stumbled over Him." He was the stumbling block, but they were at fault. For they did not believe in Him (Matthew 13:58).[10]

Give and Take

Another way to explain this important distinction is to say that the active voice means "to *give* offense," while the passive denotes "to *take* offense."[11] A proverbial saying captures this difference. "No offense was given, but offense was taken."

This distinction holds up when the noun form is used. One of the most familiar instances of a blameworthy stumbling block is found in

Matthew's account of an exchange between Simon Peter and Jesus. "'God forbid it, Lord! This shall never happen to You.' But He turned and said to Peter, 'Get behind Me, Satan! You are a *stumbling block* to Me'" (Matthew 16:22–23).[12]

On the other hand, Jesus Christ is repeatedly described as a "ROCK OF OFFENSE" over which people stumble in unbelief (Romans 9:33; 1 Peter 2:8).[13]

In Romans 14 and 1 Corinthians 8, Paul was concerned only with those who *give* offense.[14] (The opposite thrust of taking offense will be considered again later.) In strong terms, he warned stronger brothers not to cause weaker brothers to stumble.

> And so, by sinning against the brethren and wounding their conscience when it is weak, you sin against Christ. Therefore, if food causes my brother to stumble, I will never eat meat again, so that I will not cause my brother to stumble. (1 Corinthians 8:12–13)

So, a stumbling block is an action taken by a stronger brother (or sister) that, though it would ordinarily qualify as a permissible act of freedom, influences a weaker brother (or sister) to sin against his conscience. The responsibility for the sin is charged to the stronger brother because of his insensitivity to the weaker brother's vulnerability.

A Misguided Missile

This concept is illustrated by something that happened to me when I was a boy. One evening, I was already late for supper when I started home. To make up for lost time, I planned to take a shortcut across an open field. When I arrived, I learned to my dismay that the field was no longer "open." It was occupied by several people with bows and arrows.

The route I had anticipated taking cut directly across the trajectory of the arrows. Yet to detour around the archers would cost precious minutes. I made a decision to stick to my original flight plan. When I discerned what I thought was a lull in the missile traffic, I took off. Next thing, I heard a whish just behind my head and then the gasp of the spectators. What I did, in my juvenile immaturity, was stupid. But the guy who let that arrow fly almost caused me to stumble. Shooting an arrow is perfectly legitimate when done within legal restrictions. So a man may take target practice at an archery range with complete freedom. He is not compelled to do so; neither is he prohibited from practicing.

However, if a small boy in his ignorance wanders onto the archery range, the situation changes. The archer is no longer free to release the arrow, even if he has followed all the rules. It is not his fault that the child has crossed the line of fire. Still, he is required to refrain from shooting until the boy is out of danger. There is nothing wrong with shooting an arrow in itself. But if such an act resulted in injury or death to a "weaker" child, the archer would be held accountable. Even on an archery range, the man with the bow must look before he shoots. The safety of others is of greater importance than the freedom to shoot an arrow.

Paul's logic follows similar lines of thought. Earlier I said that something is more important than enjoyment of my Christian freedom. Now we can see what that something is—the spiritual well-being of a weaker brother.

SOME ESSENTIAL DEFINITIONS

Weaker brother: a Christian who, because of the weakness of his faith, knowledge, conscience, and will, can be influenced to sin against his conscience by the example of a differing stronger brother.

Stronger brother: a Christian who, because of his understanding of Christian freedom and the strength of his conviction, exercises his liberty in good conscience without being improperly influenced by the differing opinions of others.

Stumbling block: an action taken by a stronger brother that, though it would ordinarily qualify as a permissible act of freedom, influences a weaker brother to sin against his conscience.

A Pound of Prevention

Having defined our key terms, we can now turn our attention to the stronger brother's responsibility to let his liberty be limited by love. An analysis of Romans 14:13–15:2 reveals an even balance between negatives and positives. Paul begins this segment with a negative exhortation, and so will we.

HOW TO CARE FOR WEAKER BROTHERS
ROMANS 14:13–15:2

Do Not...

1. Put a **stumbling block** in his way (14:13)
2. **Destroy** with food (14:15)
3. Let your good thing become **evil** (14:16)
4. **Tear down** God's work (14:20)
5. **Give offense** (14:20)
6. Cause a brother to **stumble** (14:21)
7. Just **please yourself** (15:1)

By now, we are accustomed to the meaning of "stumbling block" and "give offense." But the severity of the other terms is startling—"destroy," "evil," "tear down." That impression is further reinforced in 1 Corinthians 8: "ruined" a brother for whom Christ died (verse 11); "sinning" against the brethren (12); "sin against Christ" (12). I conclude that Paul considered this stumbling block business to be pretty serious, but why?

The answer lies in the nature of the weaker brother's vulnerability. In the first place, he is liable to *sin against his conscience* (1 Corinthians 8:10). To some, that might not sound as serious as the violation of God's law. But God makes no such distinction! (Romans 14:23).

Our Moral Guidance System

The conscience is that part of a man's soul that judges right from wrong. It tells him when he is about to veer off his moral course with some improper thought or action. When he ignores that warning and does what he senses to be wrong, the conscience hauls him into court and condemns him for his transgression. That transaction is experienced as guilt.

At any given point, the standard by which the conscience judges is absolute. It may not be precisely correct in comparison to God's perfect holiness. But the conscience declares guilt or acquittal on the basis of what it construes to be right and wrong at that moment, and does so unequivocally.[15]

Understanding these things can help us appreciate the seriousness of sinning against the conscience. For even if the standard by which the conscience is judging is not as perfect as God's moral law, the individual reacts *as though it is.* Therefore, to disregard the warnings of the conscience is to choose self over God. And that constitutes rebellion—the sin of going our own way (Isaiah 53:6).

The Danger of Moral Drift

That's bad enough. But there is a second potential threat to the spiritual life of a weaker brother. The sin against the conscience can lead just as easily to *sin against God's commands.* Author Jerry White cites an infamous case in point:

> Former presidential aide Jeb Stuart Magruder, commenting on the Watergate scandal said, "We had conned ourselves into thinking we weren't doing anything really wrong, and by the time we were doing things that were illegal, we had lost control. We had gone from poor ethical behavior into illegal activities without even realizing it."[16]

This tendency of the flesh to edge us over the line from liberty into license is one of Paul's themes in 1 Corinthians 8–10. Here is the flow of his thought. In chapter 8, he responds to a question about the propriety of eating meat offered to idols. Though such food was free from any spiritual contamination, Paul declared, many believers were unaware of that fact (8:1–7). So rather than influencing these weaker brothers to sin against their conscience, those with knowledge should refrain from eating this meat (8:8–13).

Chapter 9 consists of Paul's personal testimony establishing his rights as an apostle (9:1–14). He then explains how he had chosen to forgo those rights for the spiritual benefit of others (9:15–27). In contrast is the example of Israel. Though they had been given tremendous spiritual privileges (10:1–4), they experienced a moral erosion that degenerated from discontent to disobedience to destruction (10:5–10). Their example warns us all that no one is immune to such failure (10:11–13).

The Seduction of Idolatry

The Corinthian believers were in danger of succumbing to Israel's besetting sin: idolatry (10:14). For while there was nothing wrong with eating meat previously offered to idols, there was something very wrong with partaking of the temple feasts in which that meat was offered as a sacrifice. In that culture, to participate in a meal dedicated to a deity was tantamount to worshipping that god. Furthermore, the Corinthian "gods" were, in fact, demons. So to share in a pagan feast was to have communion with the archenemies of Christ (10:14–22).

That is why, back in 1 Corinthians 8:10, Paul asserted that a stronger brother shouldn't be seen eating in a pagan temple (even when an official feast is not occurring). For a weaker brother imitating his example would sin against his conscience. Moreover, he might not possess the spiritual insight to discern any significant difference between obtaining meat at the temple and eating it at a pagan feast.[17]

To sum up: The reason the stronger brother must be careful about harming a weaker brother through his liberty is twofold: (1) the weaker brother might be influenced to sin against his conscience, which is to sin against God; and (2) such an act could be the first step in the downhill slide from liberty into license.

Bricks Are for Building, Not Throwing

So far, I have emphasized Paul's preventative instruction. He intentionally stressed restraint in the exercise of freedom to keep from hurting a brother. And yet, a mature Christian could conscientiously limit his freedom by love and still fall short of his obligations to his brother. The reason, plainly, is that love is not merely preventive in its expression—it is constructive. That positive side of the currency of love is readily seen in the rest of the verbs Paul employs.

HOW TO CARE FOR WEAKER BROTHERS
ROMANS 14:13–15:2

Do Not...	Do...
1. Put a **stumbling block** in his way (14:13)	1. Walk according to **love** (14:15)
2. **Destroy** with food (14:15)	2. **Serve** Christ (14:18)
3. Let your good thing become **evil** (14:16)	3. Pursue **peace** (14:19)
4. **Tear down** God's work (14:20)	4. **Build up** one another (14:19)
5. **Give offense** (14:20)	5. **Bear** the weaknesses of the weak (15:1)
6. Cause a brother to **stumble** (14:21)	6. **Edify** him (15:2)
7. Just **please yourself** (15:1)	7. **Please** your neighbor for his good (15:2)

Though not expressly stated, it is implied throughout that the weaker brother's lack of strength is temporary. He is, as they say, under construction, and God isn't finished with him yet (Romans 14:19–20). The responsibility of the stronger brother, then, is twofold: he is to refrain from tearing down what God is building, and he is to participate constructively in God's work in his brother's life.

> Paul is really not as concerned about "not being a stumbling block" as he is about "becoming a stepping stone." In so many words, then, Paul is saying that to not be a stumbling block is good, but to seek to be a stepping stone is even better. To be a stepping stone means that you are actively seeking ways to help others draw closer to Christ. Being a stepping stone implies that you will be walked on.[18]

The key to a proper attitude, it seems, is perspective. The stronger brother could technically comply with Paul's admonition to limit his freedom and go around muttering to himself about how much he had "given up for this weakling." But Paul wasn't looking for martyrs. He was recruiting investors to contribute to God's work. The initial investment, the incalculable cost of Christ's life, has already been made (Romans 14:15; 1 Corinthians 8:11). The stronger brother is invited to chip in his two cents' worth to assist in the completion of the project.

That Man in the Hard Hat Is Paul

For Paul, this matter of being a builder, a stepping-stone, an investor, was more than just a good preaching point. It was a matter of personal practice:

> For though I am free from all men, I have made myself a slave to all, so that I may win more. To the Jews I became as a Jew, so that I might win Jews; to those who are under the Law, as under the Law though not being myself under the Law, so that I might win those who are under the Law; to those who are without law, as without law, though not being without the law of God but under the law of Christ, so that I might win those who are without law. To the weak I became weak, that I might win the weak; I have become all things to all men, so that I may by all means save some. (1 Corinthians 9:19–22)

> Give no offense either to Jews or to Greeks or to the church of God; just as I also please all men in all things, not seeking my own profit but the profit of the many, so that they may be saved. (1 Corinthians 10:32–33)

Accordingly, Paul could write: "Be imitators of me, just as I also am of Christ" (1 Corinthians 11:1). F. F. Bruce offers this insightful summary:

> Paul enjoyed his Christian liberty to the full. Never was there a Christian more thoroughly emancipated from un-Christian inhibitions and taboos. So completely emancipated was he from spiritual bondage that he was not even in bondage to his emancipation. He conformed to the Jewish way of life when he was in Jewish society as cheerfully as he accommodated himself to Gentile ways when he was living with Gentiles. The interests

of the gospel and the highest well-being of men and women were paramount considerations with him, and to these he subordinated everything else.[19]

Careful Enjoyment

To be faithful to Paul's instruction about weaker brothers, I need to add a couple of qualifying, and very practical, footnotes. The first is recorded in 1 Corinthians 10:25–27:

> Eat anything that is sold in the meat market without asking questions for conscience' sake; FOR THE EARTH IS THE LORD'S, AND ALL IT CONTAINS. If one of the unbelievers invites you and you want to go, eat anything that is set before you without asking questions for conscience' sake.

Essentially, Paul's message was, "Enjoy your freedom." The stronger brother is not required to go around taking surveys to determine if a weaker brother is in the vicinity. If the coast appears to be clear, he may proceed to do anything endorsed by his conscience, without worrying about phantom "weaker brothers."[20] Of course, if a weaker brother identifies himself, or if it appears that one may be present, then immediate restraint is in order as the subsequent verses declare (1 Corinthians 10:28–30).

The second qualification provides the appropriate balance to the first one without canceling it out. It consists of two words: "with discretion." Enjoy your freedom with discretion. Put negatively, don't flaunt your freedom. This piece of wisdom lies behind the rhetorical question, "For if someone sees you, who have knowledge, dining in an idol's temple, will not his conscience, if he is weak, be strengthened to eat things sacrificed to idols?" (1 Corinthians 8:10).

One problem, as Paul saw it, with eating in an idol's temple was that one was more likely to be seen by a weaker brother. To exercise that freedom *with discretion* entailed eating the meat at home or at the private residence of a friend (1 Corinthians 10:25–27). In an environment where there is widespread disagreement over some matter of conscience, the mature Christian will exercise great care about where and how he enjoys his freedom.

Recognizing Weaker Brothers

As Jews and Gentiles were brought together in the first-century Church, one clear evidence of God's grace was the replacement of hostility and prejudice with a spirit of compassion. The Gentile believers showed sensitivity for their Jewish brothers by avoiding practices that were offensive to them because of their strict upbringing (Acts 15:28–29). And the Jewish saints came to appreciate the revulsion that many Gentile Christians had for certain aspects of their pagan background (1 Corinthians 8:7). In short, they learned where to watch out for weaker brothers.

In our day, there are at least four categories of Christians that merit our loving attention. First, a young adult leaving the parental nest will need some time to sort out his own convictions. Extra sensitivity is especially appropriate when the young adult comes from a strict, legalistic environment.

The second group is composed of relatively recent converts out of a background of licentiousness. Often, such babes in Christ immediately reject virtually every aspect of their former lifestyle, including some practices that may be perfectly within the believer's sphere of freedom. Such radical purging of the "old" is probably necessary for self-protection until these new converts can responsibly discern their own perimeters of freedom. It would be a mistake to push these spiritual infants too quickly toward liberty.

A third category includes believers from another country or culture. It is impossible to comprehend the impact our societal milieu has on our convictions until we spend some time in an alien culture. While we would not wish to be offensive when moving to or traveling in some other region, the weaker brother with whom we have contact is more likely to be the foreigner in our midst. His adjustment to our standards may take some time. And we will help if we are sensitive to those areas that he finds difficult.

The fourth group is made up of dependent children of convinced, differing brothers. For example, two fathers may hold differing positions on attending movies and still accept one another fully. But each man needs to remain alert to his influence on his brother's children. That is especially true when children are seeking external justification to rebel against parental standards and authority.

COPING WITH PHARISEES

There are actually three categories of differing Christians we must properly relate to. Consider Mr. Tucker, the man who decided he could take his children to carefully selected movies. How should he regard Mr. Timm, his fellow church board member who stays away from movies? They are both "stronger brothers" who are convinced of their differing viewpoints. Mr. Tucker should accept Mr. Timm and not look down on him for his convictions. But Mr. Tucker should also be careful about the influence he might have on Mr. Timm's son, Josh. Prior to the father-and-son chat, Josh was probably a "weaker brother," and Mr. Tucker would not want to do or say anything that might tempt the boy to sin against his conscience.

But then there's Mr. Stagg. He agrees with Mr. Timm that it is inappropriate to go to movies of any kind. But he takes it a step further. He maintains that it is wrong for any Christian to attend movies. He takes his personal conviction and universalizes it to apply to every one. So he takes offense at Mr. Tucker's liberty and condemns him for it. Of this kind of person C. S. Lewis wrote, "One of the marks of a certain type of bad man is that he cannot give up a thing himself without wanting every one else to give it up. That is not the Christian way."[21]

In terms of stumbling blocks, Mr. Stagg *takes offense* when no offense is *given*. The cause of the offense is his pride or unbelief, rather than improper behavior on the part of others. He becomes upset, but is not "destroyed." He is not a weaker brother for he is strong in his convictions and will not blindly follow a contrary example. Nor is he a stronger brother, for he is not strong in understanding. He has not fully grasped the nature and reality of Christian freedom and responsibility, especially as it affects relationships with other Christians.

Though not given the same systematic treatment in Romans and 1 Corinthians as the weaker brother, this third character appears frequently on the pages of the New Testament. I call a believer who fits this category simply *the pharisee* since the Pharisees were the classic example.

The pharisee is a professing believer with strong convictions who, because of his pride, takes offense at those who resist his pressure to conform to his point of view. By his nature, the pharisee is most in need of the correctives set forth in Romans 14:1–12. Of the three types of differing brothers, he is also the most difficult to get along with. Sometimes he will even claim he is a weaker brother as a way to force you to change. For this reason, Joe Aldrich calls the pharisee a "professional weaker brother."[22]

Since definitions are often clarified through comparison, I have prepared the following diagram to reveal significant differences and similarities.

CATEGORIES OF DIFFERING BROTHERS		
Weaker Brother	**Stronger Brother**	**Pharisee**
He differs from my opinion at times.	He differs from my opinion at times.	He differs from my opinion at times.
He is not fully convinced.	He is fully convinced.	He is fully convinced.
He is sincere.	He is convinced and humble.	He is convinced and proud.
He needs teaching and is open to it.	He has been taught, but is open to correction.	He has been taught, but is not open to correction.
He is surprised at my use of freedom.	He accepts me with my differing opinion.	He judges or rejects me for my differing conviction.
He does not think he can teach me.	He is willing to discuss why he differs.	He seeks to make me conform to his viewpoint.
He is influenced by my example.	He is not improperly influenced by my example.	He is not influenced by my example.
I can cause him to stumble into sin.	I cannot cause him to stumble into sin.	His pride will cause him to be offended.
He is caused to sin by my wrong use of freedom.	He is not caused to sin by my use of freedom.	He becomes upset by my use of freedom.
When I cause him to stumble it is an "offense given."	Since he does not stumble, there is no offense at all.	When he stumbles over my freedom, it is an "offense taken."

Jesus' Thorns in the Flesh

When it comes to responding properly to pharisees, we would do well to observe the Lord Jesus. For through His interaction with the Pharisees of His day, Christ provided a model that determined the outlook of His apostles.[23] A survey of Jesus' encounters with the Pharisees reveals a pattern of increasing hostility. That is, as Jesus refused to conform to the worldview and lifestyle of the Pharisees, their antagonism toward Him intensified through several levels.

Level 1—*Observation:* When Jesus emerged on the religious landscape, Pharisees observed Him and His disciples doing things (or not doing things) that violated their tradition: dining with "sinners," not fasting on prescribed days, and picking grain on the Sabbath (Mark 2:16, 18, 23–28). The Pharisees expressed their amazement in the form of a question: "Why?" In each case, Jesus simply gave the reasons for His actions.

Level 2—*Scrutiny:* The Pharisees began watching for infractions of their tradition in order to accuse Him (Mark 3:2). Jesus' emotional reaction to their hardened hearts was grief and anger (Mark 3:5). He publicly justified an act of healing on the Sabbath, and then He did it in their presence (Matthew 12:11–13).

Level 3—*Conspiracy:* From that point, the Pharisees "conspired against Him, as to how they might destroy Him" (Matthew 12:14). Jesus responded by withdrawing from them (Matthew 12:15).

Level 4— *Slander:* When Jesus expelled a demon from a man who was blind and mute, the Pharisees made their rejection of Him official by attributing His miraculous works to Satan (Matthew 12:22–37). Jesus refuted their faulty logic and rebuked them personally for the first time.

Level 5—*Accusation:* The conflict escalated as Pharisees accused Jesus' disciples of violating the tradition of the elders (Matthew 15:1–2). Jesus' response was frontal and for the first time He directly called them "hypocrites" (Matthew 15:7) and challenged them on their cardinal error of breaking the commandment of God for the sake of their tradition (Matthew 15:3). Now He spoke of the Pharisees directly to His disciples:

> Then the disciples came and said to Him, "Do You know that the Pharisees were offended when they heard this statement?"

> But He answered and said, "Every plant which My heavenly Father did not plant shall be uprooted. Let them alone; they are blind guides of the blind. And if a blind man guides a blind man, both will fall into a pit." (Matthew 15:12–14)

Level 6—*Manipulation:* Thereafter, all questioning by the Pharisees was designed to incriminate Jesus with the authorities or alienate Him from the people (Matthew 22:15; Mark 10:1–12; 12:13–17). Jesus skillfully parried all attempts to impale Him on the horns of a dilemma (Luke 20:26, 39–40). He also began to warn His disciples and the multitudes about the hypocrisy and false teaching of the Pharisees (Matthew 16:6–12; 21:33–46; Mark 8:15; Luke 12:1; 18:9–14).

Level 7—*Destruction:* As the Pharisees plotted with the rest of the religious establishment to kill Jesus, He delivered a scathing denunciation of them and their form of "religion" (Matthew 23).

Fencing with Pharisees

Jesus' conflict with Pharisees was greater than ours and gives good guidelines on how to properly respond to them.

1. Jesus did not avoid doing things that He knew would offend the Pharisees.
2. The Pharisees always took the initiative in the confrontations.
3. During the early stages, when questioned or accused by the Pharisees, Jesus simply answered their questions and explained the reasons for His actions.
4. When the Pharisees began to dissuade people from following Him, Jesus rebuked them with greater force.
5. He also, at that point, warned His followers about them, instructing the multitudes in parables about their teaching.
6. Jesus' specific instructions for His disciples were: Beware, and leave them alone.
7. When Jesus challenged the Pharisees personally, the target of His attack was the content of their *doctrine* (i.e., when they supplanted the commands of God with their own tradition), the phoniness of their *practice* (hypocrisy), and the destructive effect of their *influence* in the lives of others.

Bending Over Backwards

Now, by placing the pertinent apostolic exhortations alongside the patterns of Christ's example, we can establish some guidelines for relating to the pharisaic brethren among us.

1. *Beware* of becoming a pharisee (Matthew 16:12; Luke 12:1; Romans 14:3). Basically, a pharisee fails to distinguish between divine command and personal application. He absolutizes the application—not just for himself, but for everyone else as well.
2. When questioned by a pharisee, graciously *explain* the reasons for your convictions (Colossians 4:6; 2 Timothy 2:24–25; 1 Peter 3:14–16).
3. Don't *capitulate* to his pressure to conform to his absolutes (Colossians 2:8, 16–23), especially if they undermine the gospel of grace (Galatians 2:3–5).
4. Pursue *peace* (Romans 12:18; 14:19). If a pharisee rejects your efforts to establish harmony, leave him alone and commit him to God (Matthew 15:12–14).
5. *Admonish* the church to beware of the dangers of pharisaism (Romans 15:14). Instruct and exhort the pharisee in public ministry to the body.[24]

Pulling the Thorn

The first five guidelines are applicable to relationships with "passive pharisees"—those who take offense at the liberty of others but don't otherwise create division in the church. The final two steps are reserved for the "aggressive pharisee."

6. When the pharisee begins to cause spiritual damage to others, the church, or the reputation of the Lord, *confront him* privately and seek to help him change (Matthew 18:15; Galatians 6:1; 1 Thessalonians 5:14; 2 Thessalonians 3:14–15).
7. If private reproof does not restore the brother, then the steps that Christ spelled out for *church discipline* are called for (Matthew 18:15–20). The final step of excommunication is equivalent to Christ's public rebuke of those who so vigorously opposed Him (Matthew 23).

As the family of God and fellow members of His body, we have responsibilities to one another. When correction is called for, the straying brother will more readily respond with repentance when confronted by someone who has earned the reputation of a servant. The pharisee also needs the love of a caring family.

To conclude this portion of our study, let's return to a comparison of the three categories of differing brothers. This time, our focus is on how the mature believer is to relate to each of the three differing brothers.

RELATING TO DIFFERING BROTHERS		
Weaker Brother	**Stronger Brother**	**Pharisee**
I need never give him offense.	I will not be able to give him offense.	I will not be able to prevent his taking offense.
I become a willing slave to his conscience.	I am free to exercise my freedom.	I will not allow him to enslave me to his standards.
I must limit my freedom to avoid sinning against him.	I need not limit my freedom on his account.	I may choose to limit my freedom to keep him from getting upset at me.

The Bunker Hill Principle

What should I do if I'm not sure whether my differing brother is a weaker brother or a pharisee? Apply the Bunker Hill Principle: Don't fire until you see the whites of his eyes. That is, assume he is a weaker brother and refrain from exercising your freedom until the person in the line of fire is correctly identified or removed from danger. Even if he proves to have pharisaic tendencies, you may find it best to sacrifice your freedom for the sake of removing obstacles to his spiritual growth (cf. Acts 15:28–29).

DECISION MAKING WHEN CHRISTIANS DIFFER

ROMANS 14:1–15:13

1. Learn to distinguish between matters of command and matters of freedom (14:14, 20).
2. On debatable issues, cultivate your own convictions (14:5).
3. Allow your brother the freedom to determine his own convictions, even when they differ from yours (14:1–12).
4. **Let your liberty be limited, when necessary, by love (14:13–15:2).**

CONCENTRATING ON CHRIST

PRINCIPLE 5: *Follow Christ as the Model and Motivator of Servanthood.* Paul's principles are strikingly contrary to human nature. In truth, unless men adopt a servant mentality, Paul's exhortation is hopelessly unrealistic. Men want to be sovereigns, not servants. But then the supernatural character of Christianity enters. When a believer is infused with the divine presence, the quest for sovereignty is superseded by a compulsion to serve. In fact, the more the saint becomes like his Savior, the more servant minded he becomes. So, as in Romans 15, the apostles frequently point to the Example.

> Each of us is to please his neighbor for his good, to his edification. For even Christ did not please Himself; but as it is written, "THE REPROACHES OF THOSE WHO REPROACHED YOU FELL ON ME." For whatever was written in earlier times was written for our instruction, so that through perseverance and the encouragement of the Scriptures we might have hope. Now may the God who gives perseverance and encouragement grant you to be of the same mind with one another according to Christ Jesus, so that with one accord you may with one voice glorify the God and Father of our Lord Jesus Christ.

> Therefore, accept one another, just as Christ also accepted us to the glory of God. For I say that Christ has become a servant to the circumcision on behalf of the truth of God to confirm the promises given to the fathers, and for the Gentiles to glorify God for His mercy. (Romans 15:2–9)

Christ's School for Servants

There are a number of reasons for this apostolic habit of clinching a point by focusing on Christ as the Prime Example. The first concerns *perspective* and is well described in Everett F. Harrison's comments on verses 5–6:

> So Paul prays for a spirit of unity (like-mindedness) that will minimize individual differences as all fix their attention on Christ as the pattern for their own lives (cf. v. 3). This does not mean that believers are intended to see eye-to-eye on everything, but that the more Christ fills the spiritual vision, the greater will be the cohesiveness of the church. The centripetal magnetism of the Lord can effectively counter the centrifugal force of individual judgment and opinion.[25]

The second reason for pointing to Christ is *motivation*. The beneficiaries of the Servant's love ought to be compelled to accept and serve others (Romans 15:7). The Master Model shows us how. When Paul says, "Christ has become a servant" (Romans 15:8), we are reminded of His self-humiliation (Philippians 2:5–11).

> Make my joy complete by being of the same mind, maintaining the same love, united in spirit, intent on one purpose. Do nothing from selfishness or empty conceit, but with humility of mind regard one another as more important than yourselves.... Have this attitude in yourselves which was also in Christ Jesus. (Philippians 2:2–3, 5)

What the apostle is saying to these people is that the next time they find themselves squaring off in a fighter's stance they should switch to a servant's posture. For that is what the mind of Christ is more than anything else—a posture, kneeling and washing one another's feet. It's loving and giving as we have been loved and given to.[26]

Only the Strong Serve

The final point may be the most important: The ability, the *enablement* to serve others as Christ serves comes from God Himself. "Now may the God who gives perseverance and encouragement grant you to be of the same mind with one another according to Christ Jesus" (Romans 15:5). Jesus is not only the Model, but also as the Motivator of our obedience. For all the instructions would only mock us if His enablement was lacking. With His enablement, motivation is abundant.

DECISION MAKING WHEN CHRISTIANS DIFFER

Romans 14:1–15:13

1. Learn to distinguish between matters of command and matters of freedom (14:14, 20).
2. On debatable issues, cultivate your own convictions (14:5).
3. Allow your brother the freedom to determine his own convictions, even when they differ from yours (14:1–12).
4. Let your liberty be limited, when necessary, by love (14:13–15:2).
5. **Follow Christ as the model and motivator of servanthood (15:3–13).**

---

1. Martin Luther, "On the Freedom of a Christian Man," quoted in F. F. Bruce, *The Epistle of Paul to the Romans: An Introduction and Commentary* (Grand Rapids, MI: Wm. B. Eerdmans Publishing Co., 1963), 246 (cf. 1 Corinthians 9:19).
2. In his consistent use of masculine terminology, Paul may be reflecting not only a patriarchal culture but a theological construct. All Christians are "brothers," not because we are all male, but because we are "all sons of God" (Galatians 3:26). The connotation of "son" encompasses more than "child." For a son had (among other things) the rights

of inheritance (Galatians 3:29), a precious blessing granted to all believers. So it is important that all Christians retain our identity of "sonship," even though in Christ "there is neither male nor female" (Galatians 3:28). In that culture, sonship was not about gender. So Paul could address all believers as brothers without being chauvinistic. I, on the other hand, living in another time and culture, want to be sensitive to my sisters in Christ. So while I use Paul's vocabulary, I intend to be inclusive in scope. (See Scot McKnight, *The NIV Application Commentary: Galatians* [Grand Rapids, MI: Zondervan, 1995], 195–214.)

3. Frank E. Gaebelein, gen. ed., *The Expositor's Bible Commentary,* vol. 10: "Romans" by Everett F. Harrison (Grand Rapids, MI: Zondervan, 1976), 145.
4. Bruce, *Romans,* 253.
5. Colin Brown, ed., *The New International Dictionary of New Testament Theology* (Grand Rapids, MI: Zondervan, 1976), s.v. "Offence, Scandal, Stumbling Block."
6. W. E. Vine, *Expository Dictionary of New Testament Words,* vol. 3 (Old Tappan, NJ: Fleming H. Revell Co., 1940), 129.
7. Ibid.
8. Brown, *Dictionary of NT Theology,* s.v. "Offence, Scandal, Stumbling Block."
9. Other verses where *skandalizo* occurs in the active voice with the sense of "to cause to stumble" include Matthew 5:29–30 and the parallel passages in Mark and Luke.
10. Other verses where *skandalizomai* occurs in the passive voice with the sense of "to stumble over" include Matthew 11:6; 15:12; 26:31, 33; and other parallel passages in Mark and Luke.
11. Brown, *Dictionary of NT Theology,* s.v. "Offence, Scandal, Stumbling Block."
12. Other verses where *skandalon* represents a stumbling block that causes others to stumble include Matthew 18:7; Romans 16:17; Revelation 2:14; and parallel passages.
13. Other verses where *skandalon* represents something at which others take offense include 1 Corinthians 1:23 and Galatians 5:11.
14. In Romans 14:13, the synonym to stumbling block, translated "obstacle" is *proskomma,* which is literally something someone may strike his foot against. The verb, *proskopto,* is found in 1 Corinthians 10:32, and is translated "to give offense." Paul used these synonyms in the same way that he employed *skandalon* and *skandalizo.*
15. Jerry White, *Honesty, Morality and Conscience* (Colorado Springs: NavPress, 1979), 28–29, 35–36. White's second and third chapters, "Your Conscience—Friend or Foe" and "How to Use and Respond to Your Conscience" are recommended for his exploration of the biblical data about the conscience.
16. Ibid., 83.
17. This paragraph offers one possible view of harmonizing 1 Corinthians 8:10 and 10:19–22. In the former, eating in an idol's temple is considered a sin because it causes the weak to stumble. However, in 10:19–22 the eating of meat sacrificed to idols in the temple context is viewed as idolatry and always wrong. The view suggested in this book takes 8:10 to be eating in the temple apart from a pagan festival and thus not worshipping demons (1 Corinthians 10:20). It is possible to harmonize also by saying that eating in the festival was not pagan worship if the believer had no part in the sacrifice of the food. Even better is the alternative suggested by Hodge that eating in the idol temple in 8:10 is wrong for two reasons (hurting the weak and idolatry), but Paul only mentions its harm of the weak until he gets to the second problem of idolatry in chapter 10. "Here he views the matter simply under the aspect *of an offence,* or in reference to its effect on the weaker brethren, and therefore says nothing of the sinfulness of the act in itself." Charles Hodge, *An Exposition of the First Epistle to the Corinthians* (Grand Rapids, MI: Wm. B. Eerdmans Publishing Co., n.d.), 147–48.

18. Fritz Ridenour, *How to Be a Christian in an Unchristian World* (Glendale, CA: Regal Books, 1967), 136.
19. Bruce, *Romans,* 243.
20. This is supported by C. K. Barrett's observations on Romans 14:21: "This does not mean that all Christians should take vows of abstinence. The infinitives 'to eat' and 'to drink' are aorists, and the meaning seems to be that if on any particular occasion it seems likely that to eat flesh or to drink wine will cause a brother to stumble, it is right on that occasion to abstain. Eating and drinking are not wrong in themselves, and on other occasions the danger may not arise." C. K. Barrett, *A Commentary on the Epistle to the Romans* (New York: Harper and Row, 1957), 266.
21. C. S. Lewis, *Mere Christianity* (New York: Simon & Schuster, 1996), 76.
22. Joseph C. Aldrich, *Life-Style Evangelism* (Portland, OR: Multnomah Press, 1981), 43.
23. A systematic treatment of Christ's encounters with the Pharisees is found in John R. W. Stott's excellent volume, *Christ the Controversialist* (Downers Grove, IL: InterVarsity Press, 1970).
24. In the New Testament Epistles, admonition is a form of exhortation, often with the idea of warning. Most of the time it refers to preventive warning rather than confrontation over a specific problem. In every instance but one (2 Thessalonians 3:15), where *admonish* is used in the sense of "reprove"), the admonition is directed toward a *group* of people. Of primary concern in admonition is the attitude of the one doing the exhorting. Key verses on this ministry include Romans 15:14; Acts 20:31; 1 Corinthians 4:14; Colossians 1:28–29 and 3:16. See also the very practical discussion by Gene A. Getz in *Building Up One Another* (Wheaton, IL: Victor Books, 1979), 51–59.
25. Gabelein, *Expositor's Bible Commentary,* vol. 10: "Romans," by Everett F. Harrison, 152–53.
26. Ben Patterson, "A Small Pump at the Edge of the Swamp?" *Leadership: A Practical Journal for Church Leaders* 1 (Spring 1980): 45.

CONCLUSION

We have covered a lot of terrain in this book. It would probably be helpful to quickly review where we have been.

Part 1 was an honest attempt to present the main beliefs of the traditional view of God's guidance. In the first edition I presented it in more detail, but in this second edition an outline of the traditional view was deemed sufficient.

Part 2 was a critique of the strengths and weaknesses of the traditional view. There we saw that God does not have an ideal individual will as the traditional view asserts. Such an "individual will of God" cannot be established by reason, experience, biblical example, or biblical teaching (chapters 3 and 4). We saw that the practice of looking for a dot in the center of God's will (a dot that does not exist) has created needless frustration in decision making.

We saw further that the traditional view contains several applicational difficulties (chapters 5 and 6). First, the traditional view must be abandoned in the ordinary decisions of life. Second, it provides no adequate means for dealing with genuinely equal options. Third, it tends to promote immature approaches to decision making. Finally, the traditional view can appeal only to subjective sources of knowledge and thus objective certainty in finding God's individual will is not possible.

Part 3 proposed an alternative to the traditional view, which I have called the "way of wisdom" and is summarized by the following chart.

PRINCIPLES OF DECISION MAKING
THE WAY OF WISDOM

1. Where God commands, we must obey (chapter 8).
2. Where there is no command, God gives us freedom (and responsibility) to choose (chapter 9).
3. Where there is no command, God gives us wisdom to choose (chapters 10 and 11).
4. When we have chosen what is moral and wise, we must trust the sovereign God to work all the details together for good (chapters 12 and 13).

The way of wisdom avoids the weaknesses of the traditional view while it builds upon its strengths. The priority of the moral will of God and the reality of the sovereign will of God is maintained. The idea that God has an ideal individual will for each believer that must be discovered in order to make right decisions is abandoned along with all the difficulties it created. God-given freedom in noncommanded decisions is recognized as biblical, and the use of that freedom is regulated by God's moral will and wisdom.

Finally, *part 4* took us from the quiet study of God's guidance principles to the noisy reality of everyday decision making. The way of wisdom was applied to the specific, concrete, and often difficult decisions of life. These included marriage choices, mission involvement, vocational choices, giving priorities, and disagreement on debatable issues. Part 4 not only fleshed out the principles of part 3, but added further scriptural support for the way of wisdom.

You have one of three possible responses to the wisdom view presented here. You may agree. You may disagree. Or you may want to think further before making a decision.

If you agree, you need to love and fully accept every believer who holds to the traditional view. You should not condemn, criticize, or look down on the one who disagrees (Romans 14:4). Rather, you should discuss the Scriptures together, always remembering that the goal is to honor and understand God's Word, not to win the argument.

If you disagree with the wisdom view, you should love and accept the brother who wrote it. And you are to love and accept those who agree with it even though you consider them mistaken in their understanding of Scripture.

If you are not sure whether you agree or disagree, your response is most crucial. First, you should make it your goal to search the Scriptures concerning guidance so that you may become fully convinced before the Lord. Second, you should not follow this new presentation of guidance until you *are* fully convinced. You should continue to follow your previous conviction so that your actions will be of faith and not of doubt (Romans 14:23). If you are not sure, but go ahead and attempt to follow the way of wisdom, doubts and self-condemnation are likely to follow (Romans 14:22–23). You should follow the traditional view until you are convinced of another view.

As evangelicals we must love Scripture—not our interpretation of it. When our view is questioned we are tempted to be upset, defensive, careless with our words, and more desirous of winning an argument than honoring and discussing the Bible. Discussions then look surprisingly like arguments. Being fully convinced (Romans 14:5) does not require us to be defensive, argumentative, or closed to differing opinions. The searcher for scriptural truth wants to hear the best arguments against his view so that he may strengthen the weaknesses in his position, properly understand the views of others, and change his own view when truth so dictates.

My relationship with Jack, a pastor and close spiritual brother, is a constant reminder to me that love and unity among believers who disagree can and should exist. We do not agree completely on the teaching of guidance and God's will, but God has blessed our ministry and unity with each other. I so enjoy ministering with Jack that when he asks me to speak at a church retreat I can never think of the word "no." Some of his church family have said to us that we should minister together permanently because of our joy and unity. The world will not identify true believers by their view of guidance, but by their love for one another (John 13:35).

A student who knew my view of guidance once approached me

looking very concerned. With some difficulty he said, "You know you're going to hurt a lot of people if you go ahead and write a book with this wrong view of God's will." I had the presence of mind to answer little and listen much to this brother. But his statement stuck in my mind. Would I be hurting some people by writing this book? If so, how could I justify my efforts to have it published? I was not able to give him a good answer on the spot, but I have since found answers to those questions.

First, Romans 14 recognizes that we will have differences of opinion that will not result in harm if we love and accept one another and continue to search the Scriptures to be fully convinced in our own minds.

Second, this book does not claim to speak with the authority of Scripture, but only to be the teaching of a concerned believer who is fully convinced that the way of wisdom is what the Bible teaches.

Finally, if the way of wisdom is wrong and the traditional view correct, this book will help the traditional view by raising questions that it must answer to strengthen its position.

It is for this purpose—the clarification of scriptural truth so that God's people might better fulfill His moral will—that I have written this book. It is my hope that the way of wisdom will become a way of life for many, for the glory of God.

appendix one

REVIEWS OF BOOKS ON FINDING GOD'S WILL

In the Introduction to the first edition of *Decision Making*, I made this observation: "Solomon's lament that 'the writing of many books is endless' (Ecclesiastes 12:12) seems especially applicable to volumes on the subject of knowing God's will." If I had entertained any fantasy that my "definitive statement" on the topic of guidance would serve as the last word…well, let's just say that Solomon's reputation for astute observation remains intact. I don't know how many books on knowing God's will have been published since 1980, but I know that choosing fifteen of them to review is only a representative effort.

The continuing stream of books on God's guidance testifies to two things, at least. One is the importance of the subject and the hunger that people have to understand how God intends for them to live. The other is that no human commentator is going to provide the final word on the subject. There is plenty of room for fresh insight as capable writers grapple with the Scriptures and the challenges of daily living. One of the things that struck me as I read each of these books is how much I learned from other authors on a subject in which I have some expertise—even when (sometimes *especially* when) I disagree with them.

My intention in writing these reviews is constructive examination of biblical truth. The key word in that sentence is "constructive." I have had some experience at being on the receiving end of criticism that was less than charitable. When *Decision Making* was first published, it was immediately dubbed as "controversial." In some quarters, that was putting it mildly. While the book was assigned as a required text in Christian institutions from high school through seminary, it was actually banned on other campuses. Seminars were conducted and articles were written to refute this "alternative to the traditional view." I received emotional letters from folks who were intent on setting me straight. One disgruntled soul expressed his frustration with this Parthian shot: "Everything you know is wrong!"

Of course, not all criticism that I received was inflammatory. Some of it really was constructive—and correct! I think this edition of *Decision Making* is better than the first one. And that is due, in no small measure, to the insights of those who pointed out weaknesses in the original presentation. So it is appropriate for me to begin by expressing my gratitude to the writers of these books, among others, for the things they have taught me about decision making and the will of God. And I commend them for having the courage to put their convictions in print.

Constructive critique is an exercise in applying the principles from the last two chapters of this book. I assume that all of the authors engaged here are "stronger brothers" and that the discussion of points of disagreement is a legitimate exercise. I think that those who expound the traditional view of guidance are wrong at certain points, and I will point those out. I believe that identifying those points will help all of us to think more clearly and critically about the subject at hand. And I expect that my brothers and sisters agree with me about that.

I am assuming that you have already read *Decision Making and the Will of God*, so I will content myself with pointing out the places where our viewpoints diverge and limiting my "corrective" comments to brief summary statements. My hope is that my commentaries on these fine books will help you to become more discerning when reading about God's will and decision making.

And to those authors whose books are not included in these reviews, I didn't mean to slight you. I couldn't keep up with everything worthwhile that has been written about guidance. I would have included more, but my editor drew the line. And you know how editors can be… (Additional reviews are available on my website.)

The reviews that follow have been categorized according to my analysis of the authors' governing views. They appear in this sequence:

1. *Traditional View*: Henry Blackaby and Claude King, Jack Deere, Tim LaHaye.
2. *Traditional View with Wisdom Leanings*: Elisabeth Elliot and Charles Swindoll.
3. *Synthesis of Traditional and Wisdom Views:* Dallas Willard.
4. *Wisdom View in Traditional Vocabulary*: John MacArthur, J. I. Packer, M. Blaine Smith, and Bruce Waltke.
5. *Wisdom View*: James Montgomery Boice, Sinclair Ferguson, Os Guinness, James Petty, and Haddon Robinson.

TRADITIONAL VIEW

Experiencing God: *How to Live the Full Adventure of Knowing and Doing the Will of God*

Henry Blackaby and Claude King

(Nashville: Broadman and Holman Publishers, 1994)

Experiencing God has swept through Christian circles. Its beautiful cover shows the burning bush of Moses in place of the *O* in the word *God.* This is a fitting graphic, because God's revelation to Moses is presented as the pattern for His interaction with believers today.

The authors elaborate on seven principles intended to help readers to "experience God":

1. God is always at work around you.
2. God pursues a continuing love relationship with you that is real and personal.
3. God invites you to become involved with Him in His work.
4. God speaks by the Holy Spirit through the Bible, prayer, circumstances, and the church to reveal Himself, His purposes, and His ways.

5. God's invitation for you to work with Him always leads you to a crisis of belief that requires faith and action.
6. You must make major adjustments in your life to join God in what He is doing.
7. You come to know God by experience as you obey Him and He accomplishes His work through you.

Six of these principles make up the basic Christian life. Depending on how you understand them, they can be biblical and helpful. In their exposition of these principles, the authors have captured my heart and thousands of others. God's love relationship with us is beautifully portrayed. The greatness of our God is extolled so that our faith grows. The book motivates our desire to give full dedication and absolute obedience in response to such love. God is not only always at work around us, but we are touched deeply by God's names and nature so that we see Him at work in us as never before. My heart is warmed and my faith grows at each reading of this book. The fact that I have reasons to critique the book at certain points does not change that reality.

The authors begin with an explanation of biblical examples of God speaking. I will call this *Pattern A*. In these instances, when God spoke, those who heard knew it was God. They knew what He was saying. They knew what they were to do in response (p. 31). Are these examples of God's direct revelation to Moses, Isaiah, or Paul the normal ways believers experience God? I don't believe they are.

In their fourth principle, the authors maintain: "God speaks by the Holy Spirit through the Bible, prayer, circumstances, and the church to reveal Himself, His purposes, and His ways." I will call this *Pattern B*. And it reflects the traditional view of finding God's will. Patterns A and B are not the same, yet Blackaby and King seem to treat them as though they are.

CRITIQUE #1—Experiencing God *uses examples of supernatural direct revelation as the norm.*

Like other proponents of the traditional view, this book sets forth examples of direct, supernatural revelation to specific biblical characters (Pattern A) as normative experience. "Surely the Lord GOD does nothing unless He reveals His secret counsel to His servants the prophets" (Amos 3:7). Then these examples are said to substantiate the idea that God speaks through the Bible, prayer, circumstances, and the church (Pattern B). I believe this is a confusion of categories that are not the same.

In the Bible, God gave His prophets special revelation to pass on to His people (Pattern A). The prophets were uniquely set apart by God for this purpose. And Moses was unique even among the prophets. God gave him direct revelation without dreams and visions. He was given direct access to the voice of God and saw God's form (Numbers 12:6–8).

But when Blackaby and King explain how God speaks to people today, they describe something very different. God is said to "reveal" His will to us through the Bible, circumstances, the church, and prayer (Pattern B). These signs all should be checked against each other. But that is not what happened with Moses. In Exodus 3, Moses had no Bible. He was not praying, he was minding his own business, tending sheep. Circumstances were never conducive to Moses' new task. The nation of Israel was the closest thing to the church—and it didn't want him.

This tendency to superimpose Pattern A illustrations onto Pattern B experience is an example of the "imprecise hermeneutics" I described at the conclusion of chapter 4, "Does Scripture Teach the Dot?" In my judgment, this is a significant weakness of the traditional view.

CRITIQUE #2—*This book encourages believers to wait until they receive a clear revelation from God before acting.*

This book assumes that some details of God's will are not contained in the Bible. God will tell you what He is doing and then you are to join in with Him. God is the one who initiates. He reveals to each believer what He is doing and what we should do. God took the initiative with Noah, Abraham, and Moses (p. 54). "When God starts to do something in the world, He takes the initiative to come and talk to somebody" (p. 66). It is this "agenda" (p. 68) that we must know if we are to act in harmony with His purposes.

I see two potential problems with this approach. The first is the assertion that God's assignment to us (through the Bible, prayer, circumstances, church) will be as clear to us as His assignment was to Moses. But I don't think it works out that way in practice—as the authors seem to admit with their illustration from the life of George Mueller. Mueller did not claim to have direct revelation. He went through steps in the process of finding God's will. In the end, he says, "I come to a deliberate judgment according to the best of my ability and knowledge" (p. 72).

Blackaby and King acknowledge that this process may seem "vague." Clearly the experiences of Moses and Mueller were different.

The second potential problem is that waiting for a clear message from God before acting can be a prescription for inaction. The Bible, of course, does not call us to passivity. As I elaborated in chapter 14, "Guidance: A Biblical Model," the apostle Paul provides an excellent model for us to follow. In making a major ministry decision to visit Rome, he *took the initiative* in making plans which were subsequently submitted to the sovereign will of God. If Paul waited for God's explicit direction, as the traditional view advises, he doesn't mention it in the explanation of his decision making (Romans 1 and 15).

CRITIQUE #3—Experiencing God *offers an unusual view of spiritual gifts.* Blackaby and King teach that waiting to discover your spiritual gifts before you accept an assignment from God is backward (p. 46). The gift comes after you accept the ministry, not before. You should listen to God and He will tell you what to do. He will supply the miraculous power to do it successfully. The power He gives you is the spiritual gift.

This explanation fits Moses well. God gave him not only a task, but three miraculous signs and ten plagues to carry it out. But Peter and Paul taught that each Christian *has been given* one or more spiritual gifts that must be discovered and used (1 Peter 4:10; see Romans 12:6–8 and 1 Corinthians 12–14). Stewardship of our spiritual gifts is to be a factor in the decisions that we make about ministry. (For elaboration of this point, see chapter 23 in *Decision Making.*)

CRITIQUE #4—*This view seems to expect all our assignments will be successful if not miraculous.*

When illustrating applications of their principles, the authors naturally chose instances where failure in ministry was followed by success. For example, they tell how a church tried to start a Bible study as an outreach to seekers (pp. 44–45). For two years they got nowhere. They then reversed their method. This time they just asked God to show them what He was doing so they could join in. Within three days someone asked a member of the group: "Do you know somebody who can lead us in a Bible study?" They conclude, "For almost two years we tried to do something for God and failed. For three days we looked to see where God was working and joined Him" (p. 45).

The implication that following such leading will inevitably lead to success seems to be supported by direct statements by the authors: "When God purposes to do something, He guarantees that it will come to pass" (pp. 152, 168). When you know this success in ministry, you are "experiencing God." This conclusion fits the logic of the traditional view. If a plan comes from God, then He will accomplish the results.

I have no problem with this reasoning when the plan in question is communicated by supernatural revelation (Pattern A). But I see a very different paradigm in Scripture for noncommanded decisions. James 4:13–16 teaches both the appropriateness of planning and of humble submission to God's sovereign will (see chapter 13, "God's Sovereign Will and Decision Making"). I see no promise nor requirement of a successful outcome to all of our plans and decisions. And I am concerned that implications to the contrary may unintentionally discourage many who serve God in hard places that produce little by way of observable results. Our efforts are pleasing to God if they are done with right motives and attitudes, and exhibit faithfulness in our stewardship of God's resources (1 Corinthians 4:2)—regardless of the outcome.

The authors maintain that your "assignments" from God will be "God-sized" (p. 135). "I have come to the place in my life that, if the assignment I sense God is giving me is something that I know I can handle, I know it probably is not from God. The kind of assignments God gives in the Bible are always God-sized" (p. 138). I agree with the authors that no one should ever rely on his or her own strength to accomplish spiritual results. Dependence on God is always required. But I believe it is going too far to say that every ministry assignment must be of miraculous proportions. We need to remember that the biblical illustrations are often the exception to the rule. The Bible's teaching on stewardship instructs us to match our resources to the task under consideration (Luke 14:28–30; 2 Corinthians 8:12). It is not unspiritual to evaluate a potential challenge with the question: "Is this something I can handle (by God's grace)"? That is wisdom. It is good to stretch our faith, but God's power is as necessary for "routine faithfulness" as it is for Herculean tasks.

CRITIQUE #5—*The book teaches that believers can discern personal messages from God through the Bible, prayer, and circumstances.*

"Only the Holy Spirit can reveal to you which truth of Scripture is a word from God in a particular circumstance" (p. 88). In this statement, the authors seem to mean more than personal application of general truths. When Blackaby's daughter had cancer, he says that God used John 11:4 ("This sickness is not unto death, but for the glory of God") to show him that Carrie would not die of the cancer. The verse is about Lazarus, but the personal message from God was that this daughter would not die of her disease.

It is wonderful that he received encouragement from this verse during a distressing time. But I don't think it's appropriate to claim a historical statement as a personal promise, even if it is deeply impressed upon my mind. Not only does this approach lack support from accepted principles of interpretation, but it potentially could set up vulnerable believers for disillusionment. The stories that don't pan out—where someone believed that God gave a promise through a verse, and it didn't come true—don't make it into published testimonies. But those cases may be as devastating as this one was encouraging. We should not hold God to supposed promises He has not obligated Himself to keep.

I see a similar difficulty with the "exegesis" of circumstances. These authors agree that circumstances are notoriously difficult to read. But God will tell you what they mean. "You will be watching circumstances and asking God to interpret them by revealing to you His perspective" (p. 152).

My own view, set out in detail in chapter 13, "God's Sovereign Will and Decision Making," is that the reading of providence is more than difficult—it is not sanctioned by the Bible as a means of discerning God's will.

The Bible, prayer, and circumstances are important factors in decision making. But the promise of personal messages through specific revelations is not their proper role.

CRITIQUE #6—*The main theme of the book is taken from what I believe to be a misreading of John 5.*

The authors say that we should see what God is doing and join in. Look at the circumstances that surround you and God will show you what He is doing. Then you can join what God is planning and doing, not what you want to plan and do. The pattern is based upon the statement of Christ in John 5:19: "The Son can do nothing of Himself, unless it is something He sees the Father doing; for whatever the Father does, these things the Son also does in like manner."

However, this verse is not about Christ looking at circumstances around Him and "joining the Father's work." This is John's introduction to proving that Jesus is equal to the Father (John 5:18) since He can do all the works of the Father, including resurrection and final judgment (John 5:21–22). His apprehension of the Father is intimate and direct as a member of the Godhead. He did not learn God's plan by viewing circumstances. (This passage is more completely expounded in chapter 4 of *Decision Making.*)

Conclusion

Despite my criticisms, I still find much in the book to be very helpful. It is edifying as a devotional appeal to sincere faith in God. The reader who "translates" the vocabulary and illustrations of this book through the interpretive grid of the way of wisdom will benefit greatly from genuine spiritual insight. Those who try to apply those examples and explanations literally will try to live a life that was not even the norm for Moses...who actually did see a burning bush.

SURPRISED BY THE VOICE OF GOD: *How God Speaks Today Through Prophecies, Dreams, and Visions*

Jack Deere

(Grand Rapids, MI: Zondervan, 1996)

In *Surprised by the Voice of God,* Jack Deere takes up where he left off in *Surprised by the Power of the Spirit.* Some have discounted him offhand, but I think he should be taken seriously.

For those still trying to figure out whether God intervenes miraculously in the life of the church today, Deere's books may be very convincing. They are carefully written with evidence of good research and editing. Deere has studied a vast number of Scripture passages from which he has developed a theology of the miraculous in the church. In his writing he exhibits humility and teachability. He asks the same from his readers, and effectively opens our minds to consider his understanding. Above all else he is careful and credible in the examples of miracles he describes. They are often depicted in moving stories of God's power in the Church. His words provide a devotional challenge to the reader to love God, believe God, and humbly expect God to work.

I am receptive to Deere's argument since I am open to the possibility of the miraculous gifts being present in the church today. I also respect Deere's integrity and accept his miracle stories at face value. He may be mistaken about the legitimacy of some purported miracles, but it is not because he has been dishonest or careless in confirming their reliability. His background at Dallas Theological Seminary makes him aware of both the strengths and weaknesses of the cessationist view. (Cessationists hold that God's activity of giving supernatural or sign gifts ceased with the passing of the apostles.) My concerns are stated within the context of my respect for the author and his writings.

CRITIQUE #1—*Deere presents the revelation given to Jesus, apostles, and prophets as the norm for the church age.*

Deere produces a thorough review of the incidents of divine revelation in the life of Jesus and the book of Acts. He notes that every chapter in Acts (except 17) records some instance of supernatural revelation given to the church. He correctly observes that the speeches of Peter and Paul were inspired and thus were products of revelation. Other individuals, like Philip, also received revelation. From this he concludes that all believers should expect extrabiblical revelation to be a common part of their life. "In fact, I have come to count on the voice of God to such a degree that I can no longer conceive of trying to live the Christian life without it" (p. 17).

I would have expected Deere to argue from the experiences of Jesus, the apostles, and the prophets that *some* in the church will continue to get supernatural revelation. But he contends that "hearing God in dreams, visions, impressions and in other ways is simply normal New Testament Christianity" (p. 50). "Anyone who sincerely asks will eventually hear the voice of God (James 1:5–8)" (p. 235). From the examples in the Gospels and Acts he believes that all Christians should expect to receive revelation from God.

The basis for this surprising conclusion is Acts 2:17–21. Deere takes the list of those who will receive revelation as applying to all believers in the present age. It is not that some are gifted as prophets, but that the church is in an "age of revelation." This goes beyond normal charismatic teaching, which links such revelation with the gift of prophecy given to a few. The universal scope of revelation is confirmed when Deere lists the qualifications to hear God's voice. The recipient does not need a special gift; rather, one must have humility and openness (in contrast to the pride of the cessationist "Pharisees").

In addition to the key passage in Acts 2, Deere marshals further support from the assertion that Jesus is our example in everything. The fact that He is the Son of God does not invalidate this reality. Deere argues that Jesus did not perform His miracles or receive God's revelation because He was a prophet or Son of God. Rather, it was because He was completely yielded to His Father and the Spirit. Thus, examples of Jesus' ministry and revelation He received are the norm since we, like Jesus, have the Spirit.

In my judgment, Deere is going beyond the teaching of Scripture—and even charismatic doctrine. His attempt to sidestep the ramifications of the uniqueness of Jesus' person and relationship to the Father fails to convince. It is true that as a man, Jesus was like us. But there are a host of ways in which He was also different. I will not repeat here the discussion of the "example of Christ" detailed at the conclusion of chapter 3 of *Decision Making.* Suffice it to say, there are significant reasons to conclude that the communication connection between Christ and His Father was something beyond "normal." He Himself linked His miracles with His unique identity (John 14:11). And when the Epistles set forth Christ as our example, they indicate the specific ways He is our pattern—and the reception of revelation is not included.

Likewise, the other recipients of divine revelation—the apostles and the prophets—clearly occupy a distinctive place in the formation of the church. Paul called them "the foundation" (Ephesians 2:20). Since the recorded recipients of New Testament revelation played a strategic function in the establishment and expansion of the church (Acts), and since the Epistles assign a distinctive status to those individuals (apostles and prophets), it is hard to escape the conclusion that in that setting, *revelation was a function of role.* And in the body of Christ "all are not apostles...[or] prophets" (1 Corinthians 12:29). (Again, for further elaboration, see chapter 3, "Does God Have Three Wills?")

Furthermore, Deere's use of examples from the Gospels and Acts does not harmonize with what we find in the Epistles. The Epistles do not teach that every believer should expect extrabiblical revelation as a normal feature of the Christian life. First Corinthians 12–14 deals with the use of the gifts, but prophecy (for which revelation is a prerequisite) is not the prerogative of everyone in the church. Deere appeals to Galatians 2:1–2 and Philippians 3:15. The Galatians passage demonstrates that Paul, an apostle, occasionally made decisions based on revelation. But this does not prove that everyone gets revelation to make decisions. And Philippians 3 is not about revelation at all. Paul is reminding the believer of the convicting work of the Spirit that shows us when our thoughts are not in harmony with the teaching of Scripture. God will reveal our sins so that we might change. This is not extrabiblical revelation, but conviction according to what God has already revealed.

To sum up: A comprehensive cataloging of the instances of revelation in the Gospels and Acts is still only a record of the experiences of Jesus, the apostles, and the prophets. Deere does not succeed in proving that they did not occupy a distinctive role in the foundation of the church for which divine revelation was necessary. Nor does he successfully counteract the fact that the Epistles do not teach the expectation of revelation for every Christian. The examples still illustrate the exception rather than the rule.

CRITIQUE #2—*Deere's modern-day examples of revelation are very restricted.*

Deere has diligently searched for examples and has told moving stories of God's revelation. Strict cessationists may discount these narratives as exaggeration. Others, like myself, accept the stories unless contradictory evidence is produced. (I am less inclined to accept every explanation for reportedly miraculous events.) Some examples are impressive, but only because they are selective. That is, the stories where a "revelation" proved to be true with dramatic results are showcased. For instance, a student comes to Deere for counseling, and Deere "sees" the word *pornography* superimposed on the young man's countenance. He confronts the student with this supernaturally endowed insight and that exposure becomes the key to the student's confession and restoration. That may have been a genuine revelation; but then again, what is the likelihood that a male student who is troubled enough to come for counseling might be plagued by pornography? It seems to me that a guess along those lines is going to yield a pretty high percentage of success.

This example must be put into the context of what Deere believes about "false revelation." He knows of many examples where a similar intuition proved to be wrong. What if Deere sensed "pornography" and he was mistaken? Deere would admit that he misread God's revelation and he would explore other avenues in the counseling session. Wrong revelation is expected in his theology. I could add to Deere's stories.

Sometimes my impressions have worked out very well, but most have not. If I tell them selectively, they appear to be revelation.

Some of Deere's examples are impressive, but impossible to confirm. Several people get "revelations" that Deere's daughter, Elese, is going to die. By comparing the several sources, they determine that the revelation is credible. By further revelation they learn that the devil is trying to kill her. They conclude that they should raise the level of protection around her through increased prayer. After a time, the group senses the attack is over, and she returns safely to normal life. The story is moving, but there is no way to confirm objectively its validity.

For those still deciding about miraculous gifts, Deere's examples are very persuasive. And they have an implied conclusion. If you do not get revelations from God, you will not be able to help hurting people like you should.

On the other hand, if the revelation of extrabiblical truth is available to and intended for every believer, the number of credible examples in the book is small. These cases should not be automatically denied, but neither do they prove that God is giving new revelation to all Christians. He is sovereign and can do miracles whenever He desires. Deere's enumeration of these occurrences is the most impressive and credible out there; but his examples fall short of establishing what he is trying to prove. If true revelation is being given, it still appears to be transmitted to and through a small number of people. Deere's case would be more convincing if, instead of telling individual stories, he would list the names of acknowledged prophets and healers. Then legitimate testing could be done. But that is not the point he is trying to make.

CRITIQUE #3—*Deere's concept of Fallible Prophecy is the faulty assumption to his view.*

Deere accepts the notion that a revelation from God can become degraded en route to the recipient. Unlike biblical prophets, their modern day counterparts are susceptible to confusion at several points. The problem cannot be with the revelation as it comes from God, for God cannot lie (p. 193). But there is no assurance that the revelation gets to the believer in a pure form. So much of Deere's book is devoted to working out how prophecy can be profitable if it is sometimes right and sometimes wrong.

The first problem is that the believer who gets a divine message is never sure that it really is God's revelation. Never, never, never. That is to say that the process of communication can break down at three different points. For the recipient has to decipher whether an impression is a revelation from God; then one must discern the correct interpretation; then the application has to be discovered. The prospects for accuracy at all three levels are daunting indeed.

A second challenge is developing an ear for messages from God. Revelation is only "acquired through careful cultivation" (p. 40). You must give God a chance to speak or there will be no communication (p. 63). The revelation can come in words, phrases, or inarticulate impressions. Understanding God's revelatory voice is like learning to acquire a new language. God may even give you a "dream vocabulary" where certain images that appear in one's sleep point to concrete realities. There is no set of rules for discerning God's voice, but "those who are His friends will recognize His voice" (p. 338).

All of this takes practice. "Only those who are willing to try and fail will ever become proficient at understanding which impressions come from God and which arise merely from their own soul" (p. 170). This experimentation with revelations is best done in a nonthreatening atmosphere such as a small group where people can risk the process. "All over the room people began to raise their hands to 'try out' their impressions or visions. They knew [they] weren't going to be punished for failing" (p. 173).

If revelations are fallible (at the receiving end), it is necessary to establish all sorts of guidelines to keep the foolish and false "revelations" from hurting the church and to insure that genuine prophetic pronouncements are spiritually profitable. Deere says to avoid phrases like, "Thus says the Lord," and, "the Lord showed me that you are supposed to…" Instead say, "I think the Lord might be indicating…" or "I feel impressed to…" (p. 193). Share your revelation only if God gives you permission since most revelation is given only for the purpose of prayer (p. 194). Avoid giving revelations in large meetings. "In large public services I haven't found 'prophecy' from the congregation to be all that profitable" (p. 196). Revelations about marriage, children, money "should never be delivered in a controlling or authoritative way" (p. 185).

How does a Christian group determine which revelations are reliable? If the prophesying person has a good track record, "we will automatically begin to take the word more seriously." If it is "someone who habitually gets things wrong, then we will tend not to take it so seriously. The problem with these tendencies is that the credible person could be wrong and the stranger could be right" (pp. 197–98). You should not expect infallibility even from the best prophets. "I don't know any prophetic people today who are 100 percent accurate" (p. 208).

What Deere is describing is far removed from the experience of biblical prophets and the teaching of the New Testament. As I have noted repeatedly in this book (see, for instance, chapter 15, "Special Guidance and Decision Making"), God's spokespersons were never confused about whether they had heard from God. They were clear on their message and their audience. The veracity of their prophecy was supernaturally confirmed not only to them but to their listeners. Their message could be tested by God-given criteria (Deuteronomy 13:1–5; 18:20–22; 1 Samuel 3:19–20). The biblical prophets did say, "Thus says the Lord," and their audience knew to take that seriously.

It is harder to take seriously a message like, "Thus says the Lord, maybe." If someone delivers a prophecy and it turns out to be true, then "it was from the Lord." But if someone "misreads" the impression and gets it wrong, then it didn't count. As a standard of evaluation, Deere replaces the Bible's insistence on 100 percent fulfillment of predictions with a beneficial, fruitful outcome.

Deere has redefined what it means for God to speak through revelation and prophecy. It is sort of like revelation plus water. It has the appearance of the supernatural, but it is not supernatural in the same way we see in the New Testament. Deere seems to be defining revelation not by what happened in the New Testament, but by what is happening in his church. When someone sees a purple caterpillar eating four pebbles and vomiting them up, Deere has no real way of knowing if it is revelation or not (p. 172). Yet he does not want to discourage such sincere attempts at seeing visions, because it is by such practice and risking that believers learn to receive revelations.

The Old and New Testaments present true revelation as supernatural. If God supernaturally speaks, you could not miss it if you wanted to. He is the One who initiates the revelation, not sincere believers trying to get revelations or discern impressions. God assures that the revelation is delivered accurately and received authoritatively so that the message is, "Thus says the Lord." Deere has tried to create nonmiraculous and nonauthoritative revelation. This is an unhelpful detour in an important discussion. The real question is whether supernatural revelation and prophecy occur today.

FINDING THE WILL OF GOD IN A CRAZY, MIXED-UP WORLD
Tim LaHaye
(Grand Rapids, MI: Zondervan, 1989)

Tim LaHaye has been a great advocate for the truth of the Scriptures wherever he has ministered.

This book is a clear, interesting, and straightforward presentation of the traditional view of guidance, though less nuanced than other traditional books. LaHaye opens with eleven complex counseling situations from his ministry. As the book unfolds he seeks to show each person how God's will applies to his or her situation. He does not add any new arguments for the existence of God's individual will, but draws the reader's attention to many passages where he thinks this concept is taught.

While not directly identifying *Decision Making,* he is probably referring to it under the subtitle: "Beware the New Fad" (p. 51). He writes, "Recently a somewhat controversial book emerged, suggesting, in essence, that God doesn't have an individual or specific will for each Christian; the book suggests that once you've responded to the moral or universal will of God, you then can use your own judgment and proceed as you wish" (p. 51). He thinks that the wisdom view ignores Proverbs 3:5–6 so that "it's only a matter of time before we begin to function independently from God" (p. 52).

He holds an unusual view on Romans 12:2, even from the traditional viewpoint. The final phrase of Romans 12:2 reads, "that you may prove what is that *good and acceptable and perfect will of God,*" (NKJV). He says, "Most Bible teachers accept the three words...as modifiers of one will of God. By contrast, I view them as *three levels* of that one will." The terms "good" and "acceptable" describe "God's will for the people who fall into sin but then repent and still desire to do God's basic will" (p. 59). This corresponds to the idea of God's "second best" held by other proponents of the traditional view. LaHaye gives it great emphasis and even includes nine charts to show how specific individuals related to the three levels of God's will.

By falling into sin you can forfeit God's "perfect" will forever so you have to settle for only His "acceptable" will. If you stay in sin too long, then only God's "good" will is left for you. "Don't misunderstand," he pleads, "God's good will is a worthy option for the Christian who has rebelled against the Lord and has made many major decisions during that rebellious time" (p. 66). When most traditional proponents try to avoid or downplay this "second best" category of the individual will, LaHaye makes it a centerpiece of his presentation.

One of his signposts to finding God's perfect will is inward peace. "Inner peace is God's supernatural sign that decides 'safe' or 'out' as we attempt to discern His will" (p. 107). "It's wise never to make major decisions unless the umpire, the Holy Spirit-inspired peace of God that surpasses all understanding, calls the decision 'safe'!" (p. 108). In practice he is more shrewd than his principle, for he realizes that often lack of peace is the result of immature anxiety, not supernatural guidance. The "melancholic" in particular needs encouragement to move forward because he rarely feels peace. "His lack of peace was more a function of his melancholy temperament than a sign from God not to marry" (p. 162).

As we would expect of the maestro of temperament teaching, LaHaye includes a section on the four temperaments as they relate to decision making. I have always found his insights helpful in this area, and his chapter 12 gives some excellent wisdom on the subject. He also refutes those traditional view proponents who maintain that God's perfect will always leads to success unhindered by difficulties. He shows how great ministry is often accompanied by great trials. He has experienced the same and so have the characters of the Bible.

If you want a book presenting the traditional view, this is a good and acceptable one—but not quite perfect.

TRADITIONAL VIEW WITH WISDOM LEANINGS

GOD'S GUIDANCE: *A Slow & Certain Light*
Elisabeth Elliot
(Old Tappan, NJ: Fleming H. Revell Co., 1997)
(Originally published as *A Slow and Certain Light: Some Thoughts on the Guidance of God*)

The subtitle of the first edition accurately describes the flow of this book. It consists of some thoughts on God's guidance without trying to be a systematic, exhaustive presentation. Once she has proven that God is our guide, Elliot assumes the traditional view of guidance. Yet, you will hardly notice that she holds the traditional view unless you are looking for it.

Instead, you find a book full of insight and depth. The first half of the book is really about obeying and believing God. It is saturated with jewels of well-stated truth crafted by an excellent writer. Only the last chapter ("The Means") gives clear clues that Elliott holds to the traditional view. Even there the wisdom that fills the pages makes it a book that can be read with enrichment by all.

In her examples of discovering guidance, she does not often explain exactly why she knew a certain decision was the right one. This is not a case of mysticism being propounded as certain revelation. The examples give a sense of confidence that God will be our guide without emphasizing how the decision was made. When the method is evident, the approach differs little from obeying God's moral will and seeking wisdom to serve God in the best way possible.

In Elliot's view, supernatural means of guidance are not promised, but may be given whenever God sees the need. This includes visible signs, audible signs, angels, dreams/visions, prophets. She acknowledges the "possibility of miracles anywhere, anytime" (p. 85). She notes that when miracles were given they were not usually requested. She strikes a beautiful balance. "Supernatural phenomena were given at the discretion of the divine wisdom. It is not for us to ask that God will guide us in some miraculous way. If, in his wisdom, he knows that such means are what we need, he will surely give them" (p. 86).

What we are to expect from God are *natural* means of guidance. We are to do our duty and "Do the next thing" (p. 87). We should expect that God's guidance will come in God's timing. She emphasizes the helpful role of "human agents" in decision making (p. 95). This includes both dutiful submission to those in authority and receiving counsel from the wise. Our gifts and abilities help us to make good decisions. "What is in my hand? What is my function in the Body of Christ? Have I something to give? Can I see a place where it is needed now?" (p. 99). Desires can give us insight since God is working in our lives and "my real wants are becoming more like his."

In her comments in the final chapter, much of her insight harmonizes well with the wisdom view. She refers to 1 Corinthians 10:27 with its instruction to follow our desires when invited to a meal (p. 100). "Paul was writing to Christians, and he assumes that if they went, they went with God. It was nothing to pray and fast over" (p. 99). Circumstances are controlled by God, but they are not signs to read, but are to be evaluated by wisdom. "[W]e have to use our heads. I hope that in studying the divine principles we have not forgotten the importance of the human principle of common sense. The intelligence we have is a gift from God" (p. 104).

Further, she notes the connection between wisdom and circumstances. Jesus withdrew when He heard that John had been arrested (p. 105). He preached a sermon when He saw the crowds (p. 106). Concerning Abraham's servant she says, "No angel, no vision, no word was given. The man was doing his duty, using his head, keeping his eyes open, and trusting in the Lord" (p. 108). When making a difficult decision she was "forced to sit down again, weigh all the evidence, count the cost, note the risks, and take them all to God in prayer" (p. 111). However, Elliot seems to take one of the immature actions of the traditional view when two options seem morally equal. "Choose the harder of the two ways" (p. 115). This seems to go against Paul's wisdom to avoid unnecessary trouble (1 Corinthians 7:28).

It may sound paradoxical, but people from both views of guidance can read this book with equal benefit. Both will receive insights that will harmonize with their understanding of guidance. Elliot holds the traditional view, but does not emphasize its weak points. Rather her focus is strongly on God's moral will and wisdom.

The Mystery of God's Will:
What Does He Want for Me?
Charles Swindoll
(Nashville: Thomas Nelson, Inc., 1999)

This is a typical Swindoll book—wonderfully written, edifying, and full of practical wisdom and illustrations.

The emphasis in the book is on the "Mystery." The book is almost exclusively about God's sovereign will. The key to understanding sovereignty is that you cannot. It is a mystery held in the hands of a faithful

God. Swindoll divides the sovereign will into what God decrees and what He permits (p. 26). What He permits includes evil things, but He is sovereign over all.

Swindoll believes in the moral will of God. He says that the will of God in the Christian life is all contained in the Scriptures (1 Thessalonians 4:3; 5:16–18; 1 Peter 2:13–15) (pp 28–30). Much of the book focuses on trusting God, and so Swindoll draws excellent teaching from the Scriptures to increase our trust.

He also believes in the individual will of God espoused by the traditional view. How does God lead today? (1) Through His Word; (2) through the inner prompting of the Holy Spirit (Philippians 2:12–13; Jude 3; Proverbs 16:9; Psalm 32:8; "The inner prompting is crucial, because much of the time we just can't figure it out" [p. 48]); (3) through the counsel of wise, qualified, trustworthy people; (4) through an inner assurance of peace (Colossians 3:15). Later he repeats this theme: "God wants us to understand what His will is" (p. 103). And he repeats similar guidelines: openness, Bible investigation, clarification from the Holy Spirit ("an inner compulsion"), peace, and God's "surprises" (pp. 103–9).

The book follows the traditional view, but it only incidentally addresses the moral and individual will of God. Swindoll's main purpose is to explain the *mystery of God's sovereign will.* How can things go wrong when we obey? Why do bad things happen? Why are we constantly surprised at what God brings into our lives?

These questions cannot be fully explained, so Swindoll wisely urges us, "Run toward Him. And rather than looking for someone to blame for the pain that you're now enduring or the change that's on the horizon, look heavenward and realize that this arrangement is sovereignly put together for your good and for His glory" (p. 181). And what about our unanswered questions? "It's called God's inscrutable plan. I suggest it's time we stopped trying to unscrew it. Face it. It's beyond us. So? Deal with it. That's my advice, plain and simple" (p. 216).

Since Swindoll does not delineate the three ways he uses the term "God's will," the reader may well become confused. He defines God's sovereignty as His "decretive will," but does not use the term again. He normally just talks about "God's will." Yet the subject matter switches back and forth between God's sovereign will, moral will, and individual will. He uses the categories of the traditional view, but he mainly pursues a topic that is common to all views of guidance—God's unexplainable sovereignty.

While this book can be confusing, it is also very comforting. It addresses well our interaction with a God who can be trusted but never answers all our whys. Think of it as a primer on relating to a sovereign God when things go badly. From that perspective you will find a book filled with reality, hope, comfort, and no easy answers.

SYNTHESIS OF TRADITIONAL AND WISDOM VIEWS

HEARING GOD:
Developing a Conversational Relationship with God
Dallas Willard
(Downers Grove, IL: InterVarsity Press, 1999)
(Originally published as *In Search of Guidance*)

Those looking for a simple formula for finding the "will of God" will not find it in this book. It covers much wider turf as indicated in the subtitle: "Developing a Conversational Relationship with God." Willard is a good thinker who loves tangents. He is widely read. The author index contains a wonderful feast of quotes. I would love to invite him to be a member of our Eagle and Child Reading Group.

His view is hard to describe using conventional categories. His "conversational relationship" with God is at least mildly quietistic as he listens for the inner voice. (To be fair, it's a "thinking man's" quietism.) He offers dozens of pages on how to know when God is speaking through your own feelings, impressions, and thoughts. His perspectives contrast sharply with the point of view reflected in chapter 6 of this book, "Impressions Are Impressions." The most disquieting feature is his use of prophets and inspired writers as a model of how to recognize God's voice. "It is essential to the strength of our faith that we be in some measure capable of inwardly identifying with Samuel's experience as he conversed with the Lord" (p. 218). However, in contrast to Willard's description of the inner voice, Samuel's experience was of direct revelation that was so clear he thought Eli was audibly calling him (1 Samuel 3:4–5).

The premise of the "conversation with God" theme is that every friendship has clear, two-way communication. "All the guidance which we are going to receive from God, no matter what the external or internal accompaniments may be, will ultimately take the form of our own thoughts and perceptions. We must learn to find in them the voice of that God in whom we live and move and have our being" (p. 210). "In summary, then, what we learn when we learn to recognize God's voice in our heart is a certain *weight or force*, a certain *spirit*, and a certain *content*" (p. 209).

He quotes E. Stanley Jones. "The inner voice of God does not argue, does not try to convince you. It just speaks and it is self-authenticating. It has the feel of the voice of God within it" (p. 203). Willard adds, "The content or meaning of His specific and individualized communications to us always finally takes the form of the 'inner voice'" (p. 225).

He reminds us that there is "*no formula* for making decisions" (p. 200). In the process he criticizes F. B. Meyer's classic metaphor of the "three lights" that must line up: Bible, circumstances, inward impressions (p. 196). Checking one by the other will not work, and Willard even questions the reading of these signs. "For one does not know merely by looking at these 'doors' who is opening or closing them, God or Satan or human effort" (p. 199).

Throughout the book he quotes approvingly from proponents of the traditional view such as F. B. Meyer, E. Stanley Jones, Bob Mumford, and Andrew Murray. Then he takes a different tack from the typical traditional approach. He disagrees that we can know this individual will infallibly no matter how sincere we are (p. 226).

He further departs from the traditional view by saying that specific guidance will not be given for every decision. When none is given, guidance from Scripture will be enough. "[God] calls us to responsible citizenship in His kingdom by—in effect or reality—saying, as often as possible: MY WILL FOR YOU IS FOR YOU TO DECIDE ON YOUR OWN" (p. 233, emphasis his). We are to act as "God's mature children, friends and co-workers" (p. 234).

The traditional view says "wait on the Lord" until He reveals His individual will. Willard instead says that if one is afraid to go ahead, "So far from honoring God, such an attitude is blasphemous, idolatrous, and certain to prevent us from ever entering into that conversational relationship with God wherein sensible guidance is given as is appropriate and is clearly revealed and reliably understood" (p. 235).

Well, then, where does the "perfect will of God" come into this guidance? When God gives no further individual leading, "then whatever lies within His moral will and is undertaken in faith is *His perfect will*" (p. 236). Furthermore "Many different things, then, may each be His perfect will in a given circumstance" (p. 236). This changes the definition of "perfect will" as used by the traditional view into something most proponents would not recognize. How could there be more than one individual "perfect" will? "All are 'perfect' in His will because there is none better than the others and all are good" (p. 236). Willard uses the same key term as the traditional view ("perfect will"), but endows it with quite a different meaning.

It is in this context that he says that *Decision Making and the Will of God* "has done a masterful job of critiquing the view that God always has one particular thing for you to do in a given case, and that correct decision making depends upon your 'finding out' what that thing is" (p. 236). He concludes, "So the perfect will of God may allow, for a particular person, a number of different alternatives" (p. 237). I'm afraid that both the traditional view and the wisdom view will disagree. Both will contend that Willard has grafted together two concepts ("perfect will" and "different alternatives") that are mutually exclusive.

Willard seems to be trying to amalgamate the "freedom" of the wisdom view with the "perfect will" of the traditional view. Moreover, most traditionalists will find his explanations of how one hears God's voice to be more subjective than they are comfortable with.

This results in an interesting, mystical presentation of the traditional view with a concept of freedom attached. On a continuum I would place it halfway between the traditional and wisdom views. The viewpoint appears flawed by an internal contradiction, but the result is something much easier to live out than the traditional view's concept of one "perfect will" for each decision.

WISDOM VIEW IN TRADITIONAL VOCABULARY

FOUND: *God's Will*
John MacArthur
(Colorado Springs: Cook Communications Ministries, 1998)
(Originally published as: *God's Will Is Not Lost*)

In *Reckless Faith*, MacArthur summarizes the objective guidelines of God's will. It is God's will that: (1) we be saved (1 Timothy 2:3–4); (2) we be

Spirit filled (Ephesians 5:17–18); (3) we be sanctified (1 Thessalonians 4:3); (4) we be submissive (1 Peter 2:13–15); (5) we suffer (1 Peter 4:19; Philippians 1:29; 2 Timothy 3:12) (*Reckless Faith*, 190).

"If all those objective aspects of God's will are realities in your life, you needn't fret over the other decisions you must make. As long as the options you face do not involve issues directly forbidden or commanded in Scripture, you are free to do whatever you choose" (*Reckless Faith*, 190).

In this booklet he says the same thing. "If you are doing all five of the basic things…do whatever you want! If those five elements of God's will are operating in your life, who is running your wants? God is!" (*Found*, 31).

MacArthur supports this idea of freedom and doing what you want from Psalm 37:4, "Delight yourself in the LORD; and He will give you the desires of your heart." God will *put* the right desires in your heart when you are obeying the five objective guidelines of God's will. "God does not say He will fulfill all the desires that are there. He says He will put the desires there! If you are living a godly life, He will *give you* the right desires, *His* desires" (p. 31). But as I noted at the end of chapter 17, Psalm 37:4 is not claiming that God will put specific desires in our heart, but that God will give us what we desire—that is, will answer our prayers.

MacArthur says, "I reject modern revelatory prophecy because the New Testament canon is closed and Scripture is sufficient" (*Reckless Faith,* 181). He then refutes subjective impressions as a form of God's revelation. Included are arguments against Wayne Grudem's view of revelation as "something God brings to mind." (Those following Grudem do not equate their impressions with the authority of Scripture. But in what Grudem calls a new concept of prophecy, God is understood to be genuinely speaking through impressions at some level. MacArthur rejects this idea.)

MacArthur quotes and agrees with *Decision Making* on the issue of subjective impressions. They are not revelation and thus do not have authority to give us God's guidance. He concludes "Surely this is the true path of biblical wisdom" (*Reckless Faith,* 192).

MacArthur quotes from Jonathan Edwards against equating impressions and revelation. Delusions come by giving too much weight "on impulses and impressions, as if they were immediate revelations from God, to signify something future, or to direct them where to go, and what to do" (*Reckless Faith,* 187).

MacArthur seems to agree that there is an individual will of God in addition to His sovereign and moral wills. "Most of us acknowledge that God has a plan for the life of every believer" (p. 3). This plan includes individual decisions more detailed than Scripture. "Can you know what job to seek, what school to attend, what girl or guy to love, what decision to make in any given situation? YES" (p. 4). God communicates this in the Bible. "Therefore, I believe that what one needs to know about the will of God is clearly revealed in the pages of the Word of God" (p. 4).

These two statements about God's will seem to contradict each other: (1) God's will includes what school to attend and (2) all we need to know about God's will is communicated in the Bible. Yet MacArthur does not say the Bible will tell you what school to attend. These statements can be harmonized in MacArthur's presentation. The key is what "we need to know." MacArthur says that all you need to know is God's will in Scripture and do it. Then your desires will be in harmony with His. Thus, what you desire is by definition what He desires in specific decisions. With one verse (Psalm 37:4) he solves the knowledge problem of the traditional view. We don't need to search for or know God's individual will for certain before a decision. If you obey His revealed will (Scripture) you can do what you want and your desires will automatically lead you safely into His individual will.

This is not simply an adjustment to the traditional view, but it is really the wisdom view in disguise. MacArthur teaches everything that the wisdom view teaches. He disagrees at every major point with the traditional view. In theory he still holds to an individual will of God, but it is in name only. He teaches that you need to know and obey only the moral will of God. Then you are free to make the decision you desire. Wisdom is not excluded since it is part of being Spirit-filled. He then calls your decision God's specific will by definition.

MacArthur's presentation is short, so he does not cover all issues. If he did, it would be necessary to prove that Scripture uses the term "God's will" of an individual will for each believer. He would need to explain why Scripture uses the term "free" for decisions within the moral will of God. He would need to explain to the traditional view why we don't need to know God's individual will ahead of time. He would need to address the Scripture passages put forward by the traditional view in support of the individual will.

For some who are comforted by the concept of God's individual will, this presentation may be easier to swallow than *Decision Making*. If they follow MacArthur's paradigm, they will make godly, wise, and free decisions and call the result "finding God's individual will." The better term for such decisions would be godly, wise, and free decisions, but the end result will be practically the same.

"Thou Our Guide"
J. I. Packer
Chapter 20 in *Knowing God*
(Downers Grove, IL: InterVarsity Press, 1973)

Like most evangelical Christians, I highly respect J. I. Packer. So naturally I was interested in his view of God's guidance. This chapter from his classic work, *Knowing God*, was published in 1973, several years before *Decision Making* was released. Not having the specific issues of the traditional and wisdom views in mind, his vocabulary does not always match the categories that have emerged in the current discussion. At points he seems to hold the traditional view and at others the wisdom view.

He discusses the question, "Has God a plan for individuals?" (p. 210). "Indeed, He has." In his explanation he cites references that clearly refer to God's sovereign will (Ephesians 3:11; 1:10–11). Specific examples include God's plan for Jesus whose "whole business" was to do His Father's will (John 4:34; 6:38), and for Paul whose apostleship was "by the will of God" (Acts 21:14; 22:14; 26:16–19; 1 Timothy 1:16).

When he demonstrates God's ability to communicate His will, Packer refers to instances of direct revelation with the qualification that these must be "judged exceptional and not normal" (p. 210). He thinks that for many Christians, "their basic mistake is to think of guidance as essentially *inward prompting by the Holy Spirit, apart from the written Word*" (p. 212). But in vocational decisions, where the Bible will not make the final decision, he observes: "the factor of God-given prompting and inclination, whereby one is drawn to commit oneself to one set of responsibilities rather than another, and finds one's mind settled in peace as one contemplates them, becomes decisive" (p. 213). This last comment could be claimed by either the traditional or wisdom camp.

Packer contends that God's primary means of guidance is Scripture. "The fundamental mode whereby our rational Creator guides His rational creatures is by rational understanding and application of His written Word" (p. 214). He then emphasizes believers thinking, planning ahead, accepting wise advice, and examining one's heart to avoid selfish motives.

He quotes a wisdom view author, Oliver Barclay, with approval. His strongest comment that supports the wisdom view is: "We need to ask ourselves why we 'feel' a particular course to be right, and make ourselves give reasons—and we shall be wise to lay the case before someone else whose judgment we trust, to give his verdict on our reasons" (p. 216).

In this chapter, Packer does not neatly line up with one camp or the other. But with his emphasis on the application of wisdom and giving reasons for one's decisions, the reader who follows his advice will likely avoid the pitfalls that often attend the traditional view.

Knowing God's Will: *Finding Guidance for Personal Decisions* (Revised and Expanded)

M. Blaine Smith

(Downers Grove, IL: InterVarsity Press, 1991)

Discipleship Journal contacted me about doing a point-counterpoint article on God's will. My counterpoint author was to be M. Blaine Smith of Nehemiah Ministries. I immediately read his book *Should I Get Married?* and the new edition of his *Knowing God's Will.* The latter book contains an appendix titled: "Does God Have a Will for Our Personal Decisions? (With Reflections on Garry Friesen's *Decision Making and the Will of God*)."

I enjoyed reading Smith's books. I like his thinking and his writing style. When we conversed over the phone, I instinctively liked the author himself. After reading his books, I wrote my article, but the journal editors did not like it. I was supposed to be "counterpoint" and I was agreeing with Smith's position. I had come to the conclusion that we held practically identical views though we were using different terminology. Smith did not think so, but it sure looks that way to me.

Some critics of *Decision Making* have said, "It is just semantics. The traditional view looks for the perfect will of God and you look for the wisest decision." But there really are substantial differences between the views. The fact that *Decision Making* stirred up such controversy testifies to the reality of the differences. But with Smith's book—well, I am ready to make an exception.

At first there appears to be a great difference. He argues for the "individual will" in God's guidance, and I argue long and hard against the concept. Smith accepts this foundational concept of the traditional view, but looks for this individual will *just as if he were seeking a wise decision.* Every time Smith says "individual will" you could pencil in "godly, wise decision" and our two books would be nearly identical.

For example, he writes, "First, we should study Scripture.... Then we have a responsibility to use our reason to make a logical choice about God's will, as opposed to looking for supernatural indications or purely intuitive impressions of his guidance" (p. 103). "Human reason was the channel through which God's will was normally known. In most cases discerning his will boiled down to a matter of making a sound, logical choice" (p. 115). "For Paul, discerning God's will was mainly a matter of making sound, logical judgments, in light of what course appeared most glorifying to God" (p. 123).

We should make clear that the differences between Smith's conclusions and those of the traditional view are substantial.

1. The key to the traditional view is knowing God's individual will. They say that God has promised to make it 100 percent clear, and you must discern it to know what God wants you to do. In contrast, Smith says that it is the believer's responsibility to take the initiative. Furthermore, he says that you can proceed even when you are confused about what to do. If you are obeying His Word and seeking wisdom, you can trust God to automatically bring you to His individual will. "Where we lack understanding, he'll so arrange our circumstances that we still end up doing what he desires. He's simply too big to allow our lack of understanding to keep him from leading us in the path of his will" (p. 60).

Smith has solved the knowledge problem of the traditional view by saying that you don't have to know the will of God before a decision. With his solution he has jettisoned the traditional view and in practice is following the way of wisdom.

In all the small decisions, Smith commends praying at the start of the day for God to guide you. "Then go ahead and apply yourself to the day's decisions in the faith and confidence that God is answering your prayer." Through prayer we have "confidence that our decision process is being guided by him and that what we decide reflects his will" (p. 75).

2. The traditional view usually regards personal desires with suspicion and warns against being unduly influenced by them as one seeks to know God's individual will. Smith says, "Remember that Christ is even more concerned that you understand and respond to the desires he has put within you than you are" (p. 182). Other immature practices of the traditional view are also set aside by Smith with humor, wisdom, and grace.

3. The traditional view understands inward impressions of the heart as the voice of the Holy Spirit. Smith says that they can never be equated. Impressions often reflect your personal feelings, needs, and wisdom, but they don't equal the voice of God.

Smith got to his view by good exegesis of the key passages and by large amounts of personal wisdom. I not only agree with his discussions of inward impressions and "putting out a fleece," but I often found them to be more insightful and better explained than my own.

4. The traditional view interprets circumstances as a sign from God pointing to His perfect will. Smith rejects even highly coincidental circumstances as signs from God. Circumstances should be judged by wisdom as to the effect they will have on the decision at hand.

If Smith does not hold the traditional view, what does he hold? As earlier stated, Smith believes in the "individual will" of God, but goes about seeking it exactly as you would seek to make a wise decision. He seems to equate the two. Regarding the prayer for wisdom in James 1:5, he writes: "In the New Testament the most explicit command to pray for a knowledge of God's will is given in James 1:5–6." God's will is not mentioned here, but the prayer for wisdom is. Smith has in practice equated the two.

His second appendix specifically critiques *Decision Making*. In it he raises some interesting questions about God's individual will and wisdom. He suggests that *Decision Making* has overlooked the implications of spiritual gifts as an indicator of each believer's individual distinctiveness. I discussed spiritual gifts under the moral will of God since we are commanded to use our gifts. When this command is obeyed by each Christian, its expression will be very specific and individual. The beauty of God's moral will and of wisdom is that they guide each individual in their particular situation. The command to obey one's father and mother is a general command, but in practice, that obedience will be given to a specific father and mother with their specific directives. The command to be wise or modest is very general. In application, however, it will be very specific and very different for each individual. None of this demands an individual will of God; it only requires an individual response to the moral will of God and wisdom.

Smith believes that to jettison the concept of God's individual will leads to a loss of confidence in God's personal care. In *Decision Making* I argue that God's care is individual and detailed. But it is not an expression of His individual will, but rather of His sovereign will. We have the direct assurance that "God causes all things to work together for good to those who love God, to those who are called according to His purpose" (Romans 8:28). But that does not require an individual will that the Christian must discover in order to please God. It requires a loving Father sovereignly working out His purposes in the life of each individual believer (Matthew 6:25–34).

Smith also argues that the concept of wisdom itself is evidence of the existence of an individual will. He reasons that if God applied wisdom to a decision, would He not come to the wisest choice? If He did, would He not prefer it? Would He not want to reveal this best choice to the believer? Smith concludes that this choice is the same as the individual will of God. He has a good argument. In *Decision Making* I acknowledge that it is reasonable that God *could* guide by creating and revealing an individual will. But reason does not require an individual will. And the clincher, for me, is that Scripture doesn't teach the individual will of God for each decision. What it does teach is the second principle in *Decision Making*: Where there is no command the believer is free to choose. And this is what is missing from Smith's treatment of the will of God. He does not discuss the passages, such as Genesis 2:16, that plainly teach freedom within the moral will of God: "Of every tree of the garden you may freely eat." There are many passages in which this freedom is explicitly taught. What does this freedom mean if God has one individual will for each decision? To say you are free when the believer must always find the one decision required by God's individual will is a contradiction in terms.

Smith should also explain why the apostles described their decisions in terms of wisdom if they really meant they had found God's individual will (1 Thessalonians 3:1). Why would Paul write a chapter on the decision of marriage and not mention God's individual will? (1 Corinthians 7).

Really, the only point of disagreement between *Knowing God's Will* and *Decision Making* is the concept of God's individual will. This sounds significant, but in Smith's presentation it makes little difference. If you apply Scripture and wisdom to every decision, you will practice sound decision making. Smith will call the final decision God's individual will, and I will call it making a godly, wise decision. I believe the latter terminology is more biblically accurate, but the end result under either method will be a godly, wise decision.

Despite its traditional terminology, I am convinced that *Knowing God's Will* does not teach the traditional view. I recommend it as a practical expression of the wisdom view. So if you believe in the wisdom view but don't want to drop the traditional terminology, this may be the book for you.

Finding the Will of God:
A Pagan Notion?
Bruce Waltke
(Grand Rapids, MI: Wm. B. Eerdmans Publishing Co., 2002)

The title of Bruce Waltke's book makes it look like the traditional approach—*Finding the Will of God.* The subtitle, however, reverses that impression—*A Pagan Notion?* Waltke concludes that seeking to find God's will for a decision is a form of unbiblical, pagan divination.

Waltke uses *divination* as a neutral term meaning to seek the will of a supernatural being. Thus there is bad divination (pagan practices) and good divination. In the Old Testament, good divination includes prophets, Urim and Thummim, sacred lots, dreams, signs, and direct words from God. He concludes that none of these avenues to God's will is appropriate for today. "The common idea of divining God's will is either a pagan notion that we Christians need to let go of or a mode of administration that God no longer uses."

Waltke's view of guidance is summarized in six principles.

1. Follow the Word of God.
2. Follow your heartfelt godly desires.
3. Listen to wise counsel.
4. Take circumstances into consideration.
5. God expects us to use our good judgment.
6. God does not normally intervene with direct revelation.

These principles could be interpreted either in the traditional fashion or, more likely, the way of wisdom. Waltke's book clearly comes much closer to the thesis of *Decision Making* than to the traditional view. He agrees with the traditional view that there is a will of God for guidance that is different than His sovereign will and more specific than God's moral will. He differs by saying that we should not try to find it or use divination.

Waltke gives four definitions for God's will: (1) "God's plan and decrees" (which I have called God's sovereign will); (2) God's "desire or consent" (which I have called God's moral will); (3) God's "general providence" (which I have included as the outworking of God's sovereign will); and (4) God's "specific choices in perplexing situations" (pp 8–10), which seems to fall into the category of the individual will of the traditional view—that is, God's perfect will or the center of God's will.

A quick look at his six principles shows an emphasis on wisdom in "wise counsel" and "sound judgment." While Haddon Robinson (see below) recognizes a concept of "freedom," Waltke seems to assume that there is one right decision for each situation. So in that sense he seeks an individual will in each decision, but disagrees with the traditional view on how it is to be found.

His second principle says to follow heartfelt, godly desires. I argued that personal desires should be viewed as an aspect of wisdom. What we desire to do is often a reflection of our gifts and talents, our temperament and our circumstances. Vocational counselors say that the one best question to ask someone choosing a vocation is, "What would you like to do?" Waltke, however, gives desires a more important role than simply being a source of wisdom.

His argument is this: God has desires for our life decisions. As we grow closer to God our personal desires become more and more like His desires. As we gain intimacy with Him, our desires will ultimately become exactly like His. At that point, the believer only needs to ask, "What do I desire to do?" and the answer will be God's will for him. This view could be paraphrased as "Love God, and whatever you please will be God's individual will for your life." Psalm 37:4 is used as a foundation for the concept: "Delight yourself in the LORD; and He will give you the desires of your heart."

As I stated at the end of chapter 17, I think this view of desires will work very well in heaven. But for now, we must examine and filter desires to be sure they are godly. They will never be perfectly righteous until we are with God. What about desires that are in harmony with Scripture, but not with sound judgment? A desire to sing solos for God without the ability is not ungodly, but it is unwise. So we should evaluate our desires in the light of Scripture and wisdom. If a desire does not harmonize with Scripture or wisdom, it should be ignored—not viewed as a new source of truth.

It is better to say that our desires are never perfectly godly or wise, but they do often reflect wisdom about ourselves, which is very helpful in making a godly, wise decision. The more godly and wise a person is, the more his desires will reflect godliness and wisdom. Waltke's view is an improvement on the view that says, "Empty yourself of all desires before you seek God's will." But elevating personal desires to a place where they equal God's individual will is probably going too far.

In practice, Waltke's view is a great improvement over the standard traditional view. It emphasizes wisdom in areas where the Scripture does not determine our specific choices. However, it still seems to be looking for "God's will"—but trying to get there through the back door. In essence, it says, if you do the right things you will be in God's will without officially looking for it. This approach uses the categories of the traditional view, but in practice it will usually act like the wisdom view.

WISDOM VIEW

ROMANS: *An Expositional Commentary*
VOLUME 2: *The Reign of Grace (Romans 5–8)*
James Montgomery Boice
(Grand Rapids, MI: Baker Book House, 1992)

When James Montgomery Boice gets to Romans 8:27 in his four-volume commentary on Romans, he makes some generous remarks about *Decision Making.*

> My own evaluation of this book is that it is extremely helpful and is a significant breakthrough in cutting away many of the

> hang-ups on this subject that have nearly incapacitated some Christians. Its exposure of the weakness of subjective methods of determining guidance is astute. Its stress on the sufficiency of Scripture in all moral matters is essential. Its proposal of a 'way of wisdom' in (most) decision-making matters is liberating. My only reservation is that it does not seem to deal adequately with special (and therefore also very important) situations (p. 895).

Boice then discusses Romans 8:27, which reads: "And he who searches our hearts knows the mind of the Spirit, because the Spirit intercedes for the saints in accordance with God's will" (NIV). Boice equates "God's will" in verse 27 with the "purpose" of God in Romans 8:28 ("called according to His purpose"). The sovereign will of God overlaps His moral will as God is sovereign over the process that is conforming us to "the likeness of His Son."

According to Boice, the Spirit is praying for us concerning God's sovereign will. It will come to pass since "God has decreed it and because the Holy Spirit is praying for us in this area" (p. 896). By way of personal example, Boice includes his "call to the ministry" when God gave him a specific sign to confirm this vocation. He did not regard the sign as special revelation and he did not give it revelatory authority. But he did follow it and received additional confirmation (p. 897).

The sovereign will of God is detailed. Boice concludes, "There is a perfect will of God for all people and all events, and therefore there is also a perfect will of God for each individual believer" (p. 897). He does not think that *Decision Making* denies this (and he is correct). I tried to use the term "individual will" only as the traditional view used it—to specify a plan that must be discovered in advance. That sense of an individual will I contested as unbiblical. However, God's sovereign will is detailed and thus applies to each person individually.

God's sovereign will thus includes a perfect plan for each individual. This cannot be found nor do we need to try. The Spirit is praying for each of us that God's sovereign will be realized perfectly as it will.

Finally, Boice does not deny that God may give His will by special revelation, but says this is not normative guidance, a view that is in harmony with *Decision Making*.

Discovering God's Will
Sinclair B. Ferguson
(Carlisle, PA: Banner of Truth, 1982)

This book exudes reformed theology, so you get Scripture, Scripture, Scripture, and a little Westminster Confession thrown in. Actually, the title is surprising since Ferguson does not think the will of God is hidden. So "discovering" does not mean what you would expect in most books on God's will.

Most readers who come at this book from the framework of the traditional view will think the author never answers the question of how to discover God's will. He raises hopes by using the traditional terms of "perfect will" (p. 25), and "centre of God's will" (p. 85). But his meaning is different from what some readers expect. He assumes that God desires one thing in each decision, but he does not define this or show it from Scripture. Ferguson argues that when the Scriptures are correctly applied to individual situations, the end result is living in God's will.

Ferguson says the will of God is found by (1) direct commands of Scripture, (2) principles of Scripture, and (3) illustrations in Scripture. "We find that there are choices to make; we find that now we have to apply God's word to our situation. *The chief need we have, therefore, is that of increased familiarity with and sensitivity to the wisdom of his word*" (p. 31). He says, "We need supernatural help...to understand and apply our only rule of life, our only source of the knowledge of God and his will—the Holy Scriptures" (p. 32). He thinks that even subconscious thoughts show the work of the application of Scripture (p. 33).

Thus, he encourages listing the "pros and cons of the situation" (p. 36). He discusses the "subjective element in coming to know God's will" (p. 39). Here he means a sensitive, humble, submissive heart to receive the Scriptures and make personal application. From Ephesians (5:5ff.) he concludes, "To live in the will of God is to walk in love, to walk in light and to walk in wisdom" (p. 54). This is clearly equivalent to what I have called the moral will of God.

He asks, "What is the will of God in this particular, unique situation in which I find myself?" (p. 64). He turns again to scriptural principle and asks a series of questions: (1) Is it lawful? (2) Is it beneficial (that is, edifying) to me? (3) Is it enslaving? (4) Is it consistent with Christ's Lordship? (5) Is it helpful to others? and (6) Is it consistent with biblical example? (pp. 64–74).

All of these questions fall either under the moral will of God or the moral imperative of being wise. At the end of his list, he concludes, "Here again we are driven back to our great principle: we discover the will of God by a sensitive application of Scripture to our own lives" (p. 72).

I can almost hear the traditional view reader saying, "Yes of course, but you must go further and answer the question of finding God's perfect will." For Ferguson, God's Word is His perfect will. Ferguson never does answer the question, "What do I do if I have applied Scripture to my personal situation and I still have more than one good option?" He holds the wisdom view, but has not taken it to its natural conclusion. His answer seems to be "wait on the Lord" and you will eventually find the one right choice.

This book propounds the wisdom view in slightly defective form. It won't cause a stir because it does not clearly distinguish itself from the traditional view. Ferguson uses the approach of the older writers before the traditional view made its entry into the evangelical mainstream in the late 1800s. Unless the reader realizes that the book is not propagating the traditional view, he or she will think, "Sure, the Bible contains the will of God, but I'm looking for the perfect individual will. I guess I'll have to find another book that deals with that." Nothing could be more practical than application of the Scripture to every situation, but many readers may not realize that this is the message of his book.

The Call:
Finding and Fulfilling the Central Purpose of Your Life
Os Guinness
(Nashville: W Publishing Group, 2003)

From the title, one might expect that Guinness's book is an exposition of the traditional view. For "the call" is the term used by the traditional view to describe God's individual will for the life work of each person. But Guinness does not hold the traditional view. For him, "the call" is the very bedrock of Christian life and commitment. It is almost equated with the moral will of God.

He defines calling as "the truth that God calls us to himself so decisively that everything we are, everything we do, and everything we have is invested with special devotion and dynamism lived out as a response to his summons and service" (p. 4).

The call is primarily to Jesus Himself. Jesus expresses the call by His commands, and He bids us come and die with Him. God initiates this call and seeks us. We are, in the title of chapter 2, "Seekers Sought." "Responding to the call means rising to the challenge, but in conversation and in partnership—and in an intimate relationship between the called and the Caller" (p. 24).

It is possible to read the traditional view into this book (p. 46), but Guinness's understanding of the individual nature of the call is different from that of the traditional view. He emphasizes that God individually presents His call to us. We must individually use the spiritual gifts and the endowed abilities given to us in the place where God has sovereignly placed us to His glory. All areas of the world are God's domain, and He utilizes John Newton's preaching as much as William Wilberforce's politicking (p. 29).

While our primary calling is to Christ Himself, "our secondary calling, considering who God is as sovereign, is that everyone, everywhere, and in everything should think, speak, live and act entirely for him" (p. 31). Guinness goes on to quote Oswald Chambers: "The one aim of the call of God is the satisfaction of God, not a call to do something for Him" (p. 42).

God can give a "special calling," which refers to "those tasks and missions laid on individuals through a direct, specific, supernatural communication from God" (p. 49). But this special call is not given to everyone. So Guinness disputes the traditional view's contention that everyone receives a special call to a particular vocation or to certain tasks. This understanding wrongly makes everyone a "prophet" by calling (p. 50).

What everybody does have is the call to follow Jesus. From the parables we learn "our responsibility to exercise a high degree of 'capitalistic-style' enterprise about how we live our lives" (p. 50). That sounds a lot like freedom and responsibility.

The most inspiring portions of the book are the wisdom and life stories. These accounts display the breadth and depth of Guinness's understanding of art and history. Through his narratives we meet Solzhenitsyn, Michelangelo, William Perkins, Dostoyevsky, Walker Percy, Kierkegaard, Lawrence of Arabia, Alexis de Tocqueville, Leonardo da Vinci, Simone Weil, Malcolm Muggeridge, Augustine, C. S. Lewis, G. K. Chesterton, Václav Havel, Bonhoeffer, Nietzsche, Wilberforce, Thomas Aquinas, Luther, Abraham Kuyper, Calvin, Oswald Chambers, saxophonist John Coltrane, Gerard Manley Hopkins, Puritan John Cotton, King Xerxes, Francis of Assisi, Churchill, and so on. When you finish reading *The Call*, you want to go find books about a dozen other people who illustrated his points.

Guinness insightfully and incisively applies the moral will of God's call into every area of life. With Kuyper he tells us that God says of every person, moment, and thing, "This is Mine." His kingdom principles are to be applied to every nook of society. Our time, money, devotion, hearts, energy, gifts, ability are for Him. "Do you long to know the overriding passion and purity of heart of willing one thing? Listen to Jesus of Nazareth; answer his call" (p. 181). Each chapter concludes with a similar challenge that summarizes the content of the chapter. But the ending is always the same—"Listen to Jesus of Nazareth; answer his call."

Since this book uses the older and more biblical sense of the word *call*, it harmonizes well with *Decision Making*. It is a book that urges us to obey Christ and His commands as the key to a fulfilled and meaningful life. This book is a primer on obeying the moral will of God by obeying the One whose will it is that gives the only purpose worth living for.

Step by Step:
Divine Guidance for Ordinary Christians
James C. Petty
(Phillipsburg, NJ: P&R Publishing, 1999)

If you are going to read just one other book on guidance, this is the book. (Dan Turner and the rest of the pastoral staff at Clear Creek Chapel, Springboro, Ohio, told me this might be a better presentation of the way of wisdom than *Decision Making!*)

Petty presents three models of guidance: traditional view, charismatic view, and the wisdom view. He deals briefly with the first two and finds them unbiblical. Those who find it fairly easy to jettison the traditional view will appreciate the relative brevity of Petty's critique. Others may need a more thorough refutation to loosen their grip on the traditional view.

I have a quibble about a detail of Petty's introduction to part 2:

"Understanding Guidance." Petty tells the story of Rick, a graphic designer wrestling with decisions about the future of his career. As he reflects on how he got to where he is now, Rick becomes disturbed by the thought that he might have veered from God's will during college. Maybe he got stuck in Plan B—a "disobedient" plan from which there was no escape. Petty says that "one of Rick's major problems is confusing two very different uses of the term 'the will of God' in the Bible"—"the *plan* of God" and "the *commandments* of God" (p. 56). Here's my quibble: Rick's problem is not confusion between the two biblical uses of the term 'will of God,' but rather his belief in a third use that is not biblical—the so-called individual will of God. Even when they understand that the sovereign will ("plan") of God cannot be missed or learned in advance, believers like Rick still worry about the ramifications of being disobedient to what God wants them to do (the individual will of God). They still focus their energies on trying to discern that guidance for future decisions. Later in the book Petty clarifies that Rick's dilemma is caused by his misguided search for "the individual will of God" (p. 98).

Apart from that, I find little else to critique in this book. Petty's discussion of God's sovereign will is insightful and exegetically satisfying. He gives all believers confidence that God is guiding with the "left hand" of providence (pp. 55–78, 169–76) and working all things together for good. This is wonderful material no matter what your viewpoint.

Petty traces God's activity of guidance through biblical history, using examples of special guidance from both testaments to demonstrate that God guides specifically and personally. The methodology of God's leading has changed in the church age, and believers are not to expect direct revelation. But God is still our guide. Impressions are not revelation, but are "works of God's providence" to help judge the current situation (p. 90). "God's guidance helps us to discern the best and right among choices that qualify as lawful" (p. 92).

Petty quotes *Decision Making* on whether there is an individual will of God (p. 97) and praises its "good analysis" of passages that have been used to support the traditional view (p. 99). He argues against hybrid versions that retain an individual will but try to avoid the implications of it (Smith, Geiser are examples, p. 100). "What is often called the 'individual will of God' should be seen simply as the application of God's commands and character to the specifics of our lives. It is not a separate and distinct (nonmoral) sense of God's will" (p. 101). "Guidance is discerning God's moral and spiritual preferences as they apply to our life situations. It is not a detailed plan to be discovered or communicated by God in extra-scriptural communications" (p. 101).

Petty sees a weakness in one aspect of the presentation in *Decision Making*. He divides the moral will of God into two distinct circles: (1) prohibitions that are constant and absolute, and (2) positive commands for which we must establish priorities so we know which command to obey in what order (p. 104). It is in the area of positive commands that he thinks *Decision Making* falls short.

> This second circle of God's moral will covers areas just as critical to our moral and spiritual well-being as the inner circle of God's prohibitions. Garry Friesen sees this area as governed by the principle of 'spiritual expediency,' not morality (Friesen 1980, 151–281). Friesen has made an enormous contribution in exposing the unbiblical concept of the 'individual will of God.' However, while heading in the right direction, the term 'spiritual expediency' needs to be greatly strengthened. In my view, this second circle is where believers work out all the positive commands of Scripture. There is more than 'spiritual expediency' at stake here: the very heart of moral integrity is involved (p. 105).

By way of clarification, I did not say "spiritual expediency" was the key to the positive commands of Scripture. Rather, wisdom (spiritual expediency) is the key in the *area of freedom*. All commands are to be obeyed—including the command to be wise in how we keep them. Setting priorities is a good application of wisdom! So I think we're in agreement there.

I agree that there is a problem with the term *expediency*. I intended that the word be taken in the sense of "advantageous," "suitable," or "beneficial." But too many readers were troubled by negative connotations indicating that the advantage in view was motivated by self-interest. From that angle, expediency would promote doing whatever you want. That, of course, is the opposite of what I wanted to say. So in this edition, I dropped the use of *expediency*. Petty equates the term with that which is "spiritually neutral and pragmatically controlled" (p. 106). My intention was to describe the moral will of God and its command that we must be wise.

The proof of our agreement comes when Petty gives practical application of his concepts. His explanations about giving (p. 105), spiritual gifting (p. 106), use of time (p. 110), and marriage cause me to say, "Amen—that's just what I said/meant in *Decision Making*." He explains Romans 14 and 1 Corinthians 8–9 and the only difference that I can see is that he took three pages and I took two chapters. (My mother would prefer Petty's brevity.) I agree with him that wisdom is not neutral. It is commanded—a moral, spiritual issue. We must not only obey the positive commands, but do them with wisdom.

Petty says, "I believe that guidance comes when you learn to apply the Word of God to your life in the wisdom provided by the Holy Spirit" (p. 11). "Guidance is given by God when he gives us insight into issues and choices so that we make the decisions with divinely inspired wisdom. Guidance comes, in short, by God making us wise." (p. 33). "He chooses to guide mediately because of the illuminating power of that Spirit" (p. 34). Amen.

"God, I believe, does far more than reveal his general purposes and then leave us to link ourselves to them or pragmatically calculate the most edifying outcomes" (p. 41). "The Bible, properly understood and applied by the Holy Spirit, is completely sufficient for the guidance of the believer" (p. 90). "Knowing God's will is the fruit of a transformed mind" (pp. 48–49). "Guidance is knowledge of the will of God, which comes by wisdom and understanding" (p. 138). Amen.

I am certain that we are saying the same thing. Petty, however, emphasizes how God, by giving wisdom, helps us to make specific decisions in our specific circumstances. He emphasizes how the order and priority of obeying God's moral will is important—yes, that is wisdom. In part 4 Petty does an excellent job of showing how the Spirit helps us to work through seven elements of decision making and apply wisdom (pp. 189–216). His presentation shows effectively how the way of wisdom is personal and helps us with specific decisions.

Petty's pastor's heart has helped him to express many of the issues in a very helpful, fresh way. I highly recommend this book. Petty's slightly different approach to describing the way of wisdom may help some readers grasp the concepts better.

Decision Making by the Book
Haddon Robinson
(Grand Rapids, MI: Discovery House, reprint edition, 1998)

I was not surprised to find that I resonated with this book. After all, I had earlier asked this articulate speaker to write the foreword to the first edition of *Decision Making and the Will of God.* In his own book Robinson argues for God's sovereign and moral wills and against the traditional view's individual will of God. His title shows the same emphasis on God's Word as the key to decision making. Along the way he gives a slightly different emphasis, which is helpful. His decision-making principles are:

1. Make decisions in submission to God's sovereign will.
2. Make decisions in submission to God's moral will.
3. Make love and concern for the good of others the motive.
4. Focus on your strengths and gifts.
5. Consider circumstances, but don't be mastered by them.
6. We must base our decisions on wise counsel.

His first principle is equal to my fourth principle: When you have done what is moral and wise, trust the sovereign God to work the details together for good.

His second and third principles correspond to my first principle: Where God commands, we obey; that is the moral will of God. It can be summarized by the command to love God and others. Emphasizing love is a helpful focus because anyone following the moral will of God and wisdom will profit from asking, "In this situation, how can I best show others love?" That question is an embodiment of doing what is moral and wise.

His last three principles are included in my third principle: In the area of freedom, the believer must be wise. Wisdom builds on personal strengths/gifts, considers circumstances, and seeks wise counsel. Robinson contributes additional wisdom ideas: (1) Avoid making a decision in a mood; (2) separate facts from problems; (3) pursue your choice; (4) set a time limit on making the decision.

Robinson, thus, specifically states three of my four principles in his own way. The one he doesn't include is my second one on freedom: Where there is no command, God gives freedom (and responsibility) to choose. Nevertheless, this principle is expounded in chapter 3, "The Freedom to Decide." He uses similar scriptural proofs for this concept and concludes, "If we make our decisions within the boundaries of God's sovereign and moral will, we have a great deal of freedom" (p. 53). It may have been prudent for Robinson to put less emphasis on freedom because it is hard to describe that freedom without someone saying, "Oh, you mean God doesn't care what we decide," or "Oh, you mean God doesn't really guide us."

Robinson echoes Bruce Waltke when he argues that inward impressions do not equal the voice of the Spirit. "When we lift our inner impressions to the level of divine revelation, we are flirting with divination" (p. 18). "Informed hunches may be helpful, but it is close to blasphemy to raise inner impressions to the level of God's special revelation" (p. 135).

His discussion of circumstances matches *Decision Making* precisely and offers fresh illustrations. In particular he draws on three scenes from Paul's life when he faced opposition: assassins in Damascus (Acts 9), Roman prison in Philippi (Acts 16), assassins in Greece (Acts 20:1–3). "Once he fled. Once he stayed. Once he avoided the problem" (p. 112). Robinson rightly concludes that circumstances should be considered to identify the parameters of a decision, but not viewed as a secret message from God. "You cannot know, or even confirm, God's will by trying to decipher circumstances" (p. 107).

This book is written in a speaking style with many excellent illustrations and general discussions of the key passages. I recommend the book, and I know my mother would have appreciated its shorter length.

AFTERWORD
A NOTE TO FUTURE AUTHORS ON GOD'S WILL

I am no prophet, but I am reasonably certain that *Decision Making and the Will of God* will not be the last book published on this subject. I also do not expect to persuade everyone else to adopt the way of wisdom.

That said, my survey of books written over the past two decades has clarified key questions that should be addressed by future authors on the subject of knowing God's will. *Decision Making* has challenged the conventional thinking at several points. Those who intend to make a serious contribution to the discussion will need to offer well-crafted positions on the following issues.

1. What is our authority? Is it Scripture or is it our experience (or, more precisely, our interpretation of our experience)? Those who hold the traditional view need to make a case for the individual will of God on the basis of the passages analyzed in context. *Decision Making* argues that every single applicable text is better explained as either God's moral will or God's sovereign will. If this challenge to the existence of the individual will of God is to be answered, it must be done with credible exegesis. Most proponents of the traditional view simply assume the individual will of God. And some proponents of the wisdom view are still using a borrowed vocabulary that is confusing. Either prove it from Scripture, or discard it as unnecessary.

2. In particular, advocates of the traditional view need to account for the plethora of "freedom" passages in the Bible. If there is an individual will that must be discovered in advance for each decision, what can the biblical statement "do as you wish" possibly mean? And traditionalists must account for the fact that *most* of the decisions the apostles made were choices freely made by the application of wisdom; and that *all* of the apostolic instruction on decision making advocates freely made choices on the basis of wisdom. Of less importance, perhaps, but worth attention is the complete absence of any of the distinctive vocabulary of the traditional view in decision-making contexts.

3. Those who insist on linking biblical illustrations of divine revelation and the "speaking" of the Holy Spirit through inner impressions must come to terms with the confusion of categories. If there is some hermeneutical principle by which these two can be equated, it needs to

be established. Is there any passage that clearly indicates that God communicates directions for believers in noncommanded decisions by means of an inner impression? I haven't found one. Most of the argument for inner impressions as authoritative guidance is by analogy to incidents of special revelation. But they differ in the means of communication, the means of confirmation, the clarity of the message, and the certainty on the part of the hearer. The argument from analogy is proving apples by means of oranges and calling it fruit. But I don't think it's valid. If it is, somebody needs to make a cogent case for it.

4. Finally, some seem to want a hybrid of the two views. They want to say that while most noncommanded decisions fall in the area of freedom, there are some (especially important) decisions where God's guidance into the so-called individual will (e.g. His leading into a specific choice of a marriage partner) needs to be sought. This position is simply a variation on #3 above. Maybe it is true, but if it is, it must be demonstrated by legitimate exegetical proof that doesn't superimpose examples of revelation onto general statements about God's will or God's leading.

Of course no one is obligated to adopt this agenda for interaction. But if we are going to genuinely help men and women who sincerely want to make decisions that are pleasing to God, the readers of our books deserve our best effort to bring forward the clearest arguments for the positions presented. May God, our Guide, be honored by the integrity and tenor of our inquiry into His truth.

---

1. For reviews of further books see http://www.gfriesen.net. Books reviewed include: Oliver R. Barclay, *Guidance: What the Bible Says About Knowing God's Will*; J. Grant Howard, *Knowing God's Will and Doing It!*; Robert Jeffress, *Hearing the Master's Voice*; Ron Kincaid, *Praying for Guidance: How to Discover God's Will*; Gary Maeder, *God's Will for Your Life*; Lloyd John Ogilvie, *God's Will in Your Life*; Gerald Sittser, *The Will of God As a Way of Life*; R. C. Sproul, *God's Will and the Christian*; Knofel Staton, *How to Know the Will of God*; George Sweeting, *How to Discover the Will of God*; Philip Yancey, *Guidance*.

appendix two

PAINLESS SCRIPTURE MEMORY

Scripture memory is like humility. Everyone speaks highly of it, but few rush to wash feet. Likewise, most Christians believe in the value of a spiritual bank of memorized Scripture, but few make regular deposits.

I speak from experience. I've started dozens of Scripture memory programs. I've also quit dozens of times. I may have the world's record for the most Bible verses forgotten. By the time I entered seminary, I'd memorized nearly two thousand verses—and also forgotten nearly all of them.

I had many good reasons to memorize Bible verses. I found I could conquer doubts about the security of my salvation by quoting verses emphasizing faith in Christ alone. Learning inspirational verses from Psalms and Isaiah helped produce the Spirit's fruit of joy in my life. I saw I could more easily share my faith when I knew verses that explained the gospel or answered common questions. Other key verses often satisfied my own questioning mind.

I tried to be consistent in memorizing, but I was most consistent in quitting. My problem, I know now, was failure to conquer four basic mental blocks.

BLOCK 1: *Expecting Scripture memory to be some sort of secret formula to spiritual success.*
For the growing Christian, a good Bible study program and regular prayer life are more important than any memory program. Only when you can maintain a daily time of Bible study and prayer are you ready for regular Scripture memory. Jumping into it before is like trying to parallel park before you can handle a steering wheel.

BLOCK 2: *Thinking you should set a Goliath-size Scripture memory goal.*
I surprise people when I encourage them to aim low and avoid failure. A good goal for Scripture memory is not *x* number of verses, but a reasonable, regular, daily commitment of time. I began with fifteen minutes a day, and that small goal made regular memory work possible for me.

One of my students selected five minutes a day as her Scripture memory goal. A week later she told me she was meeting it but apologized for aiming so low. I told her if she could regularly spend five minutes each day, she would develop a lasting discipline and perhaps later could aim for a longer time.

Selecting a time goal is like the fable of the tortoise and the hare. The regular pace of the tortoise was much wiser and helped him beat the erratic hare to the finish line.

BLOCK 3: *Believing you have to memorize one verse word perfect before you go on to another.*
Many people use the "force method" of memorization, tackling a verse phrase by phrase until they can patch the phrases together. It may work, but it's definitely hard work.

In some ways, Scripture memory is like jogging. We know it's good for us because it keeps us in shape and our hearts and lungs healthy. But we can jog two ways: either by running in place (which is hardly fun) or by running down an interesting path.

Near my home in Oregon I can jog through a beautiful golf course. Though running is hard work and I finish the run perspiring, it's not drudgery. But when I go home to Michigan for Christmas, jogging through Detroit's frigid, snow-slick streets would be suicidal. Instead I go to my parents' not-so-hazardous basement and run in place. I get my exercise but the sense of drudgery sets in quickly.

We don't have to force memorize any more than we have to run in place when there's a better place to run. A more natural method of Bible memory calls for careful, thoughtful reading of selected verses written out on 3 x 5 cards.

Sound too simple? You've probably memorized many things unintentionally this way. Maybe you can recall part of a poem you've read over and over or verses you've heard repeatedly. Dr. John G. Mitchell, one of the founders of Multnomah Bible College, memorized great portions of Scripture simply by reading his Bible repeatedly. As a young man, he often stayed up all night munching apples and reading his Bible. Because of his regular, repeated reading of Scripture, he could remember the exact words of many passages.

To memorize five new verses, read them carefully and thoughtfully three times each. Then put them away for the day. You won't memorize them that day, but they'll be like cars in a quality assembly line steadily being built rather than thrown together in a hurry.

Then the next day, repeat the process. Each day, you'll find the verses easier to quote. After about three weeks, you'll have them on the tip of your tongue. Soon you'll find it natural to quote a verse after seeing its reference.

BLOCK 4: *Failing to include a simple review system.*

Why memorize only to forget? You will forget, you know.

The only sure dike against verse leakage is regular review. Eventually you will spend 80 percent of your Scripture memorization time commitment in review. I currently spend about sixteen minutes in review and four minutes on new verses.

I've found that review works by the law of increasing returns. The longer you review a verse, the less time you must spend to keep it fresh. A verse reviewed daily will soon need review only weekly. One reviewed weekly will soon need review only once every three weeks.

If you are willing to invest fifteen minutes a day in Scripture memory, then the following system will work for you. It's one I've passed on to many friends and students as a tool for ministry and personal growth. This system allows you to review as much and as little as you must. It works on the principle of three review categories: *daily, weekly,* and *tri-weekly*. Further time categories can be added when needed.

Begin by looking for verses of inspirational, evangelistic, or theological value. Record each one on a 3 x 5 card, putting the reference on the flip side. Be sure to understand the verse in its context so you can later apply it properly.

Get an index box and at least twenty-nine division tabs. One will be labeled "Daily," seven will be labeled with the days of the week, and twenty-one will be numbered consecutively.

Daily. Begin by placing your new verses behind this tab. You will want to add four to ten verses a week until you have ten to twenty-five verses. Read these verses three times each day. You will be able to quote them after a week or two. Then quote them one time daily for several weeks. At that point, you will be ready to move them to the *weekly* category.

Weekly. As verses are moved from the *daily* to the *weekly* category, they should be distributed evenly in each of the seven subdivisions (Monday, Tuesday, and so on) until you have a maximum of twenty verses each day. Then after reading through your daily verses, quote the verses behind the appropriate weekly tab from their references. When all the weekly tabs have the maximum twenty verses (total 140), you may begin a *triweekly* category.

Triweekly. The twenty-one subdivisions give you one for each day of the three-week period. They are numbered 1–21, and you review the verses in them on consecutive days. As verses enter this category, they are distributed evenly among the twenty-one subdivisions.

Now, let's review these instructions. Each daily time block for memory will have you reviewing all the daily verses, up to twenty of the weekly verses (chosen by day of the week), and up to twenty of the triweekly verses (taken by order of tab).

When you get more than twenty verses in each triweekly category, you may want to further subdivide. But the full memory review box will help you keep 350 verses fresh in your mind.

The first two or three months you use this system, you may experience some mental strain. But once you get over this psychological hump, you'll find yourself memorizing faster and easier.

And you may actually find it fun.

appendix three

GUIDELINES FOR BIBLE MARATHONS

Purposes:

- To set aside quality time in a busy culture to drink deeply from God's Word.
- To read through a Bible book in one sitting as it was meant to be read.
- To follow the sweep of themes and interrelatedness of the Bible.
- To experience the Word with the encouragement of community.

Leadership:

- Have one leader with an assistant, who helps with food and other issues that come up.
- Take ten minutes at the start for orientation and opening prayer.

Participants:

- Participants must commit to the full marathon, and come rested.
- Any size group works, but fifteen people in a large living room is ideal.

- Invite specific people you think would enjoy the marathon; then give a general announcement for any spaces still open.

Schedule:

- Length is from two to eighteen hours in one day. (See example schedules below.)
- Have a five-minute "response time" every one to two hours. (See below.)
- Take five-minute breaks every one to two hours for bathroom, food, and so on.

Reading:

- Have everyone bring common translations (NIV and NASB), not paraphrases.
- Reading Aloud: Willing readers stand to read one chapter to the group. Chapters longer than twenty verses should be divided among readers.
- Print an order of readers and the order in which you will read the Bible books.
- Use a good Scripture audiotape or CD for selected portions. Use it to end breaks and during meals.
- Reading order: Do not feel restricted to the New Testament order of the books. Alternate long books with short. Read Revelation last.
- Have everyone stand for the reading of every seventh chapter. On this chapter each person reads one verse around the room.

Length of Marathon:

Any reading of two or more hours is a marathon. For high schoolers and older adults, it is best to begin with a two- to five-hour marathon. College students like the challenge of eight- to sixteen-hour marathons, as well as shorter ones. At the end is a chart of reading times for specific books of the Bible. See examples below for some sample schedules.

Learning/Sharing:

- Encourage participants to bring a notebook to record insights. Have everyone look for two things during the reading: (1) A theme (love, fear, submission, hope, evangelism, God's glory, nature of God, etc), and (2) verses that relate to a specific personal problem or issue.
- Stop reading for five minutes before breaks and stand together. Have volunteers read a significant verse from that reading and pray a response to the verse (thanksgiving, confession, petition for help, praise, etc). This will probably be the most significant time.
- For the first sharing time, select several capable people ahead of time. Have them read a verse from that section and pray their response. Then keep the time open to any others willing to read and pray.

> Sharing example: "They went on their way from the presence of the Council, rejoicing that they had been considered worthy to suffer shame for His name" (Acts 5:41, read by a volunteer). "Dear Lord, the book of Acts makes it clear that the gospel will never get out to the world without suffering. Help me to accept suffering from your hand and be willing to take risks to share the gospel with my friends at school."

> Sharing example: "Be anxious for nothing, but in everything by prayer...let your requests be made known to God" (Philippians 4:6, read by a volunteer). "Dear God, I'm anxious about money and my job. Let me trust you by praying every time I feel anxious and trusting you to meet all my needs."

Miscellaneous:

- If meals are involved, keep them simple.
- Each person should bring a drink, snack, and money for any meals served.

- Have the assistant be responsible to organize any food and meals.
- Have a place for people to lie down if needed.

Example Marathons:

Gospel of Mark takes 1.5 hours (use a 2-hour block).

- Orientation and welcome: 10 minutes
- Read aloud: 50 minutes
- Response prayers: 5 minutes
- Break: 5 minutes
- Read aloud: 40 minutes
- Response prayers: 10 minutes

Hebrews through Revelation takes just under 3 hours (use a 4-hour block).

- Orientation and welcome: 10 minutes
- Read aloud: 60 minutes
- Response prayers: 5 minutes
- Break: 5 minutes
- Read aloud: 60 minutes
- Response prayers: 5 minutes
- Break: 5 minutes
- Read aloud: 60 minutes
- Response prayers: 20 minutes

Daniel and the Minor Prophets takes 4.6 hours (use a 6-hour block).
Acts through Philemon takes 6.9 hours (use an 8-hour block).

AVERAGE READING TIMES

BOOKS	HOURS	BOOKS	HOURS
Genesis–Deuteronomy	14.3	Psalms	6.1
Genesis	3.7	Proverbs	1.7
Exodus	2.9	Ecclesiastes–Song of Solomon	0.9
Leviticus	2.2	Isaiah–Malachi	17.4
Numbers	3.0	Isaiah–Daniel	13.7
Deuteronomy	2.5	Isaiah	4.3
Joshua–Esther	18.4	Jeremiah–Lamentations	4.9
Joshua–2 Chronicles	16.2	Ezekiel	3.6
Joshua	1.7	Daniel	1.1
Judges–Ruth	1.9	Hosea–Malachi	3.5
1 Samuel	2.3	New Testament	18.1
2 Samuel	1.9	Gospels	8.1
1 Kings	2.2	Matthew	2.4
2 Kings	2.0	Mark	1.5
1 Chronicles	2.1	Luke	2.5
2 Chronicles	2.3	John	1.9
Ezra, Nehemiah, Esther	1.7	Acts–Philemon	6.9
Job–Song of Solomon	11.0	Acts–Revelation	9.8
Job	2.2	Hebrews–Revelation	2.9

INDEX OF FREQUENTLY ASKED QUESTIONS

- In the first edition of *Decision Making*, you did not discuss Acts 22:14–15, in which Ananias told Paul that he would know God's will for him. Doesn't that indicate that God had an individual will for Paul? And if God intended for Paul to know His will, shouldn't we expect the same for all believers? [Chapter 3]
- In this chapter [8] you state that the moral will of God is fully revealed in the Bible. But wouldn't special revelation expand the content of God's moral will beyond what is contained in the Bible? [Chapter 8]
- Are you saying that God doesn't care about decisions that aren't specified in the Bible? For instance, does He really not care whom I might choose as a marriage partner? [Chapter 9]
- Are you saying that two options are really equal or that they only seem equal? Wouldn't God know how each would turn out and know that one was really better? [Chapter 9]
- How can you speak of the believer's freedom when God is sovereign over every detail of life including our decision making? [Chapter 9]

- In the first edition of *Decision Making,* you spoke of decisions within the area of freedom as "nonmoral" decisions. You also described the believer's freedom as "moral" freedom. In this edition you have not used this terminology. Why? [Chapter 9]
- Isn't your desire for freedom just an irresponsible worldview that does not want to be restricted? [Chapter 9]
- In a chapter that explains the believer's freedom in noncommanded decisions, I couldn't help but notice that you occasionally inserted the words "and responsibility" (usually in parentheses) when describing this freedom. The point would be that if we are free to choose in such instances, we're also responsible to choose. But if we're not trying to find the individual will of God, on what basis are we to make our choices? How is our responsibility exercised and evaluated? [Chapter 9]
- This all sounds like a matter of semantics to me. Isn't wisdom just another way of talking about God's individual will? [Chapter 11]
- If I conclude that one choice is wiser than another, am I free to choose either option? [Chapter 11]
- A person could prolong the quest for wisdom indefinitely. How can you ever have enough wisdom? [Chapter 11]
- What if I make a decision that I believe to be wise, but then feel no peace afterwards? [Chapter 11]
- What if two choices seem equally wise? [Chapter 11]
- Doesn't the traditional view also commend wisdom just like the wisdom view? What's the difference? [Chapter 11]
- You argued against the concept of a dot, but isn't there a sovereign dot? Wouldn't you agree that God's sovereign will applies to individuals as well as every individual thing that happens? How can you say there is no individual will of God? [Chapter 12]
- If God has a sovereign will that is perfect, doesn't it follow that God has a perfect plan for each believer? [Chapter 12]
- God's sovereign will seems so cold and impersonal to me. [Chapter 12]
- First Corinthians 7:17 and 20 speak of God's "calling" and "assigning." How does this fit with the thesis of your book? [Chapter 12]
- Our pastor recently presented his ministry plans. He has resigned to accept a position in another church. His explanation to the

congregation sounded spiritual, but vague: "God is leading me to another ministry." I wonder what his real reasons were. [Chapter 14]

- In your principles of decision making according to the way of wisdom, you describe how the believer should respond to God's moral guidance, wisdom guidance, and sovereign guidance. Why is there no similar principle for God's *special* guidance? [Chapter 15]
- God gave special guidance through prophets in both the Old and New Testaments. So when men and women claim to issue prophetic pronouncements today, what are we to make of that? [Chapter 15]
- So how do you respond in a private conversation when a friend says, "God told me to do thus and such," or "I felt led by the Spirit to do thus and such"? [Chapter 15]
- Is it ever appropriate to "cast lots" to make a decision? [Chapter 15]
- Isn't it true that some recent writers have elevated the role of personal desires in decision making based on Psalm 37:4? [Chapter 17]
- The wisdom view maintains that pastors are not required to have a mystical call to be qualified. How does this square with Acts 20:28, which says that the elders of the Ephesian church were "appointed" (NLT) by the Holy Spirit? [Chapter 21]
- This chapter [22] focuses on the decision each believer must make about his or her involvement in missions. But who should send missionaries? It seems as if mission agencies have taken over this function from local churches. Is there any way to restore the role of the local church as the sending agency? [Chapter 22]
- The funding of the missionary enterprise is always challenging. How might wisdom be applied to raising financial support for missions? [Chapter 22]

SCRIPTURE INDEX

A bold (**141**) number indicates that there is some discussion of the verse on that page. An *n* after a number indicates that the reference is in an endnote.

ROMANS

1 CORINTHIANS

STUDY GUIDE

Introduction

Decision Making and the Will of God presents an alternative to the traditional view of discovering God's will by reexamining this important issue from a solidly biblical basis. This guide will help you to examine the traditional view—as well as a biblical alternative—so that you can come to your own conclusions. It also suggests ways to apply the ramifications of the wisdom approach to guidance.

What's in This Guide?

This guide is divided into thirteen sessions. Ideally, the study can be completed in three months. Churches will find this study easy to use as the foundation for a course in either their Sunday school or small-group programs.

Each session is divided into several parts. The *Purpose* for each session is stated at the beginning. After this there are thoughts and questions to *Consider. Case Studies* give students a chance to apply what they are learning to life situations. *Exercises* provide opportunities for preliminary study before reading particular chapters. *Projects* extending over several sessions aid students in seeing how God's will relates to their own decisions. *Discussion* questions explore the implications of these exercises and projects.

How Do We Begin?

If your group isn't already established as a class or small group, invite six to sixteen Christians (high school age on up) to join you for a weekly study of *Decision Making and the Will of God.* Commitment and active participation by each person is essential for meaningful group study. Each member should be willing to regularly attend the weekly meetings and to do the appropriate lesson before each session. (Most lessons will take less than two hours to complete.)

Don't plan to discuss session 1 at your first meeting. Take this opportunity to get to know each other. Discuss the topic and purpose of this study. If the members of your group agree, they can pay for the books ahead of time so that you can have these materials ready to distribute at your first meeting. Also be sure to discuss the format of the study, which involves both personal study and group interaction. This will ensure that everyone knows session 1 should be completed *before* the second meeting.

Who Should Lead?

The democratic leader ensures that the group studies effectively together without dominating the study himself. He provides direction for each session without stifling the discussion of opposing viewpoints. The leader who tends to use this approach will be the most effective in leading a group study of *Decision Making and the Will of God.*

How Should We Interact?

Leaders should spend the first five minutes of each session (no more!) summarizing the content of the chapters to be discussed. Then ensure that each group member has an equal opportunity to share. "Speaking the truth in love" entails the careful wording of statements, a gentle voice, expressions of acceptance, extension of equal friendliness to all in the group, and the assumption of pure motives and sincerity on the part of those who differ. You may wish to make overhead transparencies from the charts in *Decision Making and the Will of God.* Permission to reproduce these charts is granted by the publisher, provided the transparencies are made solely for private use as a teaching tool.

Session 1

ANOTHER LOOK: YOU HAVE HEARD IT SAID

Forewords, Introduction, Chapters 1–2

Purposes

- To understand the overall plan of *Decision Making and the Will of God*
- To get an overview of the way of wisdom
- To get an overview of the traditional view

Getting Started

1. Skim *Decision Making and the Will of God.* What are the four major sections of the book? What direction does the book seem to take?
2. Read the two forewords. What do these contributors say about the question, "How can I know the will of God?" What two crippling extremes can be avoided by properly understanding God's will?
3. Read the rest of the introduction. What are the basic tenets of the way of wisdom?

Project

Take one sheet of notebook paper and draw a vertical line down the middle. Label the left column, "Successful Decision." Label the right column, "Unsuccessful Decision." Think over significant decisions you have made recently. Select a decision you were pleased with, and one that proved to be less than satisfactory. Respond to the following evaluation questions for each decision in the appropriate column.

Note: In later lessons you will be referring to this project. A thorough evaluation now will benefit your entire study.

1. What was the decision? What did you have to decide?
2. What were your options?
3. Did you have a deadline? How much time did you have to make the decision?
4. Describe the decision-making process. List the steps you took leading up to your decision (research, advice, etc.).

5. What were the positive signs that pointed in favor of the decision you made?
6. What were the negative signs that pointed against the decision you made? Did these factors favor some other option?
7. What part did your emotions play in the decision-making process?
8. What biblical principles were you able to apply to your decision? Did you overlook any?
9. How did you evaluate your decision in terms of finding God's will? How do you evaluate it now?
10. How did the decision turn out? How do you account for the outcome of your decision? Why did (or didn't) it succeed?
11. If you had the decision to make over again, knowing what you know now, what decision would you make?

Exercise

1. Before reading chapter 2, read the summary chart of the traditional view's main principles on p. 110. Restate each point in your own words.
2. As you read chapter 2, ask yourself, "Do I agree with this teaching?" Put a plus (+) in the margin when you agree, a minus (–) when you disagree, and a question mark (?) when you are not sure.

Discussion

1. How do you account for the differing outcomes of the two decisions you evaluated in the project above? Would you attribute the outcomes to circumstantial factors or to the application of decision-making principles on your part?
2. Read chapter 1. What was Ted Bradford's dilemma? Is his struggle unique? Based on your experiences, how would you advise Ted if he came to you for counsel?
3. Based on your reading of chapter 2, do you think the traditional view outline essentially agrees with what you have heard or read in the past? If not, at what points did it differ from what you have usually heard?
4. What questions do you have about the way of wisdom that will be presented in the book?

Session 2

IN SEARCH OF THE MISSING DOT

Chapters 3–4

Purposes

- To look at the three aspects of God's will suggested by the traditional view
- To examine the validity of the *individual* will of God
- To explore relevant Scripture passages to determine whether or not the Bible teaches that God has an individual will for each person

Consider

1. Read chapter 3. What was your initial reaction to the suggestion that there is no individual will of God? Check all answer(s) that apply.

❑ shocked	❑ hopeful	❑ afraid
❑ excited	❑ angry	❑ interested
❑ disconcerted	❑ confused	❑ other: ____________
❑ doubtful	❑ open	

2. If there is no individual will of God, there are some significant ramifications. Which ones come to your mind?
3. What are three arguments to support the traditional view of God's individual will for each person? What is your evaluation of these three arguments and my critique of them? In your opinion, how strong is each of the three arguments for the traditional view?

Exercises

The heart of part 2 is chapter 4, a discussion of the fourth argument for the traditional view—biblical teaching. This chapter contains careful exposition of the Scripture passages most often cited by those who hold the traditional view. Therefore, some preliminary study will be helpful. Before reading chapter 4, take two sheets of notebook paper and record your notes as you survey the Scripture passages listed below.

A. Review the definitions and summaries of the three aspects of God's will presented in outline form on p. 28. Title the first sheet, "The Traditional View of God's Will." On this sheet write out the definition for each aspect of God's will. Under the definition for the *individual* will of God, also record the characteristics that are given to describe it.

B. Title your second sheet, "Does Scripture Teach the Individual Will of God?" Several passages are commonly used to support the existence of an individual will of God, such as Psalm 32:8; Proverbs 3:5–6; 16:9; Isaiah 30:20–21; John 5:19; Romans 12:1–2; Ephesians 2:10; 5:15–17; Colossians 1:9; 4:12. List each of these ten references on the left hand side of your sheet, spacing about three lines apart. As you read each passage, answer these questions: (1) In this passage does the individual will of God make sense? The sovereign will? The moral will? (2) Is there anything in the passage or its context that would rule out one of the three aspects of God's will? (3) Which aspect of God's will do you think the biblical writer had in mind?

C. Now read chapter 4. Record in the right hand margin of your second sheet which aspect of God's will the author concludes is referred to by each passage.

Discussion

1. Based on your study for exercise A above, what are the similarities and differences of the three aspects of God's will?
2. What positive principles of guidance did you discover from the study of the Scriptures considered in chapter 4?
3. Now that you have considered a critique of the traditional view of God's individual will, what is your reaction? Check the best answer.

❑ I still feel convinced that God has an individual will for each person.

- ❑ I still think God has an individual will, but not as strongly now.
- ❑ I have serious questions about whether or not God has an individual will.
- ❑ I am fairly convinced that Scripture does not teach that God has an individual will.
- ❑ If there is no individual will of God, I sure would like to know how I am supposed to make decisions that are pleasing to God!
- ❑ Other: ________________________________

Session 3

MORE DOUBTS ABOUT THE DOT
Chapters 5–6

Purposes

- To take a look at the applicational difficulties of the traditional view
- To examine the source and value of impressions

Consider

1. Read chapters 5 and 6. Consider what is said about each of these applicational difficulties.

    - abandoning the traditional approach in ordinary decisions
    - finding it difficult to choose between apparently equal options
    - justifying a questionable decision on the grounds that "God told me to do it"
    - postponing a decision too long because of uncertainty about God's individual will
    - choosing the less desirable of two options as a guard against selfish motives
    - using a circumstantial fleece to determine a decision
    - experiencing frustration because of uncertainty over the source or message of "road signs"
    - seeing the work of a group hampered by the inability to agree on what is God's perfect will for the group

2. Which applicational difficulties of the traditional view have you observed or experienced? Which difficulties seem the most serious to you? The least serious?
3. Review chapter 6. Have you ever followed a strong inner impression with very positive results? Have you ever followed a similar impression with negative results?
4. How do you explain impressions that do not yield positive results? Check the appropriate answer(s) below.

- ❑ The impression must have come from a source other than the Holy Spirit.
- ❑ The message God intended was misunderstood.
- ❑ Inner impressions are not very reliable sources of guidance.
- ❑ Something went wrong, but I'm not sure of the problem.
- ❑ Other: ______________________________

5. What level of authority does the author conclude impressions deserve? What level do you think they deserve?

Discussion

1. How has the book helped account for any difficulties you've experienced in the past in decision making?
2. How do you rate the book's critique of the traditional view?

- ❑ It has been accurate both biblically and experientially.
- ❑ It has disagreed agreeably, showing respect and love for those who hold the traditional view.
- ❑ It has been unnecessarily disturbing in some of its implications.
- ❑ It has failed to adequately present and challenge the traditional view.
- ❑ Other: ______________________________

3. At this point, what is your emotional response to the material studied thus far? Mark where you are on the following continuum.

enthusiastic	open	giving it a chance	listening but unsettled	feeling threatened	upset	upset and closed

A personal word. Teaching this material has brought greatly varying responses from sincere believers in Christ. Think about your interaction as a group to this study. In what ways have you demonstrated maturity and loving acceptance of one another in the midst of differing opinions? How might you better present your opinions with maturity and accepting love in future studies?

Session 4

LEADING OF THE SPIRIT
Chapters 7–8

Purposes

- To consider passages about the leading of the Spirit
- To see God's moral will as the foundation for all decisions

Consider

1. Do the passages about the Spirit's leading make sense as guidance into the moral will of God? (Nehemiah 2:12; John 16:12–14; Romans 8:14–16; Galatians 5:18; Colossians 3:15)
2. Before reading chapter 8, mentally review the definition of God's moral will. What are five ways the moral will of God could affect your decision making?
3. Read chapter 8. After considering the four "way of wisdom" principles, what questions come to mind? Which principle seems the most unclear to you?
4. The moral will of God is the expression of what? What are some of the traits that are to characterize the believer? Why?
5. "The imperatives of God's moral will *touch every aspect and moment of life*" (p. 124). Discuss how God's moral will affects each of the decisions listed below.

   - which shoes to buy
   - how to utilize leisure time
   - where to live
   - which person to marry
   - what to do on a date
   - how to get work

Consider

1. How much of God's moral will is revealed in the Bible? What are you doing to increase your understanding of God's moral will?

2. Are you interested in trying any of the suggestions for learning the Scriptures? Interested in trying a Bible Marathon? If so, see the "Guidelines for Bible Marathons" in appendix 3.

Session 5
FREEDOM WITHIN GOD'S MORAL WILL
Chapter 9

Purpose

- To understand the area of freedom within God's moral will

Project

Take one sheet of notebook paper and label it, "An Upcoming Decision." Describe this decision (it should be significant), and the deadline you face (preferably within the next two months). Include the main elements of this decision and any questions you have that you hope the rest of this study will answer. Try to be thorough, for you will be referring to this project in later sessions.

Case Study

The following situation presents a couple working through the decision-making process. After reading it, discuss the questions below.

Situation: Martha Brown is twenty-seven years old and the mother of two children (ages two and four). Her husband, Charlie, is a truck driver. At times work is plentiful; at other times it is scarce. Charlie supports his family, but there isn't much money available for extras. Martha has been offered a part-time job at a fabric store. She likes the idea of getting out of the house more, as well as contributing to the family income. But Charlie doesn't care much for the idea of Martha working outside the home.

What specific elements of God's moral will do Charlie and Martha need to consider as they face this situation? (Be sure to include matters relating to goals and attitudes as well as means to their ends.) What options within the moral will of God are open to them?

Consider

1. Read chapter 9. Are you convinced that there are noncommanded decisions in which the believer is free and responsible to choose his

own course of action? If you are not convinced, how do you account for the Scripture passages that teach such freedom of choice?

2. What is your personal reaction to the idea that you are free to make your own choices in noncommanded areas? Check the best answer below.

❑ liberated	❑ relieved	❑ amazed
❑ relaxed	❑ hesitant	❑ doubtful
❑ apprehensive	❑ afraid	❑ other: ________

3. How does the concept of an "area of freedom" resolve the applicational difficulty the traditional view has with equal options?
4. During the past week, what decisions did you make that would fit in this category of noncommanded decisions?
5. Try to recall a past decision in which your main objective was to find the dot of God's individual will. What practical difference would it have made if you had viewed the decision as lying within the area of freedom?

Discussion

For the project in this lesson you identified an upcoming decision that you must make. Is it a decision that is addressed directly by Scripture, or is it a noncommanded decision? If it is noncommanded, what options do you have that lie within the area of freedom? At this point, which questions that you recorded earlier have been answered to your satisfaction?

Session 6

WISDOM FOR DECISION MAKING
Chapters 10–11

Purpose

- To discover the importance of making wise decisions on the basis of spiritual benefit

Consider

1. What Old Testament examples best support wisdom as the basis of making godly decisions? Moses (Exodus 18), David (2 Samuel 18:1–4), the axe (Ecclesiastes 10:10).
2. What teaching by Jesus is strongest in supporting the necessity of wisdom? "Two Foundations" (Matthew 7:24–27), "Counting the Cost" (Luke 14:25–32), "Ten Virgins" (Matthew 25:1–13), wise as serpents (Matthew 10:16).

Discussion

1. According to the Scripture passages cited in chapter 10, on what basis did the apostles make most of their noncommanded decisions? In their instruction, on what basis did they exhort other believers to make noncommanded decisions? (See chapter 11.)
2. Did the apostles demonstrate any acquaintance with the tenets or vocabulary of the traditional view? Do you believe that the third principle of the way of wisdom (Where there is no command, God gives us wisdom to choose) accurately summarizes the apostolic practice and instruction?
3. What are the similarities between looking for the dot and seeking the way of wisdom? What are the differences?
4. How does the goal of making wise decisions resolve the following applicational difficulties of the traditional view?

   - Adoption of two approaches to decision making—one for major decisions and one for minor decisions (pp. 81–82)

- Justification of unwise decisions on the grounds that "God told me to do it" (pp. 84–85)
- Costly delays because of uncertainty of God's individual will (p. 85)
- Rejection of personal preferences when faced with apparently equal options (pp. 85–86)
- Utilization of a circumstantial fleece as the final determiner of God's leading (p. 86)

5. Review the successful decision you evaluated as part of the project for session 1. How can the process (project question 4) be accounted for from the perspective of the way of wisdom?

Project

Review your project sheet from session 5 labeled "An Upcoming Decision." As a result of reading this chapter, what further questions could you apply to your decision? Record these questions on your sheet. As you continue to work on this project, make a list of the sources of wisdom available to you.

Session 7
THE SOVEREIGNTY OF GOD
Chapters 12–13

Purposes

- To understand the nature of God's sovereign will
- To see how the Bible relates God's sovereignty to such important considerations as planning, circumstances, open doors, and fleeces

Consider

1. Read chapters 12 and 13. Do you agree that God has a sovereign will that ultimately determines everything that happens? If you disagree, do you have an alternative interpretation of the Scripture passages cited in these chapters? If you agree, do you believe that your decisions are real? Does it really matter what decisions you make?
2. What do you think about the sovereign will of God and its role in your decisions? Check the appropriate response below.

❑ comforted	❑ unchanged	❑ puzzled
❑ threatened	❑ encouraged	❑ other: ________

3. All planning accepts the reality of risks. What distinguishes a step of faith from presumptuous foolishness?
4. How is the term "open door" (and related phrases) used in the New Testament? What do these expressions usually refer to? Did the apostle Paul feel compelled to enter every open door he encountered (pp. 208–212)?
5. Have you ever used a circumstantial fleece to help you come to a decision? What happened? Does the discussion on pp. 213–216 adequately account for your experience? If you had it to do over again, how would you approach that decision differently?

6. Even though these chapters focus on the unknowable sovereign will of God, they contain some valuable insights for decision making. Which of the principles regarding God's sovereign will and decision making have increased your understanding the most?

Case Studies

The situations below are examples of how the sovereign will of God relates to planning in everyday life. After reading each situation, discuss the questions that follow.

Situation one: Mike is a senior at a local university. He will be finishing his studies in three months, yet he has made no plans for employment or housing once he graduates. He tells you, "If God's sovereign will determines everything that happens, there is no point in planning."

How would you respond to Mike's statement?

Situation two: Two years ago Lisa Miller discovered she could not have any children. Last Tuesday she and her husband, John, told the members of their fellowship group, "We are planning to adopt a child, and we just know the Lord is going to work it out. By faith we are starting to buy baby furniture."

How would you evaluate their actions based on James 4:13–16?

Situation three: First Community Church is outgrowing its present facilities. Yet the giving is barely meeting expenses. What factors should the planning committee consider as they begin thinking about constructing a larger building? What do you think they should do?

Discussion

1. Review your unsuccessful decision from the project in session 1. Was the outcome due to your failure to acquire wisdom? (That is, did you err through poor judgment that could have been corrected?) Or was the outcome determined by circumstances beyond your control? How does this relate to the new insights you have gained from the discussion of James 4 on pp. 201–205?

Session 8

MAKING A GOOD THING BETTER

Chapters 14–16

Purposes

- To take a good look at the biblical model of guidance
- To consider the possibility of special guidance
- To compare and contrast the traditional view with the way of wisdom (review)

Exercises

A. Read chapter 14. Using the chart "Four Distinctive Ways God Guides" (p. 221) and pages 224–230 for reference, explain how God guided Paul in his decision to travel to Rome. Be sure to cover all four categories of guidance.

B. Study Nehemiah 1:1–2:8 for another biblical illustration of wise decision making. How many of the steps Paul followed ("Steps in Paul's Decision-Making Process" chart, p. 230) did Nehemiah also take? What was God's involvement in the process?

C. Prepare a decision-making worksheet that can be used as a step-by-step guide through virtually any decision. For ideas, consult the material presented in the sections titled "Biblical Guidance Described" and "Biblical Guidance Demonstrated," pp. 222-230; the evaluation questions you've already compiled for "An Upcoming Decision"; plus the outline of "Steps in Paul's Decision-Making Process" (p. 230).

Consider

1. As far as you can tell, how accurately does the way of wisdom explain what the Bible teaches about decision making and the will of God?
2. Why do some people believe that God is not personally involved in wisdom guidance?

3. If a person changes in his conviction from the traditional view to the way of wisdom, some adjustments in his understanding of the Christian walk may be required. What do you think some of these adjustments might be?
4. "There is no place for God's involvement in decision making according to the way of wisdom." How would you respond if someone said that to you?
5. Read chapter 16. Mentally review and evaluate each of the contrasts between the traditional view and the way of wisdom. Then respond to this statement: "The way of wisdom is just the traditional view in different terminology. The differences are not significant."
6. If you have become convinced of the wisdom view of guidance, what do you think would happen if you attempted to persuade others who have not had exposure to this book? How should you relate to others who do not share your viewpoint?

Session 9
A NEW WAY OF SEEING
Chapters 17–18

Purposes

- To compare the traditional view with the way of wisdom
- To recognize how God is personal in His guidance

Discuss

1. In chapter 17 how do the two views look at the following with different perspectives: common sense, counselors, personal desires, circumstances, results, impressions, inner peace?
2. Before reading chapter 18, consider the following comment. "Wisdom guidance seems so impersonal to me. I feel as though God is no longer involved with me as a person." Have you had similar thoughts as you have studied *Decision Making and the Will of God*? Explain.
3. "Hands-On Guidance" (pp. 271–272) gives five ways that God is involved in our decision making. Do these convince you that God is closely involved with us? If not, what more would God need to do to convince you of His involvement?
4. Why is "less better" (pp. 275–277) when it comes to God's revelation (Old Testament versus New Testament)?
5. See the section titled "A Personal Relationship" (p. 274). According to the book, on what basis may a believer be assured of God's personal involvement in his life? How can a believer actively cultivate his fellowship with the Lord? What insights does this suggest to you in understanding the spiritual life?

Session 10

SINGLENESS, MARRIAGE, AND WISDOM
Chapters 19–20

Purpose

- To understand how the way of wisdom approaches decisions about singleness and marriage

Exercises

A. Before reading chapters 19 and 20, list three advantages and three disadvantages of singleness. On the same sheet of paper do the same for marriage. Then read 1 Corinthians 7 and write down how Paul would complete the lists.

B. Discuss the following questions with an adult raised in an Asian or Middle Eastern culture: "What are some of the advantages of living in a culture where the parents select your mate and wedding date? How could these advantages be gained in our culture?" Write down the answers you receive and be prepared to share them with your group.

Consider

1. Read chapters 19 and 20. In our culture, what disadvantages are encountered by a nineteen-year-old who decides to get married? How can these disadvantages be overcome?
2. What are the differences between *lust, romantic love, and biblical love?* Define these terms and discuss the impact each can have on the marriage decision.
3. Those involved in courtship tend to be consistently considerate, affectionate, and loving. How can a wisdom-seeking person determine how a prospective spouse will act after the honeymoon is over?

Exercises

C. If you are married, interview a single adult and ask, "How do married people make it hard for you to enjoy your single state?" If you are single, interview a married person and reverse the question. What insights did you discover?

D. If you are single, interview a married couple that you respect and ask them these questions: "Do you find that it takes hard work to preserve a good marriage relationship? What personal traits should I look for in a potential mate that will help us to overcome the stresses of married life? What traits should I seek to develop in my own life?"

Case Studies

Read the following situations and record your counsel for each one. (The footnoted situation in this lesson is based on a real incident. Do not read the comments in the footnote until after your group discussion. Consider this a test of your ability to resist temptation!)

Situation one: An eighteen-year-old woman, Julie, has received a proposal of marriage from a man she loves. But she does not want to get married for at least three years. If she says no, Julie fears she will lose him. And if she waits another three years, she may not be able to find such a fine marriage prospect.

Situation two: To her great dismay, a Christian woman who thought her marriage was "made in heaven" is experiencing increasing dissatisfaction and unhappiness. Amy explains to you how both she and her husband, Glen, thought they had found God's perfect will when they decided to marry each other. After months of mounting doubts, they now fear that their problems stem from the fact that they missed God's will. Amy explains, "We each married the wrong person. Now we are trapped in God's second best, or worse, with no escape." The thought of such a barren situation reduces her to tears.

Situation three: Herb and Carol are "engaged to be engaged," but have not announced anything yet because Carol's mother is dead set against the wedding. Carol's mother is concerned about Herb's background. He came from a broken home and was on drugs before his conversion. Herb has been clean for three years, but Carol's mother wants another three years of probation. (Actually, she wants Carol to marry someone who is a preacher type, and there is considerable doubt that another three years would make any difference.) Carol is very close to her mother emotionally, and the thought of hurting her mother would break her heart. Herb and Carol are both twenty-two years old and don't want to wait until they are twenty-five to consider marriage.[1]

Session 11

THE MINISTRY, MISSIONS, AND WISDOM
Chapters 21–22

Purpose

- To understand how the way of wisdom approaches decisions about the ministry and missions

Exercises

A. Before reading chapters 21 and 22, take a piece of paper and draw a vertical line down the middle of it. Label the left column, "Qualifications for a Pastor." List all the qualities that you think should characterize a pastor. Label the right column, "Qualifications for a Missionary," and do the same for missionaries.

B. Interview someone who has served on a committee to find a new pastor. Ask this person the following questions: "How did you determine if a prospect was qualified to serve as pastor of your church? What qualifications were you looking for?"

Consider

1. Read chapter 21. Have you ever attended an ordination council? Were you satisfied that the council adequately determined that the candidate was qualified for the ministry?
2. Pastors who leave one church at the invitation of another tend to move to bigger churches. Evaluate that tendency from the perspective of the traditional view and from that of the wisdom view.

Case Studies

Read the situations and answer the questions that follow, based on the wisdom view.

Situation one: At an areawide rally, Stan challenged the junior and senior high students to "come forward to commit your life to the service of Christ, if you know in your heart that He is calling you into full-time Christian service."

What would you tell a student who came to you for counsel after going forward at such a rally? How could Stan change the wording of his challenge in a manner compatible with the wisdom view?

Situation two: A young man, Tim, does not desire to go into full-time Christian work, and he doesn't feel qualified. Yet Tim believes that the Lord spoke to his heart during a missionary conference and called him into full-time ministry. How would you counsel Tim?

Consider

3. Read chapter 22. This chapter seems to imply that all Christians should consider involvement in missions a top vocational priority until hindered. In view of the needs of the local church and community, is such an emphasis too strong? How should the "average" Christian respond to the great commission?
4. Discuss the reasons most Christians do not seriously consider becoming cross-cultural missionaries. Then read Luke 14:25–35. Which of the reasons are rebuked by the words of Jesus?
5. If you are not suited for a career in missions, how can you be personally involved in fulfilling the great commission?

Exercises

C. As you survey the youth in your church, do any of the high school– or college-age members demonstrate qualities that would be well suited to full-time ministry or missions? If so, have someone convey your group's observations to those young people, or send notes encouraging each of them to consider such a career.

Session 12

VOCATION, EDUCATION, GIVING, AND WISDOM
Chapters 23–24

Purpose

- To understand how the way of wisdom approaches decisions about vocation, education, and giving

Consider

1. Read chapter 23. What would be the advantages of living in a culture where parents choose their children's mate and vocation?
2. "If a student in America is industrious and selects a reputable school, he cannot go wrong on his choice." Do you agree or disagree? Why?
3. Discuss the advantages and disadvantages of attending each of the following institutions: a secular university, a Christian liberal arts college, a Bible college, a vocational-technical school.
4. In the section "Vocational Decision Making: A Case Study," (pp. 347–352), the author's decision was made by wisdom guidance. Did you sense that God was left out of his decision? Why or why not?
5. If a believer consistently obeyed the moral will of God at his job ("God's Will for Your Work," pp. 343–345), in what ways would he please his employer? In what ways might his obedience to God's moral will displease his employer?

Case Studies

Read the situations below and answer the questions that follow based on the way of wisdom.

Situation one: A friend of yours, Peter, calls you after work one day. He tells you about his frustrations with his present job: "I just can't take it there much longer. When I accomplish the near impossible, my boss only says, 'It's about time you got something done.' His unreasonableness creates such stress, I've got to quit before I blow up or break down." What would you tell Peter? What options has he failed to mention? What would be the advantages and disadvantages of each option?

Situation two: Fred, a college student, is working at a well-paying summer job. A union representative informs him that an unofficial walk-out is scheduled for next Monday to create bargaining leverage on a new contract. A strike is illegal, so everyone is going to call in sick. Refusal to participate could prove detrimental to the well-being of one's car or body. And relations with fellow workers would be strained when the others return to work.

What guidance would Fred find in the Bible about God's moral will in this situation? What wisdom can he apply?[2] (Discuss this situation in your group before consulting the endnote to learn what happened in this real situation.)

Consider

6. Read chapter 24. Have you ever been motivated more by guilt than by love to give? What situations tend to promote guilt-induced giving? How might wisdom giving resolve such difficulties in motivation?
7. Have you ever participated in a faith promise program? How did you select the amount you pledged? Did the amount come in? Was your experience mostly positive or negative? Does this chapter adequately account for your experience?
8. How do you determine the amount that you presently give to the Lord's work? Do you give a percentage of your income? Do you adjust that figure with a raise, a bonus, inflation, unexpected income, or unexpected loss?
9. "Most Christians will view grace giving as an excuse to give less than ten percent, rather than a challenge to give more 'as the Lord prospers.' More money will be given if we teach people to tithe." Do you agree or disagree with this sentiment? Why?

Session 13

DIFFERING OPINIONS AND WISDOM

Chapters 25–26, Conclusion

Purpose

- To understand how the way of wisdom approaches decisions about matters where Christians disagree

Case Studies

Read chapters 25 and 26. Then apply the principles of these chapters to the situations below, answering the questions that follow each situation. (Read the notes only after discussing the situations in your group.)

Situation one: Bob, the church youth director, made creative use of sports to attract the unsaved and to provide recreation for his young people. Football, in particular, played a key role in youth activities. One Sunday a guest speaker delivered a convincing, moving message warning against worldliness. To illustrate, he waxed eloquent on the spiritual perils of football. He said that football is time consuming, dangerous to physical health, violent, and has become a god to Americans. Those who would be separated from the world should abstain from playing or watching football. When the service ended, the young people flocked around Bob. "Is he right?" they asked. "Is it really wrong for us to play football?"

Identify the status of those involved (weaker brother, stronger brother, pharisee). Must Bob stop playing football out of love for the guest minister? What should he tell the youth?[3]

Situation two: A Bible teacher prefaced an illustration with this remark: "For the sake of illustration, you will have to assume the validity of my conviction that smoking cigarettes is sinful." Later, a class member raised his hand and said, "I don't think the illustration was fair. I have researched both the Bible and scientific studies carefully, and I disagree that smoking is sinful. So I am continuing to smoke."

Identify the status of the characters. Should the class member stop smoking for the sake of the teacher? Is there anything further that should be done by any other Christians present?[4]

Situation three: Bill, a vacationing Bible college student, was invited by the pastor to sing and give a word of testimony during the Sunday evening church service. Bill wore an earring in one ear and had a goatee. He expressed his love for the Lord and then accompanied himself with a guitar as he sang a Christian praise song. After the service, one board member told the pastor, "That was great! Let's encourage our college students to share more often. I really appreciated the freshness and genuineness of his message." Moments later, another board member took the pastor aside. "I like Bill as a Christian, but his presentation tonight was offensive. He looked like a rebel, and his song sounded more secular than worshipful. I told him that kind of music has no place in this church. I'm going to insist that we establish some policy at next Thursday's board meeting so this never happens again."

Identify the status of the characters. Who should do what? Must Bill shave and remove his jewelry? How should the two board members relate to each other at the meeting? How can the one man's offense be removed? What should the pastor do?[5]

Situation four: Kristi and Amy participate in a study group that is discussing *Decision Making and the Will of God.* Kristi gets more excited every week as she experiences increasing liberation from the frustrations of the traditional view. Amy, however, finds discussion growing more difficult. Inner leading has always been one of her greatest evidences of a personal, intimate relationship with God. She has always felt comfortable with the traditional view.

Identify the status of Kristi and Amy. How should they relate to each other? How can love and acceptance be expressed with their differing views?[6]

Consider

1. Read the conclusion. What do you think would happen if you tried to persuade everyone in your church to adopt the wisdom view of guidance?
2. How often do you see differing brothers discuss their differences with the attitude advocated in the conclusion? Why is it so difficult? How are you going to relate to others who differ from you on the question of guidance?

1. The moral issue for Herb and Carol concerns parental authority. In other words, must children be submissive to their parents for all of their lives? Must a sixty-year-old woman decline marriage because her ninety-year-old mother is against it?

   Christians differ on their positions about this issue, but Herb and Carol (not their real names) were counseled that the authority-submission relationship ends when a child becomes of legal age *and* chooses to leave the parental home. The obligation to honor one's parents is lifelong, but does not entail obedience to parental demands. Thus Herb and Carol were biblically free to marry each other. They were also free to consider the option of breaking off the relationship and going their separate ways.

   The question Herb and Carol were asked to consider was this: What way would wisdom choose? It was pointed out to them that even if they waited three years and received the approval of Carol's mother (which was unlikely), the mother would continue to exert an unhealthy influence on that marriage.

   If they chose to disregard the mother's wishes and marry in spite of her, the emotional cost to Carol would damage their marriage relationship. The emotional tie between the woman and her mother was such that the mother would continue to be a powerful force in Carol's life for some time to come.

   Herb and Carol were counseled to break up and seek other partners. (It is not known to what degree this counsel was a factor, but this couple did choose to break off their relationship and go their separate ways.)
2. The moral will of God forbade Fred to defraud his employer or to lie by calling in "sick." He was morally free to quit his job, or go to work and face the consequences from his fellow workers. Fred opted for going to work, but applied wisdom to reduce the difficulties with the other workers.

   He called the union representative and said, "I plan to go to work on Monday because I will not lie about being sick. I am doing this because I am a Christian, and I must not disobey God. I am not working to earn extra money or because I am afraid of losing my job. To prove this, I am willing to split my earnings from that day with the other workers. If they doubt my motives, I will quit my job. Please talk to the other workers and let me know if you want me to divide my earnings or quit. I will do either." The union representative was stunned, and simply said, "That's okay. I'll let the others know."

   Fred not only reported for work, but he worked at top speed to compensate for the absence of the others. He completed his work for the morning and was excused for the rest of the day by the boss. The "unofficial" walkout failed, but Fred was not hassled by the other workers. If anything, his stand gave more credibility to his testimony.

   The boss showed his appreciation to Fred for saving the company from a substantial loss by saying absolutely nothing by way of thanks. (That's real life!) On Tuesday, however, Fred was spared the humiliation of having to apologize to the boss—a requirement to which all the other workers had to submit.
3. Both Bob and the guest minister are strong, convinced brothers, neither of whom will cause the other to sin. The teens, however, have been made weaker brothers through the sermon. They have been made to doubt the correctness of their previous understanding, and are vulnerable to sinning against their doubting consciences.

   Bob need not desist from football for the preacher's sake. Further conversation between them would likely confirm that the guest minister would not be tempted to play or watch football because of Bob's example. The young people, on the other hand, merit special care.

   It is legitimate for Bob to express to them his disagreement with the preacher in a loving and accepting manner. He should explain why other Christians do not regard football as being sinful. Then the young people should be urged to become convinced one way or the other. If some still express doubts and could be made to sin against their consciences by subsequent games, Bob should temporarily suspend football—at least until the "weaker" youth are no longer vulnerable to sin. If this is necessary, the situation creates an opportunity for Bob to model self-sacrificing love by voluntarily restricting his own freedom for the sake of others.

4. Again we have two strong, convinced brothers—the teacher and the student. There may be a weaker brother present in the class who could be influenced to sin against his conscience by smoking. Thus the student's declaration of his freedom to smoke was unnecessary and insensitive. He could have stated his objection more tactfully: "Not all Christians agree that it is sinful to smoke. Why did you conclude that it is a sin?" The student does not need to stop smoking for the sake of the teacher, since the teacher will not be tempted to start smoking because of his example.

   If, however, the student encounters a genuine weaker brother responding to his comment, he should discontinue smoking until that brother is no longer endangered by his example. Meanwhile, the teacher and student would do well to elaborate that they had carefully thought through the issue. Whether they ever agree or not, they should both make clear their acceptance of and love for each other.

5. So far, there are no weaker brothers evident. The second board member is set in his opinion and will not be tempted to get an earring, grow a goatee, or sing a Christian praise song in violation of his conscience. Bill is not obligated to remove his earring and shave for the sake of a weaker brother since none is present. He may voluntarily make a change if he considers it wisest for all involved. The board members must love and accept one another with their differing viewpoints.

   The offended man, however, becomes a pharisee if he insists on conformity to his viewpoint on the part of Bill, the pastor, or the other board members. He has a right to express his opinion on policy for special music in the church, but he must be willing to accept the decision of the board if the other members disagree with him. The pastor should try to promote an atmosphere in the board meeting which allows each man the opportunity to freely express his conviction. He should then encourage everyone to follow the wisdom of the board's decision. Bill did not "give offense" to the second board member; that man "took offense." Only he can prevent offense by resisting the temptation to become upset when others differ, allowing God to be the judge of their convictions.

6. The discussion of *Decision Making and the Will of God* need not be hindered if both girls are willing to fully accept one another. As was pointed out in the introduction of this study guide, the goal of discussion must always be the clarification of truth, not the winning of an argument. "Speaking the truth in love" entails the careful wording of statements, a gentle voice, expressions of acceptance, extension of equal friendliness to all in the group, and the assumption of pure motives and sincerity on the part of those who differ. A person who becomes upset or is offended by a convincing argument is reflecting emotional immaturity at best, or expressing the sin of pride at worst.

   If you feel a relationship has been hurt or broken because of an aborted discussion over a debatable matter, a private conversation is in order. You could begin by saying, "I've sensed that our open discussion on this controversial subject has resulted in a cooling of our relationship. Our unity and friendship are too important to me to sacrifice over one issue."

   On the other hand, if you feel that a brother has sinned against you in the way he has discussed you or your opinion, you must be ready to confront him about it and fully forgive him (Matthew 18:15ff.). You may find that you were oversensitive, and he may discover his need to be more sensitive and careful in how he speaks. It is very difficult for believers to discuss debatable issues with the attitudes set forth in Romans 14 and 15. Few do it well. But it is not only possible, it is commanded (Romans 14:1–5).

To sign up for a weekly
paragraph update from Garry Friesen,
send your e-mail request to:

gfriesen@multnomah.edu

For more information on the author and
this book, visit:

www.gfriesen.net